Sunset

BEST HOME PLANS

Encyclopedia

Behind the expansive covered porch of this comfortable five-bedroom
home lies an equally inviting interior designed for modern living. See plan
AHP-9360 on page 310.

Sunset Publishing Corporation ■ **Menlo Park, California**

SUNSET BOOKS
President and Publisher:
  Susan J. Maruyama
Director, Finance & Business
  Affairs: Gary Loebner
Director, Manufacturing & Sales
  Service: Lorinda Reichert
Director, Sales & Marketing:
  Richard A. Smeby
Editorial Director:
  Kenneth Winchester
Executive Editor:
  Bob Doyle
Assistant Editor:
  Kevin Freeland
Contributing Editor:
  Don Vandervort

**SUNSET PUBLISHING
CORPORATION**
Chairman: Jim Nelson
President/Chief Executive
  Officer: Robin Wolaner
Chief Financial Officer:
  James E. Mitchell
Publisher:
  Stephen J. Seabolt
Circulation Director:
  Robert I. Gursha
Editor, Sunset Magazine:
  William R. Marken

Photographers: Mark Englund/
HomeStyles: 4, 5; Philip Harvey:
10 top, back cover; Stephen Marley:
11 top left and right; Russ Widstrand:
10 bottom; Tom Wyatt: 11 bottom.

Cover: Cover design by Naganuma
Design & Direction. Photography by
Debora Cartwright.

First printing April 1995
Copyright © 1995, Sunset Publishing
Corporation, Menlo Park, CA 94025.
First edition. All rights reserved, including
the right of reproduction in whole or in part
in any form.

ISBN 0-376-01138-6. Library of Congress
Catalog Card Number: 94-069960.
Printed in the United States.

For more information on Sunset's *Best Home
Plans Encyclopedia* or any other Sunset book,
call (800) 227-7346. For special sales, bulk
orders, and premium sales information, call
Sunset Custom Publishing Services at (415)
324-5577.

♻ Printed on recycled paper

A Dream Come True

Planning and building a house is one of life's most creative and rewarding challenges. Whether you're seriously considering building a new home or you're just dreaming about it, this book offers a wealth of inspiration and information to help you get started.

On the following pages, you'll learn how to plan and manage a home-building project—and how to ensure its success. Then you'll discover more than 400 proven home plans, designed for families just like yours by architects and professional designers. Peruse the pages and study the floor plans; you're sure to find a home that's just right for you. When you're ready to order blueprints, you can simply call or mail in your order, and you'll receive the plans within days.

Enjoy the adventure!

Contents

Blending Early American design and old-world charm, this compact house is loaded with interesting features. The bay-windowed dining room with its stepped ceiling is separated from the great room by a columned arch. The master bedroom has a tray ceiling, and the breakfast room's ceiling is vaulted. See plan AX-93304 on page 123.

A Book of Dreams

I f you've been searching for the perfect home plan, look no further! This book, filled with more than 400 of the best-selling home plans available, will become your most valued resource, rich in ideas and comprehensive in scope. You'll discover a myriad of great designs, whether you're looking for a traditional home, a striking contemporary, a country charmer, an affordable starter, or a rustic vacation retreat. All of the plans are proven designs created by some of America's foremost architects and designers.

The two keys to success in building are capable project management and good design. The next few pages will walk you through some of the most important aspects of project management: you'll find an overview of the building process, directions for selecting the right plan and getting the most from it, and methods for successfully working with a builder and other professionals.

The balance of the book presents professionally designed stock plans. Once you find a plan that will work for you— perhaps with a few modifications made later to personalize it for your family— you can order construction blueprints for a fraction of the cost of a custom design, a savings of many thousands of dollars (see pages 12–15 for information on how to order).

Floor-to-ceiling windows round the corner of this distinctive home's formal living room, filling the space with warmth and light. Entertaining and family living areas are on the main floor; bedrooms are upstairs. See plan CDG-2019 on page 374.

Gracefully arching windows accent this expansive, single-story family home. The living room, family room, and master bedroom open onto a large covered lanai at the rear of the house. See plan DD-2802 on page 143.

Victorian beauty, enhanced by gingerbread detailing, masks a thoroughly modern interior complete with a luxurious master suite and an island kitchen. See plan V-2440 on page 349.

Covered porch and a façade punctuated with Palladian windows distinguish this 1,724-square-foot home, designed for easy construction. See plan B-129-8510 on page 240.

The Art of Building

As you embark on your home-building project, think of it as a trip—clearly not a vacation but rather an interesting, adventurous, at times difficult expedition. Meticulous planning will make your journey not only far more enjoyable but also much more successful. By careful planning, you can avoid—or at least minimize—some of the pitfalls along the way.

Start with realistic expectations of the road ahead. To do this, you'll want to gain an understanding of the basic house-building process, settle on a design that will work for you and your family, and make sure your project is actually doable. By taking those initial steps, you can gain a clear idea of how much time, money, and energy you'll need to invest to make your dream come true.

The Building Process

Your role in planning and managing a house-building project can be divided into two parts: prebuilding preparation and construction management.

■ **Prebuilding preparation.** This is where you should focus most of your attention. In the hands of a qualified contractor whose expertise you can rely on, the actual building process should go fairly smoothly. But during most of the prebuilding stage, you're generally on your own. Your job will be to launch the project and develop a talented team that can help you bring your new home to fruition.

When you work with stock plans, the prebuilding process usually goes as follows:

First, you research the general area where you want to live, selecting one or more possible home sites (unless you already own a suitable lot). Then you choose a basic house design, with the idea that it may require some modification. Finally, you analyze the site, the design, and your budget to determine if the project is actually attainable.

If you decide that it is, you purchase the land and order blueprints. If you want to modify them, you consult an architect, designer, or contractor. Once the plans are finalized, you request bids from contractors and arrange any necessary construction financing.

After selecting a builder and signing a contract, you (or your contractor) then file the plans with the building department. When the plans are approved, often several weeks—or even months—later, you're ready to begin construction.

■ **Construction management.** Unless you intend to act as your own contractor, your role during the building process is mostly one of quality control and time management. Even so, it's important to know the sequence of events and something about construction methods so you can discuss progress with your builder and prepare for any important decisions you may need to make along the way.

Decision-making is critical. Once construction begins, the builder must usually plunge ahead, keeping his carpenters and subcontractors progressing steadily. If you haven't made a key decision—which model bathtub or sink to install, for example—it can bring construction to a frustrating and expensive halt.

Usually, you'll make such decisions before the onset of building, but, inevitably, some issue or another will arise during construction. Being knowledgeable about the building process will help you anticipate and circumvent potential logjams.

Selecting a House Plan

Searching for the right plan can be a fun, interactive family experience—one of the most exciting parts of a house-building project. Gather the family around as you peruse the home plans in this book. Study the size, location, and configuration of each room; traffic patterns both inside the house and to the outdoors; exterior style; and how you'll use the available space. Discuss the pros and cons of the various plans.

Browse through pictures of homes in magazines to stimulate ideas. Clip the photos you like so you can think about your favorite options. When you visit the homes of friends, note special features that appeal to you. Also, look carefully at the homes in your neighborhood, noting their style and how they fit the site.

Mark those plans that most closely suit your ideals. Then, to narrow down your choices, critique each plan, using the following information as a guide.

■ **Overall size and budget.** How large a house do you want? Will the house you're considering fit your family's requirements? Look at the overall square footage and room sizes. If you have a hard time visualizing room sizes, measure some of the rooms in your present home and compare.

It's often better for the house to be a little too big than a little too small, but remember that every extra square foot will cost more money to build and maintain.

■ **Number and type of rooms.** Beyond thinking about the number of bedrooms and baths you want, consider your family's life-style and how you use space. Do you want both a family room and a living room? Do you need a formal dining space? Will you require some extra rooms, or "swing spaces," that can serve multiple purposes, such as a home office–guest room combination?

■ **Room placement and traffic patterns.** What are your preferences for locations of formal living areas, master bedroom, and children's rooms? Do you prefer a kitchen that's open to family areas or one that's private and out of the way? How much do you use exterior spaces and how should they relate to the interior?

Once you make those determinations, look carefully at the floor plan of the house you're considering to see if it meets your needs and if the traffic flow will be convenient for your family.

■ **Architectural style.** Have you always wanted to live in a Victorian farmhouse? Now is your chance to create a house that matches your idea of "home" (taking into account, of course, styles in your neighborhood). But don't let your preference for one particular architectural style dictate your home's floor plan. If the floor plan doesn't work for your family, keep looking.

■ **Site considerations.** Most people choose a site before selecting a plan—or at least they've zeroed in on the basic type of land where they'll situate their house. It sounds elementary, but choose a house that will fit the site.

When figuring the "footprint" of a house, you must know about any restrictions that will affect your home's height or proximity to the property lines. Call the local building department (look under city or county listings in the phone book) and get a very clear description of any restrictions, such as setbacks, height limits, and lot coverage, that will affect what you can build on the site (see "Working with City Hall," at right).

When you visit potential sites, note trees, rock outcroppings, slopes, views, winds, sun, neighboring homes, and other factors. All will impact on how your house works on a particular site.

Once you've narrowed down the choice of sites, consult an architect or building designer (see page 8) to help you evaluate how some potential houses will work on the sites you have in mind.

Is Your Project Doable?

Before you purchase land, make sure your project is doable. Although it's too early at this stage to pinpoint costs, making a few phone calls will help you determine whether your project is realistic. You'll be able to learn if you can afford to build the house, how long it will take, and what obstacles may stand in your way.

To get a ballpark estimate of cost, multiply a house's total square footage (of livable space) by the local average cost per square foot for new construction. (To obtain local averages, call a contractor, an architect, a realtor, or the local chapter of the National Association of Home Builders.) Some contractors may even be willing to give you a preliminary bid. Once you know approximate costs, speak to your lender to explore financing.

Working with City Hall

For any building project, even a minor one, it's essential to be familiar with building codes and other restrictions that can affect your project.

■ **Building codes,** generally implemented by the city or county building department, set the standards for safe, lasting construction. Codes specify minimum construction techniques and materials for foundations, framing, electrical wiring, plumbing, insulation, and all other aspects of a building. Although codes are adopted and enforced locally, most regional codes conform to the standards set by the national Uniform Building Code, Standard Building Code, or Basic Building Code. In some cases, local codes set more restrictive standards than national ones.

■ **Building permits** are required for home-building projects nearly everywhere. If you work with a contractor, the builder's firm should handle all necessary permits.

More than one permit may be needed; for example, one will cover the foundation, another the electrical wiring, and still another the heating equipment installation. Each will probably involve a fee and require inspections by building officials before work can proceed. (Inspections benefit *you*, as they ensure that the job is being done satisfactorily.) Permit fees are generally a percentage (1 to 1.5 percent) of the project's estimated value, often calculated on square footage.

It's important to file for the necessary permits. Failure to do so can result in fines or legal action against you. You can even be forced to undo the work performed. At the very least, your negligence may come back to haunt you later when you're ready to sell your house.

■ **Zoning ordinances,** particular to your community, restrict setbacks (how near to property lines you may build), your house's allowable height, lot coverage factors (how much of your property you can cover with structures), and other factors that impact design and building. If your plans don't conform to zoning ordinances, you can try to obtain a variance, an exception to the rules. But this legal work can be expensive and time-consuming. Even if you prove that your project won't negatively affect your neighbors, the building department can still refuse to grant the variance.

■ **Deeds and covenants** attach to the lot. Deeds set out property lines and easements; covenants may establish architectural standards in a neighborhood. Since both can seriously impact your project, make sure you have complete information on any deeds or covenants before you turn over a spadeful of soil.

It's a good idea to discuss your project with several contractors (see page 8). They may be aware of problems in your area that could limit your options—bedrock that makes digging basements difficult, for example. These conversations are actually the first step in developing a list of contractors from which you'll choose the one who will build your home.

Recruiting Your Home Team

A home-building project will inject you and your family into the building business, an area that may be unfamiliar territory. Among the people you'll be working with are architects, designers, landscapers, contractors, and subcontractors.

Design Help

A qualified architect or designer can help you modify and personalize your home plan, taking into account your family's needs and budget and the house's style. In fact, you may want to consider consulting such a person while you're selecting a plan to help you articulate your needs.

Design professionals are capable of handling any or all aspects of the design process. For example, they can review your house plans, suggest options, and then provide rough sketches of the options on tracing paper. Many architects will even secure needed permits and negotiate with contractors or subcontractors, as well as oversee the quality of the work.

Of course, you don't necessarily need an architect or designer to implement minor changes in a plan; although most contractors aren't trained in design, some can help you with modifications.

An open-ended, hourly-fee arrangement that you work out with your architect or designer allows for flexibility, but it often turns out to be more costly than working on a flat-fee basis. On a flat fee, you agree to pay a specific amount of money for a certain amount of work.

To find architects and designers, contact such trade associations as the American Institute of Architects (AIA), American Institute of Building Designers (AIBD), American Society of Landscape Architects (ASLA), and American Society of Interior Designers (ASID). Although many professionals choose not to belong to trade associations, those who do have met the standards of their respective associations. For phone numbers of local branches, check the Yellow Pages.

■ **Architects** are licensed by the state and have degrees. They're trained in all facets of building design and construction. Although some can handle interior design and structural engineering, others hire specialists for those tasks.

■ **Building designers** are generally unlicensed but may be accredited by the American Institute of Building Designers. Their backgrounds are varied: some may be unlicensed architects in apprenticeship; others are interior designers or contractors with design skills.

■ **Draftspersons** offer an economical route to making simple changes on your drawings. Like building designers, these people may be unlicensed architect apprentices, engineers, or members of related trades. Most are accomplished at drawing up plans.

■ **Interior designers,** as their job title suggests, design interiors. They work with you to choose room finishes, furnishings, appliances, and decorative elements. Part of their expertise is in arranging furnishings to create a workable space plan. Some interior designers are employed by architectural firms; others work independently. Financial arrangements vary, depending on the designer's preference.

Related professionals are kitchen and bathroom designers, who concentrate on fixtures, cabinetry, appliances, materials, and space planning for the kitchen and bath.

■ **Landscape architects, designers, and contractors** design outdoor areas. Landscape architects are state-licensed to practice landscape design. A landscape designer usually has a landscape architect's education and training but does not have a state license. Licensed landscape contractors specialize in garden construction, though some also have design skills and experience.

■ **Soils specialists and structural engineers** may be needed for projects where unstable soils or uncommon wind loads or seismic forces must be taken into account. Any structural changes to a house require the expertise of a structural engineer to verify that the house won't fall down.

Services of these specialists can be expensive, but they're imperative in certain conditions to ensure a safe, sturdy structure. Your building department will probably let you know if their services are required.

General Contractors

To build your house, hire a licensed general contractor. Most states require a contractor to be licensed and insured for worker's compensation in order to contract a building project and hire other subcontractors. State licensing ensures that contractors have met minimum training standards and have a specified level of experience. Licensing does not guarantee, however, that they're good at what they do.

When contractors hire subcontractors, they're responsible for overseeing the quality of work and materials of the subcontractors and for paying them.

■ **Finding a contractor.** How do you find a good contractor? Start by getting referrals from people you know who have built or remodeled their home. Nothing beats a personal recommendation. The best contractors are usually busily moving from one satisfied client to another prospect, advertised only by word of mouth.

You can also ask local real estate brokers and lenders or even your building inspector for names of qualified builders. Experienced lumber dealers are another good source of names.

In the Yellow Pages, look under "Contractors–Building, General"; or call the local chapter of the National Association of Home Builders.

■ **Choosing a contractor.** Once you have a list of names of prospective builders, call several of them. On the telephone, ask first whether they handle your type of job and can work within your schedule. If they can, arrange a meeting with each one and ask them to be prepared with references of former clients and photos of previous jobs. Better still, meet them at one of their current work sites so you can get a glimpse of the quality of their work and how organized and thorough they are.

Take your plan to the meeting and discuss it enough to request a rough estimate (some builders will comply, while others will be reluctant to offer a ballpark estimate, preferring to give you a hard bid based on complete drawings). Don't hesitate to probe for advice or suggestions that might make building your house less expensive.

Be especially aware of each contractor's personality and how well you communicate. Good chemistry between you and your builder is a key ingredient for success.

Narrow down the candidates to three or four. Ask each for a firm bid, based on the exact same set of plans and specifications. For the bids to be accurate, your plans need to be complete and the specifications as precise as possible, call-ing out particular appliances, fixtures, floorings, roofing material, and so forth. (Some of these are specified in a stock-plan set; others are not.)

Call the contractors' references and ask about the quality of their work, their relationship with their clients, their promptness, and their readiness to follow up on problems. Visit former clients to check the contractor's work firsthand.

Be sure your final candidates are licensed, bonded, and insured for worker's compensation, public liability, and property damage. Also, try to determine how financially solvent they are (you can call their bank and credit references). Avoid contractors who are operating hand-to-mouth.

Don't automatically hire the contractor with the lowest bid if you don't think you'll get along well or if you have any doubts about the quality of the person's work. Instead, look for both the most reasonable bid and the contractor with the best credentials, references, terms, and compatibility with your family.

A word about bonds: You can request a performance bond that guarantees that your job will be finished by your contractor. If the job isn't completed, the bonding company will cover the cost of hiring another contractor to finish it. Bonds cost from 2 to 6 percent of the value of the project.

Your Building Contract

A building contract (see below) binds and protects both you and your contractor. It isn't just a legal document. It's also a list of the expectations of both parties. The best way to minimize the possibility of misunderstandings and costly changes later on is to write down every possible detail. Whether the contract is a standard form or one composed by you, have an attorney look it over before both you and the contractor sign it.

The contract should clearly specify all the work that needs to be done, including particular materials and work descriptions, the time schedule, and method of payment. It should be keyed to the working drawings.

A Sample Building Contract

Project and participants. Give a general description of the project, its address, and the names and addresses of both you and the builder.

Construction materials. Identify all construction materials by brand name, quality markings (species, grades, etc.), and model numbers where applicable. Avoid the clause "or equal," which allows the builder to substitute other materials for your choices. For materials you can't specify now, set down a budget figure.

Time schedule. Include both start and completion dates and specify that work will be "continuous." Although a contractor cannot be responsible for delays caused by strikes and material shortages, your builder should assume responsibility for completing the project within a reasonable period of time.

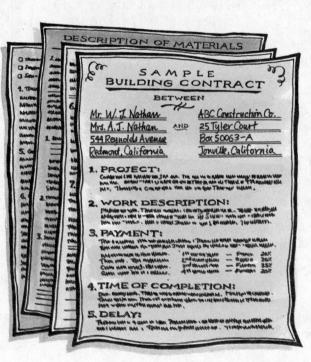

Work to be performed. State all work you expect the contractor to perform, from initial grading to finished painting.

Method and schedule of payment. Specify how and when payments are to be made. Typical agreements specify installment payments as particular phases of work are completed. Final payment is withheld until the job receives its final inspection and is cleared of all liens.

Waiver of liens. Protect yourself with a waiver of liens signed by the general contractor, the subcontractors, and all major suppliers. That way, subcontractors who are not paid for materials or services cannot place a lien on your property.

Personalizing Stock Plans

The beauty of buying stock plans for your new home is that they offer tested, well-conceived design at an affordable price. And stock plans dramatically reduce the time it takes to design a house, since the plans are ready when you are.

Because they were not created specifically for your family, stock plans may not reflect your personal taste. But it's not difficult to make revisions in stock plans that will turn your home into an expression of your family's personality. You'll surely want to add personal touches and choose your own finishes.

Ideally, the modifications you implement will be fairly minor. The more extensive the changes, the more expensive the plans. Major changes take valuable design time, and those that affect a house's structure may require a structural engineer's approval.

If you anticipate wholesale changes, such as moving a number of bearing walls or changing the roofline significantly, you may be better off selecting another plan. On the other hand, reconfiguring or changing the sizes of some rooms can probably be handled fairly easily.

Some structural changes may even be necessary to comply with local codes. Your area may have specific requirements for snow loads, energy codes, seismic or wind resistance, and so forth. Those types of modifications are likely to require the services of an architect or structural engineer.

Plan Modifications

Before you pencil in any changes, live with your plans for a while. Study them carefully—at your building site, if possible. Try to picture the finished house: how rooms will interrelate, where the sun will enter and at what angle, what the view will be from each window. Think about traffic patterns, access to rooms, room sizes, window and door locations, natural light, and kitchen and bathroom layouts.

Typical changes might involve adding windows or skylights to bring in natural light or capture a view. Or you may want to widen a hallway or doorway for roomier access, extend a room, eliminate doors, or change window and door sizes. Perhaps you'd like to shorten a room, stealing the gained space for a large closet. Look closely at the kitchen; it's not difficult to reconfigure the layout if it makes the space more convenient for you.

Above all, take your time—this is your home and it should reflect your taste and needs. Make your changes now, during the planning stage. Once construction begins, it will take crowbars, hammers, saws, new materials, and, most significantly, time to alter the plans. Because changes are not part of your building contract, you can count on them being expensive extras once construction begins.

Specifying Finishes

One way to personalize a house without changing its structure is to substitute your favorite finishes for those specified on the plan.

Would you prefer a stuccoed exterior rather than the wood siding shown on the plan? In most cases, this is a relatively easy change. Do you like the look of a wood shingle roof rather than the composition shingles shown on the plan? This, too, is easy. Perhaps you would like to change the windows from sliders to casements, or upgrade to high-efficiency glazing. No problem. Many of those kinds of changes can be worked out with your contractor.

Inside, you may want hardwood where vinyl flooring is shown. In fact, you can—and should—choose types, colors, and styles of floorings, wall coverings, tile, plumbing fixtures, door hardware, cabinetry, appliances, lighting fixtures, and other interior details, for it's these materials that will personalize your home. For help in making selections, consult an architect or interior designer (see page 8).

Each material you select should be spelled out clearly and precisely in your building contract.

Finishing touches can transform a house built from stock plans into an expression of your family's taste and style. Clockwise, from far left: Colorful tilework and custom cabinetry enliven a bathroom (Design: Osburn Design); highly organized closet system maximizes storage space (Architect: David Jeremiah Hurley); low-level deck expands living space to outdoor areas (Landscape architects: The Runa Group, Inc.); built-ins convert the corner of a guest room into a home office (Design: Lynn Williams of The French Connection); French country cabinetry lends style and old-world charm to a kitchen (Design: Garry Bishop/Showcase Kitchens).

What the Plans Include

Complete construction blueprints are available for every house shown in this book. Clear and concise, these detailed blueprints are designed by licensed architects or members of the American Institute of Building Designers (AIBD). Each plan is designed to meet standards set down by nationally recognized building codes (the Uniform Building Code, Standard Building Code, or Basic Building Code) at the time and for the area where they were drawn.

Remember, however, that every state, county, and municipality has its own codes, zoning requirements, ordinances, and building regulations. Modifications may be necessary to comply with such local requirements as snow loads, energy codes, seismic zones, and flood areas.

Although blueprint sets vary depending on the size and complexity of the house and on the individual designer's style, each set may include the elements described below and shown at right.

■ **Exterior elevations** show the front, rear, and sides of the house, including exterior materials, details, and measurements.

■ **Foundation plans** include drawings for a full, partial, or daylight basement, crawlspace, pole, pier, or slab foundation. All necessary notations and dimensions are included. (Foundation options will vary for each plan. If the plan you choose doesn't have the type of foundation you desire, a generic conversion diagram is available.)

■ **Detailed floor plans** show the placement of interior walls and the dimensions of rooms, doors, windows, stairways, and similar elements for each level of the house.

■ **Cross sections** show details of the house as though it were cut in slices from the roof to the foundation. The cross sections give the home's construction, insulation, flooring, and roofing details.

■ **Interior elevations** show the specific details of cabinets (kitchen, bathroom, and utility room), fireplaces, built-in units, and other special interior features.

■ **Roof details** give the layout of rafters, dormers, gables, and other roof elements, including clerestory windows and skylights. These details may be shown on the elevation sheet or on a separate diagram.

■ **Schematic electrical layouts** show the suggested locations for switches, fixtures, and outlets. These details may be shown on the floor plan or on a separate diagram.

■ **General specifications** provide instructions and information regarding excavation and grading, masonry and concrete work, carpentry and woodwork, thermal and moisture protection, drywall, tile, flooring, glazing, and caulking and sealants.

Other Helpful Building Aids

In addition to the construction information on every set of plans, you can buy the following guides.

■ **Reproducible blueprints** are helpful if you'll be making changes to the stock plan you've chosen. These blueprints are original line drawings produced on erasable, reproducible paper for the purpose of modification. When alterations are complete, working copies can be made.

■ **Itemized materials list** details the quantity, type, and size of materials needed to build your home. (This list is extremely helpful in obtaining an accurate construction bid. It's not intended for use to order materials.)

■ **Mirror-reverse plans** are useful if you want to build your home in the reverse of the plan that's shown. Because the lettering and dimensions read backwards, be sure to buy at least one regular-reading set of blueprints.

■ **Description of materials** gives the type and quality of materials suggested for the home. This form may be required for obtaining FHA or VA financing.

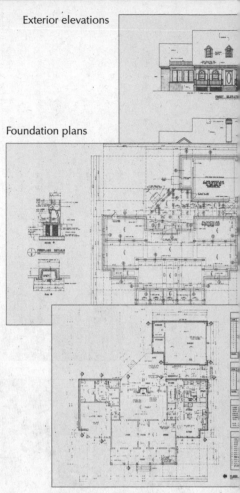

Exterior elevations

Foundation plans

Detailed floor plans

■ **How-to diagrams** for plumbing, wiring, solar heating, framing and foundation conversions show how to plumb, wire, install a solar heating system, convert plans with 2 by 4 exterior walls to 2 by 6 construction (or vice versa), and adapt a plan for a basement, crawlspace, or slab foundation. These diagrams are not specific to any one plan.

NOTE: Due to regional variations, local availability of materials, local codes, methods of installation, and individual preferences, detailed heating, plumbing, and electrical specifications are not included on plans. The duct work, venting, and other details will vary, depending on the heating and cooling system you use and the type of energy that operates it. These details and specifications are easily obtained from your builder or local supplier.

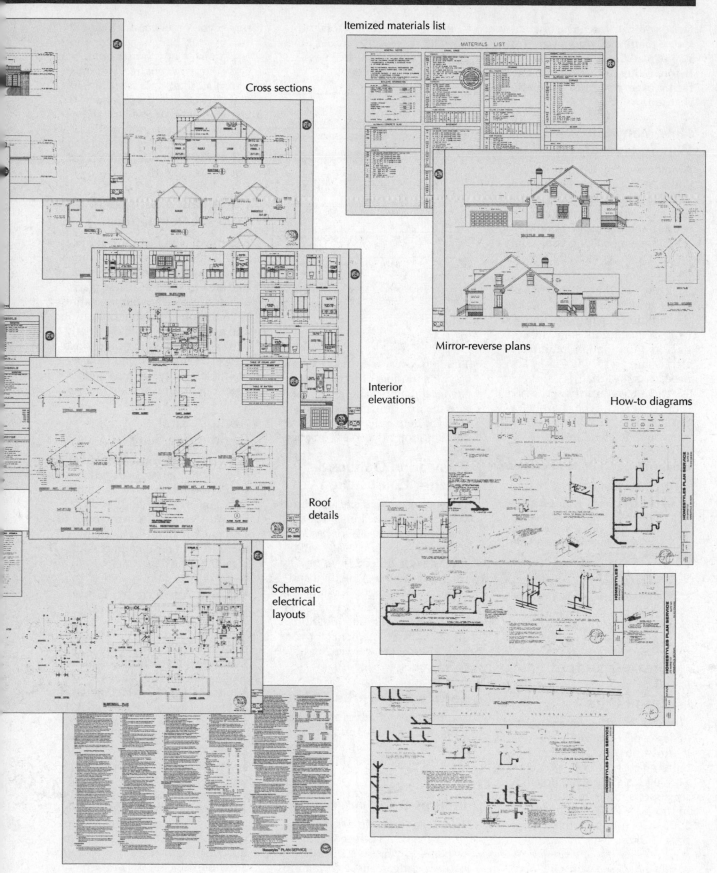

Itemized materials list

Cross sections

Mirror-reverse plans

Interior
elevations

How-to diagrams

Roof
details

Schematic
electrical
layouts

General specifications

13

Before You Order

Once you've chosen the one or two house plans that work best for you, you're ready to order blueprints. Before filling in the form on the facing page, note the information that follows.

How Many Blueprints Will You Need?

A single set of blueprints will allow you to study a home design in detail. You'll need more for obtaining bids and permits, as well as some to use as reference at the building site. If you'll be modifying your home plan, order a reproducible set (see page 12).

Figure you'll need at least one set each for yourself, your builder, the building department, and your lender. In addition, some subcontractors—foundation, plumber, electrician, and HVAC—may also need at least partial sets. If they do, ask them to return the sets when they're finished. The chart below can help you calculate how many sets you're likely to need.

Blueprint Checklist

____**Owner's set(s)**

____**Builder usually requires at least three sets: one for legal documentation, one for inspections, and a minimum of one set for subcontractors.**

____**Building department requires at least one set. Check with your local department before ordering.**

____**Lending institution usually needs one set for a conventional mortgage, three sets for FHA or VA loans.**

____**TOTAL SETS NEEDED**

Blueprint Prices

The cost of having an architect design a new custom home typically runs from 5 to 15 percent of the building cost, or from $5,000 to $15,000 for a $100,000 home. A single set of blueprints for the plans in this book ranges from $295 to $505, depending on the house's size. Working with these drawings, you can save enough on design fees to add a deck, a swimming pool, or a luxurious kitchen.

Pricing is based on "total finished living space." Garages, porches, decks, and unfinished basements are not included.

Price Code (Size)	1 Set	4 Sets	7 Sets	Reproducible Set
A (under 1,500 sq. ft.)	$295	$345	$380	$455
B (1,500-1,999 sq. ft.)	$330	$380	$415	$490
C (2,000-2,499 sq. ft.)	$365	$415	$450	$525
D (2,500-2,999 sq. ft.)	$400	$450	$485	$560
E (3,000-3,499 sq. ft.)	$435	$485	$520	$595
F (3,500-3,999 sq. ft.)	$470	$520	$555	$630
G (4,000 sq. ft. and up)	$505	$555	$590	$665

Building Costs

Building costs vary widely, depending on a number of factors, including local material and labor costs and the finishing materials you select. For help estimating costs, see "Is Your Project Doable?" on page 7.

Foundation Options & Exterior Construction

Depending on your site and climate, your home will be built with a slab, pier, pole, crawlspace, or basement foundation. Exterior walls will be framed with either 2 by 4s or 2 by 6s, determined by structural and insulation standards in your area. Most contractors can easily adapt a home to meet the foundation and/or wall requirements for your area. Or ask for a conversion how-to diagram (see page 12).

Service & Blueprint Delivery

Service representatives are available to answer questions and assist you in placing your order. Every effort is made to process and ship orders within 48 hours.

Returns & Exchanges

Each set of blueprints is specially printed and shipped to you in response to your specific order; consequently, requests for refunds cannot be honored. However, if the prints you order cannot be used, you may exchange them for another plan from any Sunset home plan book. For an exchange, you must return all sets of plans within 30 days. A nonrefundable service charge will be assessed for all exchanges; for more information, call the toll-free number on the facing page. Note: Reproducible sets cannot be exchanged.

Compliance with Local Codes & Regulations

Because of climatic, geographic, and political variations, building codes and regulations vary from one area to another. These plans are authorized for your use expressly conditioned on your obligation and agreement to comply strictly with all local building codes, ordinances, regulations, and requirements, including permits and inspections at time of construction.

Architectural & Engineering Seals

With increased concern about energy costs and safety, many cities and states now require that an architect or engineer review and "seal" a blueprint prior to construction. To find out whether this is a requirement in your area, contact your local building department.

License Agreement, Copy Restrictions & Copyright

When you purchase your blueprints, you are granted the right to use those documents to construct a single unit. All the plans in this publication are protected under the Federal Copyright Act, Title XVII of the United States Code and Chapter 37 of the Code of Federal Regulations. Each designer retains title and ownership of the original documents. The blueprints licensed to you cannot be used by or resold to any other person, copied, or reproduced by any means. The copying restrictions do not apply to reproducible blueprints. When you buy a reproducible set, you may modify and reproduce it for your own use.

Blueprint Order Form

Complete this order form in just three easy steps. Then mail in your order or, for faster service, call toll-free.

1. Blueprints & Accessories

BLUEPRINT CHART

Price Code	1 Set	4 Sets	7 Sets	Reproducible Set*
A	$295	$345	$380	$455
B	$330	$380	$415	$490
C	$365	$415	$450	$525
D	$400	$450	$485	$560
E	$435	$485	$520	$595
F	$470	$520	$555	$630
G	$505	$555	$590	$665

Prices subject to change

*A reproducible set is produced on erasable paper for the purpose of modification. It is only available for plans with prefixes A, AG, AGH, AH, AHP, APS, AX, B, C, CPS, DCL, DD, DW, E, EOF, FB, GL, GML, GSA, H, HDG, HDS, HFL, J, K, KLF, LMB, LRD, M, NW, OH, PH, PI, S, SDG, THD, U, UDG, V.

Mirror-Reverse Sets: $40 surcharge. From the total number of sets you ordered above, choose the number you want to be reversed. *Note: All writing on mirror-reverse plans is backwards. Order at least one regular-reading set.*

Itemized Materials List: One set $40; each additional set $10. Details the quantity, type, and size of materials needed to build your home.

Description of Materials: Sold in a set of two for $40 (for use in obtaining FHA or VA financing).

Typical How-To Diagrams: One set $15; two sets $25; three sets $35; four sets $40. General guides on plumbing, wiring, and solar heating, plus information on how to convert from one foundation or exterior framing to another. *Note: These diagrams are not specific to any one plan.*

2. Sales Tax & Shipping

Determine your subtotal and add appropriate local state sales tax, plus shipping and handling (see chart below).

SHIPPING & HANDLING

	1–3 Sets	4–6 Sets	7 or More Sets	Reproducible Set
U.S. Regular (4–6 working days)	$15.00	$17.50	$20.00	$15.00
U.S. Express (2–3 working days)	$27.50	$30.00	$32.50	$27.50
Canada Regular (2–3 weeks)	$15.00	$17.50	$20.00	$15.00
Canada Express (4–6 working days)	$27.50	$32.50	$37.50	$27.50
Overseas/Airmail (7–10 working days)	$52.50	$62.50	$72.50	$52.50

3. Customer Information

Choose the method of payment you prefer. Include check, money order, or credit card information, complete name and address portion, and mail to:

Sunset/HomeStyles Plan Service
P.O. Box 50670
Minneapolis, MN 55405

FOR FASTER SERVICE
CALL 1-800-547-5570

SS13

COMPLETE THIS FORM

Plan Number _____ **Price Code** _____

Foundation _____
(Review your plan carefully for foundation options—basement, pole, pier, crawlspace, or slab. Many plans offer several options; others offer only one.)

Number of Sets: $_____
    ☐ One Set   (See chart at left)
    ☐ Four Sets
    ☐ Seven Sets
    ☐ One Reproducible Set

Additional Sets _____ $_____
    ($40 each)

Mirror-Reverse Sets _____ $_____
    ($40 surcharge)

Itemized Materials List $_____
Only available for plans with prefixes AH, AHP, APS*, AX*, B*, C, CAR, CDG*, CPS, DD*, DW, E, FB, GSA, H, HDG, HFL, I*, J, K, LMB*, LRD, N, NW*, P, PH, R, S, THD, U, UDG, VL. *Not available on all plans. Please call before ordering.

Description of Materials $_____
Only available for plans with prefixes AHP, C, DW, H, HFL, J, K, LMB, P, PH, VL.

Typical How-To Diagrams $_____
☐ Plumbing ☐ Wiring ☐ Solar Heating ☐ Foundation & Framing Conversion

SUBTOTAL $_____

SALES TAX $_____

SHIPPING & HANDLING $_____

GRAND TOTAL $_____

☐ Check/money order enclosed (in U.S. funds)
☐ VISA   ☐ MasterCard   ☐ AmEx   ☐ Discover

Credit Card # _____ **Exp. Date** _____

Signature _____

Name _____

Address _____

City _____ **State** ____ **Country** _____

Zip _____ **Daytime Phone** (_____) _____
☐ Please check if you are a contractor.

Mail form to: Sunset/HomeStyles Plan Service
                P.O. Box 50670
                Minneapolis, MN 55405

Or fax to: (612) 338-1626

FOR FASTER SERVICE
CALL 1-800-547-5570

SS13

Garden Home

- This thoroughly modern plan exhibits beautiful traditional touches in its exterior design.
- A garden area leads visitors to a side door with a vaulted entry.
- A delightful kitchen/nook area is just to the right of the entry, and includes a convenient snack bar, a pantry and a nearby laundry room. The bayed breakfast nook overlooks the front yard.
- The living and dining areas share a 12½-ft.-high vaulted ceiling, making an impressive space for entertaining and family living. The stone fireplace and patio view add to the dramatic atmosphere.
- The master suite boasts a large closet and a private bath.
- Two more bedrooms share another bath off the hall.

Plans P-6598-2A & -2D

Bedrooms: 3	Baths: 2
Living Area:	
Main floor (with crawlspace)	1,375 sq. ft.
Main floor (with basement)	1,470 sq. ft.
Total Living Area:	**1,375/1,470 sq. ft.**
Daylight basement	1,470 sq. ft.
Garage	435 sq. ft.
Exterior Wall Framing:	2x4
Foundation Options:	**Plan #**
Daylight basement	P-6598-2D
Crawlspace	P-6598-2A

(All plans can be built with your choice of foundation and framing. A generic conversion diagram is available. See order form.)

BLUEPRINT PRICE CODE:	**A**

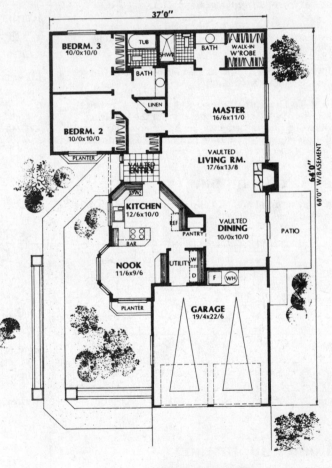

MAIN FLOOR

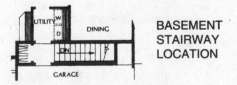

BASEMENT STAIRWAY LOCATION

TO ORDER THIS BLUEPRINT, CALL TOLL-FREE 1-800-547-5570

Plans P-6598-2A & -2D

PRICES AND DETAILS ON PAGES 12-15

Designed for Today's Family

- Compact and affordable, this home is designed for today's young families.
- The Great Room features corner windows, an impressive fireplace and a 12-ft.-high vaulted ceiling.
- The kitchen/dining room combination offers space for two people to share food preparation and clean-up chores.
- The master suite is impressive for a home of this size, and includes a cozy window seat, a large walk-in closet and a private bath.
- Another full bath serves the remainder of the main floor. The optional third bedroom could be used as a den or as an expanded dining area.

Plan B-8317

Bedrooms: 2+	Baths: 2
Living Area:	
Main floor	1,016 sq. ft.
Total Living Area:	**1,016 sq. ft.**
Exterior Wall Framing:	2x4

Foundation Options:

Slab
(All plans can be built with your choice of foundation and framing. A generic conversion diagram is available. See order form.)

BLUEPRINT PRICE CODE: **A**

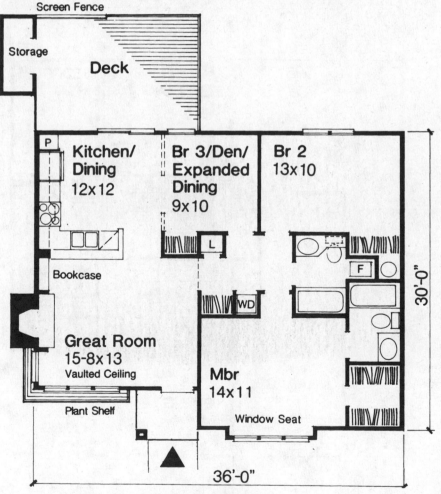

MAIN FLOOR

Country-Style Coziness

- Designed as a starter or retirement home, this delightful plan has a charming exterior and an open, airy interior.
- The spacious front porch gives guests a warm welcome and provides added space for relaxing or entertaining. The modified hip roof, half-round louver vent and decorative porch railings are other distinguishing features of the facade.
- Inside, the open dining and living rooms are heightened by dramatic vaulted ceilings. The streamlined kitchen has a snack counter joining it to the dining room. All three rooms reap the benefits of the fireplace.
- A laundry closet is in the hall leading to the three bedrooms. The main bath is close by.
- The master bedroom suite offers its own bath, plus a private patio sequestered behind the garage.

Plan APS-1002

Bedrooms: 3	**Baths:** 2

Space:	
Main floor	1,050 sq. ft.
Total Living Area	**1,050 sq. ft.**
Garage	288 sq. ft.
Exterior Wall Framing	2x4

Foundation options:

Slab

(Foundation & framing conversion diagram available—see order form.)

Blueprint Price Code	A

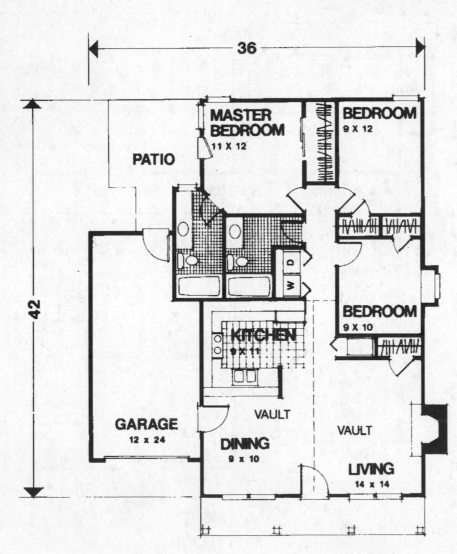

Plan APS-1002

PRICES AND DETAILS
ON PAGES 12-15

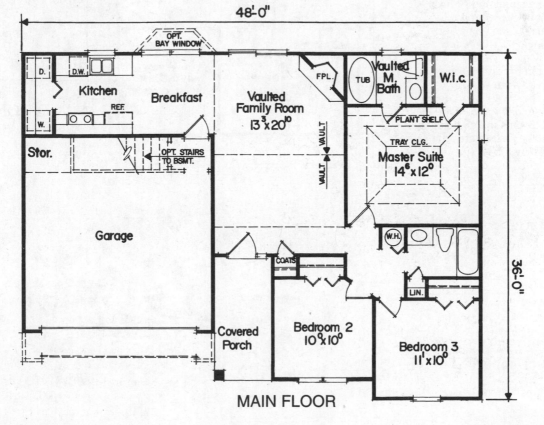

High Ceilings, Large Spaces!

- This affordable home is filled with large spaces that are further enhanced by high ceilings and lots of windows.
- The charming exterior is complemented by a combination of lap siding and brick, along with a columned front porch and a sidelighted entry door.
- Inside, the first area to come into view is the huge family room, which features a 15½-ft. vaulted ceiling and an efficient corner fireplace. Sliding glass doors open up the room to the backyard.

- The family room flows into the spacious breakfast room and kitchen. A picture window or an optional bay window brightens the breakfast room, while the kitchen offers a window above the sink and a convenient laundry closet that hides the clutter.
- The master suite leaves out nothing. An 11-ft. tray ceiling in the sleeping area gives way to the vaulted master bath, which is accented with a plant shelf above the entrance. A roomy walk-in closet is also included. The two smaller bedrooms share a hall bath.
- The optional basement doubles the home's size, providing ample expansion space.

Plan FB-1070	
Bedrooms: 3	**Baths:** 2
Living Area:	
Main floor	1,070 sq. ft.
Total Living Area:	**1,070 sq. ft.**
Daylight basement	1,070 sq. ft.
Garage	484 sq. ft.
Exterior Wall Framing:	2x4
Foundation Options:	
Daylight basement	
Crawlspace	
Slab	

(All plans can be built with your choice of foundation and framing. A generic conversion diagram is available. See order form.)

BLUEPRINT PRICE CODE: **A**

MAIN FLOOR

Adorable and Affordable

- This charming one-story home has much to offer, despite its modest size and economical bent.
- The lovely full-width porch has old-fashioned detailing, such as the round columns, decorative railings and ornamental molding.
- An open floor plan maximizes the home's square footage. The front door opens to the living room, where a railing creates a hallway effect while using very little space.
- Straight ahead, the dining room adjoins the island kitchen, while offering a compact laundry closet and sliding glass doors to a large rear patio.
- Focusing on quality, the home also offers features such as a 10-ft. tray ceiling in the living room and a 9-ft. stepped ceiling in the dining room.
- The three bedrooms are well proportioned. The master bedroom includes a private bathroom, while the two smaller bedrooms share another full bath. Note that the fixtures are arranged to reduce plumbing runs.

Plan AX-91316

Bedrooms: 3	Baths: 2
Living Area:	
Main floor	1,097 sq. ft.
Total Living Area:	**1,097 sq. ft.**
Standard basement	1,097 sq. ft.
Garage	461 sq. ft.
Exterior Wall Framing:	2x4

Foundation Options:

Standard basement
Slab

(All plans can be built with your choice of foundation and framing. A generic conversion diagram is available. See order form.)

BLUEPRINT PRICE CODE: A

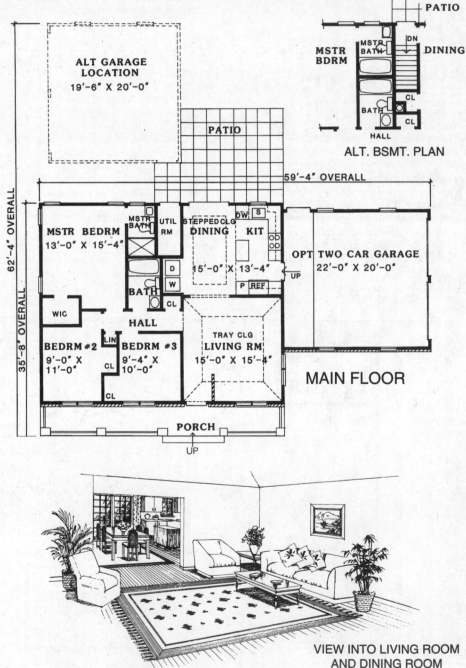

ALT GARAGE LOCATION 19'-6" X 20'-0"

PATIO

59'-4" OVERALL

62'-4" OVERALL

35'-8" OVERALL

MSTR BEDRM 13'-0" X 15'-4"

MSTR BATH

UTIL RM

STEPPED CLG DINING 15'-0" X 13'-4"

DW S

KIT

OPT TWO CAR GARAGE 22'-0" X 20'-0"

BATH

WIC

D

W

CL

P REF

UP

BEDRM #2 9'-0" X 11'-0"

LIN

HALL

BEDRM #3 9'-4" X 10'-0"

CL

CL

CL

TRAY CLG LIVING RM 15'-0" X 15'-4"

MAIN FLOOR

PORCH

UP

PATIO

MSTR BDRM

MSTR BATH

DN

DINING

BATH

CL

CL

HALL

ALT. BSMT. PLAN

VIEW INTO LIVING ROOM AND DINING ROOM

Plan AX-91316

PRICES AND DETAILS ON PAGES 12-15

Love at First Sight!

- Upon seeing its covered front porch and bright brick and siding exterior, it's easy to fall in love with this adorable home.
- Past the ornate and inviting entry, the spacious family room and its decorative plant shelf and dramatic fireplace offer an impressive introduction to the interior. Tall windows and a high 12-ft. vaulted ceiling add to the ambience.
- The adjoining dining room is great for casual or formal occasions. The sliding glass doors that access the backyard may be built into a sunny window bay for a more dramatic effect.
- The efficient galley-style kitchen offers a pantry, an attached laundry room and a door to the garage.
- Three bedrooms occupy the sleeping wing. The master bedroom includes a roomy walk-in closet. The private master bath features a 12-ft. vaulted ceiling, a garden tub, a separate shower and a dual-sink vanity.
- A second full bath services the secondary bedrooms, one of which may be expanded by a 12-ft. vaulted ceiling.

Plan APS-1103

Bedrooms: 3	Baths: 2
Living Area:	
Main floor	1,197 sq. ft.
Total Living Area:	**1,197 sq. ft.**
Garage	380 sq. ft.
Exterior Wall Framing:	2x4

Foundation Options:

Slab

(All plans can be built with your choice of foundation and framing. A generic conversion diagram is available. See order form.)

BLUEPRINT PRICE CODE: A

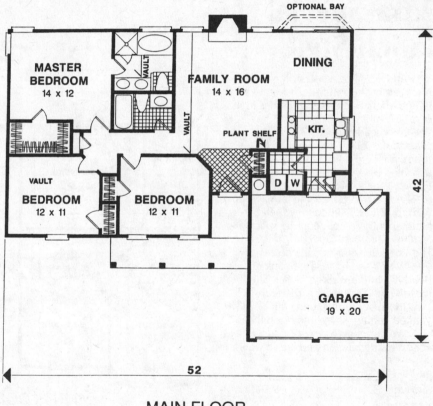

MAIN FLOOR

Extra-Special Ranch-Style

- Repeating gables, wood siding and brick adorn this ranch-style home, which offers numerous amenities in its compact interior.
- The entry leads directly into a spectacular 21-ft.-high vaulted family room, an ideal entertainment area accented by a corner fireplace and a French door to the backyard.
- A serving bar connects the family room with the efficient kitchen, which has a handy pantry, ample counter space and a sunny breakfast room.
- The luxurious master suite boasts a 10½-ft. tray ceiling, a large bank of windows and a walk-in closet. The master bath features a garden tub.
- Two more bedrooms, one with a 14½-ft. vaulted ceiling, share another full bath.
- The two-car garage provides convenient access to the kitchen and laundry area.

Plan FB-1104

Bedrooms: 3	Baths: 2
Living Area:	
Main floor	1,104 sq. ft.
Total Living Area:	**1,104 sq. ft.**
Daylight basement	1,104 sq. ft.
Garage	400 sq. ft.
Exterior Wall Framing:	2x4

Foundation Options:

Daylight basement
Crawlspace

(All plans can be built with your choice of foundation and framing. A generic conversion diagram is available. See order form.)

BLUEPRINT PRICE CODE: A

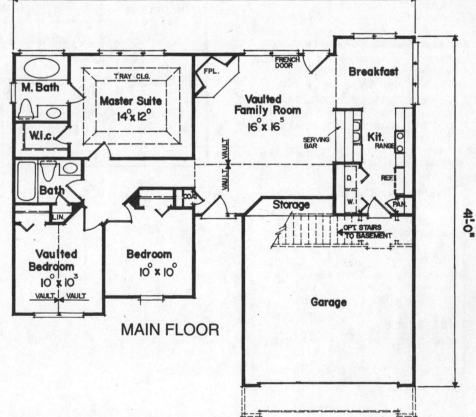

MAIN FLOOR

Plan FB-1104

PRICES AND DETAILS ON PAGES 12-15

Compact Home with Rustic Look

- While it may resemble a hunting lodge on the outside, this home is cozy and modern inside.
- The spacious living room offers sloped ceilings, a great fireplace and hearth and a view through the open dining room to the rear of the home.
- The kitchen is designed for convenience, featuring a broom closet and a double pantry.
- The master suite is luxurious for a compact home, with its large closet, compartmentalized bath and dressing room with double vanity.
- Two secondary bedrooms are on the opposite side of the home for privacy and share another full bath.
- Note the unusual wrap-around arrangement of the utility/storage area and garage.

Plan E-1106

Bedrooms: 3	Baths: 2
Space:	
Main floor	1,187 sq. ft.
Total Living Area	**1,187 sq. ft.**
Garage	440 sq. ft.
Utility & Storage	108 sq. ft.
Porch	99 sq. ft.
Exterior Wall Framing	2x6

Foundation options:

Crawlspace

Slab

(Foundation & framing conversion diagram available—see order form.)

Blueprint Price Code	A

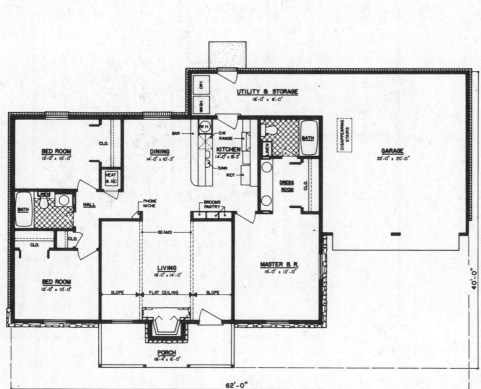

Appealing Farmhouse

- This appealing farmhouse design features a shady and inviting front porch with decorative railings.
- Inside, 14-ft. vaulted ceilings expand the living and dining rooms.
- This large area is brightened by bay windows and warmed by a unique two-way fireplace. Sliding glass doors lead to a sunny backyard patio.
- The functional kitchen includes a pantry closet, plenty of cabinet space and a serving bar to the dining room.
- The master bedroom boasts a mirrored dressing area, a private bath and abundant closet space.
- Two additional bedrooms share another full bath. The third bedroom includes a cozy window seat.

Plan NW-521

Bedrooms: 3	Baths: 2
Living Area:	
Main floor	1,187 sq. ft.
Total Living Area:	**1,187 sq. ft.**
Garage	448 sq. ft.
Exterior Wall Framing:	2x6

Foundation Options:

Crawlspace

(All plans can be built with your choice of foundation and framing. A generic conversion diagram is available. See order form.)

BLUEPRINT PRICE CODE: **A**

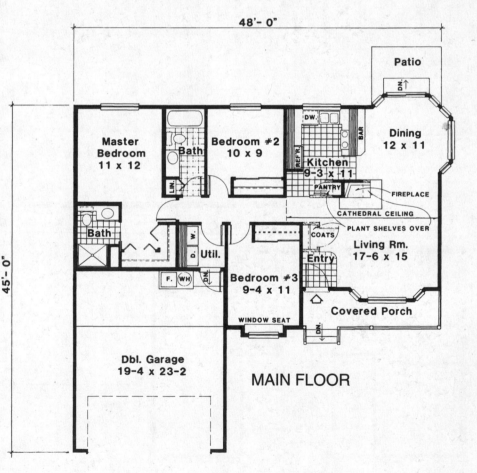

MAIN FLOOR

Plan NW-521

PRICES AND DETAILS ON PAGES 12-15

Cozy, Rustic Country Home

- This cozy, rustic home offers a modern, open interior that efficiently maximizes the square footage.
- The large living room features a 13-ft. sloped ceiling accented by rustic beams and an eye-catching corner fireplace.
- The living room flows into the adjoining dining room and the efficient U-shaped kitchen for a spacious, open feel.
- The master and secondary bedrooms are separated by the activity areas. The master suite includes a private bath and a separate dressing area with a dual-sink vanity.
- The secondary bedrooms share another full bath.

Plan E-1109

Bedrooms: 3	Baths: 2
Living Area:	
Main floor	1,191 sq. ft.
Total Living Area:	**1,191 sq. ft.**
Garage	462 sq. ft.
Storage & utility	55 sq. ft.
Exterior Wall Framing:	2x6

Foundation Options:

Crawlspace
Slab
(All plans can be built with your choice of foundation and framing. A generic conversion diagram is available. See order form.)

BLUEPRINT PRICE CODE: A

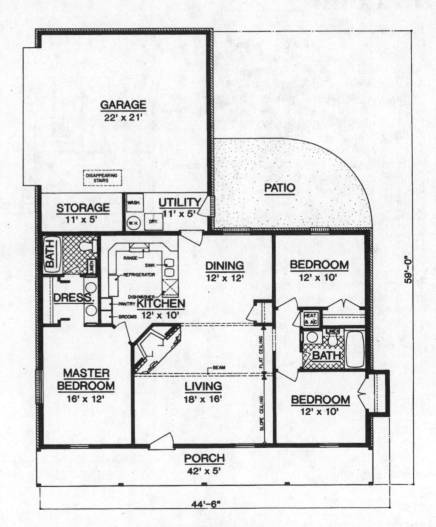

MAIN FLOOR

Family Tradition

- This home basks in tradition, with beautiful detailing on the outside and vaulted family gathering areas inside.
- A columned front porch opens to a spacious family room, where a 16-ft. vaulted ceiling soars above a striking fireplace flanked by arched windows. The 16-ft. ceiling continues into the dining room and kitchen beyond.
- The sunny dining room opens to the backyard through a French door. The vaulted kitchen offers a bright angled sink, a snack bar and a large pantry closet topped by a plant shelf.
- The master suite boasts a 10½-ft. tray ceiling in the sleeping area and a 13½-ft. vaulted ceiling in the luxurious garden bath.
- Two secondary bedrooms share another full bath. A roomy laundry area is close to the bedrooms and the garage.
- For added spaciousness, all ceilings are 9 ft. high unless otherwise specified.

Plan FB-5115-CLAI

Bedrooms: 3	Baths: 2
Living Area:	
Main floor	1,198 sq. ft.
Total Living Area:	**1,198 sq. ft.**
Standard basement	1,198 sq. ft.
Garage	484 sq. ft.
Exterior Wall Framing:	2x4

Foundation Options:

Daylight basement

Crawlspace

(All plans can be built with your choice of foundation and framing. A generic conversion diagram is available. See order form.)

BLUEPRINT PRICE CODE: A

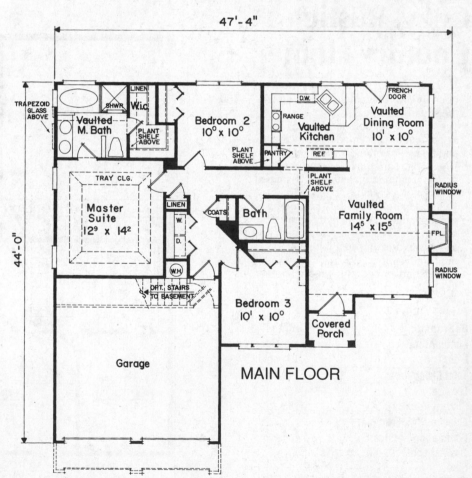

MAIN FLOOR

Affordable Amenities

- An excellent design for a young family or an empty-nest couple.
- This design is an economical, affordable size, but includes the amenities today's homeowners are looking for.
- The large country-style kitchen includes a sunny breakfast nook, garden window over the sink and a pantry.
- The master bedroom includes a private bath and large walk-in closet.
- Living and dining rooms flow together to make an impressive open space for family gatherings or entertaining.
- Living room boasts an impressive fireplace and a vaulted ceiling.
- Optional third bedroom would make a convenient home office.

Plan CDG-1001

Bedrooms: 2-3	Baths: 2
Total living area:	1,199 sq. ft.
Garage:	494 sq. ft.
Exterior Wall Framing:	2x6

Foundation options:
Crawlspace only.
(Foundation & framing conversion diagram available — see order form.)

Blueprint Price Code: A

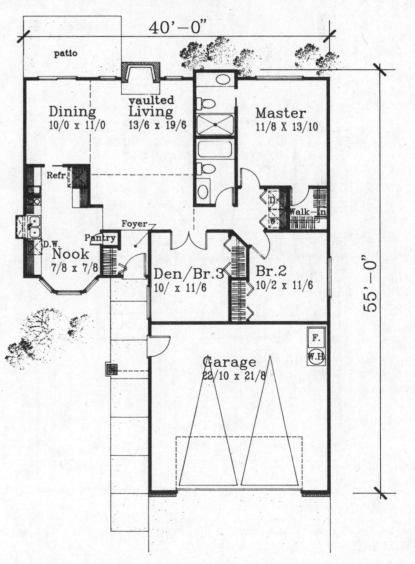

Dining 10/0 x 11/0

vaulted Living 13/6 x 19/6

Master 11/8 X 13/10

patio

Refr.

Foyer

Pantry

D.W.

Nook 7/8 x 7/8

Den/Br.3 10/ x 11/6

Br.2 10/2 x 11/6

Walk-in

Garage 22/10 x 21/8

F. W.H.

40'-0"

55'-0"

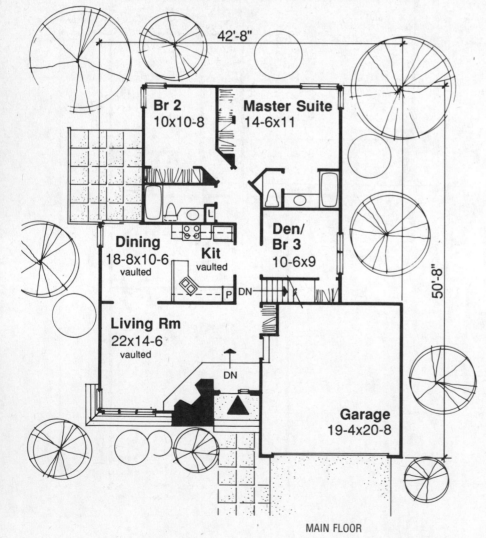

MAIN FLOOR

Br 2
10x10-8

Master Suite
14-6x11

Dining
18-8x10-6
vaulted

Kit
vaulted

Den/
Br 3
10-6x9

Living Rm
22x14-6
vaulted

Garage
19-4x20-8

42'-8"

50'-8"

Maximum Value and Excitement

- This well-planned 1,231 sq. ft. ranch design gives the first-time home buyer the most value and excitement for the dollar.
- The front porch, stone chimney, divided windows, and gable louvre all highlight a nostalgic charm.
- The interior spaces feature vaulted ceilings for an airy feel.
- The den could serve several functions, including guest quarters or a formal dining room.
- The master bedroom has a full-wall closet and a divided bath with private toilet.

Plan B-88021

Bedrooms: 2-3	Baths: 2
Space:	
Total living area:	1,231 sq. ft.
Basement:	1,231 sq. ft.
Garage:	400 sq. ft.
Exterior Wall Framing:	2x4

Foundation options:
Standard basement.
(Foundation & framing conversion diagram available — see order form.)

Blueprint Price Code:	A

Spacious Living/Dining Area

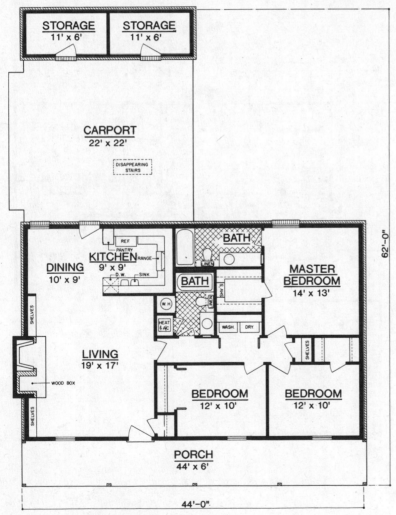

AREAS

Living	1244 sq. ft.
Porches	269 sq. ft.
Carport	484 sq. ft.
Storage	132 sq. ft.
Total	2129 sq. ft.

Exterior walls are 2x6 construction.
Specify crawlspace or slab foundation.

STORAGE 11' x 6'
STORAGE 11' x 6'
CARPORT 22' x 22'
DISAPPEARING STAIRS
DINING 10' x 9'
KITCHEN 9' x 9'
REF.
PANTRY
RANGE
D.W. SINK
BATH
LINEN
BATH
SHV'S
MASTER BEDROOM 14' x 13'
W H
HEAT & AC
WASH. DRY.
SHELVES
LIVING 19' x 17'
WOOD BOX
SHELVES
SHELVES
BEDROOM 12' x 10'
BEDROOM 12' x 10'
PORCH 44' x 6'
62'-0"
44'-0"

Blueprint Price Code A

Plan E-1219

**TO ORDER THIS BLUEPRINT,
CALL TOLL-FREE 1-800-547-5570**

**PRICES AND DETAILS
ON PAGES 12-15**

29

Comfortable L-Shaped Ranch

- From the covered entry to the beautiful and spacious family gathering areas, this comfortable ranch-style home puts many extras into a compact space.
- Straight off the central foyer, an inviting fireplace and a bright bay window highlight the living and dining area, while sliding glass doors open to a wide backyard terrace.
- The combination kitchen/family room features a large eating bar. The nearby mudroom offers a service entrance, laundry facilities, access to the garage and room for a half-bath.
- In the isolated sleeping wing, the master bedroom boasts a private bath and plenty of closet space. Two additional bedrooms share another full bath.

Plan K-276-R

Bedrooms: 3	Baths: 2+
Living Area:	
Main floor	1,245 sq. ft.
Total Living Area:	**1,245 sq. ft.**
Standard basement	1,245 sq. ft.
Garage	499 sq. ft.
Exterior Wall Framing:	2x4 or 2x6

Foundation Options:

Standard basement
Crawlspace
Slab

(All plans can be built with your choice of foundation and framing. A generic conversion diagram is available. See order form.)

BLUEPRINT PRICE CODE: **A**

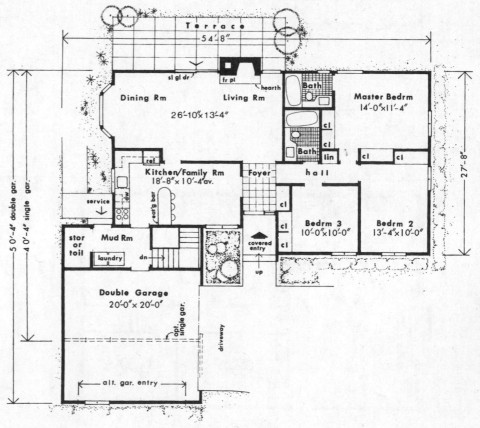

MAIN FLOOR

TO ORDER THIS BLUEPRINT, CALL TOLL-FREE 1-800-547-5570

Plan K-276-R

PRICES AND DETAILS ON PAGES 12-15

Designed for Easy Living

- A covered porch and an open foyer welcome guests to this stylish home.
- The spacious living and dining rooms merge together for a large activity or entertaining expanse. A bay window at one end and sliding glass doors at the other brighten the area, while a stone fireplace sets a comfortable mood.
- The kitchen's handy snack bar makes the dining room suitable for casual dining as well as formal entertaining. The patio is perfect for outdoor events.
- Three bedrooms make up the sleeping wing, removed from the rest of the home. The two secondary bedrooms share a hall bath. The master bedroom has its own bath, in addition to a large walk-in closet.
- An oversized laundry room is located near the garage access.

Plan LMB-2203-T

Bedrooms: 3	Baths: 2
Living Area:	
Main floor	1,248 sq. ft.
Total Living Area:	**1,248 sq. ft.**
Garage	484 sq. ft.
Exterior Wall Framing:	2x6

Foundation Options:

Crawlspace

(All plans can be built with your choice of foundation and framing. A generic conversion diagram is available. See order form.)

BLUEPRINT PRICE CODE: **A**

MAIN FLOOR

Affordable Country Charm

- A covered front porch, attached garage, and bay window add appeal to this efficient, affordable home.
- A spacious living room with fireplace and window seat offer plenty of family living space.
- The kitchen/dining room opens to a rear patio for indoor/outdoor living.
- The attached garage incorporates stairs for the optional basement.
- The plan includes three bedrooms and two baths on the same level, a plus for young families.

Plan AX-98602

Bedrooms: 3	Baths: 2

Space:

Total living area:	1,253 sq. ft.
Basement:	1,253 sq. ft.
Garage:	368 sq. ft.

Exterior Wall Framing:	2x4

Foundation options:
Standard basement.
Slab.
(Foundation & framing conversion diagram available — see order form.)

Blueprint Price Code:	A

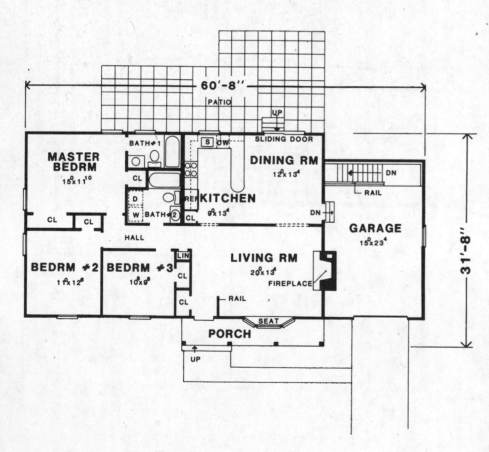

MASTER BEDRM 15⁸x11¹⁰

BATH #1

DINING RM 12⁸x13⁴

SLIDING DOOR

UP

KITCHEN 9⁸x13⁴

DN

RAIL

GARAGE 15x23⁴

DN

BEDRM #2 1⁰x12⁸

BEDRM #3 10x9⁸

HALL

LIVING RM 20⁸x13⁴

FIREPLACE

RAIL

SEAT

PORCH

UP

PATIO

60'-8''

31'-8''

TO ORDER THIS BLUEPRINT, CALL TOLL-FREE 1-800-547-5570

Plan AX-98602

PRICES AND DETAILS ON PAGES 12-15

Covered Porch Invites Visitors

- This nice home welcomes visitors with its covered front porch and its wide-open living areas.
- Detailed columns, railings and shutters decorate the front porch that guides guests to the central entry.
- Just off the entry, the bright living room merges with the dining room. The side wall is lined with glass, including a glass door that opens to the yard.
- The angled kitchen features a serving counter facing the dining room. A handry laundry closet and access to a storage area and the garage is nearby.
- An angled hall leads to the bedroom wing. The master suite offers a private bath, a walk-in closet and a dressing area with a vanity. Two additional bedrooms and another full bath are located down the hall.

Plan E-1217

Bedrooms: 3	**Baths:** 2

Living Area:	
Main floor	1,266 sq. ft.
Total Living Area:	**1,266 sq. ft.**
Garage and storage	550 sq. ft.
Exterior Wall Framing:	2x6

Foundation Options:

Crawlspace

Slab

(All plans can be built with your choice of foundation and framing. A generic conversion diagram is available. See order form.)

BLUEPRINT PRICE CODE:	**A**

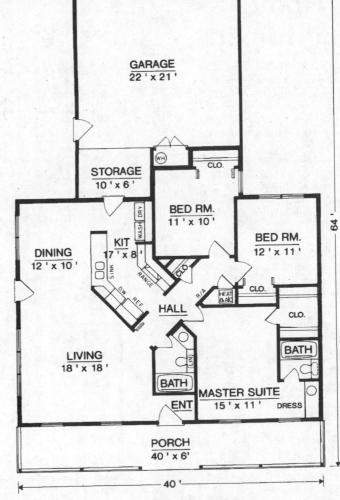

MAIN FLOOR

Small Home Has Big Impact

- Small in area but big on function, this angled, three-bedroom ranch glows with charm.
- The central foyer neatly channels traffic to the bedroom wing, the formal areas to the rear and the kitchen and family room to the left.
- Highlighted by a sloped ceiling and a stone fireplace, the living and dining rooms combine for a dramatic setting that overlooks a backyard terrace.
- The family room and kitchen also flow together smoothly for a casual family atmosphere.
- Two skylighted bathrooms and three bedrooms are secluded to the right of the home.

Plan K-696-T

Bedrooms: 3	Baths: 2½
Living Area:	
Main floor	1,272 sq. ft.
Total Living Area:	**1,272 sq. ft.**
Standard basement	1,232 sq. ft.
Garage	509 sq. ft.
Exterior Wall Framing:	2x4 or 2x6

Foundation Options:
Standard basement
Slab
(Typical foundation & framing conversion diagram available—see order form.)

BLUEPRINT PRICE CODE: A

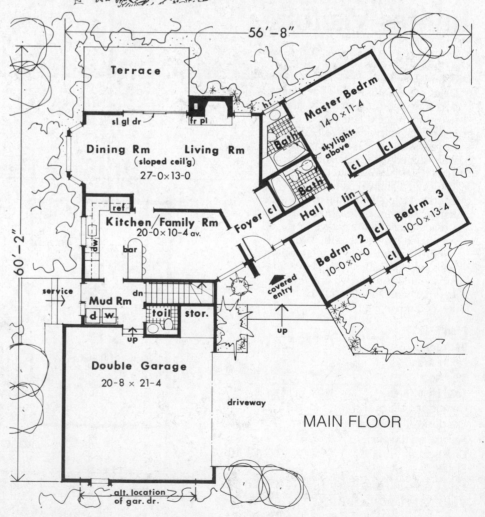

MAIN FLOOR

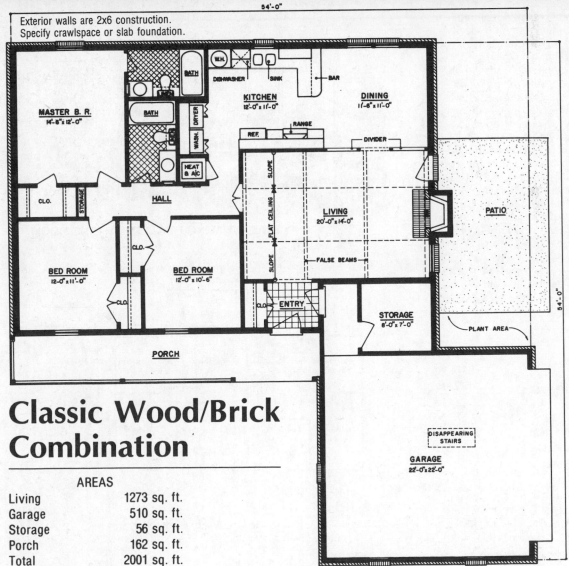

Exterior walls are 2x6 construction.
Specify crawlspace or slab foundation.

54'-0"

54'-0"

MASTER B. R.
14'-8" x 12'-0"

BATH

BATH

WASH | DRYER

HEAT & A/C

W.H.
DISHWASHER
SINK
BAR

KITCHEN
12'-0" x 11'-0"

DINING
11'-6" x 11'-0"

REF. | RANGE
DIVIDER

HALL

CLO. | STORAGE

SLOPE
FLAT CEILING
SLOPE

LIVING
20'-0" x 14'-0"

PATIO

BED ROOM
12'-0" x 11'-0"

CLO.

BED ROOM
12'-0" x 10'-6"

CLO.

FALSE BEAMS

CLO. | ENTRY

STORAGE
8'-0" x 7'-0"

PLANT AREA

PORCH

DISAPPEARING
STAIRS

GARAGE
22'-0" x 22'-0"

Classic Wood/Brick Combination

AREAS

Living	1273 sq. ft.
Garage	510 sq. ft.
Storage	56 sq. ft.
Porch	162 sq. ft.
Total	2001 sq. ft.

Blueprint Price Code A

Plan E-1212

Comfortable Ranch Design

- This affordable ranch design offers numerous amenities and is ideally structured for comfortable living, both indoors and out.
- A tiled reception hall leads into the spacious living and dining rooms, which feature a handsome brick fireplace, an 11-ft. sloped ceiling and two sets of sliding glass doors to access a lovely backyard terrace.
- The adjacent family room, designed for privacy, showcases a large boxed-out window with a built-in seat. The kitchen features an efficient U-shaped counter, an eating bar and a pantry.
- The master suite has its own terrace and private bath with a whirlpool tub.
- Two additional bedrooms share a second full bath.
- The garage has two separate storage areas—one accessible from the interior and the other from the backyard.

Plan K-518-A

Bedrooms: 3	Baths: 2
Living Area:	
Main floor	1,276 sq. ft.
Total Living Area:	**1,276 sq. ft.**
Standard basement	1,247 sq. ft.
Garage and storage	579 sq. ft.
Exterior Wall Framing:	2x4 or 2x6

Foundation Options:
Standard basement
Slab
(All plans can be built with your choice of foundation and framing. A generic conversion diagram is available. See order form.)

BLUEPRINT PRICE CODE: A

VIEW INTO LIVING ROOM AND DINING ROOM

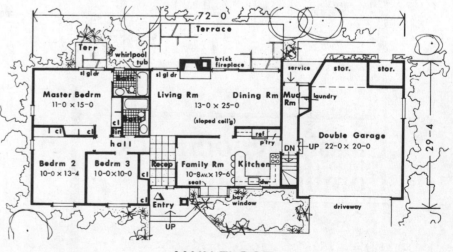

MAIN FLOOR

Cozy Home for Retirees or New Families

Total living area: 1,283 sq. ft.
(Not counting basement or garage)

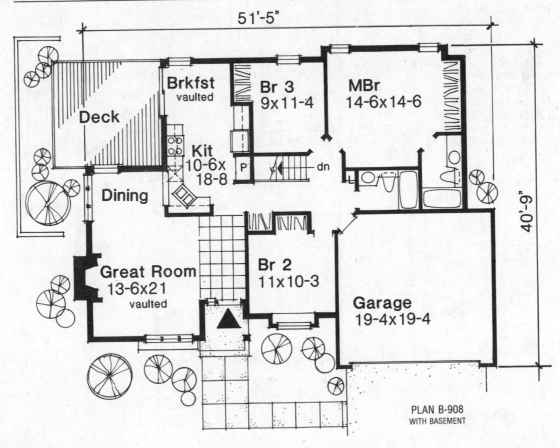

51'-5"

Deck

Brkfst
vaulted

Br 3
9x11-4

MBr
14-6x14-6

Kit
10-6x
18-8

P   dn

Dining

Great Room
13-6x21
vaulted

Br 2
11x10-3

Garage
19-4x19-4

40'-9"

PLAN B-908
WITH BASEMENT

TO ORDER THIS BLUEPRINT,
CALL TOLL-FREE 1-800-547-5570

Blueprint Price Code A
Plan B-908

PRICES AND DETAILS
ON PAGES 12-15

37

Eye-Catching Details

- This eye-catching home features a handsome exterior and an exciting floor plan that maximizes square footage.
- The covered porch leads into a vaulted foyer with an angled coat closet. Straight ahead, the 16½-ft.-high vaulted Great Room combines with the dining room and kitchen to create one expansive living and entertaining area.
- The Great Room offers a fireplace and access to the backyard. The galley-style kitchen has a 16½-ft.-high ceiling and is bordered by the vaulted dining room on one side and a breakfast area with a laundry closet on the other.
- The master suite boasts a 15-ft., 8-in. tray ceiling. The 13-ft.-high vaulted bath has a garden tub, a separate shower and a vanity with knee space.
- The two remaining bedrooms are located on the opposite side of the home and share a full bath. A plant shelf is an attention-getting detail found here.

Plan FB-1289

Bedrooms: 3	Baths: 2
Living Area:	
Main floor	1,289 sq. ft.
Total Living Area:	**1,289 sq. ft.**
Daylight basement	1,289 sq. ft.
Garage	430 sq. ft.
Exterior Wall Framing:	2x4

Foundation Options:
Daylight basement
Crawlspace
Slab
(All plans can be built with your choice of foundation and framing. A generic conversion diagram is available. See order form.)

BLUEPRINT PRICE CODE: A

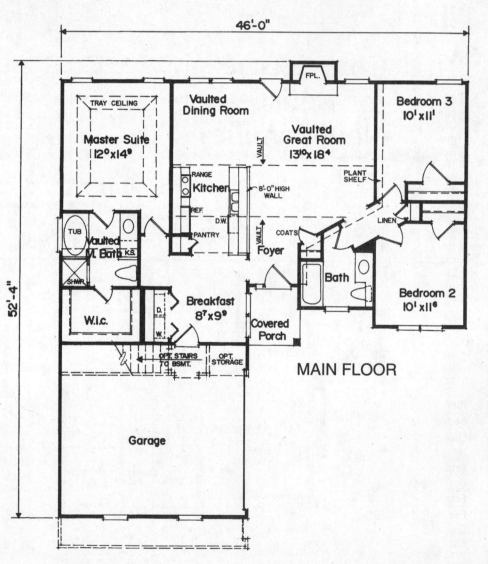

MAIN FLOOR

TO ORDER THIS BLUEPRINT,
CALL TOLL-FREE 1-800-547-5570

Plan FB-1289

PRICES AND DETAILS
ON PAGES 12-15

Charming Accents

- Traditional accents add warmth and charm to the facade of this affordable one-story home.
- Decorative, beveled oval glass adorns the elegant entry, which is flanked by sidelights.
- The tiled foyer introduces the spacious family room, which is enhanced by a 12-ft. vaulted ceiling and a nice fireplace. A French door provides easy access to the backyard.
- The galley-style kitchen flows into the sunny dining area, which can be extended with an optional bay window.
- The secluded master bedroom features plenty of closet space. The private master bath boasts a corner garden tub, a separate shower and two sinks. The bath may be expanded with a 13-ft. vaulted ceiling.
- Two additional bedrooms share a hall bath in the opposite wing. A nice-sized laundry room is centrally located.

Plan APS-1205

Bedrooms: 3	**Baths:** 2

Living Area:	
Main floor	1,296 sq. ft.
Total Living Area:	**1,296 sq. ft.**
Garage	380 sq. ft.
Exterior Wall Framing:	2x4

Foundation Options:
Crawlspace
Slab
(All plans can be built with your choice of foundation and framing. A generic conversion diagram is available. See order form.)

BLUEPRINT PRICE CODE: A

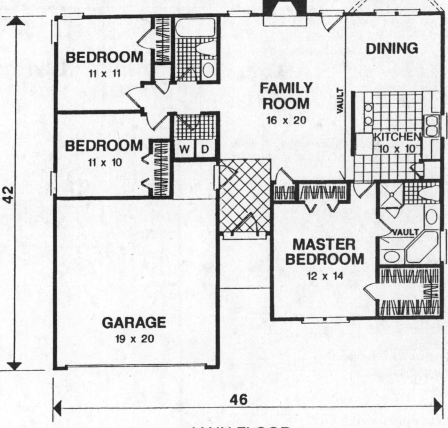

MAIN FLOOR

Bold New Economic Plan

- The inviting entry of this economical three-bedroom ranch flows directly into the spacious living room.
- Warmed by a fireplace, the living room is easily served from the kitchen's angled snack counter. The adjoining dining area enjoys access to a covered backyard patio.
- The charming master bedroom offers a private bath, a dressing area and a roomy walk-in closet.
- Two additional bedrooms boast walk-in closets and are served by a nearby hallway bath.
- The convenient laundry/utility room accesses the two-car garage, which includes extra storage space.
- At only 46 ft. wide, this design would be suitable for a narrow lot.

Plan SDG-81115

Bedrooms: 3	Baths: 2
Living Area:	
Main floor	1,296 sq. ft.
Total Living Area:	**1,296 sq. ft.**
Garage	400 sq. ft.
Exterior Wall Framing:	2x4

Foundation Options:

Slab
(All plans can be built with your choice of foundation and framing. A generic conversion diagram is available. See order form.)

BLUEPRINT PRICE CODE: A

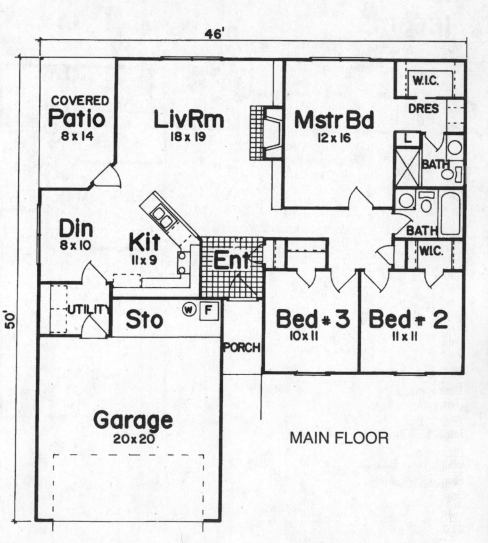

MAIN FLOOR

Plan SDG-81115

Light-Filled, Flowing Spaces

- A beautiful bay window in the living room and an open, light-filled floor plan distinguish this stylish home.
- The large combined living and dining area—equally suitable for family gatherings or for more formal entertaining—features a fireplace and a view of a covered patio.
- The sunny, bayed breakfast nook accesses the patio, while the efficient kitchen includes a sizable pantry.
- Double doors open to the spacious master suite, which features a private bath and a walk-in closet.
- The two remaining bedrooms have large windows overlooking the backyard and share a full bath. One of the bedrooms is conveniently located off the breakfast nook, and could be used as a TV room, study or guest bedroom.
- Nice laundry facilities are located near the entrance to the two-car garage.

Plan R-1028

Bedrooms: 2+	Baths: 2
Living Area:	
Main floor	1,305 sq. ft.
Total Living Area:	**1,305 sq. ft.**
Garage	429 sq. ft.
Exterior Wall Framing:	2x6

Foundation Options:

Crawlspace

(All plans can be built with your choice of foundation and framing. A generic conversion diagram is available. See order form.)

BLUEPRINT PRICE CODE: A

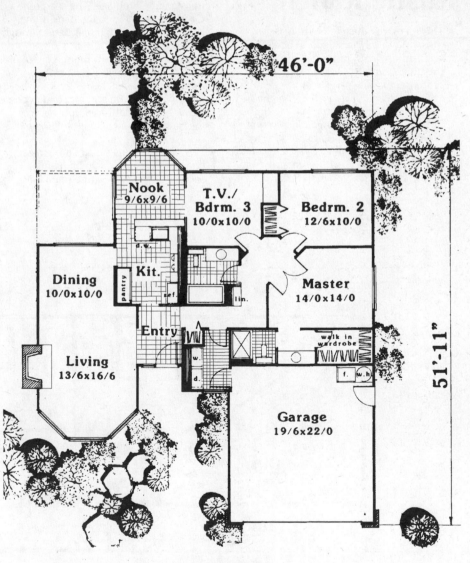

MAIN FLOOR

Rustic Ranch

- This rustic ranch-style home may be finished entirely in stucco or accented with siding. With just two bedrooms, the home is perfect for the starter or retirement family.
- Off the covered front porch, the entry unfolds directly to the primary living areas. The formal dining area is set off with a decorative planter wall.
- An angled wall discreetly separates the kitchen from the Great Room and would be an ideal location for a freestanding fireplace. The spacious Great Room flows to the back of the home and opens to a rear patio through sliding glass doors.
- The kitchen features a unique circular snack bar and a windowed sink.
- Adjacent to the kitchen is a nice-sized laundry room with a pantry and access to the backyard. Bi-fold doors across the hall open to a coat closet and extra storage space.
- The sleeping wing houses a big master bedroom with a private bath and a second bedroom near the main bath.

Plan Q-1323-1A

Bedrooms: 2	**Baths:** 2

Living Area:

Main floor	1,323 sq. ft.
Total Living Area:	**1,323 sq. ft.**
Garage	420 sq. ft.
Exterior Wall Framing:	2x4

Foundation Options:

Slab

(All plans can be built with your choice of foundation and framing. A generic conversion diagram is available. See order form.)

BLUEPRINT PRICE CODE:	**A**

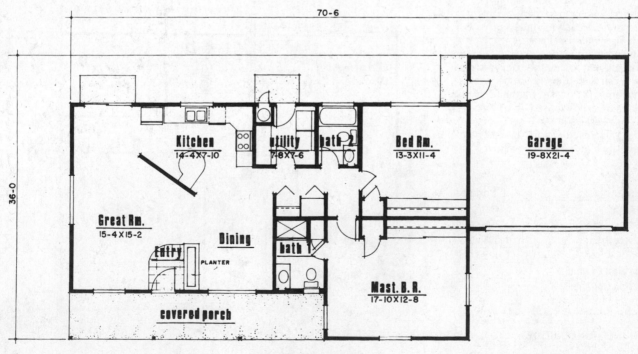

MAIN FLOOR

Plan Q-1323-1A
PRICES AND DETAILS ON PAGES 12-15

High-Profile Contemporary

- This design does away with wasted space, putting the emphasis on quality rather than on size.
- The angled floor plan minimizes hall space and creates smooth traffic flow while adding architectural appeal. The roof framing is square, however, to allow for economical construction.
- The spectacular living and dining rooms share a 16-ft. cathedral ceiling and a fireplace. Both rooms have lots of glass overlooking an angled rear terrace.
- The dining room includes a glass-filled alcove and sliding patio doors topped by transom windows. Tall windows frame the living room fireplace and trace the slope of the ceiling.
- A pass-through joins the dining room to the combination kitchen and family room, which features a snack bar and a clerestory window.
- The sleeping wing provides a super master suite, which boasts a skylighted dressing area and a luxurious bath. The optional den, or third bedroom, shares a second full bath with another bedroom that offers a 14-ft. sloped ceiling.

Plan K-688-D

Bedrooms: 2+	Baths: 2½
Living Area:	
Main floor	1,340 sq. ft.
Total Living Area:	**1,340 sq. ft.**
Standard basement	1,235 sq. ft.
Garage	484 sq. ft.
Exterior Wall Framing:	2x4 or 2x6

Foundation Options:

Standard basement

Slab

(All plans can be built with your choice of foundation and framing. A generic conversion diagram is available. See order form.)

BLUEPRINT PRICE CODE: A

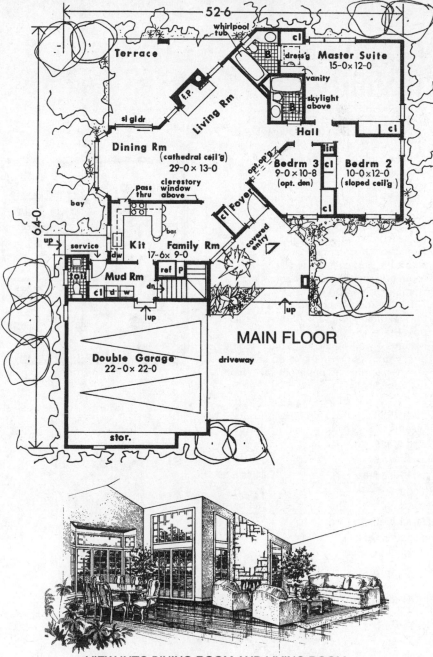

MAIN FLOOR

VIEW INTO DINING ROOM AND LIVING ROOM

Maximum Livability

- Compact and easy to build, this appealing ranch-style home is big on charm and livability.
- The entry of the home opens to a dramatic 13-ft. vaulted living room with exposed beams, a handsome fireplace and access to a backyard patio.
- Wood post dividers set off the large raised dining room, which is brightened by a stunning window wall.
- The adjoining kitchen offers a spacious snack bar and easy access to the utility room and the two-car garage. A nice storage area is also included.
- Three bedrooms and two baths occupy the sleeping wing. One of the baths is private to the master suite, which features a walk-in closet and a dressing area with a sit-down make-up table. The two remaining bedrooms also have walk-in closets.

Plan E-1305

Bedrooms: 3	Baths: 2
Living Area:	
Main floor	1,346 sq. ft.
Total Living Area:	**1,346 sq. ft.**
Garage	441 sq. ft.
Storage	44 sq. ft.
Exterior Wall Framing:	2x4

Foundation Options:

Crawlspace

Slab

(All plans can be built with your choice of foundation and framing. A generic conversion diagram is available. See order form.)

BLUEPRINT PRICE CODE:	**A**

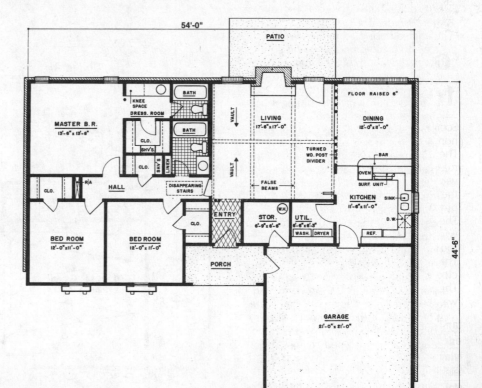

MAIN FLOOR

Plan E-1305

Roomy One-Story Home

- Economical to build and maintain, this home includes many luxurious features.
- The large living room includes a massive fireplace and a beamed, vaulted ceiling, and visually flows into the raised dining room. A French door provides access to an inviting patio.
- The U-shaped kitchen offers a windowed sink and an adjoining utility room with a washer and dryer.
- The master suite features a large walk-in closet and a private bath.
- The two secondary bedrooms also have walk-in closets and share a hall bath.

Plan E-1307

Bedrooms: 3	Baths: 2
Living Area:	
Main floor	1,346 sq. ft.
Total Living Area:	**1,346 sq. ft.**
Garage	441 sq. ft.
Storage & utility	88 sq. ft.
Exterior Wall Framing:	2x4

Foundation Options:

Crawlspace

Slab

(All plans can be built with your choice of foundation and framing. A generic conversion diagram is available. See order form.)

BLUEPRINT PRICE CODE: A

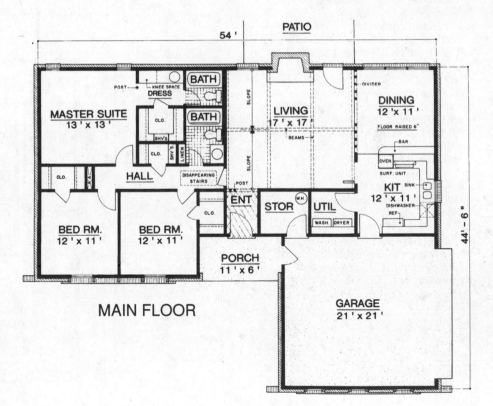

MAIN FLOOR

A Perfect Fit

- This country-style home will fit anywhere. Its charming character and narrow width make it ideal for those who value vintage styling along with plenty of yard space.
- The quaint covered front porch opens into the living room, which boasts a 12-ft., 8-in. cathedral ceiling and an inviting fireplace.
- The adjacent bay-windowed dining area features a 9-ft.-high vaulted ceiling and easy access to the efficient, galley-style kitchen.
- Off the kitchen, a handy laundry/utility room is convenient to the back entrance. The carport can accommodate two cars and includes a lockable storage area.
- The master bedroom suite offers a roomy walk-in closet, a private bath and sliding glass doors to a rear patio.
- Another full bath is centrally located for easy service to the rest of the home. Two more nice-sized bedrooms complete the plan.

Plan J-86119

Bedrooms: 3	Baths: 2
Living Area:	
Main floor	1,346 sq. ft.
Total Living Area:	**1,346 sq. ft.**
Standard basement	1,346 sq. ft.
Carport	400 sq. ft.
Exterior Wall Framing:	2x4

Foundation Options:

Standard basement
Crawlspace
Slab

(All plans can be built with your choice of foundation and framing. A generic conversion diagram is available. See order form.)

BLUEPRINT PRICE CODE: **A**

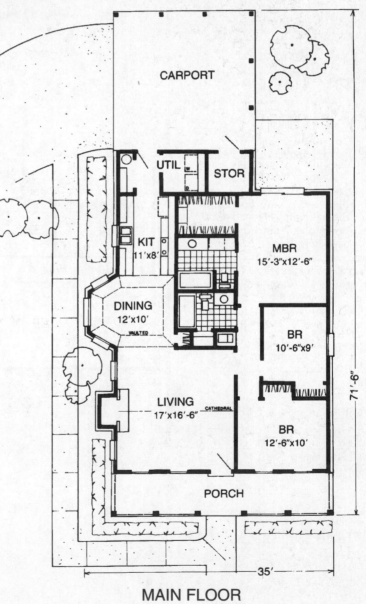

MAIN FLOOR

Plan J-86119

Exciting Great Room Featured

- A brick and wood exterior accented by multiple gables and ornate windows gives this smart-looking one-story home lots of curb appeal.
- The amenity-filled interior is just as exciting. The 17-ft. vaulted foyer leads immediately into the spacious Great Room that also features a 17-ft.-high vaulted ceiling and a handsome fireplace flanked by windows.
- The adjoining dining room flows nicely into the breakfast area and the kitchen. The impressive kitchen offers an angled serving bar and a convenient pantry, while the sunny breakfast area has a French door to the backyard.
- The master suite boasts a 10-ft. tray ceiling and a walk-in closet with a plant shelf. The vaulted master bath features a garden tub and a dual-sink vanity.
- The two remaining bedrooms are serviced by another full bath.

Plan FB-1359

Bedrooms: 3	Baths: 2
Living Area:	
Main floor	1,359 sq. ft.
Total Living Area:	**1,359 sq. ft.**
Garage	407 sq. ft.
Exterior Wall Framing:	2x4

Foundation Options:

Crawlspace

Slab

(All plans can be built with your choice of foundation and framing. A generic conversion diagram is available. See order form.)

BLUEPRINT PRICE CODE: A

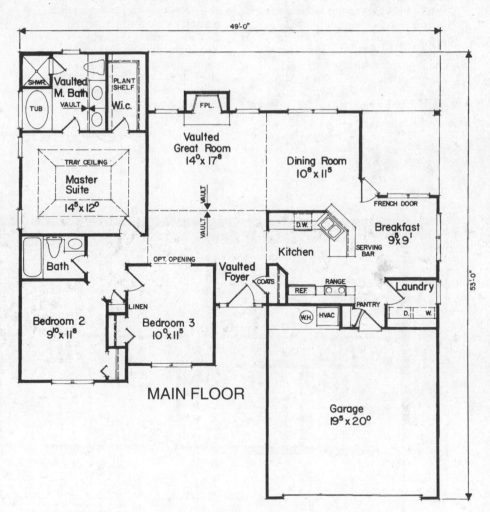

MAIN FLOOR

Economical Three-Bedroom

- A striking covered entry with stately columns adds a distinguished look to this economical one-story home.
- Inside, a spacious living and dining room combination easily and elegantly accommodates formal occasions.
- The large family room is open to the kitchen, which offers an oversized snack bar and a pantry closet. A bright eating area overlooks a lovely outdoor patio. A pocket door closes off the kitchen from the formal dining room.
- The laundry room is conveniently located near the kitchen and the carport with extra storage space.
- The sleeping wing houses a large master bedroom with a private bath, two linen closets, a walk-in closet and a separate dressing area set off with wood spindles.
- The two extra bedrooms have walk-in closets and share another full bath across the hall.

Plan E-1300	
Bedrooms: 3	**Baths:** 2
Living Area:	
Main floor	1,366 sq. ft.
Total Living Area:	**1,366 sq. ft.**
Carport and storage	470 sq. ft.
Exterior Wall Framing:	2x4
Foundation Options:	

Crawlspace
Slab
(All plans can be built with your choice of foundation and framing. A generic conversion diagram is available. See order form.)

BLUEPRINT PRICE CODE:	A

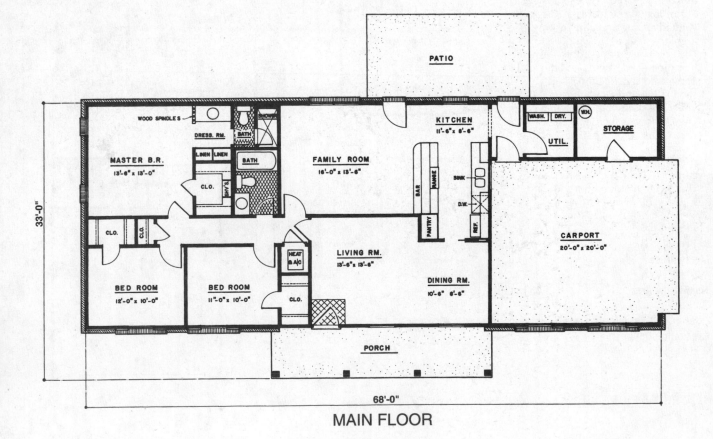

MAIN FLOOR

Plan E-1300

PRICES AND DETAILS
ON PAGES 12-15

Luxury in a Small Package

- The elegant exterior of this design sets the tone for the luxurious spaces within.
- The foyer opens to the centrally located living room, which features a 15-ft. cathedral ceiling, a two-way fireplace and access to a lovely rear terrace.
- The unusual kitchen design includes an angled snack bar that lies between the bayed breakfast den and the formal dining room. Sliding glass doors open to another terrace.
- The master suite is a dream come true, with its romantic fireplace, built-in desk and 9-ft.-high tray ceiling. The private bath includes a whirlpool tub and a dual-sink vanity.
- Another full bath serves the remaining two bedrooms, one of which boasts a cathedral ceiling and a tall arched window.

Plan AHP-9300

Bedrooms: 3	Baths: 2
Living Area:	
Main floor	1,513 sq. ft.
Total Living Area:	**1,513 sq. ft.**
Standard basement	1,360 sq. ft.
Garage	400 sq. ft.
Exterior Wall Framing:	2x4 or 2x6

Foundation Options:
Standard basement
Crawlspace
Slab
(All plans can be built with your choice of foundation and framing. A generic conversion diagram is available. See order form.)

BLUEPRINT PRICE CODE:	B

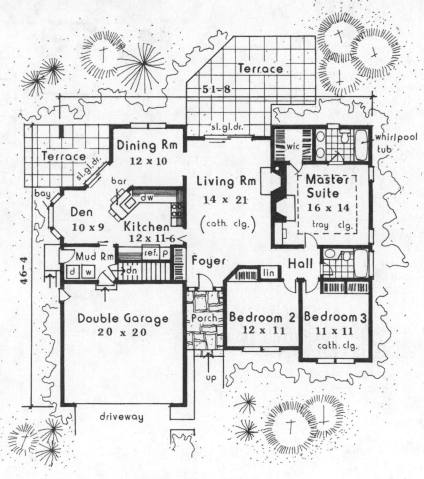

MAIN FLOOR

Outstanding One-Story

- Vaulted living spaces add to the spacious feel of this outstanding home, which would be ideal for a narrow lot.
- The focal point is the spacious Great Room and dining room area, enhanced by a 13½-ft. vaulted ceiling and a large fireplace flanked by windows to overlook the lovely patio and backyard.
- The dining room offers access to a secluded side courtyard.
- A beautiful bay window in the adjoining kitchen brightens the room and overlooks a front garden. A 10½-ft. vaulted ceiling and a functional snack bar are also featured.
- The master suite offers a sitting room with sliding glass doors to the patio. A private bath and a walk-in closet are also included.
- The two remaining bedrooms share the hall bath.

Plans P-6588-2A & -2D

Bedrooms: 3	Baths: 2
Living Area:	
Main floor (crawlspace version)	1,362 sq. ft.
Main floor (basement version)	1,403 sq. ft.
Total Living Area:	**1,362/1,403 sq. ft.**
Daylight basement	1,303 sq. ft.
Garage	427 sq. ft.
Exterior Wall Framing:	2x6
Foundation Options:	**Plan #**
Daylight basement	P-6588-2D
Crawlspace	P-6588-2A

(All plans can be built with your choice of foundation and framing. A generic conversion diagram is available. See order form.)

BLUEPRINT PRICE CODE:	**A**

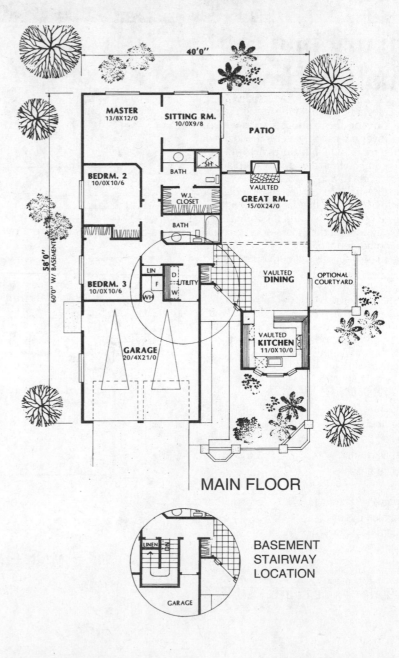

MAIN FLOOR

BASEMENT STAIRWAY LOCATION

Extra Sparkle

- A lovely front porch with a cameo front door, decorative posts, bay windows and dormers give this country-style home extra sparkle.
- The Great Room is at the center of the floor plan, where it merges with the dining room and the screened porch. The Great Room features a 10-ft. tray ceiling, a fireplace, a built-in wet bar and a wall of windows to the patio.
- The eat-in kitchen has a half-wall that keeps it open to the Great Room and hallway. The dining room offers a half-wall facing the foyer and a bay window overlooking the front porch.
- The delectable master suite is isolated from the other bedrooms and includes a charming bay window, a 10-ft. tray ceiling and a luxurious private bath.
- The two smaller bedrooms are off the main foyer and separated by a full bath.
- A mudroom with a washer and dryer is accessible from the two-car garage.

Plan AX-91312

Bedrooms: 3	Baths: 2
Space:	
Main floor	1,595 sq. ft.
Total Living Area	**1,595 sq. ft.**
Screened Porch	178 sq. ft.
Basement	1,595 sq. ft.
Garage, Storage and Utility	508 sq. ft.
Exterior Wall Framing	2x4

Foundation Options:

Daylight basement

Standard basement

Slab

(All plans can be built with your choice of foundation and framing. A generic conversion diagram is available. See order form.)

Blueprint Price Code	B

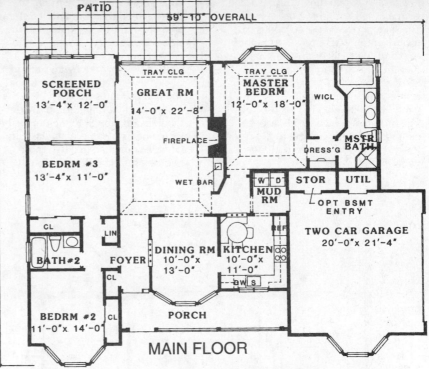

MAIN FLOOR

VIEW INTO GREAT ROOM

Rustic Comfort

- Rustic charm highlights the exterior of this design, while the interior is filled with all the latest comforts.
- The wide, covered porch opens to a roomy entry, where two 7-ft.-high openings with decorative railings view into the dining room.
- Straight ahead lies the sunken living room, which features a 16-ft.-high vaulted ceiling with exposed beams. The fireplace is faced with floor-to-ceiling fieldstone, adding to the rustic look. A rear door opens to a large patio with twin plant areas.

- The large U-shaped kitchen has such nice extras as a china niche with glass shelves. Other bonuses include the adjacent sewing/hobby room, the oversized utility room and the storage area and built-in workbench in the side-entry garage.
- The secluded master suite hosts a sunken sleeping area with built-in bookshelves. One step up is a cozy sitting area that is outlined by brick columns and a railed room divider. Double doors open to the deluxe bath, which offers a niche with glass shelves.
- Double doors conceal two more bedrooms and a full bath.

Plan E-1607	
Bedrooms: 3	Baths: 2
Living Area:	
Main floor	1,600 sq. ft.
Total Living Area:	1,600 sq. ft.
Standard basement	1,600 sq. ft.
Garage	484 sq. ft.
Storage	132 sq. ft.
Exterior Wall Framing:	2x6
Foundation Options:	
Standard basement	
Crawlspace	
Slab	

(All plans can be built with your choice of foundation and framing. A generic conversion diagram is available. See order form.)

BLUEPRINT PRICE CODE: B

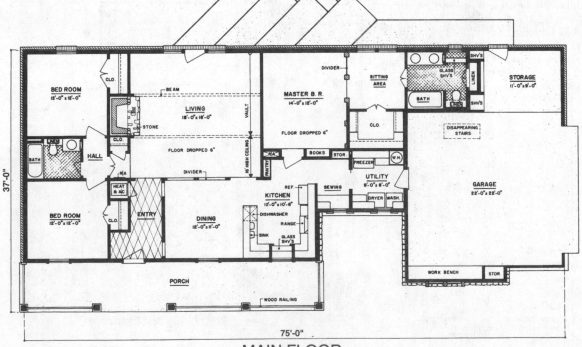

MAIN FLOOR

Plan E-1607

PRICES AND DETAILS ON PAGES 12-15

Tradition Updated

- The nostalgic exterior of this home gives way to dramatic cathedral ceilings and illuminating skylights inside.
- The covered front porch welcomes guests into the stone-tiled foyer, which flows into the living spaces.
- The living and dining rooms merge, forming a spacious, front-oriented entertaining area.

- A large three-sided fireplace situated between the living room and the family room may be enjoyed in both areas.
- The skylighted family room is also brightened by sliding glass doors that access a rear patio.
- The sunny island kitchen offers a nice breakfast nook and easy access to the laundry room and the garage.
- The master suite boasts a walk-in closet and a skylighted bath with a dual-sink vanity, a soaking tub and a separate shower. Two additional bedrooms share another full bath.

Plan AX-90303-A

Bedrooms: 3	Baths: 2
Living Area:	
Main floor	1,615 sq. ft.
Total Living Area:	**1,615 sq. ft.**
Basement	1,615 sq. ft.
Garage	412 sq. ft.
Exterior Wall Framing:	2x4

Foundation Options:

Daylight basement
Standard basement
Crawlspace
Slab
(All plans can be built with your choice of foundation and framing. A generic conversion diagram is available. See order form.)

BLUEPRINT PRICE CODE: B

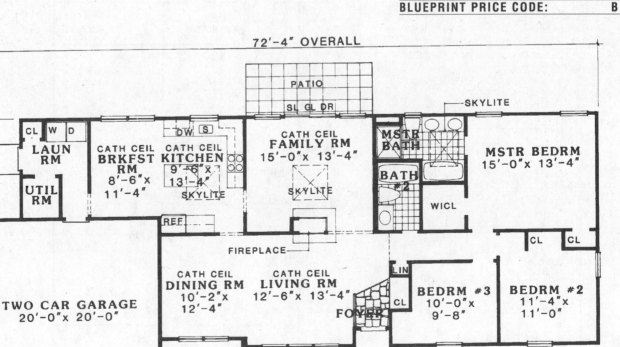

MAIN FLOOR

Design Fits Narrow Lot

- This compact, cozy and dignified plan makes great use of a small lot, while also offering an exciting interior design.
- In from the covered front porch, the living room features a warm fireplace and a 13-ft., 6-in. cathedral ceiling.
- The bay-windowed dining room joins the living room to provide a spacious area for entertaining.
- The galley-style kitchen has easy access to a large pantry closet, the utility room and the carport.
- The master suite includes a deluxe bath and a roomy walk-in closet.
- Two secondary bedrooms share another bath off the hallway.
- A lockable storage area is located off the rear patio.

Plan J-86161

Bedrooms: 3	Baths: 2
Living Area:	
Main floor	1,626 sq. ft.
Total Living Area:	**1,626 sq. ft.**
Standard basement	1,626 sq. ft.
Carport	410 sq. ft.
Storage	104 sq. ft.
Exterior Wall Framing:	2x4

Foundation Options:

Standard basement
Crawlspace
Slab
(All plans can be built with your choice of foundation and framing. A generic conversion diagram is available. See order form.)

BLUEPRINT PRICE CODE:	B

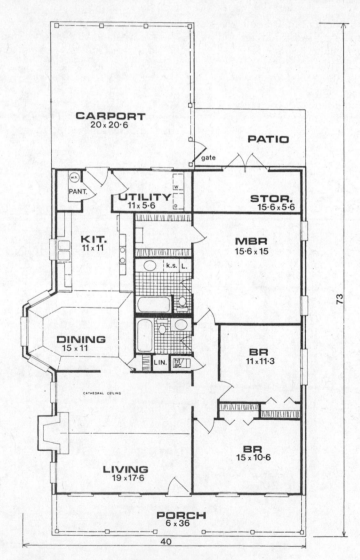

MAIN FLOOR

Plan J-86161

Friendly Country Charm

- An inviting front porch welcomes you to this friendly one-story home.
- The porch opens to a spacious central living room with a warm fireplace and functional built-in storage shelves.
- The bay window of the adjoining dining room allows a view of the backyard.

The dining area also enjoys an eating bar provided by the adjacent walk-through kitchen.
- The nice-sized kitchen also has a windowed sink and easy access to the laundry room and carport.
- Three bedrooms and two baths occupy the sleeping wing. The oversized master bedroom features a lovely boxed-out window, two walk-in closets and a private bath. The secondary bedrooms share the second full bath.

Plan J-8692	
Bedrooms: 3	**Baths:** 2
Living Area:	
Main floor	1,633 sq. ft.
Total Living Area:	**1,633 sq. ft.**
Standard basement	1,633 sq. ft.
Carport	380 sq. ft.
Exterior Wall Framing:	2x4
Foundation Options:	
Standard basement	
Crawlspace	
Slab	

(All plans can be built with your choice of foundation and framing. A generic conversion diagram is available. See order form.)

BLUEPRINT PRICE CODE:	B

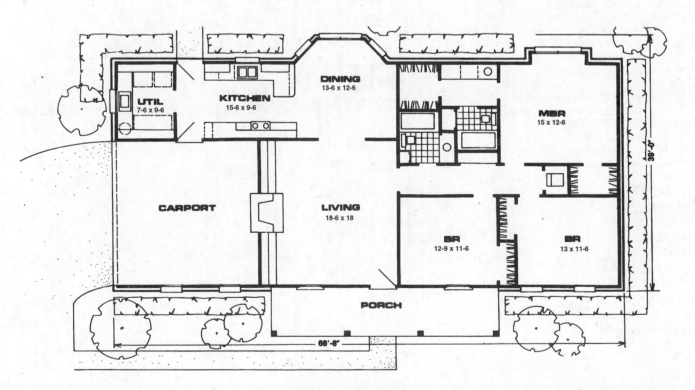

MAIN FLOOR

Planned to Perfection

- This attractive and stylish home offers an interior design that is planned to perfection.
- The covered entry and vaulted foyer create an impressive welcome.
- The vaulted Great Room features a corner fireplace, a wet bar and lots of windows. The adjoining dining room offers a bay window and access to a covered patio.
- The gourmet kitchen includes an island cooktop, a garden window above the sink and a built-in desk. The attached nook is surrounded by windows that overlook a delightful planter.
- The master suite boasts a tray ceiling that rises to 9½ ft. and a peaceful reading area that accesses a private patio. The superb master bath features a garden tub and a separate shower.
- Two secondary bedrooms share a compartmentalized bath.

Plan S-4789

Bedrooms: 3	Baths: 2
Living Area:	
Main floor	1,665 sq. ft.
Total Living Area:	**1,665 sq. ft.**
Standard basement	1,665 sq. ft.
Garage	400 sq. ft.
Exterior Wall Framing:	2x6

Foundation Options:

Standard basement
Crawlspace
Slab

(All plans can be built with your choice of foundation and framing. A generic conversion diagram is available. See order form.)

BLUEPRINT PRICE CODE: B

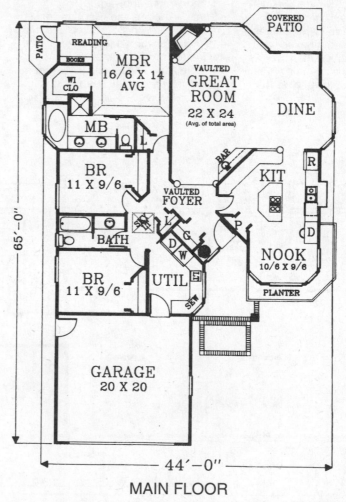

MAIN FLOOR

BASEMENT
STAIRWAY
LOCATION

TO ORDER THIS BLUEPRINT,
CALL TOLL-FREE 1-800-547-5570

Plan S-4789

PRICES AND DETAILS
ON PAGES 12-15

Photo by Mark Englund/HomeStyles

Elegant Approach

- This smart-looking design features an impressive approach, with a beautiful courtyard leading to the front door.
- The Y-shaped tiled entry efficiently directs traffic to all areas of the home.
- To the right, the combined living room and dining area offer a bow window, a fireplace and corner windows that overlook a covered sideyard patio.
- The adjacent sun room showcases a 14-ft. vaulted, skylighted ceiling and access to the patio.
- The corner kitchen has a snack bar that faces the family room, which features a 16-ft. vaulted ceiling, a woodstove and access to a second patio.
- The roomy master suite boasts a compartmentalized bath with a skylighted dressing area, a walk-in wardrobe and a shower.
- Another bath and bedroom, plus a den or possible third bedroom, complete this exciting design.

Plans P-7661-3A & -3D

Bedrooms: 2+	Baths: 2
Living Area:	
Main floor	1,693 sq. ft.
Total Living Area:	**1,693 sq. ft.**
Daylight basement	1,275 sq. ft.
Garage	462 sq. ft.
Exterior Wall Framing:	2x4
Foundation Options:	**Plan #**
Daylight basement	P-7661-3D
Crawlspace	P-7661-3A

(All plans can be built with your choice of foundation and framing. A generic conversion diagram is available. See order form.)

BLUEPRINT PRICE CODE:	**B**

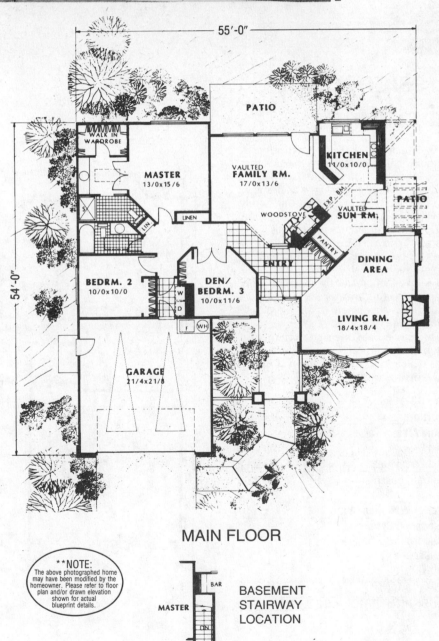

MAIN FLOOR

**NOTE:
The above photographed home may have been modified by the homeowner. Please refer to floor plan and/or drawn elevation shown for actual blueprint details.

BASEMENT STAIRWAY LOCATION

Designed for Livability

- As you enter this excitingly spacious traditional home, you see through the extensive windows to the backyard.
- This four-bedroom home was designed for the livability of the maturing family with the separation of the master suite.
- The formal dining room expands spatially to the living room while being set off by a decorative column and plant shelves.
- The bay that creates the morning room and the sitting area for the master suite also adds excitement to this plan, both inside and out.
- The master bath offers an exciting oval tub under glass and a separate shower, as well as a spacious walk-in closet and a dressing area.

Plan DD-1696

Bedrooms: 4	Baths: 2
Living Area:	
Main floor	1,748 sq. ft.
Total Living Area:	**1,748 sq. ft.**
Standard basement	1,748 sq. ft.
Garage	393 sq. ft.
Exterior Wall Framing:	2x4

Foundation Options:

Standard basement
Crawlspace
Slab
(All plans can be built with your choice of foundation and framing. A generic conversion diagram is available. See order form.)

BLUEPRINT PRICE CODE: B

MAIN FLOOR

Plan DD-1696

Cozy Covered Porches

- Twin dormers give this raised one-story design the appearance of a two-story. Two covered porches and a deck supplement the main living areas with plenty of outdoor entertaining space.
- The large central living room features a dramatic fireplace, a 12-ft. ceiling with a skylight and access to both porch areas.
- Double doors open to a bayed eating area, which overlooks the adjoining deck and includes a sloped ceiling that rises to 12 ft. in the kitchen. An angled snack bar and a pantry are also featured.
- The elegant master suite is tucked to one side of the home and also overlooks the backyard and deck. Laundry facilities and garage access are nearby.
- Across the home, two additional bedrooms share another full bath.

Plan E-1826

Bedrooms: 3	Baths: 2
Living Area:	
Main floor	1,800 sq. ft.
Total Living Area:	**1,800 sq. ft.**
Garage	550 sq. ft.
Storage	84 sq. ft.
Exterior Wall Framing:	2x6

Foundation Options:

Crawlspace
Slab
(All plans can be built with your choice of foundation and framing. A generic conversion diagram is available. See order form.)

BLUEPRINT PRICE CODE: B

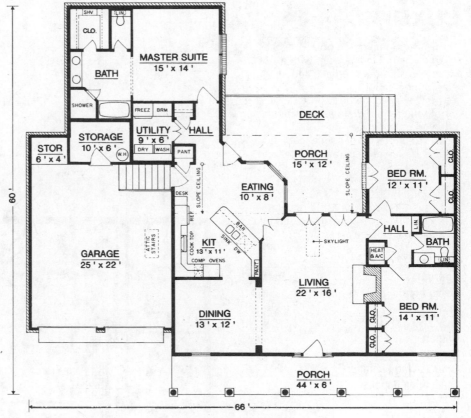

MAIN FLOOR

Attainable Luxury

- This traditional ranch home offers a large, central living room with a 12-ft. ceiling, a corner fireplace and an adjoining patio.
- The U-shaped kitchen easily services both the formal dining room and the bayed eating area.
- The luxurious master suite features a large bath with separate vanities and dressing areas.
- Two secondary bedrooms share a second full bath.
- A covered carport boasts a decorative brick wall, attic space above and two additional storage areas.

Plan E-1812

Bedrooms: 3	Baths: 2
Living Area:	
Main floor	1,860 sq. ft.
Total Living Area:	**1,860 sq. ft.**
Carport	484 sq. ft.
Storage	132 sq. ft.
Exterior Wall Framing:	2x6

Foundation Options:

Crawlspace

Slab

(All plans can be built with your choice of foundation and framing. A generic conversion diagram is available. See order form.)

BLUEPRINT PRICE CODE: B

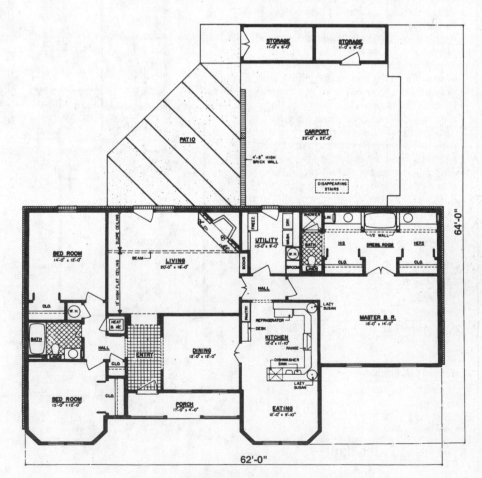

MAIN FLOOR

Plan E-1812

PRICES AND DETAILS
ON PAGES 12-15

Impressive Master Suite

- This attractive one-story home features an impressive master suite located apart from the secondary bedrooms.
- A lovely front porch opens to the entry, which flows to the formal dining room, the rear-oriented living room and the secondary bedroom wing.
- The living room boasts a large corner fireplace, a ceiling that slopes to 11 ft. and access to a backyard patio.
- A U-shaped kitchen services the dining room and its own eating area. It also boasts a built-in desk, a handy pantry closet and access to the nearby laundry room and carport.
- The wide master bedroom hosts a lavish master bath with a spa tub, a separate shower and his-and-hers dressing areas.
- Across the home, the two secondary bedrooms share another full bath.

Plan E-1818

Bedrooms: 3	Baths: 2
Living Area:	
Main floor	1,868 sq. ft.
Total Living Area:	**1,868 sq. ft.**
Carport	484 sq. ft.
Storage	132 sq. ft.
Exterior Wall Framing:	2x6

Foundation Options:
Crawlspace
Slab
(All plans can be built with your choice of foundation and framing. A generic conversion diagram is available. See order form.)

BLUEPRINT PRICE CODE: B

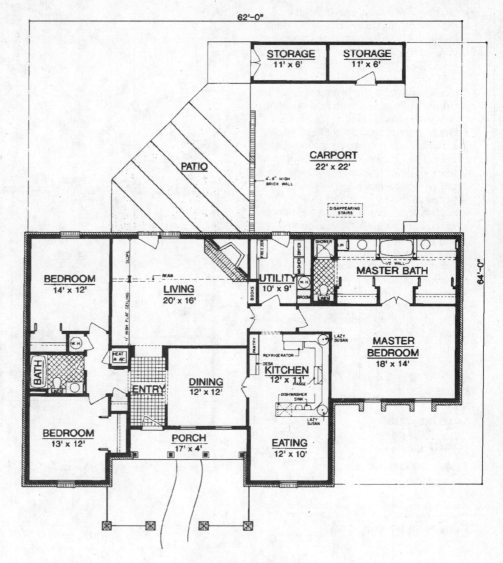

MAIN FLOOR

Showy One-Story

- Dramatic windows embellish the exterior of this showy one-story home.
- Inside, the entry provides a sweeping view of the living room, where sliding glass doors open to the backyard patio and flank a dramatic fireplace.
- Skylights accent the living room's 12-ft. sloped ceiling, while arched openings define the formal dining room.
- Double doors lead from the dining room to the kitchen and informal eating area. The kitchen features a built-in work desk and a pantry. An oversized utility room adjoins the kitchen and accesses the two-car garage.
- A 10-ft. tray ceiling adorns the master suite. The private bath is accented with a skylight above the fabulous fan-shaped marble tub. His-and-hers vanities, a separate shower and a huge walk-in closet are also featured.
- Two more bedrooms and a full bath are located at the other end of the home.
- The front-facing bedroom boasts a 12-ft. sloped ceiling.

Plan E-1830

Bedrooms: 3	Baths: 2
Living Area:	
Main floor	1,868 sq. ft.
Total Living Area:	**1,868 sq. ft.**
Garage and storage	616 sq. ft.
Exterior Wall Framing:	2x6

Foundation Options:

Crawlspace

Slab

(All plans can be built with your choice of foundation and framing. A generic conversion diagram is available. See order form.)

BLUEPRINT PRICE CODE:	**B**

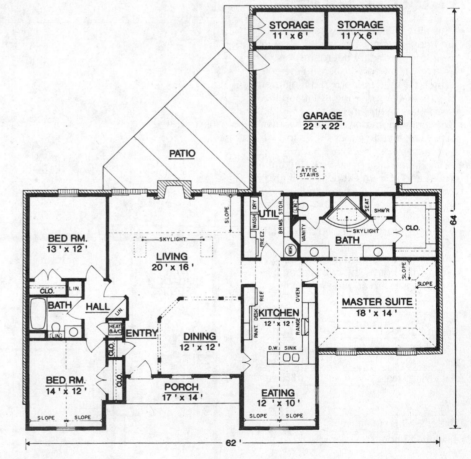

MAIN FLOOR

Plan E-1830

PRICES AND DETAILS
ON PAGES 12-15

A Real Original

- This home's round window, elegant entry and transom windows create an eye-catching, original look.
- Inside, high ceilings and tremendous views let the eyes wander. The foyer provides an exciting look at the expansive deck and the inviting spa through the living room's tall windows. The windows frame a handsome fireplace, while a 10-ft. ceiling adds volume and interest.
- To the right of the foyer is a cozy den or home office with its own fireplace, 10-ft. ceiling and dramatic windows.
- The spacious kitchen/breakfast area features an oversized snack bar island and opens to a large screen porch. Within easy reach are the laundry room and the entrance to the garage.
- The bright formal dining room overlooks the deck and boasts a ceiling that vaults up to 10 feet.
- The secluded master suite looks out to the deck as well, with access through a patio door. The private bath features a dynamite corner spa tub, a separate shower and a large walk-in closet.
- A second bedroom and bath complete the main floor.

Plan B-90065

Bedrooms: 2+	Baths: 2
Living Area:	
Main floor	1,889 sq. ft.
Total Living Area:	**1,889 sq. ft.**
Standard basement	1,889 sq. ft.
Garage	406 sq. ft.
Exterior Wall Framing:	2x6

Foundation Options:

Standard basement

(All plans can be built with your choice of foundation and framing. A generic conversion diagram is available. See order form.)

BLUEPRINT PRICE CODE: **B**

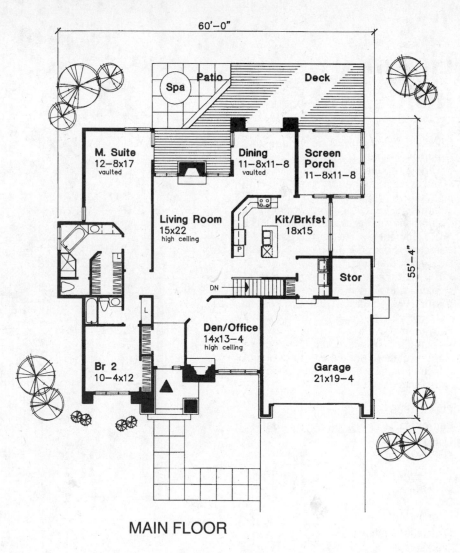

MAIN FLOOR

Elegance
Inside and Out

- The raised front porch of this home is finely detailed with wood columns, railings, moldings, and French doors with half-round transoms.
- The living room, dining room and entry have 12-ft.-high ceilings. Skylights illuminate the living room, which offers a fireplace and access to a roomy deck.
- The efficient kitchen permits easy service to both the dining room and the casual eating area.
- The master suite features a raised tray ceiling and an enormous skylighted bath with a walk-in closet, dual vanities and a large quarter-circle spa tub surrounded by a mirror wall.
- On the left, two secondary bedrooms are insulated from the more active areas of the home by an efficient hallway, and also share another full bath.

Plan E-1909

Bedrooms: 3	Baths: 2
Living Area:	
Main floor	1,936 sq. ft.
Total Living Area:	**1,936 sq. ft.**
Garage	484 sq. ft.
Storage	132 sq. ft.
Exterior Wall Framing:	2x6

Foundation Options:
Crawlspace
Slab
(All plans can be built with your choice of foundation and framing. A generic conversion diagram is available. See order form.)

BLUEPRINT PRICE CODE: B

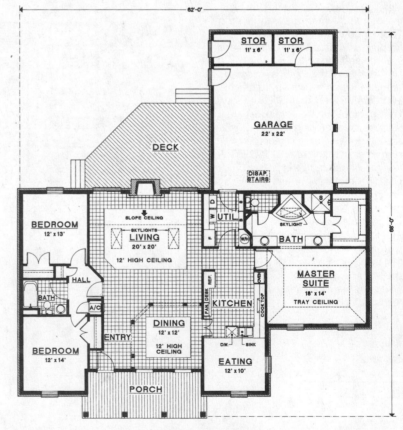

MAIN FLOOR

TO ORDER THIS BLUEPRINT, CALL TOLL-FREE 1-800-547-5570

Plan E-1909

PRICES AND DETAILS ON PAGES 12-15

All in One!

- This plan puts all of today's most luxurious home-design features into one attractive, economical package.
- The covered front porch and the gabled roofline, accented by an arched window and a round louver vent, give the exterior a homey yet stylish appeal.
- Just inside the front door, the ceiling rises up to 11 ft., making an impressive greeting. A skylight and French doors framing the fireplace flood the living room with light.
- The living room flows into a nice-sized dining room, also with an 11-ft. ceiling, which in turn leads to the large eat-in kitchen. Here you'll find lots of counter space, a handy laundry closet and a eating area that opens to a terrace.
- The bedroom wing includes a wonderful master suite, with a sizable sleeping area and a dressing area with two closets. Glass blocks above the dual-sink vanity let in light yet maintain privacy. A whirlpool tub and a separate shower complete the suite.
- The larger of the two remaining bedrooms boasts an 11-ft.-high ceiling and an arched window.

Plan HFL-1680-FL

Bedrooms: 3	Baths: 2
Living Area:	
Main floor	1,367 sq. ft.
Total Living Area:	**1,367 sq. ft.**
Standard basement	1,367 sq. ft.
Garage	431 sq. ft.
Exterior Wall Framing:	2x6

Foundation Options:

Standard basement

(All plans can be built with your choice of foundation and framing. A generic conversion diagram is available. See order form.)

BLUEPRINT PRICE CODE: A

VIEW INTO LIVING ROOM

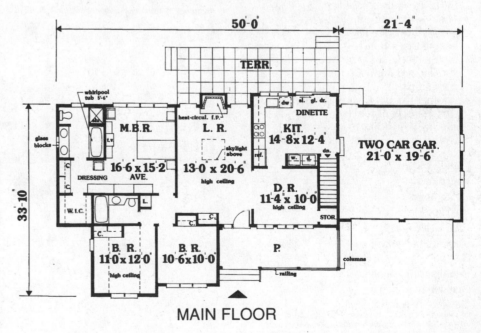

MAIN FLOOR

Inviting Windows

- This comfortable home presents an impressive facade, with its large and inviting front window arrangement.
- A step down from the front entry, the Great Room boasts a 12-ft. vaulted ceiling with a barrel-vaulted area that outlines the half-round front window. The striking angled fireplace can be enjoyed from the adjoining dining area.
- The galley-style kitchen hosts a half-round cutout above the sink and a breakfast area that accesses a backyard deck and patio. The kitchen, breakfast area and dining area also are enhanced by 12-ft. vaulted ceilings.
- The master bedroom features a boxed-out window, a walk-in closet and a ceiling that vaults to 12 feet. The private bath includes a garden tub, a separate shower and a private toilet compartment.
- Another full bath serves the two remaining bedrooms, one of which has sliding glass doors to the deck and would make an ideal den.

Plan B-902

Bedrooms: 2+	Baths: 2
Living Area:	
Main floor	1,368 sq. ft.
Total Living Area:	**1,368 sq. ft.**
Standard basement	1,368 sq. ft.
Garage	412 sq. ft.
Exterior Wall Framing:	2x4

Foundation Options:

Standard basement

(All plans can be built with your choice of foundation and framing. A generic conversion diagram is available. See order form.)

BLUEPRINT PRICE CODE: A

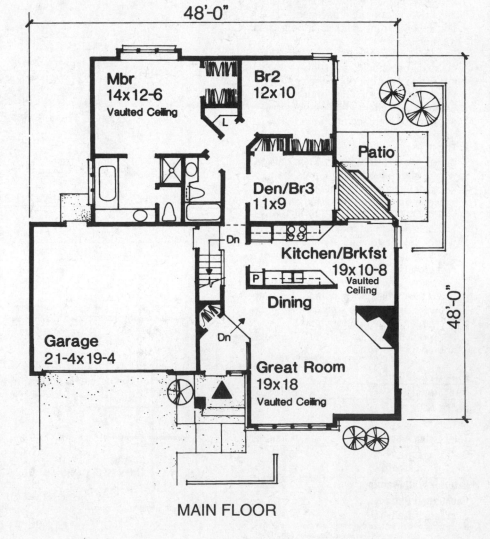

48'-0"

48'-0"

- Mbr 14x12-6 Vaulted Ceiling
- Br2 12x10
- Patio
- Den/Br3 11x9
- Kitchen/Brkfst 19x10-8 Vaulted Ceiling
- Dining
- Garage 21-4x19-4
- Great Room 19x18 Vaulted Ceiling

Dn

MAIN FLOOR

TO ORDER THIS BLUEPRINT, CALL TOLL-FREE 1-800-547-5570

Plan B-902

PRICES AND DETAILS ON PAGES 12-15

Family-Style Leisure Living

- This handsome ranch-style home features a floor plan that is great for family living and entertaining.
- In from the quaint covered porch, the spacious formal areas flow together for a dramatic impact. The living room is enhanced by a fireplace and a sloped ceiling. A patio door in the dining room extends activities to the outdoors.
- The efficient U-shaped kitchen opens to the dining room and offers a pantry, a window above the sink and abundant counter space.
- A good-sized utility room with convenient laundry facilities opens to the carport. This area also includes a large storage room and disappearing stairs to even more storage space.
- Three bedrooms and two baths occupy the sleeping wing. The master suite features a large walk-in closet and a private bath.
- The two remaining bedrooms are well proportioned and share a hall bath. Storage space is well accounted for here as well, with two linen closets and a coat closet in the bedroom hall.

Plan E-1308	
Bedrooms: 3	**Baths:** 2
Living Area:	
Main floor	1,375 sq. ft.
Total Living Area:	**1,375 sq. ft.**
Carport	430 sq. ft.
Storage	95 sq. ft.
Exterior Wall Framing:	2x4
Foundation Options:	
Crawlspace	
Slab	

(All plans can be built with your choice of foundation and framing. A generic conversion diagram is available. See order form.)

BLUEPRINT PRICE CODE: A

MAIN FLOOR

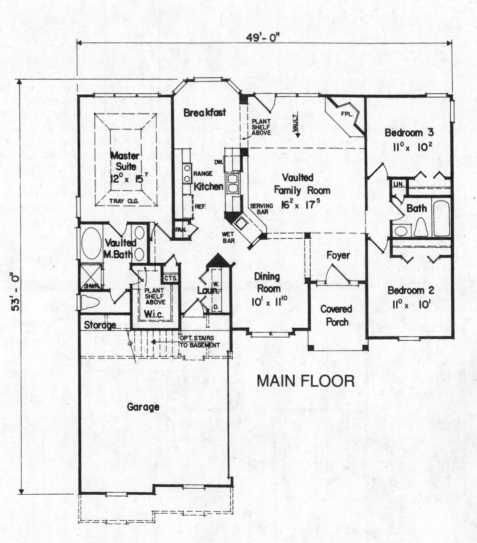

Distinctive Inside and Out

- A decorative columned entry, shuttered windows and a facade of stucco and stone offer a distinct look to this economical one-story home.
- The focal point of the interior is the huge, central family room. The room is enhanced with a dramatic corner fireplace, a vaulted ceiling and a neat serving bar that extends from the kitchen and includes a wet bar.
- A decorative plant shelf adorns the entrance to the adjoining breakfast room, which features a lovely bay window. The kitchen offers a pantry and a pass-through to the serving bar.
- The formal dining room is easy to reach from both the kitchen and the family room, and is highlighted by a raised ceiling and a tall window.
- The secluded master suite boasts a vaulted private bath with dual sinks, an oval garden tub, a separate toilet room and a large walk-in closet.
- Two more bedrooms share a second bath at the other end of the home.

Plan FB-5001-SAVA

Bedrooms: 3	Baths: 2
Living Area:	
Main floor	1,429 sq. ft.
Total Living Area:	**1,429 sq. ft.**
Daylight basement	1,429 sq. ft.
Garage	250 sq. ft.
Storage	14 sq. ft.
Exterior Wall Framing:	2x4

Foundation Options:

Daylight basement
Crawlspace
Slab
(Typical foundation & framing conversion diagram available—see order form.)

BLUEPRINT PRICE CODE: **A**

MAIN FLOOR

Plan FB-5001-SAVA

PRICES AND DETAILS
ON PAGES 12-15

Easy Living

- This cozy one-story design makes the most of its square footage by neatly incorporating features usually found only in much larger homes.
- Off the covered porch is a spacious living room with a dramatic corner fireplace, a ceiling that slopes to 13 ft., 6 in. and a long view to the backyard patio.
- The living room unfolds to a lovely dining room with a patio door.
- The adjoining kitchen features a snack bar for convenient serving and quick meals. The efficient, U-shaped kitchen also offers a pantry and a broom closet, plus a nearby utility/storage room.
- The gorgeous master suite is positioned for privacy. The bright bedroom has a ceiling that slopes to 11 ft. and a large front window arrangement. The master bath features dual sinks.
- The secondary bedrooms are located at the opposite end of the home and share a convenient hall bath.

Plan E-1311

Bedrooms: 3	Baths: 2
Living Area:	
Main floor	1,380 sq. ft.
Total Living Area:	**1,380 sq. ft.**
Garage	440 sq. ft.
Utility and storage	84 sq. ft.
Exterior Wall Framing:	2x6

Foundation Options:

Crawlspace
Slab
(All plans can be built with your choice of foundation and framing. A generic conversion diagram is available. See order form.)

BLUEPRINT PRICE CODE:	**A**

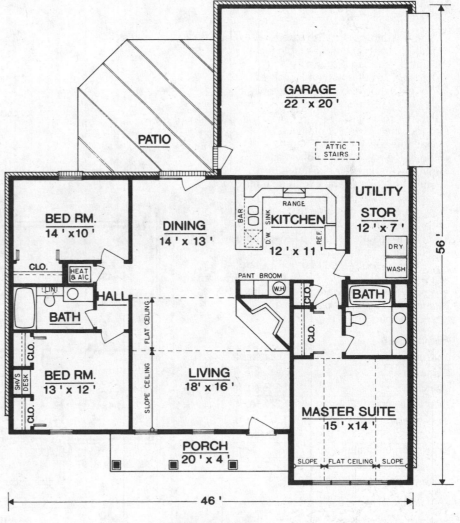

MAIN FLOOR

Stylish Exterior, Open Floor Plan

- With its simple yet stylish exterior, this modest-sized design is suitable for country or urban settings.
- A covered front porch and a gabled roof extension accent the facade while providing plenty of sheltered space for outdoor relaxation.
- Inside, the open floor plan puts available space to efficient use.
- The living room, which offers an inviting fireplace, is expanded by a cathedral ceiling. The adjoining dining area is open to the island kitchen, and all three rooms combine to create one huge gathering place.
- The master suite features a private bath and a large walk-in closet.
- Two more good-sized bedrooms share a second full bath.
- A convenient utility area leads to the carport, which incorporates extra storage space.

Plan J-86155

Bedrooms: 3	Baths: 2
Living Area:	
Main floor	1,385 sq. ft.
Total Living Area:	**1,385 sq. ft.**
Standard basement	1,385 sq. ft.
Carport	380 sq. ft.
Exterior Wall Framing:	2x4

Foundation Options:

Standard basement
Crawlspace
Slab

(All plans can be built with your choice of foundation and framing. A generic conversion diagram is available. See order form.)

BLUEPRINT PRICE CODE: A

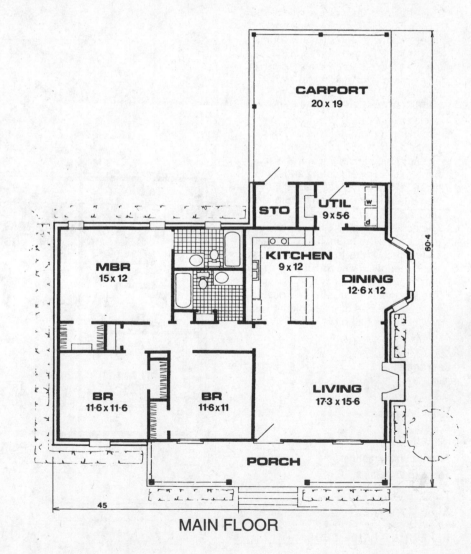

MAIN FLOOR

TO ORDER THIS BLUEPRINT, CALL TOLL-FREE 1-800-547-5570

Plan J-86155

PRICES AND DETAILS ON PAGES 12-15

Inviting Country Porch

- A columned porch with double doors invites you into the rustic living areas of this ranch-style home.
- Inside, the entry allows views back to the expansive, central living room and the backyard beyond.
- The living room boasts an exposed-beam ceiling and a massive fireplace

with a wide stone hearth, a wood box and built-in bookshelves. A sunny patio offers additional entertaining space.
- The dining room and the efficient kitchen combine for easy meal service, with a serving bar separating the two.
- The main hallway leads to the sleeping wing, which offers a large master bedroom with a walk-in closet and a private bath.
- Two additional bedrooms share another full bath, and a laundry closet is accessible to the entire bedroom wing.

Plan E-1304	
Bedrooms: 3	**Baths:** 2
Living Area:	
Main floor	1,395 sq. ft.
Total Living Area:	**1,395 sq. ft.**
Garage & storage	481 sq. ft.
Exterior Wall Framing:	2x4

Foundation Options:

Crawlspace
Slab
(All plans can be built with your choice of foundation and framing. A generic conversion diagram is available. See order form.)

BLUEPRINT PRICE CODE: A

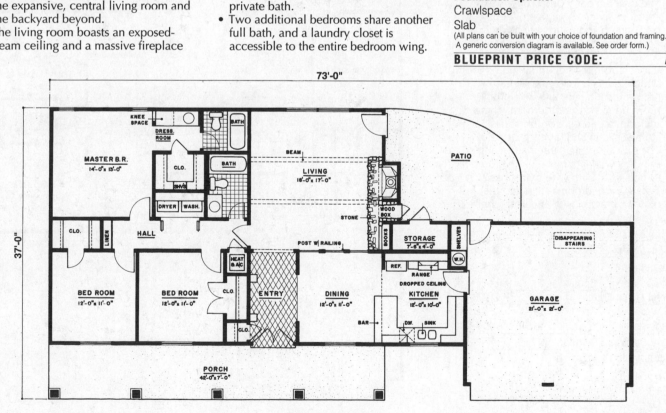

MAIN FLOOR

TO ORDER THIS BLUEPRINT, CALL TOLL-FREE 1-800-547-5570

Plan E-1304

PRICES AND DETAILS ON PAGES 12-15

Street Privacy

- If privacy from street traffic or noise is a concern, this unique home design will fit the bill. The views are oriented to the rear, leaving the front of the home quiet and protected.
- The covered entry porch opens to a spacious living room that overlooks a back porch and patio area. A dramatic corner fireplace is an inviting feature.
- A functional snack bar separates the kitchen from the adjoining dining room, which boasts a lovely bay window.
- Just off the kitchen, a deluxe utility room doubles as a mudroom. The area includes a pantry, a broom closet, a storage closet and laundry facilities.
- The private master suite has an angled window wall, a large walk-in closet and a nice-sized bath with twin sinks.
- Two more bedrooms share another full bath on the opposite end of the home.

Plan E-1424

Bedrooms: 3	Baths: 2
Living Area:	
Main floor	1,415 sq. ft.
Total Living Area:	**1,415 sq. ft.**
Garage	484 sq. ft.
Storage	60 sq. ft.
Exterior Wall Framing:	2x6

Foundation Options:

Crawlspace

Slab

(All plans can be built with your choice of foundation and framing. A generic conversion diagram is available. See order form.)

BLUEPRINT PRICE CODE: A

MAIN FLOOR

Plan E-1424

PRICES AND DETAILS ON PAGES 12-15

Charming Traditional

- The attractive facade of this traditional home features decorative fretwork and louvers in the gables, plus eye-catching window and door treatments.
- The entry area features a commanding view of the living room, which boasts a 12½-ft. ceiling and a corner fireplace. A rear porch and patio are visible through French doors.
- The bayed dining room shares an eating bar with the U-shaped kitchen. The nearby utility room includes a pantry and laundry facilities.
- The quiet master suite includes a big walk-in closet and a private bath with a dual-sink vanity.
- On the other side of the home, double doors close off the two secondary bedrooms from the living areas. A full bath services this wing.

Plan E-1428

Bedrooms: 3	**Baths:** 2

Living Area:

Main floor	1,415 sq. ft.
Total Living Area:	**1,415 sq. ft.**
Garage	484 sq. ft.
Storage	60 sq. ft.
Exterior Wall Framing:	2x6

Foundation Options:

Crawlspace
Slab

(All plans can be built with your choice of foundation and framing. A generic conversion diagram is available. See order form.)

BLUEPRINT PRICE CODE: **A**

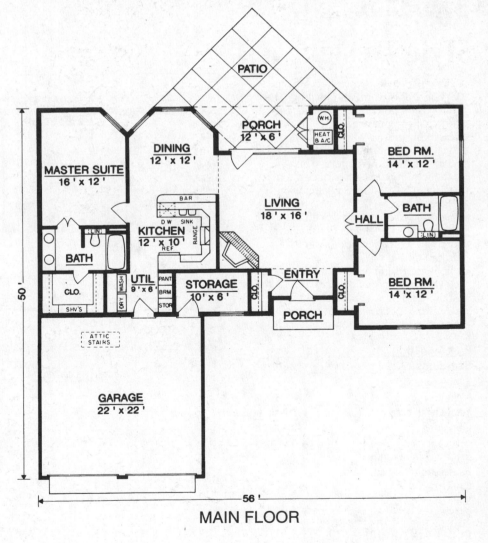

MAIN FLOOR

Rustic Ranch-Style Design

- This ranch-style home offers a rustic facade that is warm and inviting. The railed front porch and stone accents are especially appealing.
- The interior is warm as well, with the focal point being the attractive living room. Features here include an eye-catching fireplace, patio access and a dramatic 14-ft. sloped ceiling with exposed beams.
- The open dining room lies off the foyer and adjoins the efficient U-shaped kitchen, which includes a pantry and a broom closet.
- The master suite features a large walk-in closet and a roomy master bath.
- At the other end of the home, two secondary bedrooms with abundant closet space share another full bath.

Plan E-1410

Bedrooms: 3	Baths: 2

Living Area:

Main floor	1,418 sq. ft.
Total Living Area:	**1,418 sq. ft.**
Garage	484 sq. ft.
Storage	38 sq. ft.
Exterior Wall Framing:	**2x4**

Foundation Options:

Crawlspace

Slab

(All plans can be built with your choice of foundation and framing. A generic conversion diagram is available. See order form.)

BLUEPRINT PRICE CODE: **A**

MAIN FLOOR

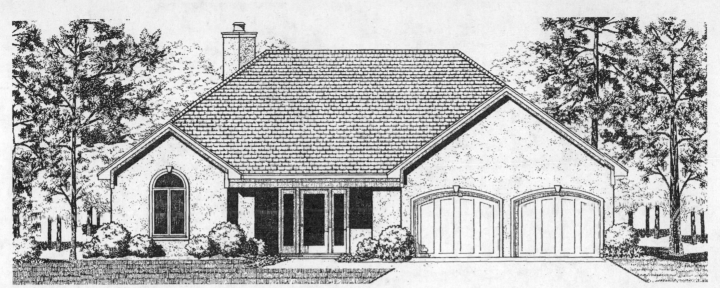

Wide Angles
Add Style

- The comfortably-sized living areas of this gorgeous home are stylishly enhanced by wide, interesting angles.
- Past the covered front porch, the sidelighted front door brightens the living room just ahead.
- The spacious living room is warmed by a dramatic corner fireplace and opens to an angled, covered back porch.
- A stunning bayed dining room merges with the kitchen and its functional angled snack bar. Laundry facilities and access to the garage are nearby.
- The master suite is removed from the secondary bedrooms and features double doors to a deluxe private bath with an angled spa tub, a dual-sink vanity and a large walk-in closet.
- Another full bath serves the two additional bedrooms at the opposite end of the home.

Plan E-1426

Bedrooms: 3	Baths: 2
Living Area:	
Main floor	1,420 sq. ft.
Total Living Area:	**1,420 sq. ft.**
Garage and storage	540 sq. ft.
Exterior Wall Framing:	2x6

Foundation Options:

Crawlspace
Slab
(All plans can be built with your choice of foundation and framing. A generic conversion diagram is available. See order form.)

BLUEPRINT PRICE CODE: A

MAIN FLOOR

Splendid Split-Foyer

- This popular split-foyer home offers soaring vaulted formal areas and a splendid master suite.
- The foyer leads up to the airy living room, which is brightened by broad windows and warmed by a fireplace
- The adjoining dining room merges with the breakfast area and accesses the back deck though sliding glass doors.

- Double windows warm the breakfast nook and provide views to the backyard. The kitchen also boasts an angled sink area with a plant shelf.
- The master suite features a large closet, a corner window and a deluxe master bath that boasts another closet, a step-up spa tub and a separate shower. Two additional bedrooms share a full bath.
- The lower level provides space for expansion with the inclusion of an unfinished family room. The tuck-under garage and the laundry room share this level.

Plan APS-1410

Bedrooms: 3	Baths: 2
Living Area:	
Main floor	1,428 sq. ft.
Total Living Area:	**1,428 sq. ft.**
Daylight basement	458 sq. ft.
Tuck-under garage	480 sq. ft.
Exterior Wall Framing:	2x4

Foundation Options:

Daylight basement
(All plans can be built with your choice of foundation and framing. A generic conversion diagram is available. See order form.)

BLUEPRINT PRICE CODE: A

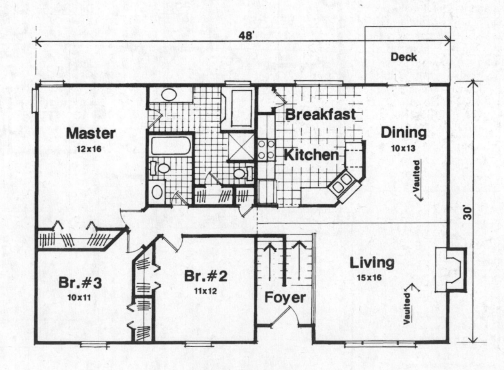

MAIN FLOOR

Plan APS-1410

Easy, Open Floor Plan

- This attractive home flaunts a mixture of vertical and horizontal wood siding, and the wide-open floor plan permits easy traffic flow.
- A large, central living room merges with a dining area at the back of the home. The skylighted living room features a 10-ft. ceiling, a handsome fireplace and a patio door to a covered side porch.
- The roomy U-shaped kitchen includes a pantry and a convenient eating bar. Nearby, a utility room offers garage access and extra freezer space.
- The isolated master suite boasts a sunny sitting area and a large walk-in closet. The private master bath has two sets of double doors and offers an exciting oval tub, a separate toilet room and his-and-hers sinks in a long, angled vanity.
- Two more bedrooms and another full bath are at the other end of the home.

Plan E-1430

Bedrooms: 3	Baths: 2
Living Area:	
Main floor	1,430 sq. ft.
Total Living Area:	**1,430 sq. ft.**
Garage and storage	465 sq. ft.
Exterior Wall Framing:	2x4

Foundation Options:

Crawlspace

Slab

(All plans can be built with your choice of foundation and framing. A generic conversion diagram is available. See order form.)

BLUEPRINT PRICE CODE: A

MAIN FLOOR

Quality Details Inside and Out

- A sparkling stucco finish, an eye-catching roofline and elegant window treatments hint at the quality features found inside this exquisite home.
- The airy entry opens to a large, central living room, which is embellished with a 10-ft. ceiling and a dramatic fireplace.
- The living room flows into a nice-sized dining area. A covered side porch expands the entertaining area.
- A functional eating bar and pantry are featured in the adjoining U-shaped kitchen. The nearby hallway to the garage neatly stores a washer, a dryer and a laundry sink.
- Secluded to the back of the home is a private master suite with a romantic sitting area and a large walk-in closet. The master bath offers dual sinks and an exciting oval tub.
- Two secondary bedrooms and another bath are located on the other side of the living room and entry.

Plan E-1435

Bedrooms: 3	Baths: 2

Living Area:	
Main floor	1,442 sq. ft.
Total Living Area:	**1,442 sq. ft.**
Garage and storage	516 sq. ft.
Exterior Wall Framing:	2x4

Foundation Options:

Crawlspace

Slab

(All plans can be built with your choice of foundation and framing. A generic conversion diagram is available. See order form.)

BLUEPRINT PRICE CODE:	**A**

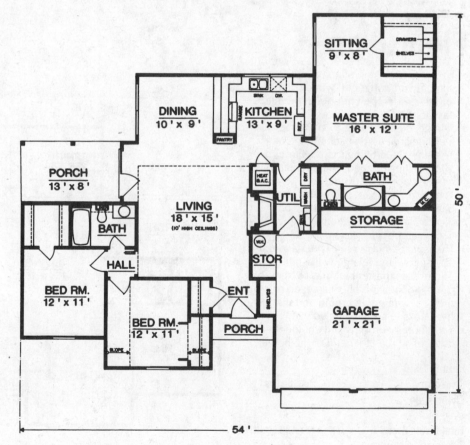

MAIN FLOOR

Plan E-1435

PRICES AND DETAILS ON PAGES 12-15

Sleek One-Story

- Steep, sleek rooflines and a trio of French doors with half-round transoms give this one-story a look of distinction.
- The covered front porch opens to the spacious living room, where a central fireplace cleverly incorporates a wet bar, bookshelves and a coat closet.
- Behind the fireplace, the adjoining dining room offers views to the backyard through an arched window arrangement. The two rooms are expanded by 11-ft. ceilings and a covered back porch.
- A snack bar connects the dining room to the U-shaped kitchen, which offers a pantry closet and large windows over the sink. Laundry facilities are nearby.
- The secluded master suite features a large walk-in closet and a private bath. Across the home, the secondary bedrooms each have a walk-in closet and share another full bath.

Plan E-1427

Bedrooms: 3	**Baths: 2**

Living Area:

Main floor	1,444 sq. ft.
Total Living Area:	**1,444 sq. ft.**
Garage and storage	540 sq. ft.
Exterior Wall Framing:	2x4

Foundation Options:

Crawlspace

Slab

(All plans can be built with your choice of foundation and framing. A generic conversion diagram is available. See order form.)

BLUEPRINT PRICE CODE:	**A**

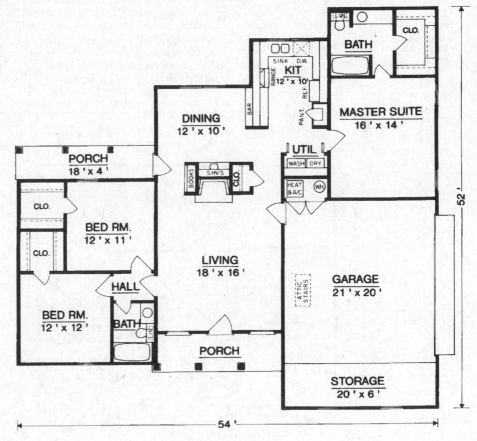

MAIN FLOOR

Extraordinary Split-Level

- This design boasts a striking arched window in an inviting facade that introduces an extraordinary split-level floor plan.
- The recessed entry opens into the expansive living room, with its fabulous windows, nice fireplace and breathtaking 12-ft. vaulted ceiling.
- The dining room, which features a 14-ft. vaulted ceiling, expands the open living area and lends an air of spaciousness to the entire main floor.
- The kitchen is a gourmet's dream, offering a wraparound counter, a double sink and a pass-through to the dining room. A 12-ft. vaulted ceiling is shared with the sunny breakfast room, which shows off a built-in desk and sliding-door access to a backyard deck.
- The sizable master bedroom, a second bedroom and a shared bath are several steps up from the main level, creating a sense of privacy.
- The third bedroom makes a great den, playroom, office or guest room.

Plan B-87112

Bedrooms: 2+	Baths: 2
Living Area:	
Main floor	1,452 sq. ft.
Total Living Area:	**1,452 sq. ft.**
Standard basement	1,452 sq. ft.
Garage	448 sq. ft.
Exterior Wall Framing:	2x4

Foundation Options:

Standard basement
(All plans can be built with your choice of foundation and framing. A generic conversion diagram is available. See order form.)

BLUEPRINT PRICE CODE: A

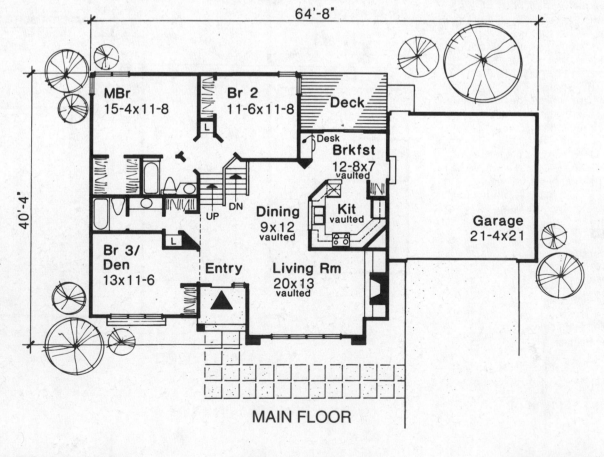

MAIN FLOOR

Plan B-87112

PRICES AND DETAILS ON PAGES 12-15

Classic Country-Style

- The classic covered front porch with decorative railings and columns make this home reminiscent of an early 20th-century farmhouse.
- Dormers give the home the appearance of a two-story, even though it is designed for single-level living.
- The huge living room features a ceiling that slopes up to 13 feet. A corner fireplace radiates warmth to both the living room and the dining room.
- The dining room overlooks a backyard patio and shares a versatile serving bar with the open kitchen. A large utility room is just steps away.
- The master bedroom boasts a roomy bath with a dual-sink vanity. The two smaller bedrooms at the other end of the home share a full bath.

Plan E-1412

Bedrooms: 3	Baths: 2

Living Area:

Main floor	1,484 sq. ft.
Total Living Area:	**1,484 sq. ft.**
Garage	440 sq. ft.
Exterior Wall Framing:	2x6

Foundation Options:

Crawlspace

Slab

(All plans can be built with your choice of foundation and framing. A generic conversion diagram is available. See order form.)

BLUEPRINT PRICE CODE: **A**

MAIN FLOOR

Charming Simplicity

- This home features a covered front porch and a simple floor plan, each enhancing the home's charming appeal.
- In the living room, the cozy fireplace offers warmth and drama. Built-in bookcases are featured on either side.
- The adjoining dining room flows into the bright island kitchen and opens to the backyard. Laundry facilities and a carport entrance are nearby.
- The secluded master bedroom features a sloped ceiling, a corner window, a walk-in closet, a dressing area and a separate bath.
- Two nice-sized bedrooms share a full bath at the opposite end of the home.

Plan J-8670

Bedrooms: 3	Baths: 2
Living Area:	
Main floor	1,522 sq. ft.
Total Living Area:	**1,522 sq. ft.**
Standard basement	1,522 sq. ft.
Carport and storage	436 sq. ft.
Exterior Wall Framing:	2x4

Foundation Options:
Standard basement
Crawlspace
Slab
(All plans can be built with your choice of foundation and framing. A generic conversion diagram is available. See order form.)

BLUEPRINT PRICE CODE: B

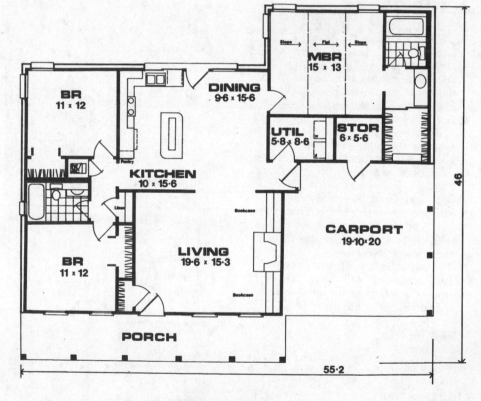

MAIN FLOOR

Plan J-8670

PRICES AND DETAILS ON PAGES 12-15

Design Harmony

- This home combines several distinct architectural styles to achieve a design harmony all its own.
- The front columns are reminiscent of ancient Greece, while the Palladian window in the master bedroom originated in the Renaissance period. The sleek rectangular shape of the home gives it an updated, contemporary look.
- The portico columns are repeated inside, where they are used to visually separate the foyer from the living room and to dramatize the 18-ft. cathedral ceiling. Columns also frame the handsome fireplace.
- Straight ahead, the dining room and kitchen share a high 10-ft. ceiling. The entire area basks in natural light from two skylights, a large bow window and sliding glass doors that open to a sizable backyard terrace.
- The master bedroom boasts a 10-ft. ceiling, a gorgeous Palladian window and a private whirlpool bath.

Plan HFL-1200-FH

Bedrooms: 3	Baths: 2
Living Area:	
Main floor	1,530 sq. ft.
Total Living Area:	**1,530 sq. ft.**
Standard basement	1,434 sq. ft.
Garage and storage	463 sq. ft.
Exterior Wall Framing:	2x6

Foundation Options:

Standard basement

Slab

(All plans can be built with your choice of foundation and framing. A generic conversion diagram is available. See order form.)

BLUEPRINT PRICE CODE: B

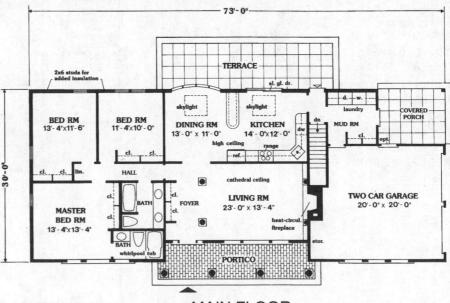

VIEW INTO LIVING ROOM

MAIN FLOOR

Exciting Exterior Options

ELEVATION A

ELEVATION B

- Two exciting elevations are available with this striking stucco design. (Both are included with blueprint purchase.)
- The stately, covered front entry and elegant window treatments are just the beginning of the excitement. Inside is a huge formal living area with volume ceilings.
- The adjoining family room offers built-in shelving and provisions for an optional corner fireplace or media center. Triple sliders open to the rear covered patio.
- The eat-in country kitchen overlooks the family room and features a handy serving counter, a pantry and a laundry closet.
- Separated from the two secondary bedrooms, the master bedroom is a quiet retreat. It offers patio access and an oversized private bath with a huge walk-in closet, a big corner tub and separate vanities that flank a sitting area.

Plan HDS-99-140

Bedrooms: 3	Baths: 2
Living Area:	
Main floor	1,550 sq. ft.
Total Living Area:	**1,550 sq. ft.**
Garage	475 sq. ft.
Exterior Wall Framing:	2x4

Foundation Options:
Slab
(Typical foundation & framing conversion diagram available—see order form.)

BLUEPRINT PRICE CODE: B

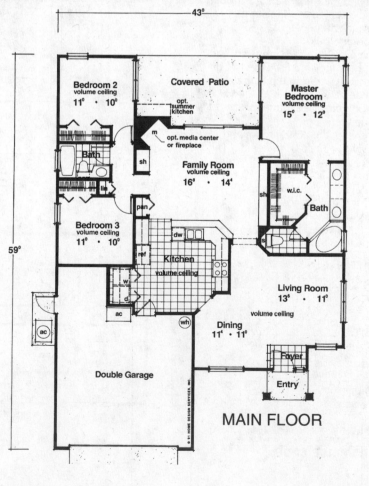

MAIN FLOOR

Plan HDS-99-140

PRICES AND DETAILS ON PAGES 12-15

One-Story
with Impact

- Striking gables, a brick facade and an elegant sidelighted entry give this one-story plenty of impact.
- The impressive interior spaces begin with an 11-ft., 8-in. raised ceiling in the foyer. To the left of the foyer, decorative columns and a large picture window grace the dining room.
- The wonderful living spaces center around a huge family room, which features a 14-ft.-high vaulted ceiling and another pair of columns that separate it from the hall. A stunning fireplace is framed by a window and a beautiful French door.
- The open kitchen and breakfast area features a built-in desk, a pantry closet and a pass-through above the sink.
- An elegant 10-ft. tray ceiling is featured in the master suite, which also boasts a 13-ft. vaulted bath with a garden spa tub, a separate shower, a big walk-in closet and an attractive plant shelf.

Plan FB-1553

Bedrooms: 3	Baths: 2
Living Area:	
Main floor	1,553 sq. ft.
Total Living Area:	**1,553 sq. ft.**
Daylight basement	1,553 sq. ft.
Garage	410 sq. ft.
Exterior Wall Framing:	2x4

Foundation Options:

Daylight basement
Crawlspace
Slab

(All plans can be built with your choice of foundation and framing. A generic conversion diagram is available. See order form.)

BLUEPRINT PRICE CODE: B

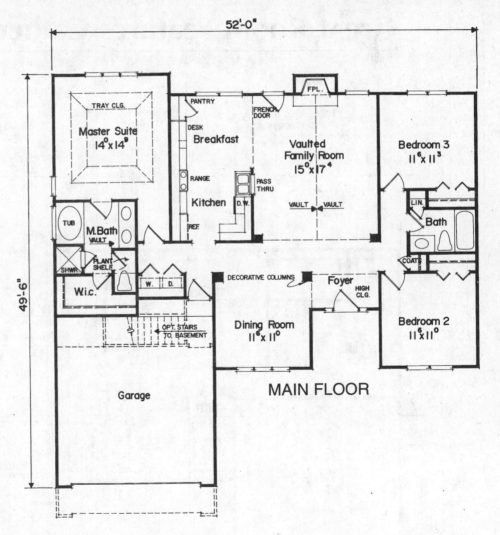

MAIN FLOOR

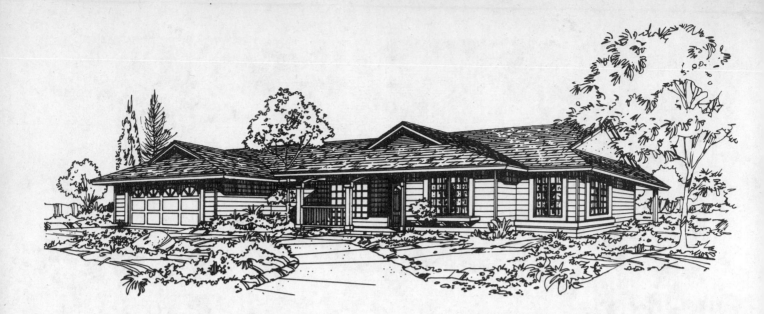

Great Room Features Cathedral Ceiling

Total living area:
(Not counting garage)

1,559 sq. ft.

PLAN Q-1559-1A
WITHOUT BASEMENT
(SLAB-ON-GRADE FOUNDATION)

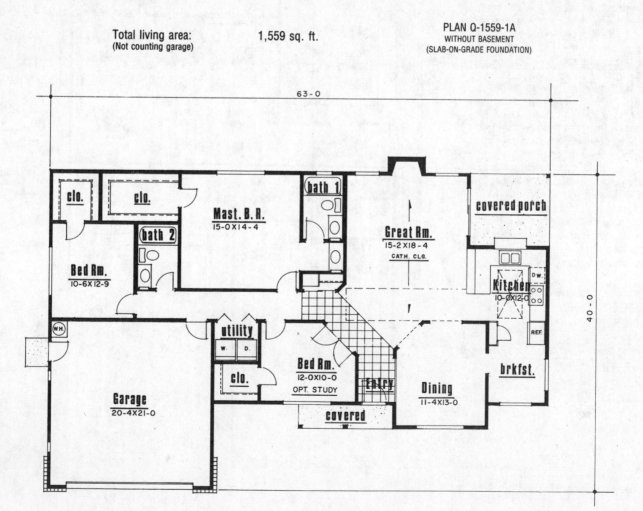

Blueprint Price Code B

Plan Q-1559-1A

Country Highlights

- This nice home has country highlights, with shuttered windows, lap siding and a quaint covered porch.
- The foyer flows into the spacious living room, which offers a 9-ft.-high ceiling, a warm fireplace and tall windows that give views to the front porch. French doors open from the adjoining dining room to a backyard terrace.
- The kitchen features a sunny dinette that accesses the terrace, plus an angled pass-through to the dining room. A nifty mudroom with laundry facilities accesses the garage and the terrace.
- The master bedroom boasts a large walk-in closet and a private bath with a dual-sink vanity, a whirlpool tub and a separate shower.
- Across the home, two secondary bedrooms share another full bath.
- Dormered windows brighten the unfinished upper floor, which provides for future expansion possibilities.

Plan HFL-1700-SR

Bedrooms: 3+	Baths: 2
Living Area:	
Main floor	1,567 sq. ft.
Total Living Area:	**1,567 sq. ft.**
Upper floor (unfinished)	338 sq. ft.
Standard basement	1,567 sq. ft.
Garage	504 sq. ft.
Exterior Wall Framing:	2x6

Foundation Options:

Standard basement

Slab

(All plans can be built with your choice of foundation and framing. A generic conversion diagram is available. See order form.)

BLUEPRINT PRICE CODE: B

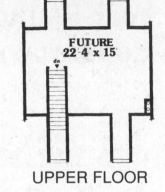

VIEW INTO LIVING ROOM

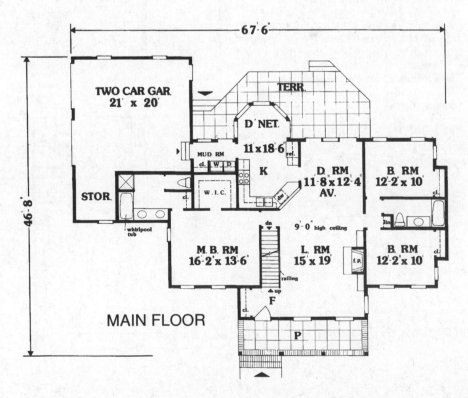

UPPER FLOOR

MAIN FLOOR

REAR VIEW

Year-Round Comfort

FRONT VIEW

- Designed for the energy-conscious, this passive-solar home provides year-round comfort with much lower fuel costs.
- The open, airy interior is a delight. In the winter, sunshine penetrates deep into the living spaces. In the summer, wide overhangs shade the interior.
- The central living and dining rooms flow together, creating a bright, open space. Sliding glass doors open to a terrace and an enclosed sun spot.
- In the airy casual space, the kitchen has an eating bar and a sunny breakfast nook. The adjoining family room boasts a woodstove that warms the entire area.
- The master bedroom suite includes a private terrace, a personal bath and a walk-in closet. Two other bedrooms share another full bath.

Plan K-392-T

Bedrooms: 3	Baths: 2½
Living Area:	
Main floor	1,592 sq. ft.
Sun spot	125 sq. ft.
Total Living Area:	**1,717 sq. ft.**
Partial basement	634 sq. ft.
Garage	407 sq. ft.
Exterior Wall Framing:	2x4 or 2x6

Foundation Options:

Partial basement
Slab

(All plans can be built with your choice of foundation and framing. A generic conversion diagram is available. See order form.)

BLUEPRINT PRICE CODE:	B

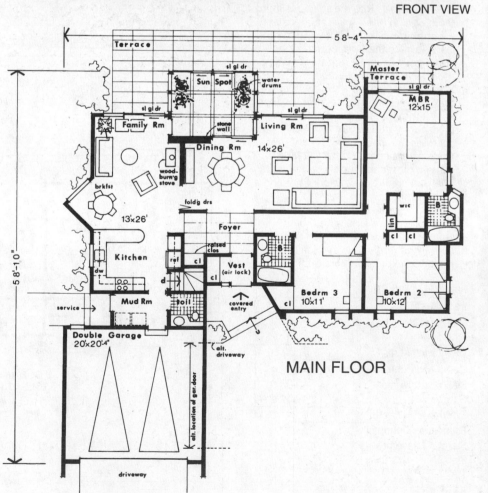

MAIN FLOOR

Captivating Colonial Transitional

- A charming cupola and a large covered porch accented by detailed columns lend this country-style home the feel of the Colonial South.
- The large foyer leads into a huge living room which features a dramatic sunken floor, a cozy fireplace and access to a beautiful rear terrace.

- An open railing looks into the roomy dining room, which features nearby kitchen access and a serving bar.
- A unique sewing room with a built-in storage unit is conveniently located close to the kitchen and the utiltity room. The utility room leads to the two-car garage.
- The ammenity-stacked master bedroom boasts a sunken floor, a built-in book shelf and dramatic mirrors. A railing flanked by brick columns opens to a sunny private sitting room with a walk-in closet. The master bath boasts a dual-sink vanity and built-in shelves.
- Two additional bedrooms on the other side of the home share a hall bath.

Plan E-1614	
Bedrooms: 3	**Baths:** 2
Living Area:	
Main floor	1,600 sq. ft.
Total Living Area:	**1,600 sq. ft.**
Standard basement	1,600 sq. ft.
Garage and storage	588 sq. ft.
Exterior Wall Framing:	2x6

Foundation Options:

Standard basement

Crawlspace

Slab

(All plans can be built with your choice of foundation and framing. A generic conversion diagram is available. See order form.)

BLUEPRINT PRICE CODE:	B

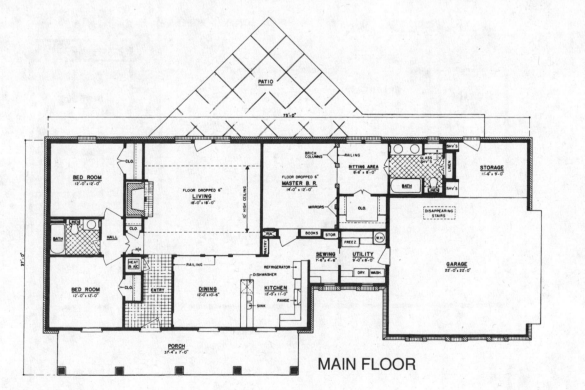

MAIN FLOOR

Designed for Relaxed Living

Wood post and railing, shutters and covered porch give a relaxed look to this country home. A fireplace lends extra appeal to the large living room. A country kitchen with center work bar is located between the breakfast room and separate dining room.

All three bedrooms are located on one side of the house. Each bedroom has good closet space.

Total living area: 1,627 sq. ft.
(Not counting basement or garage)

Specify daylight basement, crawlspace or slab foundation.

CLOSET **DRESS**

BEDROOM
15-6 × 12-0

SCREENED PORCHS
14-0 × 10-0

CLOSET   CLOSET

STORAGE
7-10 × 8-0

W D

PAN

BREAKFAST
10-0 × 9-6

KITCHEN
10-0 × 13-4

DINING ROOM
11-0 × 13-4

NEN

DOWN

BEDROOM
12-0 × 11-0

BATH

LINEN

51-0

GARAGE
20-0 × 20-4

LIVING ROOM
21-0 × 15-4

CLOSET

BEDROOM
13-0 × 11-4

COAT

PORCH
26-6 × 8-0

60-0

**TO ORDER THIS BLUEPRINT,
CALL TOLL-FREE 1-800-547-5570**

Blueprint Price Code B
Plan C-7549

*PRICES AND DETAILS
ON PAGES 12-15*

Distinctive Design

- This well-designed home is neatly laid out to provide distinctive formal and informal living areas.
- The entry guides guests into the combination living and dining room. Straight ahead, double doors open to a large family room that overlooks an inviting patio. An 11-ft. vaulted ceiling with exposed beams and a dramatic fireplace with a raised hearth give the room added appeal.
- The galley-style kitchen offers easy service to the dining room and the bayed eating area. Nearby, a deluxe utility room features laundry facilities and access to the garage.
- Three bedrooms, each with a walk-in closet, make up the sleeping wing. The master suite offers a private bath with a separate dressing area set off by a decorative half-wall.

Plan E-1601

Bedrooms: 3	Baths: 2
Living Area:	
Main floor	1,630 sq. ft.
Total Living Area:	**1,630 sq. ft.**
Garage and storage	610 sq. ft.
Exterior Wall Framing:	2x4

Foundation Options:
Crawlspace
Slab
(All plans can be built with your choice of foundation and framing. A generic conversion diagram is available. See order form.)

BLUEPRINT PRICE CODE: B

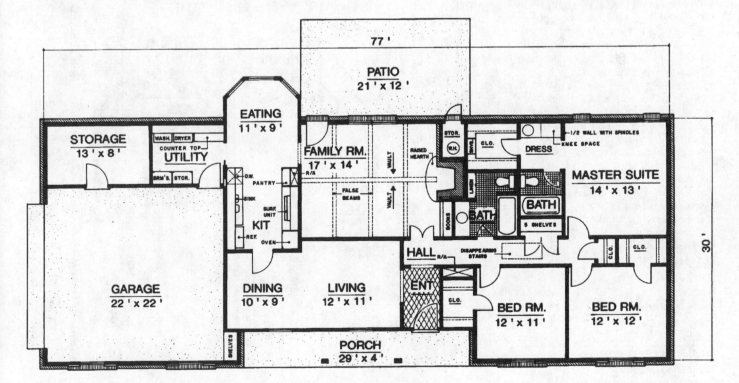

MAIN FLOOR

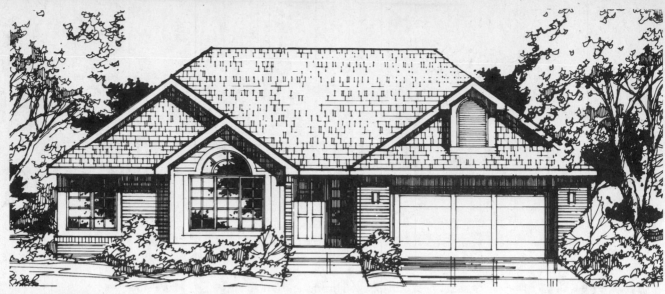

Affordable Luxury

- This stylish and enticing home combines luxury and affordability in one compact package.
- The foyer offers an immediate view of the living room's impressive fireplace and the wraparound deck beyond. The spacious living room also features a dramatic 15-ft. vaulted ceiling.
- The adjoining formal dining room is outlined by decorative wood columns. Sliding glass doors access the deck.
- A corner sink framed by a half-wall keeps the well-planned kitchen open to the sunny breakfast nook.
- The master suite is spectacular, with a bright sitting area and a distinctive ceiling that slopes up to 10 feet. A large walk-in closet and a sumptuous master bath with a dual-sink vanity, a whirlpool tub and a corner shower are other highlights.
- The third bedroom, with its beautiful Palladian window and vaulted ceiling, would serve equally well as a den or an impressive home office.

Plan B-89020

Bedrooms: 2+	Baths: 2
Living Area:	
Main floor	1,642 sq. ft.
Total Living Area:	**1,642 sq. ft.**
Standard basement	1,642 sq. ft.
Garage	455 sq. ft.
Exterior Wall Framing:	2x4

Foundation Options:

Standard basement

(All plans can be built with your choice of foundation and framing. A generic conversion diagram is available. See order form.)

BLUEPRINT PRICE CODE: B

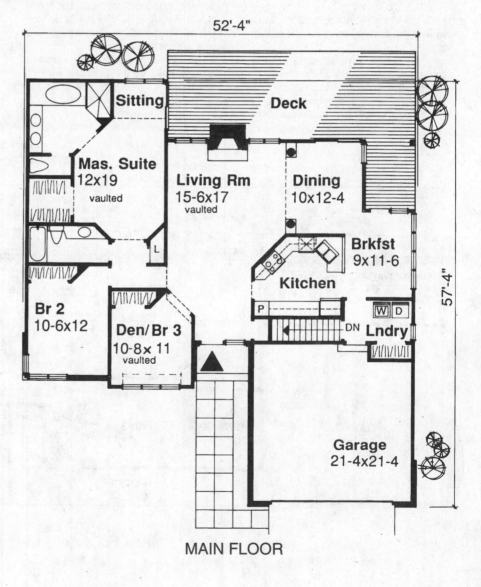

MAIN FLOOR

TO ORDER THIS BLUEPRINT, CALL TOLL-FREE 1-800-547-5570

Plan B-89020

PRICES AND DETAILS ON PAGES 12-15

Angled Solar Design

- This passive-solar design with a six-sided core is angled to capture as much sunlight as possible.
- Finished in natural vertical cedar planks and stone veneer, this contemporary three-bedroom requires a minimum of maintenance.
- Double doors at the entry open into the spacious living and dining areas.

- The formal area features a 14-ft. domed ceiling with skylights, a freestanding fireplace and three sets of sliding glass doors. The central sliding doors lead to a glass-enclosed sun room.
- The bright eat-in kitchen merges with the den, where sliding glass doors lead to one of three backyard terraces.
- The master bedroom, in the quiet sleeping wing, boasts ample closets, a private terrace and a luxurious bath, complete with a whirlpool tub.
- The two secondary bedrooms share a convenient hall bath.

Plan K-534-L	
Bedrooms: 3	Baths: 2
Living Area:	
Main floor	1,647 sq. ft.
Total Living Area:	**1,647 sq. ft.**
Standard basement	1,505 sq. ft.
Garage	400 sq. ft.
Exterior Wall Framing:	2x4 or 2x6
Foundation Options:	
Standard basement	
Slab	

(All plans can be built with your choice of foundation and framing. A generic conversion diagram is available. See order form.)

BLUEPRINT PRICE CODE: B

VIEW INTO LIVING ROOM AND DINING ROOM

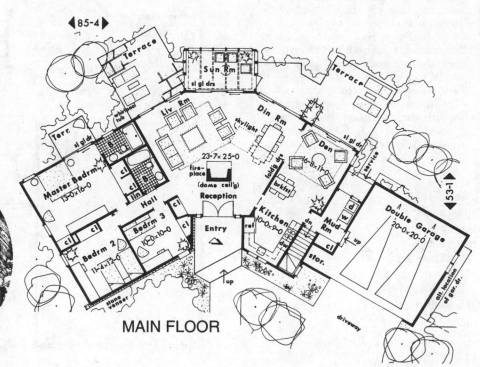

MAIN FLOOR

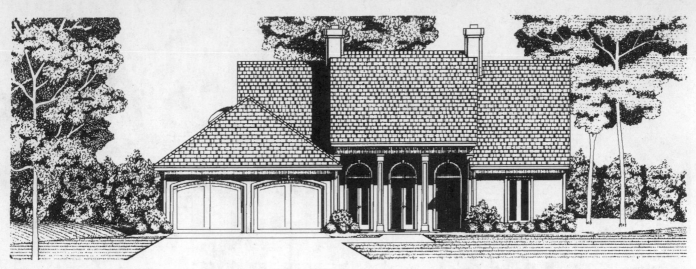

Distinctive and Elegant

- A distinctive look is captured in the exterior of this elegant one-story. Half-round transoms grace the three glass doors that open to the columned, covered front porch.
- The spacious living room at the center of the homer commands attention, with its 15-ft. ceiling and inviting fireplace. A glass door flanked by windows opens to a skylighted porch, which is also accessible from the secondary bedroom at the back of the home.
- The unique dining room overlooks the two backyard porches and boasts an elegant octagonal design, shaped by columns and cased openings.
- A 14-ft. sloped, skylighted ceiling adds drama to the gourmet kitchen, which also showcases an angled cooktop bar and a windowed sink. Laundry facilities and storage space are nearby.
- The luxurious master suite is secluded at the rear of the home, with private access to the porch. The sumptuous master bath features an oval spa tub, a separate shower, dual vanities and a huge walk-in closet.

Plan E-1628

Bedrooms: 3	Baths: 2
Living Area:	
Main floor	1,655 sq. ft.
Total Living Area:	**1,655 sq. ft.**
Garage and storage	549 sq. ft.
Exterior Wall Framing:	2x6

Foundation Options:

Crawlspace
Slab
(All plans can be built with your choice of foundation and framing. A generic conversion diagram is available. See order form.)

BLUEPRINT PRICE CODE: B

MAIN FLOOR

Plan E-1628

PRICES AND DETAILS
ON PAGES 12-15

Rustic Welcome

- This rustic design boasts an appealing exterior with a covered front porch that offers guests a friendly welcome.
- Inside, the centrally located Great Room features an 11-ft., 8-in. cathedral ceiling with exposed wood beams. A massive fireplace separates the living area from the large dining room, which offers access to a nice backyard patio.
- The galley-style kitchen flows between the formal dining room and the bayed breakfast room, which offers a handy pantry and access to laundry facilities.
- The master suite features a walk-in closet and a compartmentalized bath.
- Across the Great Room, two additional bedrooms have extra closet space and share a second full bath.
- The side-entry garage gives the front of the home an extra-appealing and uncluttered look.
- The optional daylight basement offers expanded living space. The stairway (not shown) would be located along the wall between the dining room and the back bedroom.

Plan C-8460	
Bedrooms: 3	**Baths:** 2
Living Area:	
Main floor	1,670 sq. ft.
Total Living Area:	**1,670 sq. ft.**
Daylight basement	1,600 sq. ft.
Garage	427 sq. ft.
Exterior Wall Framing:	2x4

Foundation Options:

Daylight basement
Crawlspace
Slab
(All plans can be built with your choice of foundation and framing. A generic conversion diagram is available. See order form.)

BLUEPRINT PRICE CODE:	B

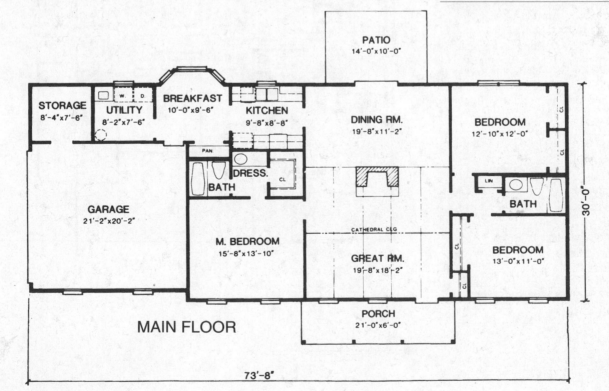

MAIN FLOOR

Smashing Master Suite!

- Corniced gables accented with arched louvers and a covered front porch with striking columns take this one-story design beyond the ordinary.
- The vaulted ceiling in the foyer rises to join the 19-ft. vaulted ceiling in the family room. A central fireplace heats the casual areas and is framed by a window and a French door.
- An angled serving bar/snack counter connects the family room to the sunny dining room and kitchen. The adjoining breakfast room has easy access to the garage, the optional basement and the laundry room with a plant shelf.
- The master suite is simply smashing, with a 10-ft. tray ceiling and private access to the backyard. The master bath has an 11½-ft. vaulted ceiling and all the amenities, while the 13-ft.-high vaulted sitting area offers an optional fireplace.

Plan FB-1671

Bedrooms: 3	Baths: 2
Living Area:	
Main floor	1,671 sq. ft.
Total Living Area:	**1,671 sq. ft.**
Daylight basement	1,671 sq. ft.
Garage	240 sq. ft.
Exterior Wall Framing:	2x4

Foundation Options:

Daylight basement
Crawlspace
(All plans can be built with your choice of foundation and framing. A generic conversion diagram is available. See order form.)

BLUEPRINT PRICE CODE: B

MAIN FLOOR

Plan FB-1671

PRICES AND DETAILS
ON PAGES 12-15

Porch Offers Three Entries

- Showy window treatments, stately columns and three sets of French doors give this Plantation-style home an inviting exterior.
- High 12-ft. ceilings in the living room, dining room and kitchen add volume to the economically-sized home.
- A corner fireplace and a view to the back porch are found in the living room. The porch is accessed from a door in the dining room.
- The adjoining kitchen features an angled snack bar that easily serves the dining room and the casual eating area.
- The secluded master suite offers a cathedral ceiling, a walk-in closet and a luxurious private bath with a spa tub and a separate shower.
- Across the home, two additional bedrooms share a second full bath.

Plan E-1602

Bedrooms: 3	Baths: 2
Living Area:	
Main floor	1,672 sq. ft.
Total Living Area:	**1,672 sq. ft.**
Standard basement	1,672 sq. ft.
Garage	484 sq. ft.
Exterior Wall Framing:	2x6

Foundation Options:

Standard basement
Crawlspace
Slab

(All plans can be built with your choice of foundation and framing. A generic conversion diagram is available. See order form.)

BLUEPRINT PRICE CODE: B

MAIN FLOOR

GARAGE 22' x 22'
ATTIC STAIRS
PATIO
DECK
BEDROOM 12' x 12'
STORAGE 16' x 6'
PORCH 16' x 8'
CLOS
BATH
HALL
WASH DRY
UTIL 8' x 8'
DINING 14' x 13' 12 ft. clg.
ATTIC STAIRS
BATH
SLOPE
SLOPE
MASTER SUITE 16' x 14'
EATING 10' x 12'
BAR
REF
KITCHEN 12' x 13' 12 ft. clg.
LIVING 18' x 18' 12 ft. clg.
BEDROOM 12' x 12'
PORCH 42' x 6'

60'
68'

Circular Dining Room Featured

- An attractive stone facade, innovative architectural features and a functional, light-filled floor plan are the hallmarks of this attractive design.
- Guests are welcomed in the skylighted gallery, which boasts an 11-ft.-high sloped ceiling. The living room features a stone fireplace and opens to the circular dining room.
- The dining room is highlighted by a curved wall of windows and an 11-ft. domed ceiling, making an expansive space for entertaining.
- The open kitchen is set up for efficient operation and adjoins the sunny dinette and the cozy family room.
- The bedrooms are zoned to the left, with the master suite including a private bath, a large walk-in closet and access to an outdoor terrace. The additional bedrooms share another full bath.

Plan K-663-N

Bedrooms: 3	Baths: 2
Living Area:	
Main floor	1,682 sq. ft.
Total Living Area:	**1,682 sq. ft.**
Standard basement	1,645 sq. ft.
Garage	453 sq. ft.
Exterior Wall Framing:	2x4 or 2x6

Foundation Options:

Standard basement
Slab

(All plans can be built with your choice of foundation and framing. A generic conversion diagram is available. See order form.)

BLUEPRINT PRICE CODE: B

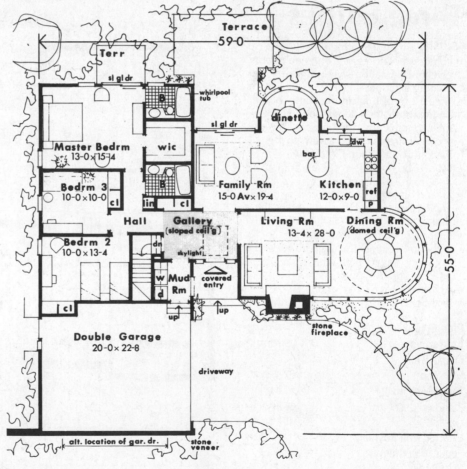

MAIN FLOOR

TO ORDER THIS BLUEPRINT, CALL TOLL-FREE 1-800-547-5570

Plan K-663-N

PRICES AND DETAILS ON PAGES 12-15

Shady Porches, Sunny Patio

- Designed with stylish country looks, this attractive one-story also has shady porches and a sunny patio for relaxed indoor/outdoor living.
- The inviting foyer flows into the spacious living room, which is warmed by a handsome fireplace.
- The adjoining dining room has a door to a screened-in porch, which opens to the backyard and serves as a breezeway to the nearby garage
- The U-shaped kitchen has a pantry closet and plenty of counter space. Around the corner, a space-efficient laundry/utility room exits to a big backyard patio.
- The master bedroom is brightened by windows on two sides and includes a wardrobe closet. The compartmentalized master bath offers a separate dressing area and a walk-in closet.
- Another full bath serves two additional good-sized bedrooms.

Plan C-7557

Bedrooms: 3	Baths: 2
Living Area:	
Main floor	1,688 sq. ft.
Total Living Area:	**1,688 sq. ft.**
Standard basement	1,688 sq. ft.
Garage	400 sq. ft.
Exterior Wall Framing:	2x4

Foundation Options:
Standard basement
Crawlspace
Slab
(All plans can be built with your choice of foundation and framing. A generic conversion diagram is available. See order form.)

BLUEPRINT PRICE CODE:	B

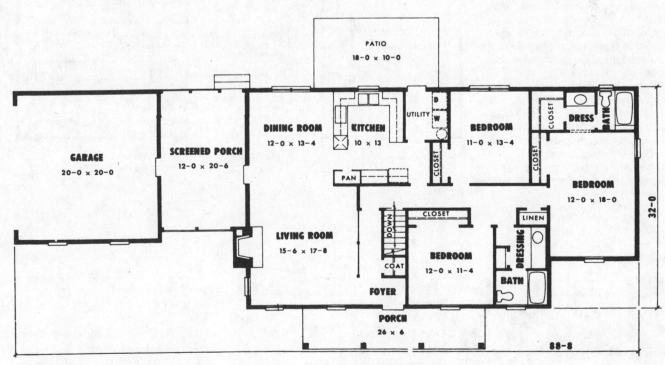

MAIN FLOOR

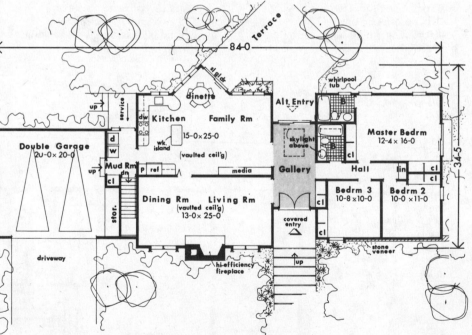

Handsome Ranch Offers Symmetry

- A dramatic facade with stone chimney, vertical siding and stone veneer accents gives this ranch a distinctive custom appearance.
- Double doors at the entry open to a skylit gallery and a well-zoned floor plan.
- The formal living and dining rooms at the front of the home are highlighted by a vaulted ceiling and a stone-finished fireplace.
- The expansive informal areas at the rear are ideal for casual family living and entertaining. A vaulted ceiling hovers above a sunny, angular dinette area, an open island kitchen and a family room with built-in media center.
- Included in the sleeping wing is an isolated master bedroom with a private terrace and a personal bath with whirlpool tub.

VIEW OF DINETTE AND FAMILY ROOM FROM KITCHEN.

Plan K-673-R

Bedrooms: 3	**Baths:** 2

Space:

Main floor	1,704 sq. ft.
Total Living Area	**1,704 sq. ft.**
Basement	1,600 sq. ft.
Garage	400 sq. ft.
Exterior Wall Framing	2x4 or 2x6

Foundation options:

Standard Basement
Slab
(Foundation & framing conversion diagram available—see order form.)

Blueprint Price Code   B

Plan K-673-R

PRICES AND DETAILS ON PAGES 12-15

Large, Stylish Spaces

- This stylish brick home greets guests with a beautiful entry court that leads to the recessed front porch.
- Beyond the porch, the bright entry flows into the Great Room, which features an 11-ft. sloped ceiling. This airy space also offers a fireplace, a sunny dining area and sliding glass doors to a backyard patio.
- The kitchen has a walk-in pantry, an open serving counter above the sink and convenient access to the laundry facilities and the garage.
- Isolated from the secondary bedrooms, the master suite boasts a 9-ft. tray ceiling, an oversized walk-in closet and an exquisite bath with two distinct sink areas, a corner garden tub and a separate shower.
- The third bedroom, which features lovely double doors and a front-facing bay window, would also make a perfect home office.

Plan SDG-91188

Bedrooms: 2+	Baths: 2
Living Area:	
Main floor	1,704 sq. ft.
Total Living Area:	**1,704 sq. ft.**
Garage	484 sq. ft.
Exterior Wall Framing:	2x4

Foundation Options:

Slab

(All plans can be built with your choice of foundation and framing. A generic conversion diagram is available. See order form.)

BLUEPRINT PRICE CODE:	B

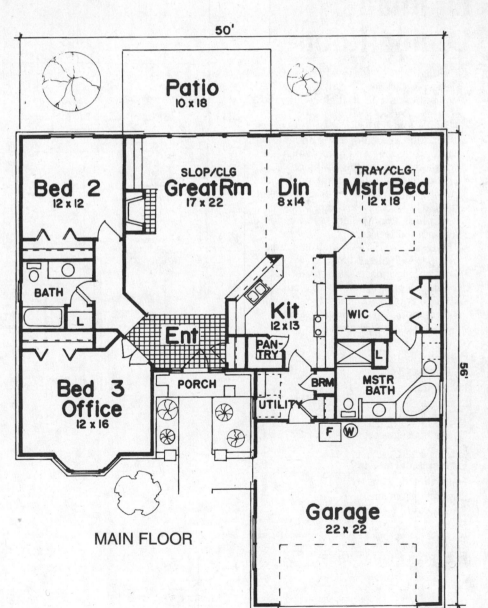

MAIN FLOOR

Dramatic Dining Room

- The highlight of this lovely one-story design is its dramatic dining room, which boasts a 14-ft.-high ceiling and a soaring window wall.
- The airy foyer ushers guests through a 14-ft.-high arched opening and into the 18-ft. vaulted Great Room, which is warmed by an inviting fireplace.
- The kitchen features a large pantry, a serving bar and a handy pass-through to the Great Room. The bright breakfast area offers a convenient laundry closet and outdoor access.
- The two secondary bedrooms share a compartmentalized bath.
- The removed master suite features a 14-ft. tray ceiling, overhead plant shelves and an adjoining 13½-ft. vaulted sitting room. An exciting garden tub is found in the luxurious master bath.

Plan FB-5008-ALLE

Bedrooms: 3	Baths: 2
Living Area:	
Main floor	1,715 sq. ft.
Total Living Area:	**1,715 sq. ft.**
Daylight basement	1,715 sq. ft.
Garage	400 sq. ft.
Exterior Wall Framing:	2x4

Foundation Options:

Daylight basement

Crawlspace

Slab

(All plans can be built with your choice of foundation and framing. A generic conversion diagram is available. See order form.)

BLUEPRINT PRICE CODE: **B**

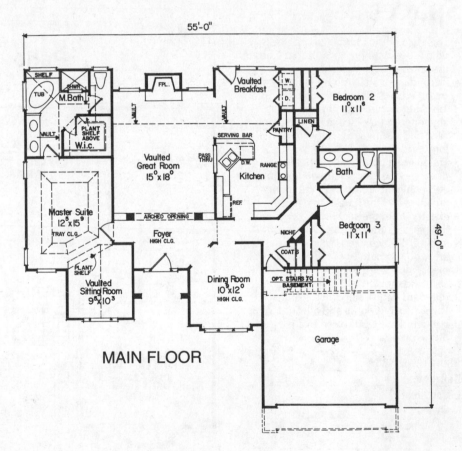

MAIN FLOOR

Plan FB-5008-ALLE

PRICES AND DETAILS ON PAGES 12-15

Breathtaking Open Space

- Soaring ceilings and an open floor plan add breathtaking volume to this charming country-style home.
- The inviting covered porch entrance opens into the spacious living room, which boasts a spectacular 21-ft.-high cathedral ceiling. Two overhead dormers fill the area with natural light, while a fireplace adds warmth.
- Also under the cathedral ceiling, the kitchen shares an eating bar with the bay-windowed breakfast area. The adjacent skylighted computer room provides access to a covered rear porch and a skylighted laundry room.
- The master bedroom has private access to another covered rear porch. The skylighted master bath has a 10-ft. sloped ceiling, a whirlpool tub and a walk-in closet.
- Optional upper-floor areas provide future expansion space for the needs of a growing family.

Plan J-9302

Bedrooms: 3	Baths: 2
Living Area:	
Main floor	1,745 sq. ft.
Total Living Area:	**1,745 sq. ft.**
Standard basement	1,745 sq. ft.
Garage	503 sq. ft.
Exterior Wall Framing:	2x4

Foundation Options:

Standard basement
Crawlspace
Slab
(All plans can be built with your choice of foundation and framing. A generic conversion diagram is available. See order form.)

BLUEPRINT PRICE CODE: B

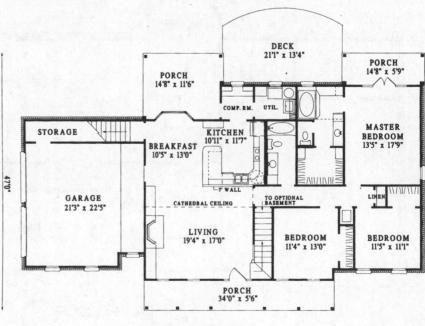

UPPER FLOOR

MAIN FLOOR

Simply Beautiful

- This four-bedroom design offers simplistic beauty, economical construction and ample space for both family life and formal entertaining—all on one floor.
- The charming cottage-style exterior gives way to a spacious interior. A 13-ft. vaulted, beamed ceiling soars above the huge living room, which features a

massive fireplace, built-in bookshelves and access to a backyard patio.
- The efficient galley-style kitchen flows between a sunny bayed eating area and the formal dining room.
- The deluxe master suite includes a dressing room, a large walk-in closet and a private bath.
- The three remaining bedrooms are larger than average and offer ample closet space.
- A nice-sized storage area and a deluxe utility room are accessible from the two-car garage.

Plan E-1702	
Bedrooms: 4	**Baths:** 2
Living Area:	
Main floor	1,751 sq. ft.
Total Living Area:	**1,751 sq. ft.**
Garage	484 sq. ft.
Storage	105 sq. ft.
Exterior Wall Framing:	2x4
Foundation Options:	
Crawlspace	
Slab	

(All plans can be built with your choice of foundation and framing. A generic conversion diagram is available. See order form.)

BLUEPRINT PRICE CODE: B

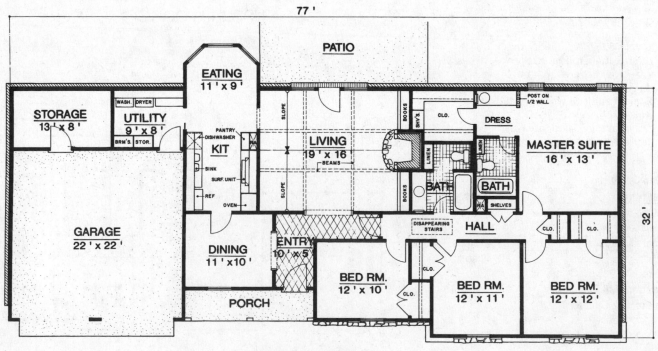

MAIN FLOOR

TO ORDER THIS BLUEPRINT, CALL TOLL-FREE 1-800-547-5570   Plan E-1702   *PRICES AND DETAILS ON PAGES 12-15*

Panoramic Rear View

- This rustic but elegant country home offers an open, airy interior.
- At the center of the floor plan is a spacious living room with a sloped ceiling, fireplace and an all-glass circular wall giving a panoramic view of the backyard.
- The adjoining dining room shares the sloped ceiling and offers sliders to the rear terrace.
- The bright kitchen has a large window, an optional skylight and a counter bar that separates it from the bayed dinette.
- The bedroom wing includes two secondary bedrooms and a large, bayed master bedroom with dual walk-in closets and a private bath with a sloped ceiling and a garden whirlpool tub.

VIEW OF LIVING AND DINING ROOMS.

Plan K-685-DA

Bedrooms: 3	Baths: 2 ½
Space:	
Main floor	1,760 sq. ft.
Total Living Area	**1,760 sq. ft.**
Basement	1,700 sq. ft.
Garage	482 sq. ft.
Exterior Wall Framing	2x4 or 2x6

Foundation options:
Standard Basement
Slab
(Foundation & framing conversion diagram available—see order form.)

Blueprint Price Code	**B**

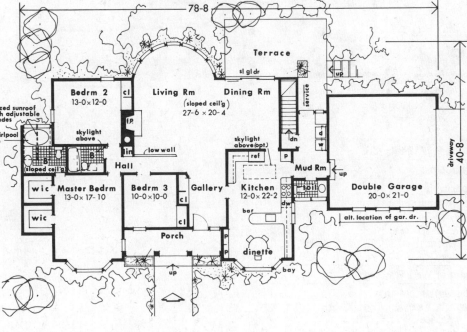

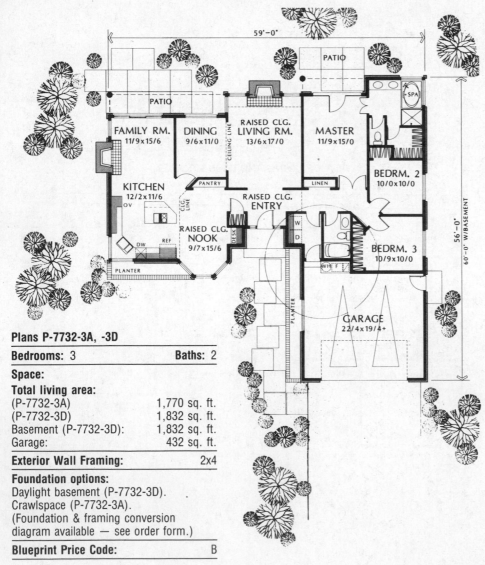

Plans P-7732-3A, -3D

Bedrooms: 3	Baths: 2

Space:

Total living area:

(P-7732-3A)	1,770 sq. ft.
(P-7732-3D)	1,832 sq. ft.
Basement (P-7732-3D):	1,832 sq. ft.
Garage:	432 sq. ft.

Exterior Wall Framing:	2x4

Foundation options:
Daylight basement (P-7732-3D).
Crawlspace (P-7732-3A).
(Foundation & framing conversion
diagram available — see order form.)

Blueprint Price Code:	B

Stately Character

- Brick with kneewall planters, stylish hip rooflines and a covered entry with transom glass give a stately character to this exciting one-story design.
- A raised ceiling at the entry and on into the living room enhances the feeling of spaciousness.
- The formal dining room flows into the living room and enjoys the fireplace view.
- The island kitchen opens to both the raised ceilinged breakfast bay with built-in desk and to the family room with second fireplace and sliders to the rear patio.
- The master suite enjoys double doors, private patio access, walk-in closet and spa bath.

LOCATION OF STAIRS IN
BASEMENT VERSION.

Plans P-7732-3A, -3D
*PRICES AND DETAILS
ON PAGES 12-15*

Rustic, Relaxed Living

- The screened porch of this rustic home offers a cool place to dine on warm summer days. The covered front porch provides an inviting welcome and a place for pure relaxation.
- With its warm fireplace and surrounding windows, the home's spacious living room is ideal for unwinding indoors. The living room

unfolds to a nice-sized dining area that overlooks a backyard patio and opens to the screened porch.
- The U-shaped kitchen is centrally located and features a nice windowed sink. A handy pantry and a laundry room adjoin to the right.
- Three large bedrooms make up the home's sleeping wing. The master bedroom boasts a roomy private bath with a step-up spa tub, a separate shower and two walk-in closets.
- The secondary bedrooms share a compartmentalized hall bath.

Plan C-8650

Bedrooms: 3	Baths: 2
Living Area:	
Main floor	1,773 sq. ft.
Total Living Area:	**1,773 sq. ft.**
Daylight basement	1,773 sq. ft.
Garage	441 sq. ft.
Exterior Wall Framing:	2x4

Foundation Options:

Daylight basement
Crawlspace
Slab
(All plans can be built with your choice of foundation and framing. A generic conversion diagram is available. See order form.)

BLUEPRINT PRICE CODE: B

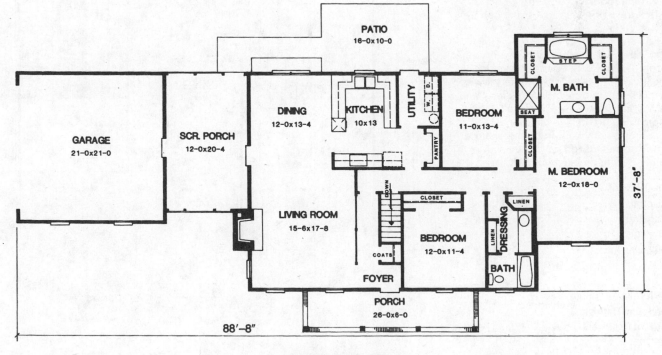

MAIN FLOOR

Country Charm, Cottage Look

- An interesting combination of stone and stucco gives a charming cottage look to this attactive country home.
- Off the inviting sidelighted entry, the formal dining room is defined by striking columns.
- The dining room expands into the living room, which boasts a fireplace and built-in shelves. A French door provides access to a backyard patio.
- The galley-style kitchen offers a sunny morning room and a pantry closet.
- All of the living areas are expanded by 10-ft. ceilings.
- The master bedroom features a 10-ft. ceiling and a nice bay-windowed sitting area. The full bath boasts an exciting oval garden tub and a separate shower, as well as a two-part walk-in closet and a dressing area with a dual-sink vanity.
- Across the home, two additional bedrooms with walk-in closets share a compartmentalized bath with independent dressing vanities.

Plan DD-1790

Bedrooms: 3	Baths: 2½
Living Area:	
Main floor	1,790 sq. ft.
Total Living Area:	**1,790 sq. ft.**
Standard basement	1,790 sq. ft.
Garage	438 sq. ft.
Exterior Wall Framing:	2x4

Foundation Options:

Standard basement
Crawlspace
Slab

(All plans can be built with your choice of foundation and framing. A generic conversion diagram is available. See order form.)

BLUEPRINT PRICE CODE:	B

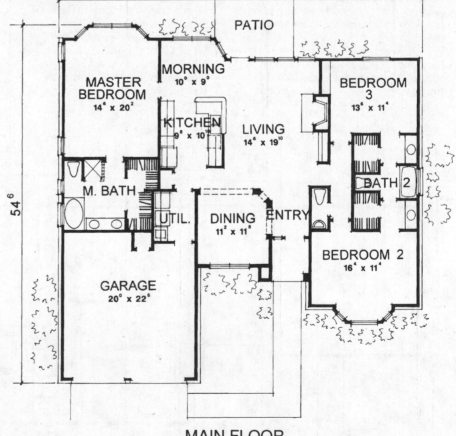

MAIN FLOOR

TO ORDER THIS BLUEPRINT, CALL TOLL-FREE 1-800-547-5570

Plan DD-1790

PRICES AND DETAILS ON PAGES 12-15

Low-profile Country Classic

Total living area:	1,790 sq. ft.
Porches:	352 sq. ft.
Carport:	474 sq. ft.
Storage:	146 sq. ft.
Total:	2,762 sq. ft.

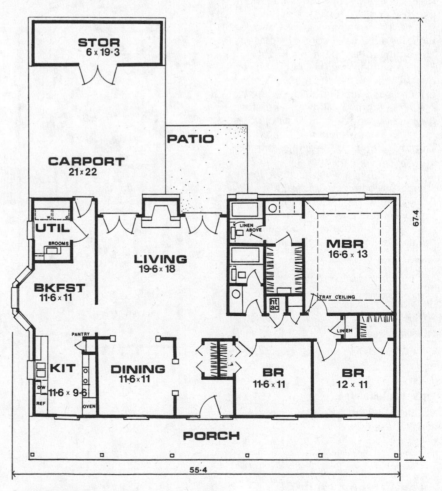

Specify basement, crawlspace or slab foundation.

Blueprint Price Code B

Plan J-8606

TO ORDER THIS BLUEPRINT,
CALL TOLL-FREE 1-800-547-5570

PRICES AND DETAILS
ON PAGES 12-15   109

Free-Flowing Floor Plan

- This exciting luxury home is characterized by a fluid floor plan with open indoor/outdoor living spaces.
- The stylish columned porch opens to a spacious living room and dining room expanse that overlooks the outdoor spaces. The breathtaking view also includes a dramatic corner fireplace.
- The dining room opens to a bright kitchen with an angled eating bar. The overall spaciousness of the living areas is increased with high 12-ft. ceilings.
- A sunny, informal eating area adjoins the kitchen, and an angled set of doors opens to a convenient main-floor laundry room near the garage entrance.
- The master suite features a 13-ft. vaulted ceiling, a walk-in closet and a sumptuous bath with an oval tub.
- A separate wing houses two additional bedrooms and another full bath.
- Attic space is accessible from stairs in the garage and in the bedroom wing.

Plan E-1710

Bedrooms: 3	Baths: 2
Living Area:	
Main floor	1,792 sq. ft.
Total Living Area:	**1,792 sq. ft.**
Standard basement	1,792 sq. ft.
Garage	484 sq. ft.
Storage	96 sq. ft.
Exterior Wall Framing:	2x6

Foundation Options:

Standard basement
Crawlspace
Slab

(All plans can be built with your choice of foundation and framing. A generic conversion diagram is available. See order form.)

BLUEPRINT PRICE CODE: B

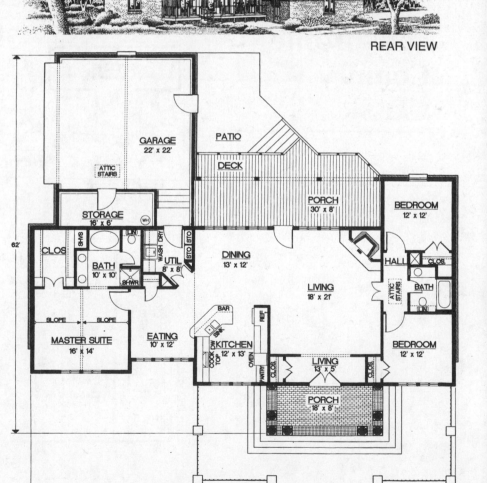

REAR VIEW

MAIN FLOOR

Plan E-1710

Fresh Air

- With its nostalgic look and country style, this lovely home brings a breath of fresh air into any neighborhood.
- Past the inviting wraparound porch, the foyer is brightened by an arched transom window above the front door.
- The adjoining formal dining room is defined by decorative columns and features a 9-ft., 4-in. stepped ceiling.
- The bright and airy kitchen includes a pantry, a windowed sink and a sunny breakfast area with porch access.
- Enhanced by an 11-ft stepped ceiling, the spacious Great Room is warmed by a fireplace flanked by sliding glass doors to a covered back porch.
- The lush master bedroom boasts an 11-ft. tray ceiling and a bayed sitting area. The master bath showcases a circular spa tub with a glass-block wall.
- The two remaining bedrooms are serviced by a second bath and a nearby laundry room. The protruding bedroom has a 12-ft. vaulted ceiling.
- Additional living space can be made available by finishing the upper floor.

Plan AX-93308

Bedrooms: 3+	Baths: 2
Living Area:	
Main floor	1,793 sq. ft.
Total Living Area:	**1,793 sq. ft.**
Standard basement	1,793 sq. ft.
Unfinished upper floor	779 sq. ft.
Garage and utility	471 sq. ft.
Exterior Wall Framing:	2x4

Foundation Options:

Standard basement
Crawlspace
Slab
(All plans can be built with your choice of foundation and framing. A generic conversion diagram is available. See order form.)

BLUEPRINT PRICE CODE: B

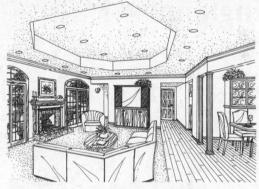

VIEW INTO GREAT ROOM

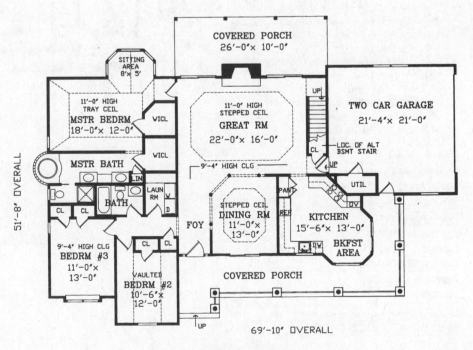

MAIN FLOOR

New England Charm

- Saltbox design motifs, divided windows, impressive entry columns and shake siding give this one-story the charm of a New England farmhouse.
- The entry gallery has a 13-ft.-high vaulted ceiling that continues into the central living room. A plant shelf and columns introduce the living room, where a dramatic three-sided fireplace and a wet bar give way to the dining room and its 11-ft. vaulted ceiling.
- The open kitchen flows into a sunny and informal family room. A sun porch with access to a large rear patio further expands this space.
- The master suite offers such exciting features as a 13-ft. vaulted ceiling, a walk-in closet and a splendid private bath with a garden tub in one corner. Another full bath serves the secondary bedroom across the hall.

Plan B-89503

Bedrooms: 2+	Baths: 2
Living Area:	
Main floor	1,797 sq. ft.
Total Living Area:	**1,797 sq. ft.**
Standard basement	1,797 sq. ft.
Garage	758 sq. ft.
Exterior Wall Framing:	2x6

Foundation Options:

Standard basement

All plans can be built with your choice of foundation and framing. A generic conversion diagram is available. See order form.)

BLUEPRINT PRICE CODE: B

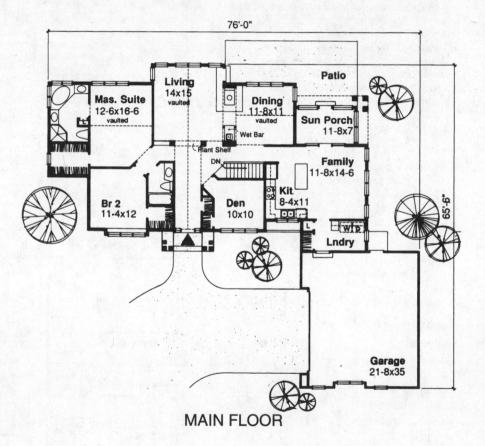

MAIN FLOOR

TO ORDER THIS BLUEPRINT, CALL TOLL-FREE 1-800-547-5570

Plan B-89503

PRICES AND DETAILS ON PAGES 12-15

Classic Country-Style

- At the center of this rustic country-style home is an enormous living room with a flat beamed ceiling, a massive stone fireplace and access to a patio and a covered rear porch.
- The adjoining eating area and kitchen provide plenty of room for casual dining and meal preparation. The eating

area is visually enhanced by a 14-ft. sloped ceiling with false beams. The kitchen includes a snack bar, a pantry closet and a built-in spice cabinet.

- The formal dining room gets plenty of pizzazz from the stone-faced wall and arched planter facing the living room.
- The secluded master suite has it all, including a private bath, a separate dressing area and a large walk-in closet with built-in shelves.
- The two remaining bedrooms have big closets and easy access to a full bath.

Plan E-1808

Bedrooms: 3	Baths: 2
Living Area:	
Main floor	1,800 sq. ft.
Total Living Area:	**1,800 sq. ft.**
Garage	605 sq. ft.
Exterior Wall Framing:	2x4

Foundation Options:

Crawlspace
Slab
(All plans can be built with your choice of foundation and framing. A generic conversion diagram is available. See order form.)

BLUEPRINT PRICE CODE: B

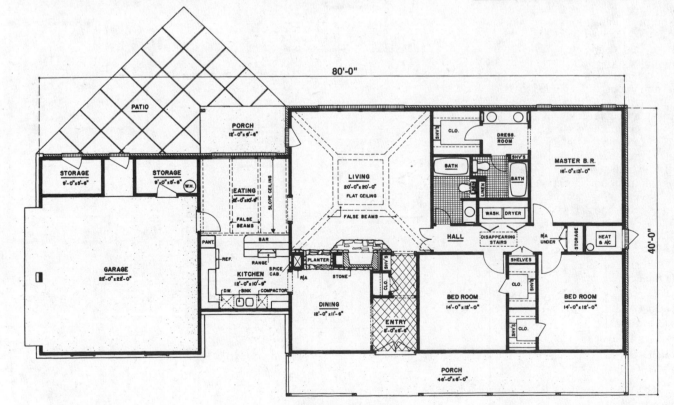

MAIN FLOOR

Masterful Master Suite

- This gorgeous home features front and rear covered porches and a master suite so luxurious it deserves its own wing.
- The expansive entry welcomes visitors into a spacious, skylighted living room, which boasts a handsome fireplace. The adjacent formal dining room overlooks the front porch.
- Designed for efficiency, the kitchen features an angled snack bar, a bayed eating area and views of the porch. An all-purpose utility room is conveniently located off the kitchen.
- The kitchen, eating area, living room and dining room are all heightened by 12-ft. ceilings.
- The sumptuous and secluded master suite features a tub and a separate shower, a double-sink vanity, a walk-in closet with built-in shelves and a compartmentalized toilet.
- The two secondary bedrooms share a hall bath at the other end of the home. The rear bedroom offers porch access.
- The two-car garage features two built-in storage areas and access to unfinished attic space above.

Plan E-1811

Bedrooms: 3	Baths: 2
Living Area:	
Main floor	1,800 sq. ft.
Total Living Area:	**1,800 sq. ft.**
Garage and storage	634 sq. ft.
Exterior Wall Framing:	2x6

Foundation Options:

Crawlspace
Slab

(All plans can be built with your choice of foundation and framing. A generic conversion diagram is available. See order form.)

BLUEPRINT PRICE CODE: **B**

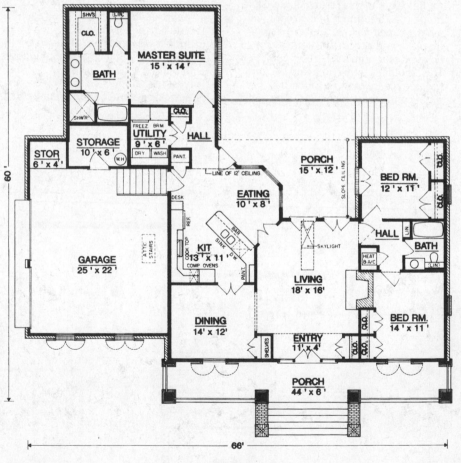

MAIN FLOOR

Plan E-1811

Updated Creole

- This Louisiana-style raised cottage features a tin roof, shuttered windows and three pairs of French doors, all of which add to the comfort and nostalgic appeal of this Creole classic.
- The French doors enter from the cool and relaxing front porch to the formal living areas and a front bedroom.
- The central living room merges with the dining room and the kitchen's eating area. A fireplace warms the whole area while more French doors access a covered backyard porch.
- The efficient kitchen offers an angled snack bar and a bay-windowed nook that overlooks the porch and deck.
- A secluded master suite showcases a private bathroom, fit for the most demanding taste. Across the home the secondary bedrooms include abundant closet space and share a full bath.
- This full-featured, energy-efficient design also includes a large utility room and extra storage space in the garage.

Plan E-1823

Bedrooms: 3	Baths: 2
Living Area:	
Main floor	1,800 sq. ft.
Total Living Area:	**1,800 sq. ft.**
Garage	550 sq. ft.
Exterior Wall Framing:	2x6

Foundation Options:

Crawlspace

Slab

(All plans can be built with your choice of foundation and framing. A generic conversion diagram is available. See order form.)

BLUEPRINT PRICE CODE: B

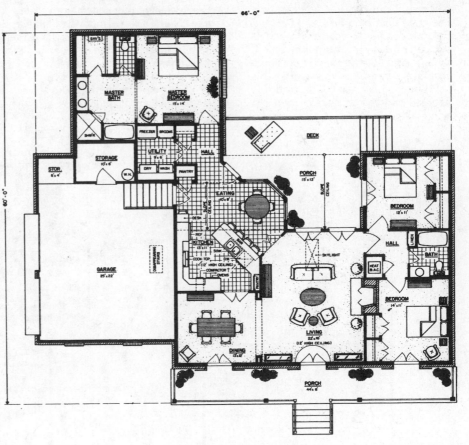

MAIN FLOOR

Stunning Style

- The stunning detailing of this three-bedroom stucco home includes a stately roofline, round louvers and a sidelighted entry door topped with a half-round transom.
- The open floor plan begins at the foyer, where a decorative column is all that separates the dining room from the living room. Lovely French doors and windows overlook the backyard, while a 13½-ft. ceiling creates a dramatic effect for this spacious area.

- A sunny breakfast room and a great kitchen with a huge serving bar adjoin a 14½-ft.-high vaulted family room.
- A laundry/mudroom lies near the garage, which is supplemented by a handy storage or shop area.
- The opulent master suite has an 11-ft. tray ceiling, a rear window wall and a French door to the outdoors. The master bath includes a spa tub, a separate shower, a spacious walk-in closet and a dual-sink vanity with a sit-down makeup area. Another full bath serves the two remaining bedrooms.

Plan FB-1802

Bedrooms: 3	Baths: 2

Living Area:	
Main floor	1,802 sq. ft.
Total Living Area:	**1,802 sq. ft.**
Garage and storage	492 sq. ft.
Exterior Wall Framing:	2x4

Foundation Options:

Crawlspace

Slab

(All plans can be built with your choice of foundation and framing. A generic conversion diagram is available. See order form.)

BLUEPRINT PRICE CODE: B

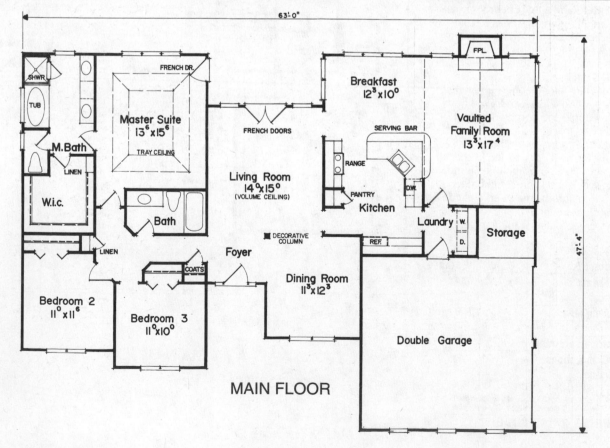

MAIN FLOOR

Outstanding One-Story

- This sharp one-story home has an outstanding floor plan, attractively enhanced by a stately brick facade.
- A vestibule introduces the foyer, which flows between the formal living spaces at the front of the home.
- The large living room features a 14-ft., 8-in. sloped ceiling and dramatic, high windows. The spacious dining room has easy access to the kitchen.

- The expansive family room is the focal point of the home, with a 16-ft. beamed cathedral ceiling, a slate-hearth fireplace and sliding glass doors to a backyard terrace.
- The adjoining kitchen has a snack bar and a sunny dinette framed by a curved window wall that overlooks the terrace.
- Included in the sleeping wing is a luxurious master suite with a private bath. A skylighted dressing room and a big walk-in closet are also featured.
- The two secondary bedrooms share a hall bath that has a dual-sink vanity. A half-bath is near the mud/laundry room.

Plan K-278-M	
Bedrooms: 3	**Baths:** 2½
Living Area:	
Main floor	1,803 sq. ft.
Total Living Area:	**1,803 sq. ft.**
Standard basement	1,778 sq. ft.
Garage and storage	586 sq. ft.
Exterior Wall Framing:	2x4 or 2x6
Foundation Options:	
Standard basement	
Slab	

(All plans can be built with your choice of foundation and framing. A generic conversion diagram is available. See order form.)

BLUEPRINT PRICE CODE:	B

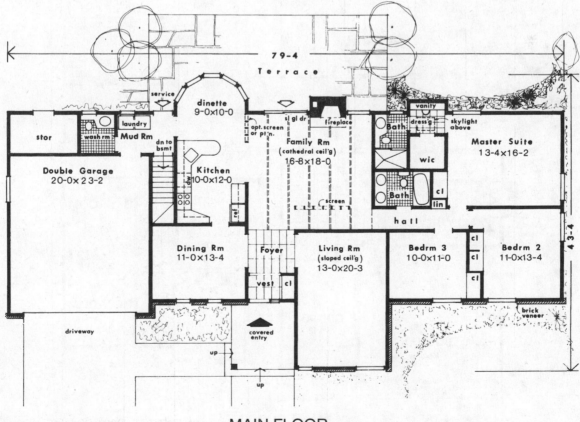

MAIN FLOOR

Functional Four-Bedroom

- This one-story's efficient design makes use of every inch of space to accommodate four bedrooms and plenty of living space.
- The ornate exterior includes an oval-glassed entry, wood columns and rich window and brick treatments.
- The foyer offers views into the living room and the dining room. The living room is enhanced by a 12-ft. ceiling and overlooks a huge deck through French doors framed by windows.
- An oversized island, a pantry and a recipe/work desk are featured in the sunny and open central kitchen.
- The family can relax in the adjoining family room, which sports a cozy fireplace and a dramatic ceiling that vaults up to a 12-ft.-high flat area. A French door provides deck access.
- Four bedrooms, two baths and a large laundry room are housed in the sleeping wing. The master bedroom boasts a walk-in closet, a private garden bath and French doors to the deck.

Plan APS-1813	
Bedrooms: 4	**Baths: 2**
Living Area:	
Main floor	1,814 sq. ft.
Total Living Area:	**1,814 sq. ft.**
Garage	380 sq. ft.
Exterior Wall Framing:	2x4

Foundation Options:
Crawlspace
Slab
(All plans can be built with your choice of foundation and framing. A generic conversion diagram is available. See order form.)

BLUEPRINT PRICE CODE:	B

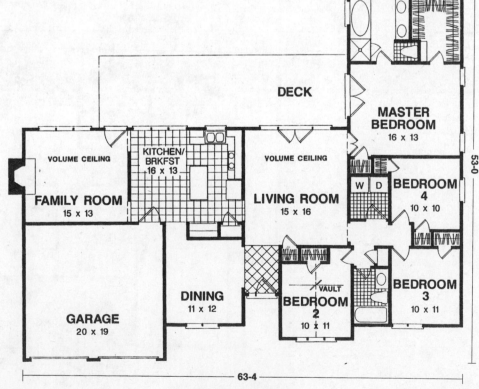

MAIN FLOOR

Plan APS-1813

PRICES AND DETAILS ON PAGES 12-15

Eye-Catching One-Story

- This eye-catching design sports cedar siding, multiple gables and a curved planter surrounding a bayed nook.
- The covered entry opens to a roomy foyer, where double doors lead to a quiet den or bedroom.
- Straight ahead, a corner fireplace in the Great Room radiates its warmth to the surrounding rooms. Glass lines the rear wall, culminating in French doors. A 14½-ft. vaulted ceiling and a wet bar are other embellishments.
- The deluxe kitchen includes a pantry, a built-in desk and a boxed-out window above the sink. The delightful nook features an 11½-ft. vaulted ceiling.
- A skylighted hall leads to the relaxing master bedroom, complete with a sitting area and private access to the outdoors. The master bath offers a garden spa tub, a separate shower and a toilet closet.
- The remaining bedroom has easy access to another compartmentalized bath.

Plan S-42093

Bedrooms: 2+	Baths: 2
Living Area:	
Main floor	1,830 sq. ft.
Total Living Area:	**1,830 sq. ft.**
Standard basement	1,765 sq. ft.
Garage	433 sq. ft.
Exterior Wall Framing:	2x6

Foundation Options:
Standard basement
Crawlspace
Slab
(All plans can be built with your choice of foundation and framing. A generic conversion diagram is available. See order form.)

BLUEPRINT PRICE CODE: B

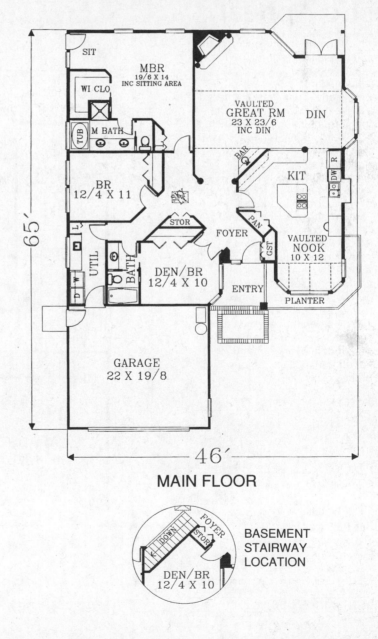

MAIN FLOOR

BASEMENT STAIRWAY LOCATION

Rustic Appeal

- The handsome stone and stucco of this charming French one-story give it a rustic cottage appeal.
- The columned porch opens into the welcoming entry, which is brightened by an arched transom window. The adjacent formal dining room, which boasts a 10-ft. ceiling, is defined by a decorative column.
- The bright and airy kitchen offers a corner pantry and an angled bar. The bay-windowed morning room provides a great space for informal meals. Both areas are expanded by 10-ft. ceilings.
- Warmed by a corner fireplace, the spacious living room features a 10-ft.-high sloped ceiling, a window wall and access to a large deck.
- Secluded for privacy, the master bedroom and bath are expanded by 10-ft. sloped ceilings. The master bath includes a garden tub, a separate shower and a dual-sink vanity.
- Three additional bedrooms and a second full bath occupy the opposite side of the home.

Plan DD-1961

Bedrooms: 4	Baths: 2
Living Area:	
Main floor	1,961 sq. ft.
Total Living Area:	**1,961 sq. ft.**
Standard basement	1,961 sq. ft.
Garage	468 sq. ft.
Exterior Wall Framing:	2x4

Foundation Options:
Standard basement
Crawlspace
Slab
(All plans can be built with your choice of foundation and framing. A generic conversion diagram is available. See order form.)

BLUEPRINT PRICE CODE: B

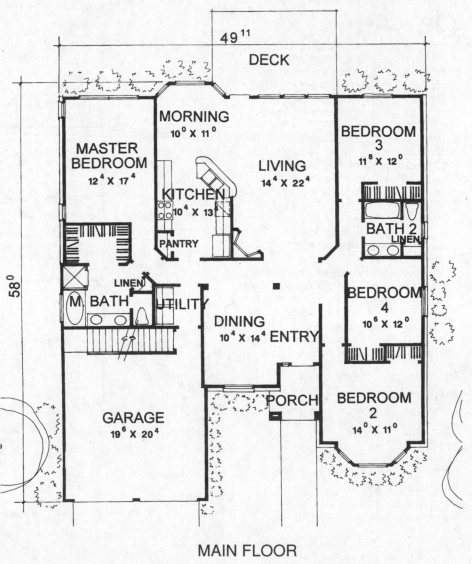

MAIN FLOOR

Plan DD-1961

TO ORDER THIS BLUEPRINT, CALL TOLL-FREE 1-800-547-5570

PRICES AND DETAILS ON PAGES 12-15

Indoor/Outdoor Delights

- A curved porch in the front and a garden sun room in the back make this home an indoor/outdoor delight.
- Inside, a roomy kitchen is open to a five-sided, glassed-in dining room that views out to the porch.
- The living room features a fireplace along a glass wall that adjoins the gloriously sunny garden room.

- Wrapped in windows, the garden room accesses the backyard as well as a large storage area in the unobtrusive, side-entry garage.
- The master suite is no less luxurious, featuring a a sumptuous master bath with a garden spa tub, a corner shower and a walk-in closet.
- Each of the two remaining bedrooms has a boxed-out window and a walk-in closet. A full bath with a corner shower and a dual-sink vanity is close by.
- A stairway leads to the attic, which provides more potential living space.

Plan DD-1852	
Bedrooms: 3	**Baths:** 2
Living Area:	
Main floor	1,852 sq. ft.
Total Living Area:	**1,852 sq. ft.**
Standard basement	1,852 sq. ft.
Garage	528 sq. ft.
Exterior Wall Framing:	2x4
Foundation Options:	
Standard basement	
Crawlspace	
Slab	

(All plans can be built with your choice of foundation and framing. A generic conversion diagram is available. See order form.)

BLUEPRINT PRICE CODE: B

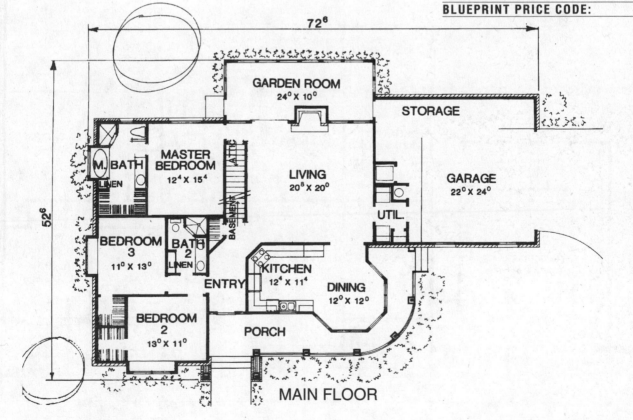

MAIN FLOOR

Rambling Ranch

- This ground-hugging ranch home was designed to make maximum use of three living areas.
- The informal area includes a spacious family room with an inviting fireplace visible from the foyer. The adjoining kitchen is fully equipped and features a large pantry and a cooktop peninsula. The bright dinette offers sliding glass doors to a nice covered porch, which has a handy built-in barbecue.

- The kitchen easily accesses the dining and living rooms at the front of the home. These formal areas flow together for gracious entertaining, and are accented by a striking partition.
- The bedrooms are set apart from the active areas of the home and achieve quiet and privacy with well-placed closets and baths.
- The master suite boasts plenty of closet space and a windowed private bath.
- The two secondary bedrooms are brightened by triple windows. The lavish hall bath offers two basins and a built-in linen closet.

Plan HFL-1400-JN

Bedrooms: 3	Baths: 2
Living Area:	
Main floor	1,859 sq. ft.
Total Living Area:	**1,859 sq. ft.**
Standard basement	1,686 sq. ft.
Garage	380 sq. ft.
Exterior Wall Framing:	2x4

Foundation Options:

Standard basement
(All plans can be built with your choice of foundation and framing. A generic conversion diagram is available. See order form.)

BLUEPRINT PRICE CODE:	**B**

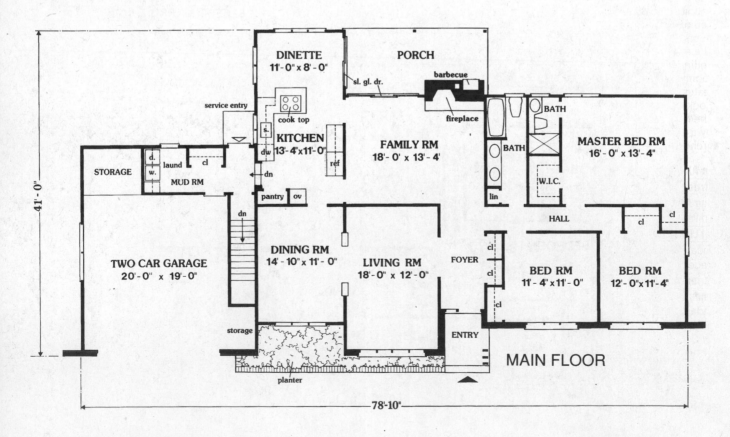

Plan HFL-1400-JN

Classic Ranch

- With decorative brick quoins, a columned porch and stylish dormers, the exterior of this classic one-story provides an interesting blend of Early American and European design.
- Just off the foyer, the bay-windowed formal dining room is enhanced by an 11-ft., 6-in.-high stepped ceiling.
- The spacious Great Room, separated from the dining room by a columned arch, features a stepped ceiling, a built-in media center and a fireplace. French doors lead to the backyard patio.
- The breakfast area, which shares an eating bar with the kitchen, boasts a ceiling that slopes to 12 feet. French doors access a covered rear porch.
- The master bedroom has a 10-ft. tray ceiling, a sunny bay window and a roomy walk-in closet. The master bath features a whirlpool tub in a bayed nook and a separate shower.
- The front-facing bedroom is enhanced by a 10-ft.-high vaulted area over an arched transom window.

Plan AX-93304

Bedrooms: 3	Baths: 2
Living Area:	
Main floor	1,860 sq. ft.
Total Living Area:	**1,860 sq. ft.**
Standard basement	1,860 sq. ft.
Garage	434 sq. ft.
Exterior Wall Framing:	2x4

Foundation Options:

Standard basement
Crawlspace
Slab
(All plans can be built with your choice of foundation and framing. A generic conversion diagram is available. See order form.)

BLUEPRINT PRICE CODE: B

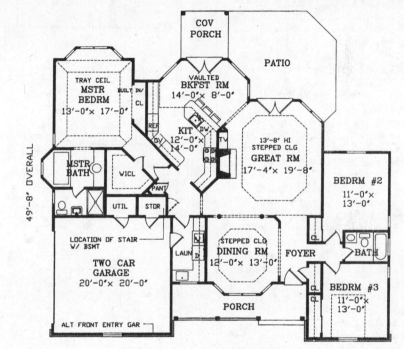

MAIN FLOOR

VIEW INTO GREAT ROOM

Upscale Charm

- Country charm with the very latest in conveniences marks this upscale home. Best of all, everything is contained on one floor, with an upper floor that may be left unfinished.
- Just inside the foyer, elegant columns embrace the dining room. Arched windows in the dining room and in the bedroom across the hall echo the delicate detailing of the covered front porch.
- Straight ahead, the family room flaunts a wall of French doors overlooking the covered back porch and the deck beyond.
- A curved snack bar smoothly joins the gourmet kitchen to the sunny breakfast area, which features a vaulted, sky-lighted ceiling. All other rooms have 9-ft. ceilings. A nearby computer room and a laundry with a recycling center are additional amenities.
- The well-appointed master suite includes a floor-to-ceiling storage unit with a built-in chest of drawers next to a dual-sink vanity. Other extras include a step-up spa tub and a separate shower.

Plan J-92100

Bedrooms: 3+	Baths: 2
Living Area:	
Main floor	1,877 sq. ft.
Total Living Area:	**1,877 sq. ft.**
Future area (upper floor)	1,500 sq. ft.
Standard basement	1,877 sq. ft.
Garage	500 sq. ft.
Exterior Wall Framing:	2x4

Foundation Options:

Standard basement
Crawlspace
Slab

(All plans can be built with your choice of foundation and framing. A generic conversion diagram is available. See order form.)

BLUEPRINT PRICE CODE:	**B**

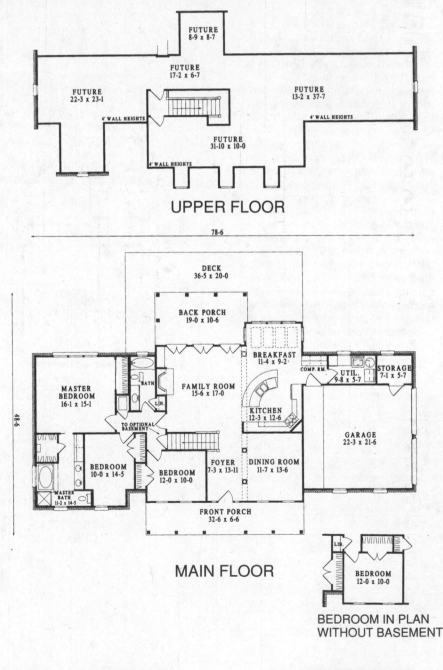

UPPER FLOOR

MAIN FLOOR

BEDROOM IN PLAN WITHOUT BASEMENT

Sweet Master Suite

- Traditional stone veneer & New England shingle exterior.
- Arch top window at bedroom/study.
- Bedroom/study can also be used as an office.
- Great Room features vaulted ceiling, fireplace & French doors to outdoor living deck.
- Kitchen includes all amenities plus breakfast eating bar.
- Main floor laundry/mudroom.
- Master suite features coffered ceiling and Master bath with walk-in closets.
- Full basement.

Plan CPS-1155-C

Bedrooms: 3	Baths: 2
Space:	
Total living area:	1,848 sq. ft.
Basement:	1,848 sq. ft.
Garage:	513 sq. ft.
Exterior Wall Framing:	2x6

Foundation options:
Standard basement.
(Foundation & framing conversion diagram available — see order form.)

Blueprint Price Code:	B

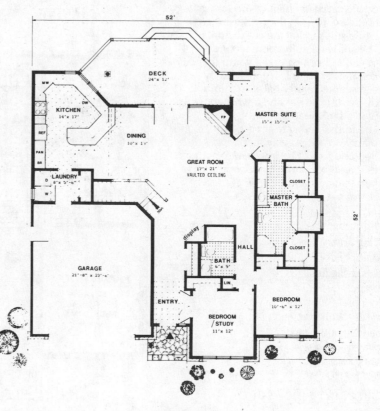

MAIN FLOOR

Garden Home with a View

- This clever design proves that privacy doesn't have to be compromised even in high-density urban neighborhoods. From within, views are oriented to a beautiful, lush entry courtyard and a covered rear porch.
- The exterior appearance is sheltered, but warm and welcoming.
- The innovative interior design centers on a unique kitchen, which directs traffic away from the working areas while still serving the entire home.
- The sunken family room features a 14-ft. vaulted ceiling and a warm fireplace.
- The master suite is highlighted by a sumptuous master bath with an oversized shower and a whirlpool tub, plus a large walk-in closet.
- The formal living room is designed and placed in such a way that it can become a third bedroom, a den, or an office or study room, depending on family needs and lifestyles.

Plan E-1824

Bedrooms: 2+	Baths: 2
Living Area:	
Main floor	1,891 sq. ft.
Total Living Area:	**1,891 sq. ft.**
Garage	506 sq. ft.
Storage	60 sq. ft.
Exterior Wall Framing:	2x4

Foundation Options:

Crawlspace
Slab
(All plans can be built with your choice of foundation and framing. A generic conversion diagram is available. See order form.)

BLUEPRINT PRICE CODE:	B

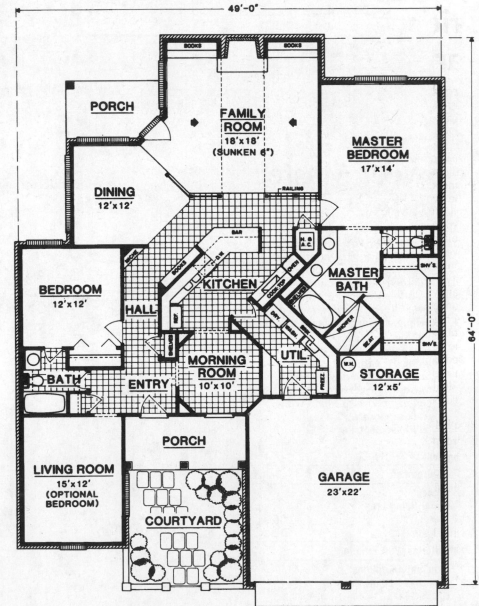

MAIN FLOOR

Plan E-1824

Friendly Farmhouse

- Reminiscent of a turn-of-the-century farmhouse, this warm, friendly home is characterized by an authentic front porch with fine post-and-rail detailing.
- The open entry provides a sweeping view of the dining room and the adjoining living room. Three columns function as an elegant divider between the two rooms. The living room features a 12-ft.-high sloped ceiling with exposed beams, an inviting fireplace, built-in bookshelves and windows overlooking the rear patio.
- A nice-sized eating area opens to the airy kitchen, which offers a snack bar, a pantry and a lazy Susan. Double doors conceal a utility room with extra storage space.
- Another set of double doors opens to the bedroom wing, where all three bedrooms have walk-in closets. The master bedroom has a private bath with a dual-sink vanity. The secondary bedrooms share another full bath.

Plan E-1813

Bedrooms: 3	Baths: 2
Living Area:	
Main floor	1,892 sq. ft.
Total Living Area:	**1,892 sq. ft.**
Carport	440 sq. ft.
Storage	120 sq. ft.
Exterior Wall Framing:	2x6

Foundation Options:

Crawlspace
Slab
(All plans can be built with your choice of foundation and framing. A generic conversion diagram is available. See order form.)

BLUEPRINT PRICE CODE:	B

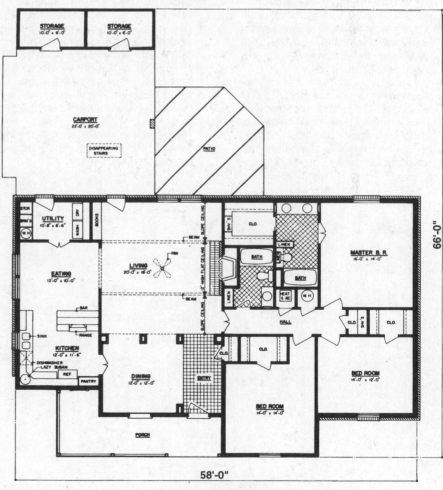

MAIN FLOOR

Playful Floor Plan

- High, hip roofs and a recessed entry give this home a smart-looking exterior. A dynamic floor plan—punctuated with angled walls, high ceilings and playful window treatments—gives the home an exciting interior.
- The sunken Great Room, the circular dining room and the angled island kitchen are the heartbeat of the home. The Great Room offers a 14-ft. vaulted ceiling, a fireplace, a built-in corner entertainment center and tall arched windows overlooking the backyard.

- An angled railing separates the Great Room from the open kitchen and dining room. An atrium door next to the glassed-in dining area leads to the backyard. The kitchen includes an island snack bar and a garden window.
- The master bedroom is nestled into one corner for quiet and privacy. This deluxe suite features two walk-in closets and a luxurious whirlpool bath.
- An extra-large laundry area, complete with a clothes-folding counter and a coat closet, is accessible from the three-car garage.
- The home is expanded by 9-ft. ceilings throughout, with the exception of the vaulted Great Room.

Plan PI-90-435

Bedrooms: 3	Baths: 2
Living Area:	
Main floor	1,896 sq. ft.
Total Living Area:	**1,896 sq. ft.**
Basement	1,889 sq. ft.
Garage	667 sq. ft.
Exterior Wall Framing:	2x6

Foundation Options:

Daylight basement
Standard basement
(All plans can be built with your choice of foundation and framing. A generic conversion diagram is available. See order form.)

BLUEPRINT PRICE CODE:	B

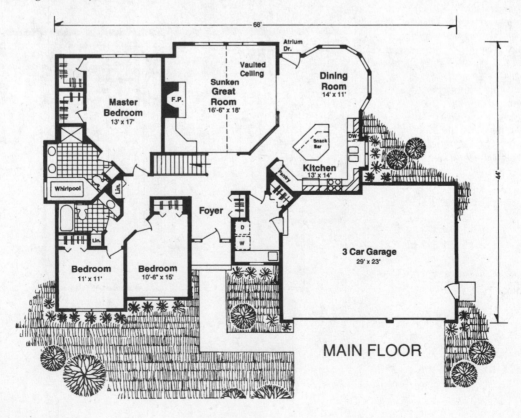

MAIN FLOOR

TO ORDER THIS BLUEPRINT, CALL TOLL-FREE 1-800-547-5570   Plan PI-90-435   **PRICES AND DETAILS ON PAGES 12-15**

French Garden Design

- A creative, angular design gives this traditional French garden home an exciting, open and airy floor plan.
- Guests enter through a covered, columned porch that opens into the large, angled living and dining rooms.
- High 12-ft. ceilings highlight the living and dining area, which also features corner windows, a wet bar, a cozy fireplace and access to a huge covered backyard porch.
- The angled walk-through kitchen, also with a 12-ft.-high ceiling, offers plenty of work space and an adjoining informal eating nook that faces a delightful private courtyard. The nearby utility area has extra freezer space, a walk-in pantry and garage access.
- The home's bedrooms are housed in two separate wings. One wing boasts a luxurious master suite, which features a large walk-in closet, an angled tub and a separate shower.
- Two large bedrooms in the other wing share a hall bath. Each bedroom has a walk-in closet.

Plan E-2004

Bedrooms: 3	Baths: 2
Living Area:	
Main floor	2,023 sq. ft.
Total Living Area:	**2,023 sq. ft.**
Garage	484 sq. ft.
Storage	87 sq. ft.
Exterior Wall Framing:	2x6

Foundation Options:

Crawlspace

Slab

(All plans can be built with your choice of foundation and framing. A generic conversion diagram is available. See order form.)

BLUEPRINT PRICE CODE: C

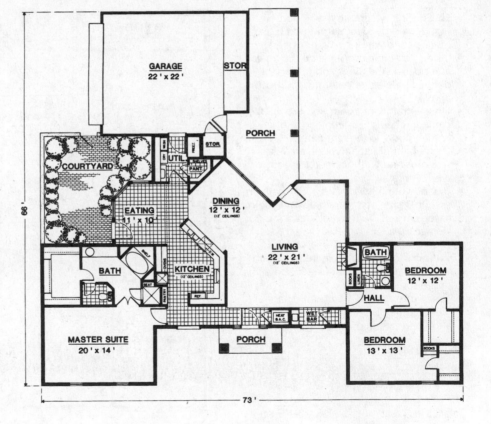

MAIN FLOOR

NOTE: The above photographed home may have been modified by the homeowner. Please refer to floor plan and/or drawn elevation shown for actual blueprint details.

Spacious Country-Style

- This distinctive country-style home is highlighted by a wide front porch and multi-paned windows with shutters.
- Inside, the dining room is off the foyer and open to the living room, but is defined by elegant columns and beams above.
- The central living room boasts a 12-ft. cathedral ceiling, a fireplace and French doors to the rear patio.
- The delightful kitchen/nook area is spacious and well planned for both work and play.
- A handy utility room and a half-bath are on either side of a short hallway leading to the carport, which includes a large storage area.
- The master suite offers his-and-hers walk-in closets and an incredible bath that incorporates a plant shelf above the raised spa tub.
- The two remaining bedrooms share a hall bath that is compartmentalized to allow more than one user at a time.

Plan J-86140

Bedrooms: 3	Baths: 2½
Living Area:	
Main floor	2,177 sq. ft.
Total Living Area:	**2,177 sq. ft.**
Standard basement	2,177 sq. ft.
Carport	440 sq. ft.
Storage	120 sq. ft.
Exterior Wall Framing:	2x4

Foundation Options:

Standard basement
Crawlspace
Slab
(All plans can be built with your choice of foundation and framing. A generic conversion diagram is available. See order form.)

BLUEPRINT PRICE CODE: C

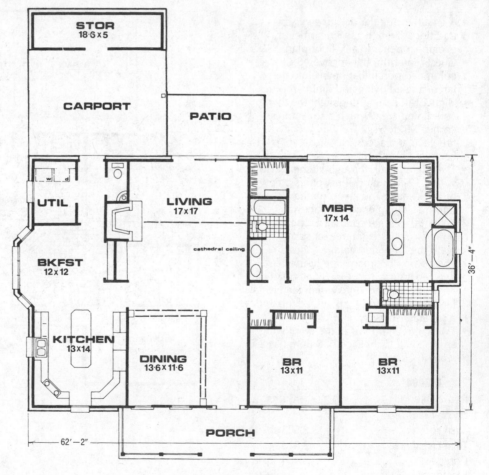

MAIN FLOOR

Plan J-86140

PRICES AND DETAILS
ON PAGES 12-15

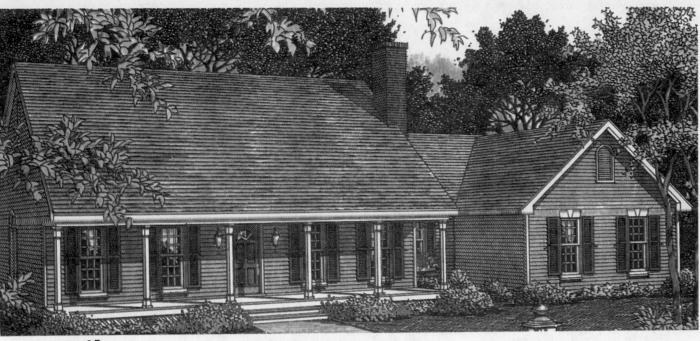

Versatile
Sun Room

- This cozy country-style home offers an inviting front porch and an interior just as welcoming.
- The spacious living room features a warming fireplace and windows that overlook the porch.
- The living room opens to a dining area, where French doors access a covered porch and a sunny patio.
- The island kitchen has a sink view, plenty of counter space, and a handy pass-through to the adjoining sun room. The bright sun room is large enough to serve as a formal dining room, a family room or a hobby room.
- The private master suite is secluded to the rear. A garden spa tub, dual walk-in closets and separate dressing areas are nice features found in the master bath.

Plan J-90014

Bedrooms: 3	Baths: 2½
Living Area:	
Main floor	2,190 sq. ft.
Total Living Area:	**2,190 sq. ft.**
Standard basement	2,190 sq. ft.
Garage	465 sq. ft.
Storage	34 sq. ft.
Exterior Wall Framing:	2x6

Foundation Options:

Standard basement

Crawlspace

Slab

(All plans can be built with your choice of foundation and framing. A generic conversion diagram is available. See order form.)

BLUEPRINT PRICE CODE:	C

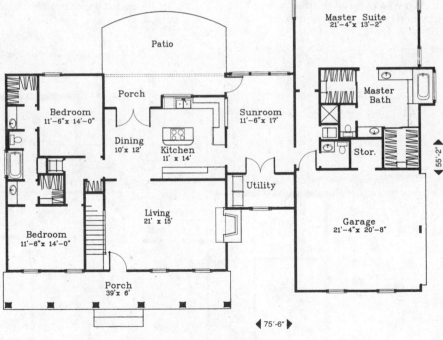

MAIN FLOOR

Classic Styling

- This handsome one-story traditional would look great in town or in the country. The shuttered and paned windows, narrow lap siding and brick accents make it a classic.
- The sprawling design begins with the spacious, central living room, featuring a beamed ceiling that slopes up to 14 feet. A window wall overlooks the covered backyard porch, and an inviting fireplace includes an extra-wide hearth and built-in bookshelves.
- The galley-style kitchen features a snack bar to the sunny eating area and a raised-panel door to the dining room.
- The isolated master suite is a quiet haven offering a large walk-in closet, a dressing room and a spacious bath.
- Three more bedrooms, two with walk-in closets, and a compartmentalized bath are located at the opposite side of the home.

Plan E-2206	
Bedrooms: 4	**Baths:** 2
Living Area:	
Main floor	2,200 sq. ft.
Total Living Area:	**2,200 sq. ft.**
Standard basement	2,200 sq. ft.
Garage and storage	624 sq. ft.
Exterior Wall Framing:	2x6

Foundation Options:
Standard basement
Crawlspace
Slab
(All plans can be built with your choice of foundation and framing. A generic conversion diagram is available. See order form.)

BLUEPRINT PRICE CODE: C

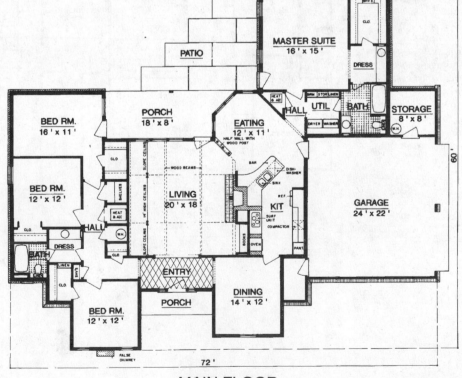

MAIN FLOOR

Plan E-2206

Photo by Mark Englund/HomeStyles

Stunning Windows

- This one-story design is enhanced by stunning window arrangements that brighten the formal areas and beyond.
- A step down from the skylighted foyer, the living room sparkles, with a tray ceiling, a striking fireplace and a turret-like bay with high arched windows.
- The island kitchen easily services the sunny bayed dining room and includes a built-in desk, a garden sink and an eating bar to the bright, vaulted nook.
- The adjoining vaulted family room is warmed by a corner woodstove and overlooks the rear patio.
- A decorative plant shelf introduces the bedroom wing. Double doors reveal the master bedroom, which boasts a tray ceiling, a rear window wall and access to the patio. The skylighted master bath includes a raised ceiling, a step-up garden spa tub and a separate shower.
- Across the hall, a den and a second bedroom share another full bath, while the utility room offers garage access.

Plans P-7754-3A & -3D

Bedrooms: 2+	Baths: 2
Living Area:	
Main floor (crawlspace version)	2,200 sq. ft.
Main floor (basement version)	2,288 sq. ft.
Total Living Area:	**2,200/2,288 sq. ft.**
Daylight basement	2,244 sq. ft.
Garage	722 sq. ft.
Exterior Wall Framing:	2x4
Foundation Options:	**Plan #**
Daylight basement	P-7754-3D
Crawlspace	P-7754-3A

(All plans can be built with your choice of foundation and framing. A generic conversion diagram is available. See order form.)

BLUEPRINT PRICE CODE:	**C**

MAIN FLOOR

**NOTE: The above photographed home may have been modified by the homeowner. Please refer to floor plan and/or drawn elevation shown for actual blueprint details.

BASEMENT STAIRWAY LOCATION

Photo by Gil Ford

Luxurious Living on One Level

- The elegant exterior of this spacious one-story presents a classic air of quality and distinction.
- Three French doors brighten the inviting entry, which flows into the spacious living room. Boasting a 13-ft. ceiling, the living room enjoys a fireplace with a wide hearth and adjoining built-in bookshelves. A wall of glass, including

a French door, provides views of the sheltered backyard porch.
- A stylish angled counter joins the spacious kitchen to the sunny bay-windowed eating nook.
- Secluded for privacy, the master suite features a nice dressing area, a large walk-in closet and private backyard access. A convenient laundry/utility room is adjacent to the master bath.
- At the opposite end of the home, double doors lead to three more bedrooms, a compartmentalized bath and lots of closet space.

Plan E-2208	
Bedrooms: 4	**Baths:** 2
Living Area:	
Main floor	2,252 sq. ft.
Total Living Area:	**2,252 sq. ft.**
Standard basement	2,252 sq. ft.
Garage and storage	592 sq. ft.
Exterior Wall Framing:	2x6
Foundation Options:	
Standard basement	
Crawlspace	
Slab	

(All plans can be built with your choice of foundation and framing. A generic conversion diagram is available. See order form.)

BLUEPRINT PRICE CODE: C

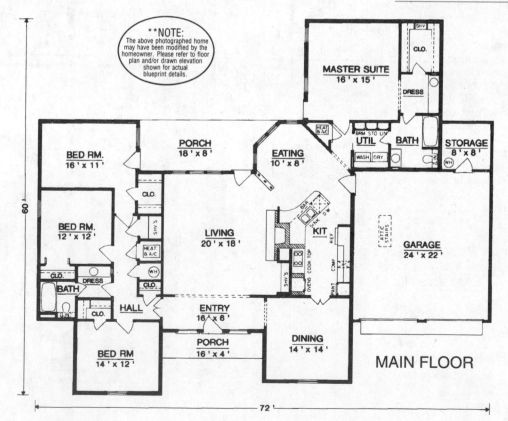

NOTE: The above photographed home may have been modified by the homeowner. Please refer to floor plan and/or drawn elevation shown for actual blueprint details.

MAIN FLOOR

TO ORDER THIS BLUEPRINT, CALL TOLL-FREE 1-800-547-5570

Plan E-2208

PRICES AND DETAILS ON PAGES 12-15

Spacious and Inviting

The four-column front porch, picture window, siding, brick, stone and cupola combine for a pleasing exterior for this three-bedroom home.

Extra features include a fireplace, screen porch, deluxe master bath and a large separate breakfast room.

Total living area: 2,306 sq. ft.
(Not counting basement or garage)

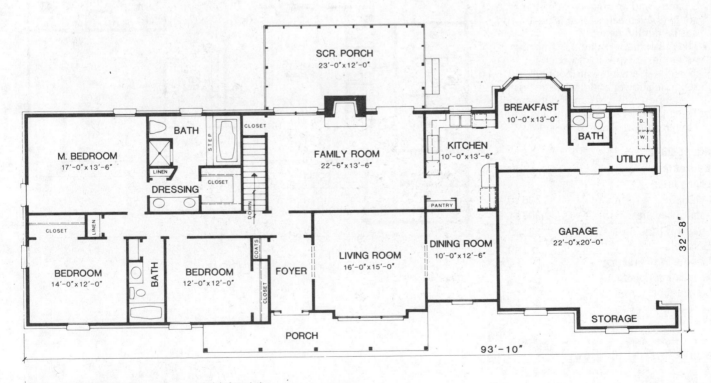

Specify daylight basement, crawlspace or slab foundation.

High Luxury in One Story

- Beautiful arched windows lend a luxurious feeling to the exterior of this one-story home.
- Soaring 12-ft. ceilings add volume to both the wide entry area and the central living room, which boasts a large fireplace and access to a covered porch and the patio beyond.
- Double doors separate the formal dining room from the corridor-style kitchen. Features of the kitchen include a pantry and an angled eating bar. The sunny, bayed eating area is perfect for casual family meals.
- The plush master suite has amazing amenities: a walk-in closet, a skylighted, angled whirlpool tub, a separate shower and private access to the laundry/utility room and the patio.
- Three good-sized bedrooms and a full bath are situated across the home.

Plan E-2302

Bedrooms: 4	Baths: 2
Living Area:	
Main floor	2,396 sq. ft.
Total Living Area:	**2,396 sq. ft.**
Standard basement	2,396 sq. ft.
Garage	484 sq. ft.
Exterior Wall Framing:	2x6

Foundation Options:

Standard basement
Crawlspace
Slab

(All plans can be built with your choice of foundation and framing. A generic conversion diagram is available. See order form.)

BLUEPRINT PRICE CODE: C

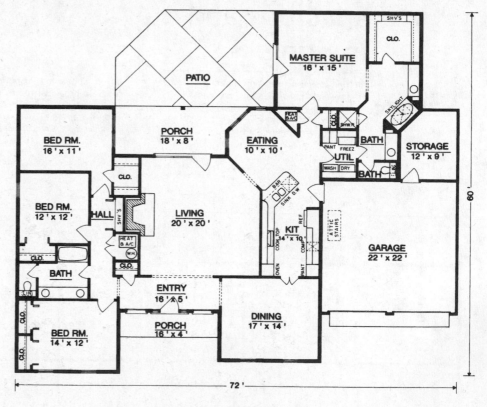

MAIN FLOOR

Plan E-2302

Wonderful Detailing

- The wonderfully detailed front porch, with its graceful arches, columns and railings, gives this home a character all its own. Dormer windows and arched transoms further accentuate the porch.
- The floor plan features a central living room with a 10-ft.-high ceiling and a fireplace framed by French doors. These doors open to a covered porch or a sun room, and a sheltered deck beyond.
- Just off the living room, the island kitchen and breakfast area provide a spacious place for family or guests. The nearby formal dining room has arched transom windows and a 10-ft. ceiling, as does the bedroom off the foyer. All of the remaining rooms have 9-ft. ceilings.
- The unusual master suite includes a window alcove, access to the porch and a fantastic bath with a garden tub.
- A huge utility room, a storage area off the garage and a 1,000-sq.-ft. attic space are other bonuses of this design.

Plan J-90019

Bedrooms: 3	Baths: 2½
Living Area:	
Main floor	2,410 sq. ft.
Total Living Area:	**2,410 sq. ft.**
Standard basement	2,410 sq. ft.
Garage	512 sq. ft.
Storage	86 sq. ft.
Exterior Wall Framing:	2x6
Foundation Options:	
Standard basement	
Crawlspace	
Slab	

(All plans can be built with your choice of foundation and framing. A generic conversion diagram is available. See order form.)

BLUEPRINT PRICE CODE:	C

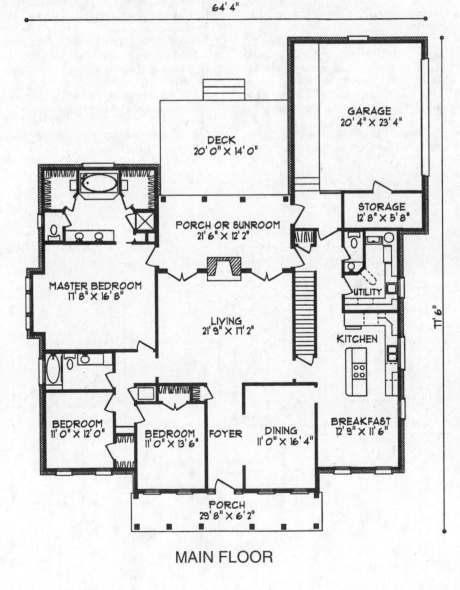

MAIN FLOOR

TO ORDER THIS BLUEPRINT,
CALL TOLL-FREE 1-800-547-5570

Plan J-90019

PRICES AND DETAILS
ON PAGES 12-15

137

Photo by Mark Englund/HomeStyles

Extraordinary Estate Living

- Extraordinary estate living is at its best in this palatial beauty.
- The double-doored entry opens to a large central living room that overlooks a covered patio with a vaulted ceiling. Volume 14-ft. ceilings are found in the living room, in the formal dining room and in the den or study, which may serve as a fourth bedroom.
- The gourmet chef will enjoy the spacious kitchen, which flaunts a

cooktop island, a walk-in pantry and a peninsula snack counter shared with the breakfast room and family room.
- This trio of informal living spaces also shares a panorama of glass and a corner fireplace centered between TV and media niches.
- Isolated at the opposite end of the home is the spacious master suite, which offers private patio access. Dual walk-in closets define the entrance to the adjoining master bath, complete with a garden Jacuzzi and separate dressing areas.
- The hall bath also opens to the outdoors for use as a pool bath.

Plan HDS-99-177	
Bedrooms: 3+	**Baths:** 3
Living Area:	
Main floor	2,597 sq. ft.
Total Living Area:	**2,597 sq. ft.**
Garage	761 sq. ft.
Exterior Wall Framing:	2x4

Foundation Options:
Slab
(All plans can be built with your choice of foundation and framing. A generic conversion diagram is available. See order form.)

BLUEPRINT PRICE CODE: D

NOTE:
The above photographed home may have been modified by the homeowner. Please refer to floor plan and/or drawn elevation shown for actual blueprint details.

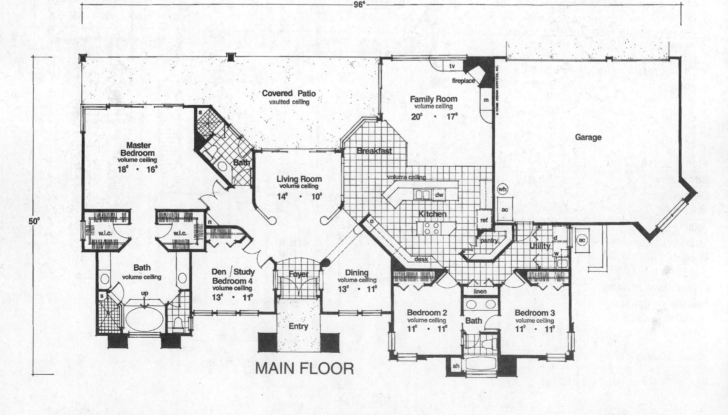

MAIN FLOOR

TO ORDER THIS BLUEPRINT,
CALL TOLL-FREE 1-800-547-5570

Plan HDS-99-177

PRICES AND DETAILS
ON PAGES 12-15

Photo by Mark Englund/HomeStyles

Alluring Arches

- Massive columns, high, dramatic arches and expansive glass attract passersby to this alluring one-story home.
- Inside, 12-ft. coffered ceilings are found in the foyer, dining room and living room. A bank of windows in the living room provides a sweeping view of the covered backyard patio, creating a bright, open effect that is carried throughout the home.
- The informal, family activity areas are oriented to the back of the home as well. Spectacular window walls in the breakfast room and family room offer tremendous views. The family room's inviting corner fireplace is positioned to be enjoyed from the breakfast area and the spacious island kitchen.
- Separated from the secondary bedrooms, the superb master suite is entered through double doors and features a sitting room and a garden bath. Another full bath is across the hall from the den, which would also make a great guest room or nursery.

Plan HDS-99-179

Bedrooms: 3+	Baths: 3

Living Area:

Main floor	2,660 sq. ft.
Total Living Area:	**2,660 sq. ft.**
Garage	527 sq. ft.
Exterior Wall Framing:	2x4

Foundation Options:

Slab

(All plans can be built with your choice of foundation and framing. A generic conversion diagram is available. See order form.)

BLUEPRINT PRICE CODE: D

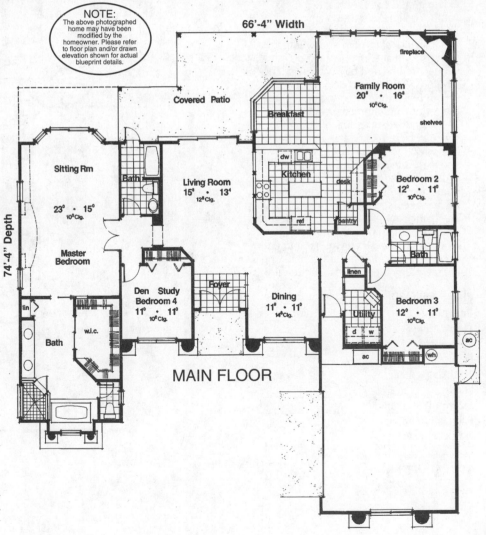

NOTE: The above photographed home may have been modified by the homeowner. Please refer to floor plan and/or drawn elevation shown for actual blueprint details.

MAIN FLOOR

Luxurious Interior

- This luxurious home is introduced by an exciting tiled entry with a 17½-ft. vaulted ceiling and a skylight.
- The highlight of the home is the expansive Great Room and dining area, with its fireplace, planter, 17½-ft. vaulted ceiling and bay windows. The fabulous wraparound deck with a step-up hot tub is the perfect complement to this large entertainment space.
- The kitchen features lots of counter space, a large pantry and an adjoining bay-windowed breakfast nook.
- The exquisite master suite flaunts a sunken garden tub, a separate shower, a dual-sink vanity, a walk-in closet and private access to the deck area.
- The game room downstairs is perfect for casual entertaining, with its warm woodstove, oversized wet bar and patio access. Two bedrooms, a full bath and a large utility area are also included.

Plan P-6595-3D

Bedrooms: 3	Baths: 2½
Living Area:	
Main floor	1,530 sq. ft.
Daylight basement	1,145 sq. ft.
Total Living Area:	**2,675 sq. ft.**
Garage	462 sq. ft.
Exterior Wall Framing:	2x6

Foundation Options:

Daylight basement

(All plans can be built with your choice of foundation and framing. A generic conversion diagram is available. See order form.)

BLUEPRINT PRICE CODE: D

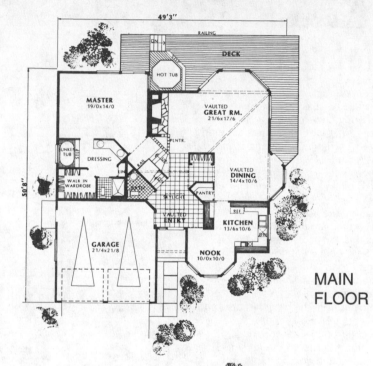

MAIN FLOOR

DAYLIGHT BASEMENT

Plan P-6595-3D

PRICES AND DETAILS ON PAGES 12-15

Easy-Living Atmosphere

- Clean lines and a functional, well-designed floor plan create a relaxed, easy-living atmosphere for this sprawling ranch-style home.
- An inviting front porch with attractive columns and planter boxes opens to an airy entry, which flows into the living room and the family room.
- The huge central family room features a 14-ft. vaulted, exposed-beam ceiling and a handsome fireplace with a built-in wood box. A nice desk and plenty of bookshelves give the room a distinguished feel. A French door opens to a versatile covered rear porch.
- The large gourmet kitchen is highlighted by an arched brick pass-through to the family room. Double doors open to the intimate formal dining room, which hosts a built-in china hutch. The sunny informal eating area features lovely porch views on either side.
- The isolated sleeping wing includes four bedrooms. The enormous master bedroom has a giant walk-in closet and a private bath. A compartmentalized bath with two vanities serves the remaining bedrooms.

Plan E-2700

Bedrooms: 4	Baths: 2½
Living Area:	
Main floor	2,719 sq. ft.
Total Living Area:	**2,719 sq. ft.**
Garage	533 sq. ft.
Storage	50 sq. ft.
Exterior Wall Framing:	2x6

Foundation Options:

Crawlspace
Slab
(All plans can be built with your choice of foundation and framing. A generic conversion diagram is available. See order form.)

BLUEPRINT PRICE CODE:	D

MAIN FLOOR

Photo by Kevin Robinson

Striking Hillside Home Design

- This striking home is designed for a sloping site. The two-car garage and sideyard deck are nestled into the hillside, while cedar siding and a shake roof blend in nicely with the terrain.
- Clerestory windows brighten the entry and the living room, which unfold from the covered front porch. The huge living/dining area instantly catches the eye, with its corner fireplace, 17-ft. sloped ceiling and exciting window treatments. The living room also offers an inviting window seat, while the dining room has sliding glass doors to the large deck.
- The adjoining nook and kitchen also have access to the deck, along with lots of storage and work space.
- The isolated bedroom wing includes a master suite with his-and-hers closets and a private bath. The two smaller bedrooms share a hall bath.
- The daylight basement hosts a laundry room, a recreation room with a fireplace and a bedroom with two closets, plus a large general-use area.

Plan H-2045-5

Bedrooms: 4	Baths: 3
Living Area:	
Main floor	1,602 sq. ft.
Daylight basement	1,133 sq. ft.
Total Living Area:	**2,735 sq. ft.**
Tuck-under garage	508 sq. ft.
Exterior Wall Framing:	2x4

Foundation Options:

Daylight basement
(All plans can be built with your choice of foundation and framing. A generic conversion diagram is available. See order form.)

BLUEPRINT PRICE CODE:	D

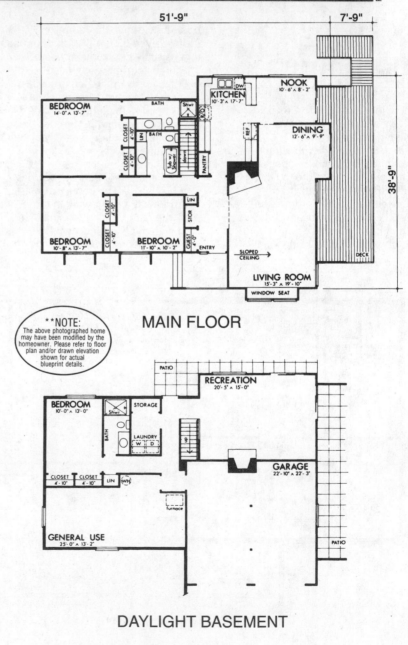

NOTE: The above photographed home may have been modified by the homeowner. Please refer to floor plan and/or drawn elevation shown for actual blueprint details.

MAIN FLOOR

DAYLIGHT BASEMENT

TO ORDER THIS BLUEPRINT, CALL TOLL-FREE 1-800-547-5570

Plan H-2045-5

PRICES AND DETAILS ON PAGES 12-15

Photo by Mark Englund/HomeStyles

Angled Interior

- This plan gives new dimension to one-story living. The exterior has graceful arched windows and a sweeping roofline. The interior is marked by unusual angles and stately columns.
- The living areas are clustered around a large lanai, or covered porch. French doors provide lanai access from the family room, the living room and the master bedroom.
- The central living room also offers arched windows and shares a two-sided fireplace with the family room.
- The island kitchen and the bayed morning room are open to the family room, which features a wet bar next to the striking fireplace.
- The master bedroom features an irresistible bath with a spa tub, a separate shower, dual vanities and two walk-in closets. Two more good-sized bedrooms share another full bath.
- A 12-ft. cathedral ceiling enhances the third bedroom. Standard 8-ft. ceilings are found in the second bedroom and the hall bath. All other rooms boast terrific 10-ft. ceilings.

Plan DD-2802

Bedrooms: 3+	Baths: 2½
Living Area:	
Main floor	2,899 sq. ft.
Total Living Area:	**2,899 sq. ft.**
Standard basement	2,899 sq. ft.
Garage	568 sq. ft.
Exterior Wall Framing:	2x4

Foundation Options:

Standard basement

Crawlspace

Slab

(All plans can be built with your choice of foundation and framing. A generic conversion diagram is available. See order form.)

BLUEPRINT PRICE CODE:	D

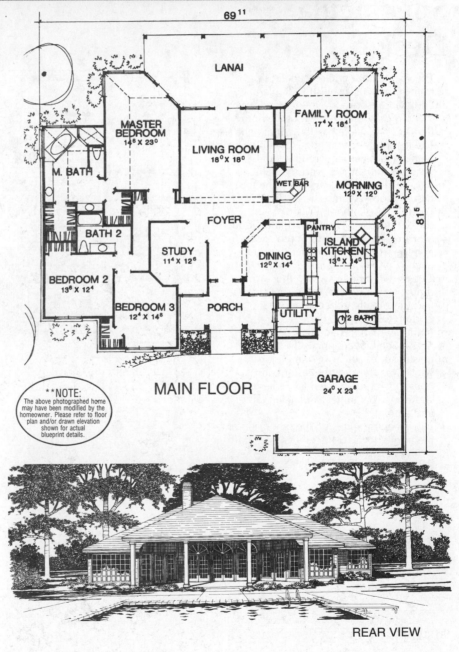

**NOTE: The above photographed home may have been modified by the homeowner. Please refer to floor plan and/or drawn elevation shown for actual blueprint details.

MAIN FLOOR

REAR VIEW

Spectacular Design

- The spectacular brick facade of this home conceals a stylish floor plan. Endless transoms crown the windows that wrap around the rear of the home, flooding the interior with natural light.
- The foyer opens to a huge Grand Room with a 14-ft. ceiling. French doors access a delightful covered porch.
- A three-sided fireplace warms the three casual rooms, which share a high 12-ft. ceiling. The Gathering Room is surrounded by tall windows; the Good Morning Room features porch access; and the island kitchen offers a double oven, a pantry and a snack bar.
- Guests will dine in style in the formal dining room, with its 13-ft. tray ceiling and trio of tall, arched windows.
- Curl·up with a good book in the quiet library, which has an airy 10-ft. ceiling.
- A 12-ft. ceiling enhances the fantastic master suite, which is wrapped in windows. The superb master bath boasts a step-up garden tub, a separate shower, two vanities, a makeup table and a bidet.
- Two sleeping suites on the other side of the home have 10-ft. ceilings and share a unique bath with private vanities.

Plan EOF-8

Bedrooms: 3+	Baths: 3½
Living Area:	
Main floor	3,392 sq. ft.
Total Living Area:	**3,392 sq. ft.**
Garage	871 sq. ft.
Exterior Wall Framing:	2x6

Foundation Options:

Slab

(All plans can be built with your choice of foundation and framing. A generic conversion diagram is available. See order form.)

BLUEPRINT PRICE CODE: E

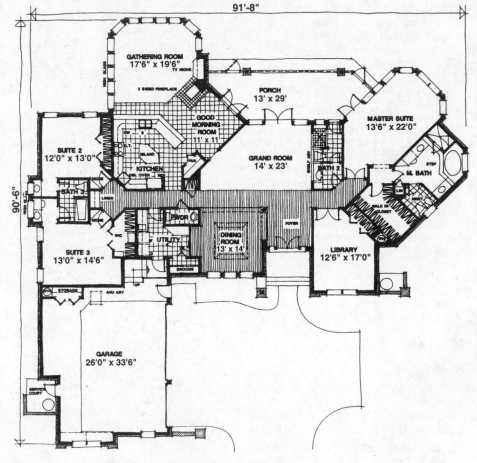

MAIN FLOOR

Plan EOF-8

PRICES AND DETAILS ON PAGES 12-15

European Charm

- This distinguished European home offers today's most luxurious features.
- In the formal living and dining rooms, 15-ft. vaulted ceilings add elegance.
- The informal areas are oriented to the rear of the home, entered through French doors in the foyer. The family room features a 12-ft. tray ceiling, a fireplace with an adjoining media center and a view of a backyard deck.

- The open kitchen and breakfast area is bright and cheerful, with a window wall and French-door deck access.
- Double doors lead into the luxurious master suite, which showcases a 14-ft. vaulted ceiling and a see-through fireplace that is shared with the spa bath. The splashy bath includes a dual-sink vanity, a separate shower and a wardrobe closet and dressing area.
- Two more bedrooms, one with private deck access, and a full bath are located on the opposite side of the home.
- Unless otherwise mentioned, 9-ft. ceilings enhance every room.

Plan APS-2006	
Bedrooms: 3	**Baths:** 2
Living Area:	
Main floor	2,006 sq. ft.
Total Living Area:	**2,006 sq. ft.**
Standard basement	2,006 sq. ft.
Garage	448 sq. ft.
Exterior Wall Framing:	2x4

Foundation Options:

Standard basement
Slab
(All plans can be built with your choice of foundation and framing. A generic conversion diagram is available. See order form.)

BLUEPRINT PRICE CODE: C

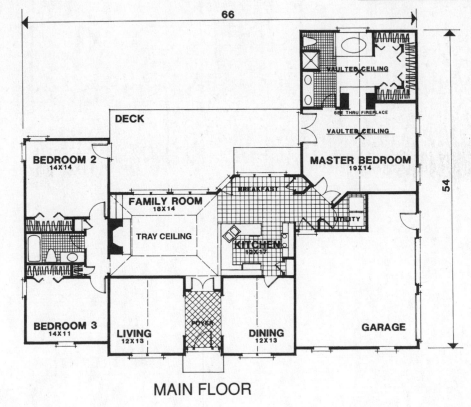

MAIN FLOOR

Sophisticated One-Story

- Beautiful windows accentuated by elegant keystones highlight the exterior of this sophisticated one-story design.
- An open floor plan is the hallmark of the interior, beginning with the foyer that provides instant views of the study as well as the dining and living rooms.
- The spacious living room boasts a fireplace with built-in bookshelves and a rear window wall that stretches into the morning room.
- The sunny morning room has a snack bar to the kitchen. The island kitchen includes a walk-in pantry, a built-in desk and easy access to the utility room and the convenient half-bath.
- The master suite features private access to a nice covered patio, plus an enormous walk-in closet and a posh bath with a spa tub and glass-block shower.
- A hall bath serves the two secondary bedrooms. These three rooms, plus the utility area, have standard 8-ft. ceilings. Other ceilings are 10 ft. high.

Plan DD-2455

Bedrooms: 3+	Baths: 2½
Living Area:	
Main floor	2,457 sq. ft.
Total Living Area:	**2,457 sq. ft.**
Standard basement	2,457 sq. ft.
Garage	585 sq. ft.
Exterior Wall Framing:	2x4

Foundation Options:

Standard basement
Crawlspace
Slab

(All plans can be built with your choice of foundation and framing. A generic conversion diagram is available. See order form.)

BLUEPRINT PRICE CODE:	C

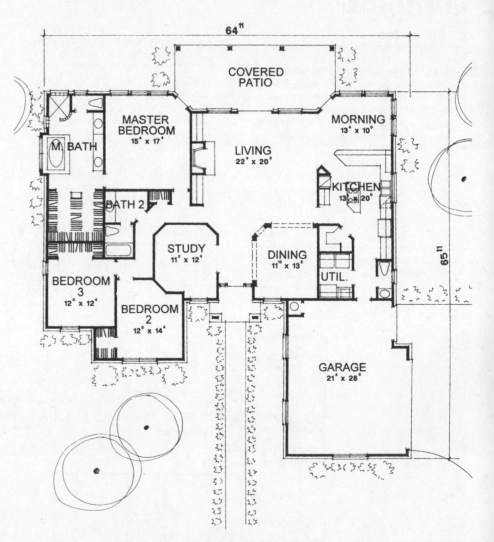

MAIN FLOOR

Plan DD-2455

PRICES AND DETAILS ON PAGES 12-15

Fashionable Detailing

- A soaring entry portico and unusual window treatments make a bold, fashionable statement for this home.
- Inside, varied ceiling heights and special features lend a distinctive look and feel to each room.
- A 14-ft. stepped ceiling in the foyer gives way to the columned formal dining room and its 12-ft. stepped ceiling. Soffit planters outline the foyer and the living room.
- Decorative columns and a 12-ft. raised ceiling also highlight the living room, where sliding doors open to an expansive covered patio.
- A huge, angular counter with a floating soffit distinguishes the kitchen from the sunny breakfast nook. The adjoining family room has a 10-ft. ceiling and a fireplace accented with high, fixed glass and built-in shelves.
- The master suite has sliding glass doors to the patio and an arched opening to the lavish bath. The raised spa tub has louvered shutters to the sleeping area.
- Across from the den is a dual-access bath. The two bedrooms at the opposite side of the home enjoy private access to another full bath.

Plan HDS-99-161

Bedrooms: 3+	Baths: 3½
Living Area:	
Main floor	2,691 sq. ft.
Total Living Area:	**2,691 sq. ft.**
Garage	520 sq. ft.
Exterior Wall Framing:	2x4

Foundation Options:

Slab

(All plans can be built with your choice of foundation and framing. A generic conversion diagram is available. See order form.)

BLUEPRINT PRICE CODE: D

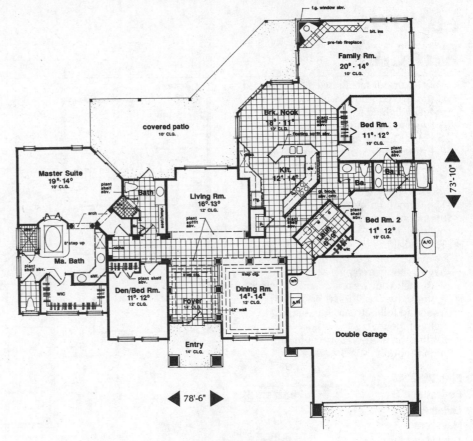

MAIN FLOOR

Luxurious Ranch

- This luxurious farmhouse is introduced by a covered front porch, which opens to a sidelighted foyer.
- A spectacular central living room with an 11-ft. ceiling and a corner fireplace lies at the center of the home. A French door accesses a wide backyard porch.
- An angled eating bar joins the living room to the kitchen and bayed nook. The formal dining room is located on the opposite end of the kitchen, overlooking the front porch.
- The lavish master suite is separated from the other bedrooms and boasts a bayed sitting area and a private bath with dual vanities and a walk-in closet.
- A study, two additional bedrooms and a second full bath are located to the right of the foyer.
- Ceilings in all rooms are at least 9 ft. high for added spaciousness.

Plan VL-2085

Bedrooms: 3+	Baths: 2½
Living Area:	
Main floor	2,085 sq. ft.
Total Living Area:	**2,085 sq. ft.**
Garage	460 sq. ft.
Exterior Wall Framing:	2x4

Foundation Options:

Crawlspace

Slab

(All plans can be built with your choice of foundation and framing. A generic conversion diagram is available. See order form.)

BLUEPRINT PRICE CODE:	C

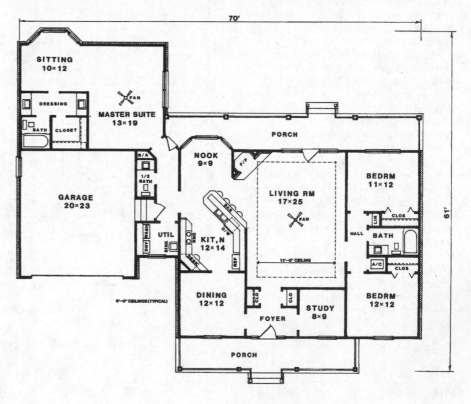

MAIN FLOOR

     Plan VL-2085   *PRICES AND DETAILS ON PAGES 12-15*

Captivating Design

- This captivating and award-winning design is introduced by a unique entry landscape that includes striking columns, an exciting fountain courtyard and a private garden.
- The beautiful, open interior commands attention with expansive glass and ceilings at least 10 ft. high throughout.
- The foyer's 15-ft. ceiling extends into the adjoining dining room, which is set off by a decorative glass-block wall.
- A step-down soffit frames the spacious central living room with its dramatic entry columns and 13-ft. ceiling. A rear bay overlooks a large covered patio.
- The gourmet kitchen shows off an oversized island cooktop and snack bar. A pass-through above the sink provides easy service to the patio's summer kitchen, while indoor dining is offered in the sunny, open breakfast area.
- A warm fireplace and flanking storage shelves adorn an exciting media wall in the large adjacent family room.
- The secondary bedrooms share a full bath near the laundry room and garage.
- Behind double doors on the other side of the home, the romantic master suite is bathed in sunlight. A private garden embraces an elegant oval tub.

Plan HDS-99-185

Bedrooms: 3+	Baths: 2½
Living Area:	
Main floor	2,397 sq. ft.
Total Living Area:	**2,397 sq. ft.**
Garage	473 sq. ft.
Exterior Wall Framing:	2x4

Foundation Options:

Slab
(All plans can be built with your choice of foundation and framing. A generic conversion diagram is available. See order form.)

BLUEPRINT PRICE CODE: C

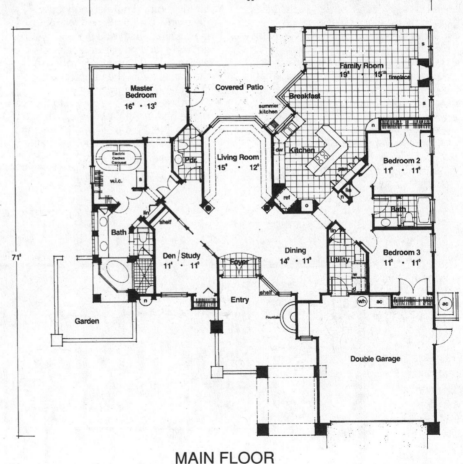

MAIN FLOOR

Ever-Popular Floor Plan

- Open living spaces that are well integrated with outdoor areas give this plan its popularity.
- The covered porch ushers guests into a roomy entry that separates the formal entertaining areas.
- Double doors open to the huge family room, which boasts a 13-ft. vaulted ceiling accented by rustic beams, a raised-hearth fireplace and built-in book-shelves. Glass doors lead to a covered porch and an adjoining patio, creating a perfect poolside setting.
- A bayed eating area is open to the family room, separated only by a decorative half-wall, and features a large china hutch and great views. The adjacent kitchen has an angled sink for easy service to the family room and the eating area. The utility room and the garage are close by.
- The master suite is secluded to the rear of the home, with a private bath and access to the patio. The two remaining bedrooms share a dual-access bath.

Plan E-2000	
Bedrooms: 3	**Baths:** 2
Living Area:	
Main floor	2,009 sq. ft.
Total Living Area:	**2,009 sq. ft.**
Garage and storage	550 sq. ft.
Exterior Wall Framing:	2x4

Foundation Options:
Crawlspace
Slab
(All plans can be built with your choice of foundation and framing. A generic conversion diagram is available. See order form.)

BLUEPRINT PRICE CODE:	C

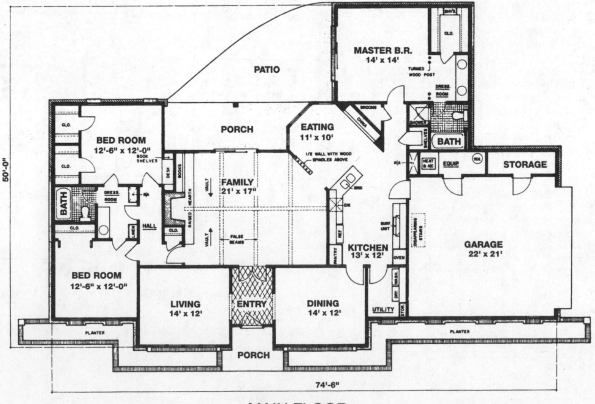

MAIN FLOOR

TO ORDER THIS BLUEPRINT,
CALL TOLL-FREE 1-800-547-5570

Plan E-2000

PRICES AND DETAILS
ON PAGES 12-15

Charming One-Story

- The charming facade of this home conceals an exciting angled interior with many accesses to the outdoors.
- At the center of the floor plan is a spacious family activity area that combines the Great Room, the breakfast room and the kitchen.
- The sunny sunken Great Room features a 12½-ft. cathedral ceiling and an exciting two-sided fireplace. The adjacent breakfast room offers French doors to a covered backyard patio.

- The unique angled kitchen has a bright sink, a serving bar and plenty of counter space. Across the hall are the dining room, the laundry room and access to the three-car garage.
- The secluded master bedroom boasts a 12½-ft. cathedral ceiling, a roomy walk-in closet and French doors to a private covered patio. The lavish master bath has a bright garden tub, a separate shower and a dual-sink vanity.
- The secondary bedrooms both have walk-in closets. The rear-facing bedroom has patio access through its own full bath. The parlor off the entry could serve as a fourth bedroom, a guest room or a home office.

Plan Q-2033-1A

Bedrooms: 3+	Baths: 3
Living Area:	
Main floor	2,033 sq. ft.
Total Living Area:	**2,033 sq. ft.**
Garage	592 sq. ft.
Exterior Wall Framing:	2x4

Foundation Options:

Slab
(All plans can be built with your choice of foundation and framing. A generic conversion diagram is available. See order form.)

BLUEPRINT PRICE CODE: C

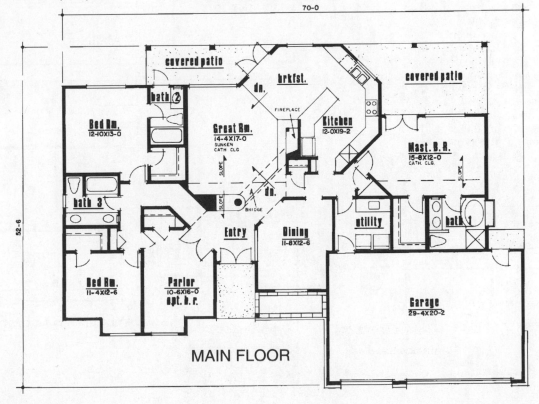

MAIN FLOOR

Well-Appointed Walk-Out Design

- The hipped roof and covered entry give this well-appointed home a look of distinction.
- Inside, the foyer leads directly into the expansive Great Room, which boasts a 13-ft. vaulted ceiling, an inviting fireplace, a built-in entertainment center and a dramatic window wall that overlooks an exciting full-width deck with a hot tub!
- A half-wall separates the Great Room from the nook, which is open to the U-shaped kitchen. The impressive kitchen includes a snack bar, a walk-in pantry and a greenhouse window.
- The isolated master suite offers a vaulted ceiling that slopes up to 9 feet. A French door opens to the deck and hot tub, while a pocket door accesses the sumptuous master bath with a spa tub under a glass-block wall.
- Two more bedrooms in the walk-out basement share another full bath. The optional expansion areas provide an additional 730 sq. ft. of space.

Plan S-41792

Bedrooms: 3	Baths: 3
Living Area:	
Main floor	1,450 sq. ft.
Partial daylight basement	590 sq. ft.
Total Living Area:	**2,040 sq. ft.**
Garage	429 sq. ft.
Unfinished expansion areas	730 sq. ft.
Exterior Wall Framing:	2x6

Foundation Options:

Partial daylight basement
(All plans can be built with your choice of foundation and framing. A generic conversion diagram is available. See order form.)

BLUEPRINT PRICE CODE: C

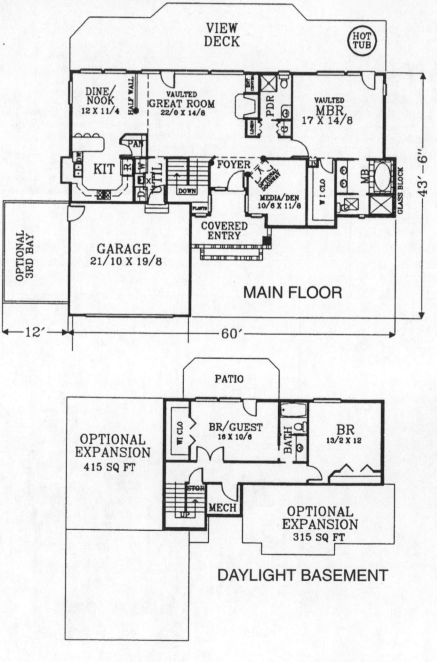

MAIN FLOOR

DAYLIGHT BASEMENT

Plan S-41792

Elaborate Entry

- This home's important-looking covered entry greets guests with heavy, banded support columns, sunburst transom windows and dual sidelights.
- Once inside, the 15-ft.-high foyer is flanked by the formal living and dining rooms, which have 10½-ft. vaulted ceilings. Straight ahead and beyond decorative columns lies the spacious family room.
- Surrounded by 8-ft.-high walls, the family room features a 13-ft. vaulted ceiling, a corner fireplace and sliding doors to a rear covered patio.
- The bright and airy kitchen has a 13-ft. ceiling and serves the family room and the breakfast area, which is enhanced by a corner window and a French door.
- The master suite enjoys a 13-ft. vaulted ceiling and features double-door patio access, a large walk-in closet and a private bath with a corner platform tub and a separate shower.

Plan HDS-90-806

Bedrooms: 4	Baths: 2
Living Area:	
Main floor	2,041 sq. ft.
Total Living Area:	**2,041 sq. ft.**
Garage	452 sq. ft.

Exterior Wall Framing:
2x4 or 8-in. concrete block

Foundation Options:
Slab
(All plans can be built with your choice of foundation and framing. A generic conversion diagram is available. See order form.)

BLUEPRINT PRICE CODE: C

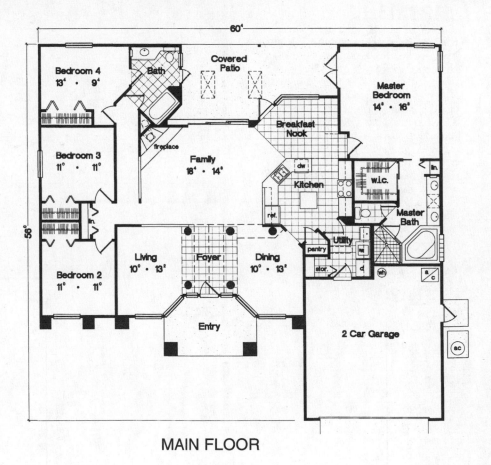

MAIN FLOOR

Modern Charmer

- This attractive plan combines country-style charm with a modern floor plan.
- The central foyer ushers guests past a study and on into the huge living room, which is highlighted by a high, flat ceiling, a corner fireplace and access to a big, covered backyard porch.
- An angled snack bar joins the living room to the bayed nook and the efficient kitchen. The formal dining room is easily reached from the kitchen and the foyer. A utility room and a half-bath are just off the garage entrance.
- The master suite, isolated for privacy, boasts a magnificent bath with a garden tub, a separate shower, double vanities and two walk-in closets.
- Two more bedrooms are located on the opposite side of the home and are separated by a hall bath.
- Ceilings in all rooms are at least 9 ft. high for added spaciousness.

REAR VIEW

Plan VL-2069

Bedrooms: 3	Baths: 2½
Living Area:	
Main floor	2,069 sq. ft.
Total Living Area:	**2,069 sq. ft.**
Garage	460 sq. ft.
Exterior Wall Framing:	2x4

Foundation Options:

Crawlspace
Slab
(All plans can be built with your choice of foundation and framing. A generic conversion diagram is available. See order form.)

BLUEPRINT PRICE CODE:	C

MAIN FLOOR

Picture Perfect!

- With graceful arches, columns and railings, the wonderful front porch makes this home the picture of country charm. Decorative chimneys, shutters and quaint dormers add more style.
- Inside, the foyer shows off sidelights and a fantail transom. The foyer is flanked by the dining room and a bedroom, both of which boast porch views and arched transoms. All three areas are expanded by 10-ft. ceilings.
- The living room also flaunts a 10-ft. ceiling, plus a fireplace and French doors that open to a skylighted porch. The remaining rooms offer 9-ft. ceilings.
- The L-shaped kitchen has an island cooktop and a sunny breakfast nook.
- A Palladian window arrangement brightens the sitting alcove in the master suite. Other highlights include porch access and a fantastic bath with a garden tub and a separate shower.
- The upper floor is perfect for future expansion space.

Plan J-9401

Bedrooms: 3+	Baths: 2½
Living Area:	
Main floor	2,089 sq. ft.
Total Living Area:	**2,089 sq. ft.**
Upper floor (unfinished)	878 sq. ft.
Standard basement	2,089 sq. ft.
Garage and storage	530 sq. ft.
Exterior Wall Framing:	2x4

Foundation Options:

Standard basement
Crawlspace
Slab

(All plans can be built with your choice of foundation and framing. A generic conversion diagram is available. See order form.)

BLUEPRINT PRICE CODE:	C

UPPER FLOOR

FUTURE 14-0 x 12-0

FUTURE 29-4 x 16-0

FUTURE 12-8 x 12-0

MAIN FLOOR

63-10

64-7

GARAGE 20-4 x 21-4

M.BATH 17-8 x 10-6

PORCH 22-0 x 12-0

STOR. 5-0x6-1

MASTER BEDROOM 19-2 x 13-7

LIVING 22-0 x 15-2

UTIL. 8-4 x 5-8

KITCHEN 12-8 x 12-0

BEDROOM 10-8 x 12-0

BEDROOM 11-6 x 11-0

FOYER 5-8x13-10

DINING 11-6 x 13-6

BREAKFAST 12-8 x 9-10

PORCH 30-8 x 6-0

Wonderful Windows

- This one-story's striking stucco and stone facade is enhanced with wonderful windows and great gables.
- A beautiful bay augments the living room/den, which can be closed off.
- A wall of windows lets sunbeams brighten the exquisite formal dining room, which is open but defined by decorative columns.
- The oversized family room offers a nice fireplace and a handy serving bar.
- The walk-through kitchen boasts a large pantry and a corner sink.
- A lovely window seat is found in one of the two secondary bedrooms.
- The magnificent master suite features a symmetrical tray ceiling that sets off a round-top window.
- Large walk-in closets flank the entry to the master bath, which offers a garden tub and two vanities. One of the vanities has knee space for a sit-down makeup area.

Plan FB-5009-CHAD

Bedrooms: 3	Baths: 2
Living Area:	
Main floor	2,115 sq. ft.
Total Living Area:	**2,115 sq. ft.**
Daylight basement	2,115 sq. ft.
Garage	517 sq. ft.
Storage	18 sq. ft.
Exterior Wall Framing:	2x4

Foundation Options:
Daylight basement
Slab
(Typical foundation & framing conversion diagram available—see order form.)

BLUEPRINT PRICE CODE: C

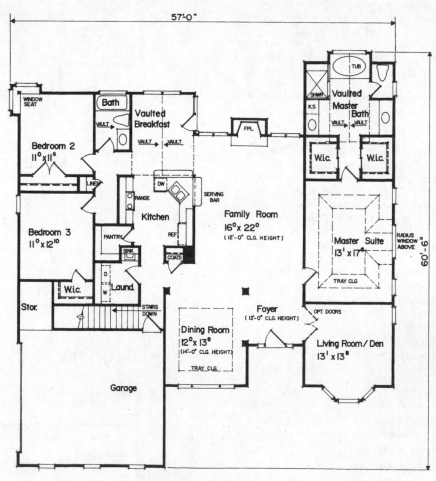

MAIN FLOOR

Plan FB-5009-CHAD

PRICES AND DETAILS ON PAGES 12-15

Vertical Dimension

- This exotic four-bedroom home is drenched in elegance and durability.
- Soaring columns, high windows and volume ceilings add a vertical dimension to the home's sprawling single-level room arrangement.
- The grand foyer reveals the formal living areas. The dining room is introduced by columns and the living room opens to a nice covered porch. All three areas have 12-ft.-high ceilings.
- The kitchen flows into a sunny breakfast nook that accesses the back porch. These areas have 12-ft. ceilings as well.
- High plant shelves surround the inviting family room, which boasts a fireplace and a 12-ft. barrel-vaulted ceiling.
- The master suite is secluded to the right of the foyer. The sleeping area features a 12-ft.-high ceiling and access to the porch. The master bath includes a huge walk-in closet and a corner step-up tub.
- At the back of the home are three more bedrooms, each with a 10-ft ceiling. The bedrooms share a full bath that can be accessed from the backyard–a nice feature if you have a pool or are entertaining outdoors.

Plan HDS-90-815

Bedrooms: 4	Baths: 2
Living Area:	
Main floor	2,153 sq. ft.
Total Living Area:	**2,153 sq. ft.**
Garage	434 sq. ft.
Exterior Wall Framing:	2x4

Foundation Options:

Slab
(All plans can be built with your choice of foundation and framing. A generic conversion diagram is available. See order form.)

BLUEPRINT PRICE CODE: **C**

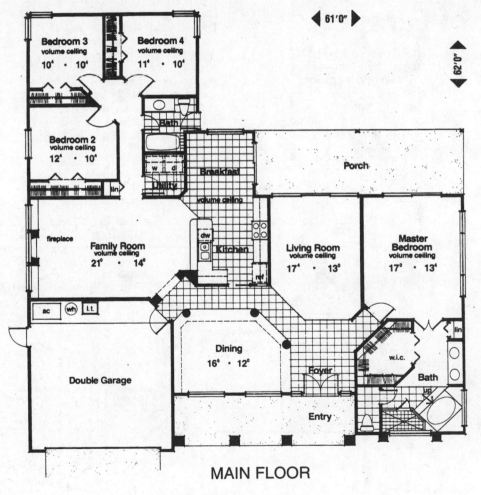

MAIN FLOOR

A Taste of Europe

- This tasteful one-story home is characterized by a European exterior and an ultra-modern interior.
- High 10-ft. ceilings grace the central living areas, from the foyer to the Great Room, and from the nook through the kitchen to the dining room.
- The inviting Great Room showcases a fireplace framed by glass that overlooks the covered back porch.
- A snack bar unites the Great Room with the bayed nook and the galley-style kitchen. A spacious utility room is just off the kitchen and accessible from the two-car garage as well.
- The secluded master suite boasts a luxurious private bath and French doors that open to the covered backyard porch.
- The master bath features a raised garden spa tub set into an intimate corner, with a separate shower nearby. A large walk-in closet and two sinks separated by a built-in makeup table are also included.
- Two additional bedrooms, a second full bath and a front study or home office make up the remainder of this up-to-date design.

Plan VL-2162	
Bedrooms: 3	**Baths:** 2
Living Area:	
Main floor	2,162 sq. ft.
Total Living Area:	**2,162 sq. ft.**
Garage	498 sq. ft.
Exterior Wall Framing:	2x4
Foundation Options:	
Crawlspace	
Slab	

(All plans can be built with your choice of foundation and framing. A generic conversion diagram is available. See order form.)

BLUEPRINT PRICE CODE: C

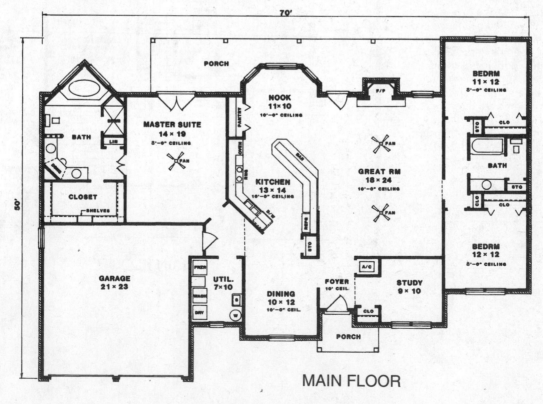

MAIN FLOOR

Plan VL-2162

Luxurious Master Suite

- The inviting facade of this gorgeous one-story design boasts a sheltered porch, symmetrical architecture and elegant window treatments.
- Inside, beautiful arched openings frame the living room, which features a 12-ft. ceiling, a dramatic fireplace and a wet bar that is open to the deluxe kitchen.
- The roomy kitchen is highlighted by an island cooktop, a built-in desk and a snack bar that faces the bayed eating area and the covered back porch.
- Isolated to the rear of the home, the master suite is a romantic retreat, offering an intimate sitting area and a luxurious bath. Entered through elegant double doors, the private bath showcases a skylighted corner tub, a separate shower, his-and-hers vanities, and a huge walk-in closet.
- The two remaining bedrooms have walk-in closets and share a hall bath.
- Unless otherwise specified, the home has 9-ft. ceilings throughout.

Plan E-2106

Bedrooms: 3	Baths: 2
Living Area:	
Main floor	2,177 sq. ft.
Total Living Area:	**2,177 sq. ft.**
Standard basement	2,177 sq. ft.
Garage and storage	570 sq. ft.
Exterior Wall Framing:	2x4

Foundation Options:

Standard basement
Crawlspace
Slab

(All plans can be built with your choice of foundation and framing. A generic conversion diagram is available. See order form.)

BLUEPRINT PRICE CODE: **C**

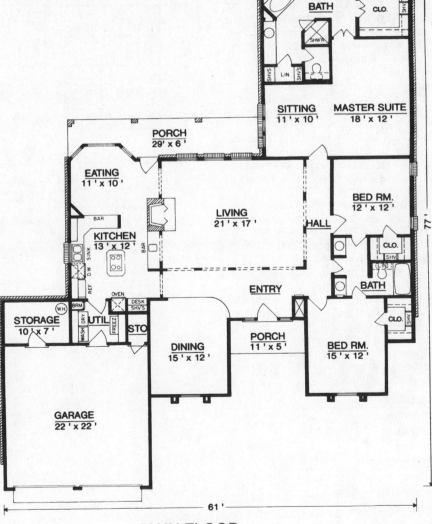

MAIN FLOOR

Arranged for Family Living

- This distinguished ranch home has a neatly arranged floor plan with a large activity area at the center and a strategically placed master bedroom.
- The formal living room and dining room flank the entry. The dining room provides views out to the covered front porch and a decorative planter with brick veneer. The living room boasts corner windows and a display niche with shelves.
- The double-doored entry also opens to a large sunken family room with a 13-ft. cathedral ceiling, a handsome fireplace, a patio view and a 10-ft-high decorative bridge.
- The huge modern kitchen offers a handy snack counter to the adjacent family room. The bayed breakfast room has French-door access to an expansive covered patio.
- Secluded to one end of the home is the deluxe master bedroom, which offers an 11-ft. cathedral ceiling, a spacious walk-in closet and French-door patio access. The master bath has a dual-sink vanity and outdoor access.
- Three additional bedrooms and two more baths are located at the opposite end of the home.

Plan Q-2266-1A

Bedrooms: 4	Baths: 3
Living Area:	
Main floor	2,266 sq. ft.
Total Living Area:	**2,266 sq. ft.**
Garage	592 sq. ft.
Exterior Wall Framing:	2x4

Foundation Options:

Slab

(All plans can be built with your choice of foundation and framing. A generic conversion diagram is available. See order form.)

BLUEPRINT PRICE CODE: C

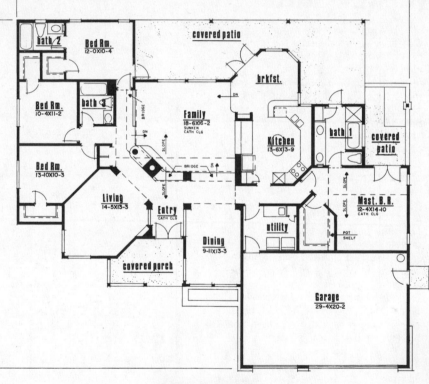

MAIN FLOOR

TO ORDER THIS BLUEPRINT,
CALL TOLL-FREE 1-800-547-5570

Plan Q-2266-1A

PRICES AND DETAILS
ON PAGES 12-15

Homey Hacienda

- This stylish home combines visual impact with an easy-living floor plan.
- Appealing arched windows attract the eye, while the low-sloping tiled roof and deep overhangs protect the home from the sun's rays.
- The tiled front entry is flanked by the dining room and a quiet study.

- Straight ahead, the spacious sunken living room features a fireplace bordered by bright windows.
- The adjoining breakfast area has sliding glass doors to a covered rear patio. The kitchen features a snack bar and a pass-through to the living room.
- The secluded master suite offers a large walk-in closet and a private bath with a luxurious spa tub. French doors lead to the patio.
- The two remaining bedrooms enjoy private access to another full bath.

Plan Q-2298-1A

Bedrooms: 3+	Baths: 2½
Living Area:	
Main floor	2,298 sq. ft.
Total Living Area:	**2,298 sq. ft.**
Garage	433 sq. ft.
Exterior Wall Framing:	2x4

Foundation Options:

Slab
(All plans can be built with your choice of foundation and framing. A generic conversion diagram is available. See order form.)

BLUEPRINT PRICE CODE: **C**

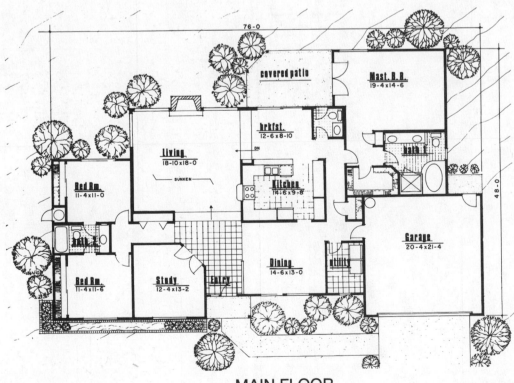

MAIN FLOOR

Ultra-Modern Mediterranean

- Soaring ceilings, a luxurious master suite and a clean stucco exterior with stylish arched windows give this nouveau-Mediterranean home its unique appeal.
- The magnificent living room and the elegant dining room combine to form one large, open area. The dining room has a tall, arched window and a 12-ft. coffered ceiling. The living room boasts a flat ceiling that is over 12 ft. high, a convenient wet bar and sliding glass doors to the covered patio.
- The informal family room is warmed by a fireplace and shares a soaring 12-ft. flat ceiling with the sunny breakfast area and the large, modern kitchen.
- The kitchen is easily accessible from the family area and the formal dining room, and features an eating bar and a spacious pantry.
- The luxurious master suite offers patio access and is enhanced by an elegant 11-ft., 6-in. tray ceiling and his-and-hers walk-in closets. The huge master bath features a dual-sink vanity, a large tiled shower and a whirlpool tub.

Plan HDS-99-158

Bedrooms: 4	Baths: 3
Living Area:	
Main floor	2,352 sq. ft.
Total Living Area:	**2,352 sq. ft.**
Garage	440 sq. ft.

Exterior Wall Framing:
8-in. concrete block and 2x4

Foundation Options:
Slab
(All plans can be built with your choice of foundation and framing. A generic conversion diagram is available. See order form.)

BLUEPRINT PRICE CODE: C

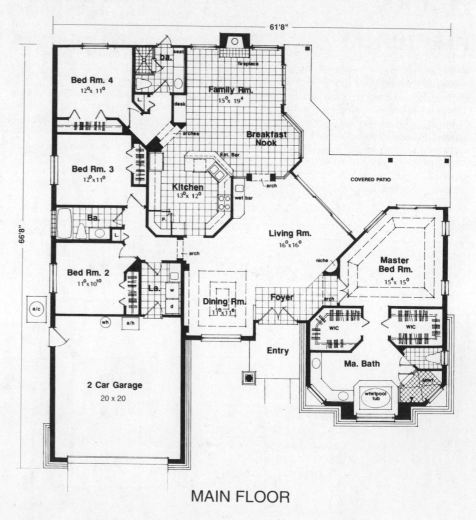

MAIN FLOOR

Light and Bright

- This outstanding home has a light, inviting facade with arched windows, unique transoms and twin dormers.
- The sheltered front porch opens to an airy entry with a dramatic view to the backyard. High 10-ft. ceilings adorn the study and the dining and living rooms.
- A well-designed kitchen is strategically placed near the entrance from the garage and adjoins a sunny morning room. The kitchen is equipped with a pantry, a central island and a nice corner window. The morning room features a lovely window seat, a built-in hutch, a snack bar and a 10-ft. ceiling.
- An inviting fireplace with a tile hearth is the focal point of the cozy family room. The niche next to the fireplace is ideal for an entertainment center. Sliding glass doors open to a large deck.
- The sleeping wing houses three bedrooms, each with a walk-in closet. The master suite has a 10-ft. ceiling and two walk-in closets, in addition to a private garden bath and deck access.

Plan DD-2372

Bedrooms: 3	Baths: 2½
Living Area:	
Main floor	2,376 sq. ft.
Total Living Area:	**2,376 sq. ft.**
Standard basement	2,376 sq. ft.
Garage	473 sq. ft.
Exterior Wall Framing:	2x4

Foundation Options:

Standard basement
Crawlspace
Slab

(All plans can be built with your choice of foundation and framing. A generic conversion diagram is available. See order form.)

BLUEPRINT PRICE CODE: C

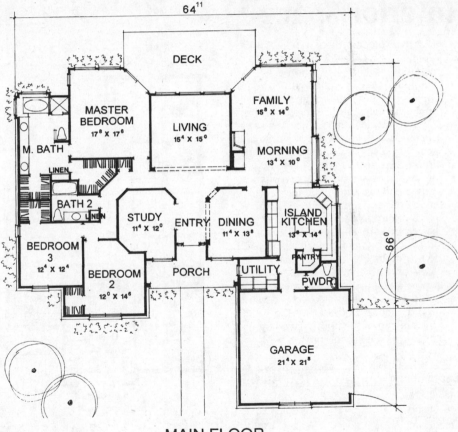

MAIN FLOOR

Captivating Interior Space

- Attractive stucco, ornate windows and tropical design accents add to the appeal of this captivating home.
- The tiled foyer has arched entries to the living room, dining room and family room. The living and dining rooms have dramatic window treatments. The spacious family room boasts a dramatic corner fireplace, a vaulted ceiling and sliding glass doors to the covered patio.
- The exciting skylighted kitchen offers a vaulted ceiling, ample counter space, a serving bar and a bayed breakfast nook with a pantry closet.
- The removed master suite boasts a romantic two-way fireplace shared with the private bath. The elegant bath shows off an oval tub, a separate corner shower and a vaulted ceiling.
- Raised 10-ft. ceilings are featured in the three secondary bedrooms at the opposite end of the home. Two large baths serve these bedrooms.

Plan HDS-99-135

Bedrooms: 4	Baths: 3

Living Area:

Main floor	2,454 sq. ft.

Total Living Area:	**2,454 sq. ft.**
Garage	448 sq. ft.

Exterior Wall Framing: 8-in. concrete block

Foundation Options:

Slab

(Typical foundation & framing conversion diagram available—see order form.)

BLUEPRINT PRICE CODE: C

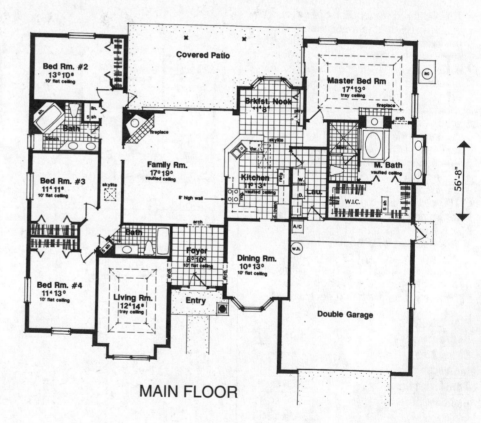

MAIN FLOOR

Farmhouse with Character

- The charm of yesterday's farmhouse and the exquisite design of a modern floor plan characterize this four-bedroom ranch.
- At the center of the floor plan is a stunning living room with an 11-ft. stepped-up ceiling, a massive corner fireplace and a door to the rear porch.
- An angled snack bar separates the living room from the adjoining kitchen and bayed breakfast nook. The formal dining room is positioned on the opposite side of the kitchen.
- The isolated master suite offers two walk-in closets and a royal bath with a sunny garden tub, twin vanities and a separate shower. It also offers private access to the porch.
- Three additional bedrooms are located at the opposite end of the home, serviced by two full baths.

Plan VL-2483

Bedrooms: 4	Baths: 3 ½
Space:	
Main floor	2,483 sq. ft.
Total Living Area	**2,483 sq. ft.**
Garage	504 sq. ft.
Exterior Wall Framing	2x4

Foundation options:

Crawlspace

Slab

(Foundation & framing conversion diagram available—see order form.)

Blueprint Price Code	C

Stunning and Sophisticated

- A well-balanced blend of brick, stucco, and glass gives this stunning one-story home a sophisticated look.
- Past the recessed entry, the 16-ft.-high foyer is highlighted by a round-topped transom window. An arched opening introduces the formal dining room.
- The spectacular living room boasts an elegant 16-ft. coffered ceiling and is brightened by a trio of tall windows topped by a radius transom.
- The spacious island kitchen includes a roomy corner pantry and a built-in desk. A serving bar is convenient to the family room and the sunny breakfast area.
- A window-flanked fireplace is the focal point of the family room, which features a 16-ft. vaulted ceiling.
- A tray ceiling adorns the luxurious master suite. The vaulted master bath has a 16-ft. ceiling and includes a garden tub, a separate shower and his-and-hers vanities and walk-in closets.

Plan FB-5074-ARLI

Bedrooms: 3+	Baths: 2½
Living Area:	
Main floor	2,492 sq. ft.
Total Living Area:	**2,492 sq. ft.**
Daylight basement	2,492 sq. ft.
Garage	400 sq. ft.
Exterior Wall Framing:	2x4

Foundation Options:

Daylight basement

Crawlspace

(All plans can be built with your choice of foundation and framing. A generic conversion diagram is available. See order form.)

BLUEPRINT PRICE CODE:	C

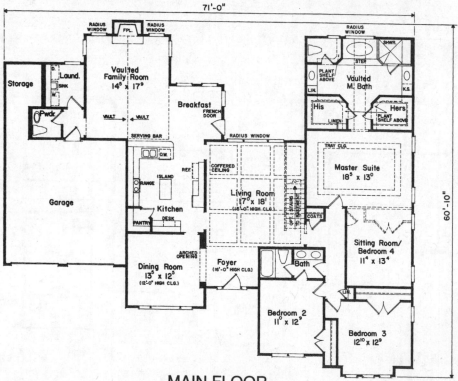

MAIN FLOOR

Plan FB-5074-ARLI

PRICES AND DETAILS ON PAGES 12-15

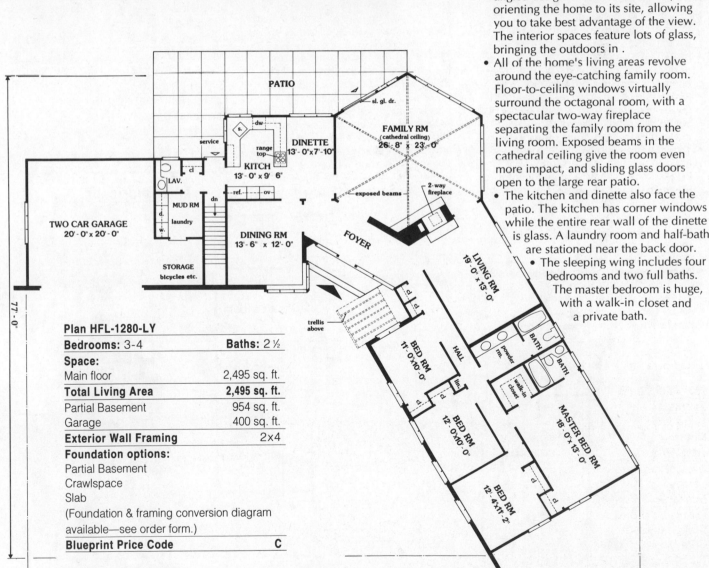

Great Garden Home

- This four-bedroom ranch home is especially great for outdoor lovers. The angled design offers more flexiblity in orienting the home to its site, allowing you to take best advantage of the view. The interior spaces feature lots of glass, bringing the outdoors in .
- All of the home's living areas revolve around the eye-catching family room. Floor-to-ceiling windows virtually surround the octagonal room, with a spectacular two-way fireplace separating the family room from the living room. Exposed beams in the cathedral ceiling give the room even more impact, and sliding glass doors open to the large rear patio.
- The kitchen and dinette also face the patio. The kitchen has corner windows while the entire rear wall of the dinette is glass. A laundry room and half-bath are stationed near the back door.
- The sleeping wing includes four bedrooms and two full baths. The master bedroom is huge, with a walk-in closet and a private bath.

PATIO

sl. gl. dr.

FAMILY RM (cathedral ceiling) 26'-8" x 23'-0"

service

s.   dw

range top

DINETTE 13'-0"x 7'-10"

KITCH 13'-0" x 9'-6"

LAV.

d

ref. — ov

MUD RM

laundry

d.
w.

dn

exposed beams

2-way fireplace

DINING RM 13'-6" x 12'-0"

FOYER

TWO CAR GARAGE 20'-0" x 20'-0"

STORAGE bicycles etc.

trellis above

LIVING RM 19'-0" x 13'-0"

BED RM 11'-0"x10'-0"

HALL

powder rm

lin.

BATH

BATH

walk-in closet

BED RM 12'-0"x10'-0"

MASTER BED RM 18'-0"x 13'-0"

BED RM 12'-4"x11'-2"

d

77'-0"

97'-10"

Plan HFL-1280-LY

Bedrooms: 3-4	Baths: 2 ½
Space:	
Main floor	2,495 sq. ft.
Total Living Area	**2,495 sq. ft.**
Partial Basement	954 sq. ft.
Garage	400 sq. ft.
Exterior Wall Framing	2x4
Foundation options:	

Partial Basement
Crawlspace
Slab
(Foundation & framing conversion diagram available—see order form.)

Blueprint Price Code	C

Stately Ranch

- This stately ranch, with its brick exterior, Palladian windows and quoin accents, is a vision of elegance.
- Inside, guests will be greeted by a dramatic living room with a 10-ft. tray ceiling, a fireplace, built-in bookcases and a unique window wall with French doors leading to an expansive deck.
- The formal dining room has mitered corners and a 10-ft. tray ceiling as well.
- Under a 14-ft. vaulted ceiling, the gourmet kitchen and the sunny breakfast room share a dramatic view of the deck through a Palladian window.

A half-bath and a laundry room are conveniently nearby.
- The inviting family room is highlighted by a 10-ft. tray ceiling, a second fireplace and deck access.
- The sumptuous master suite features his-and-hers walk-in closets, French doors leading to the deck and a 10-ft. tray ceiling. The 14-ft.-high vaulted master bath includes a garden tub, a separate shower and twin vanities.
- The adjoining bedroom would be ideal as a sitting room or a nursery.
- The second bedroom boasts a 14-ft. vaulted ceiling, while the third and fourth bedrooms have 9-ft. ceilings.

Plan APS-2410

Bedrooms: 4	Baths: 2½-3½
Living Area:	
Main floor	2,499 sq. ft.
Total Living Area:	**2,499 sq. ft.**
Standard basement	2,499 sq. ft.
Garage	456 sq. ft.
Exterior Wall Framing:	2x4

Foundation Options:
Standard basement
Crawlspace
Slab
(All plans can be built with your choice of foundation and framing. A generic conversion diagram is available. See order form.)

BLUEPRINT PRICE CODE: C

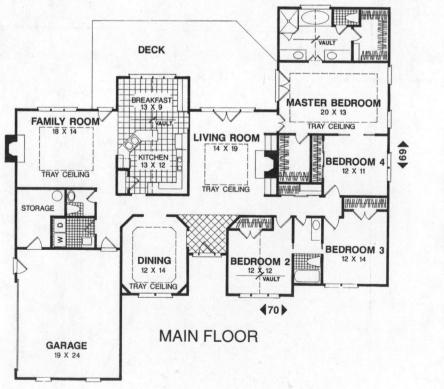

MAIN FLOOR

OPTIONAL EXTRA BATH

Plan APS-2410

PRICES AND DETAILS ON PAGES 12-15

Southern "Cracker" Style

- This Florida "Cracker" style home is warm and inviting. Its walkout lower level can accommodate a sloping lot.
- Expansive front and rear porches are ideal for entertaining. Access to the rear porch is possible from the Great Room, the dining room and the master bedroom. A second bedroom opens to the front porch.
- All three bedrooms have private baths! The master bath also offers dual walk-in closets and a luxurious garden tub.
- The huge gourmet kitchen offers a built-in desk, a pantry closet and a handy work island. Volume ceilings are found in the kitchen as well as in the dining room and Great Room.
- Adjacent to the garage on the lower level is room for a future playroom or home office. Other expansion is possible in the loft area.

Plan HDS-99-160

Bedrooms: 3	Baths: 3
Living Area:	
Main floor	2,500 sq. ft.
Total Living Area:	**2,500 sq. ft.**
Partial daylight basement	492 sq. ft.
Garage	764 sq. ft.
Exterior Wall Framing:	2x4

Foundation Options:

Partial daylight basement
(Typical foundation & framing conversion diagram available—see order form.)

BLUEPRINT PRICE CODE:	D

MAIN FLOOR

DAYLIGHT BASEMENT

Zesty Southwestern!

- Elegant arches and a bright stucco exterior add a zesty southwestern flavor to this beautiful one-story home.
- Past the columned front porch, the angled entry is flanked by the living room and the dining room, both of which feature 9½-ft. tray ceilings and lovely bay windows.
- The skylighted island kitchen offers a windowed sink, a built-in planning desk and a sunny breakfast nook.
- The adjacent family room boasts a tray ceiling and a corner fireplace. A French door opens to a covered patio.
- Double doors introduce the luxurious master bedroom, which enjoys patio access and a 9-ft.-high tray ceiling. The skylighted master bath includes a garden spa tub, a separate shower, a walk-in closet and a dual-sink vanity.
- Two additional bedrooms have built-in window seats and share a second skylighted bath. A den off the entry could easily be used as an extra bedroom or as a home office.

Plans P-7752-3A & -3D

Bedrooms: 3+	Baths: 2
Living Area:	
Main floor (crawlspace version)	2,503 sq. ft.
Main floor (basement version)	2,575 sq. ft.
Total Living Area:	**2,503/2,575 sq. ft.**
Daylight basement	2,578 sq. ft.
Garage	962 sq. ft.
Exterior Wall Framing:	2x6
Foundation Options:	**Plan #**
Daylight basement	P-7752-3D
Crawlspace	P-7752-3A

(All plans can be built with your choice of foundation and framing. A generic conversion diagram is available. See order form.)

BLUEPRINT PRICE CODE: **D**

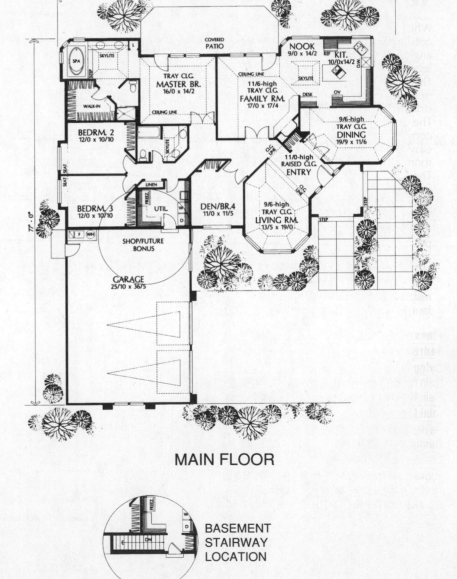

MAIN FLOOR

BASEMENT STAIRWAY LOCATION

Plans P-7752-3A & -3D

PRICES AND DETAILS
ON PAGES 12-15

Full of Surprises

- While dignified and reserved on the outside, this plan presents intriguing angles, vaulted ceilings and surprising spaces throughout the interior.
- The elegant, vaulted living room flows from the expansive foyer and includes a striking fireplace and a beautiful bay.
- The spacious island kitchen offers wide corner windows above the sink and easy service to both the vaulted dining room and the skylighted nook.
- The adjoining vaulted family room features a warm corner woodstove and sliding doors to the backyard patio.
- The superb master suite includes a vaulted sleeping area and an exquisite private bath with a skylighted dressing area, a large walk-in closet, a step-up spa tub and a separate shower.
- Three secondary bedrooms are located near another full bath and a large laundry room with garage access.

Plans P-7711-3A & -3D

Bedrooms: 4	Baths: 2
Living Area:	
Main floor (crawlspace version)	2,510 sq. ft.
Main floor (basement version)	2,580 sq. ft.
Total Living Area:	**2,510/2,580 sq. ft.**
Daylight basement	2,635 sq. ft.
Garage	806 sq. ft.
Exterior Wall Framing:	2x6
Foundation Options:	**Plan #**
Daylight basement	P-7711-3D
Crawlspace	P-7711-3A

(All plans can be built with your choice of foundation and framing. A generic conversion diagram is available. See order form.)

BLUEPRINT PRICE CODE:	D

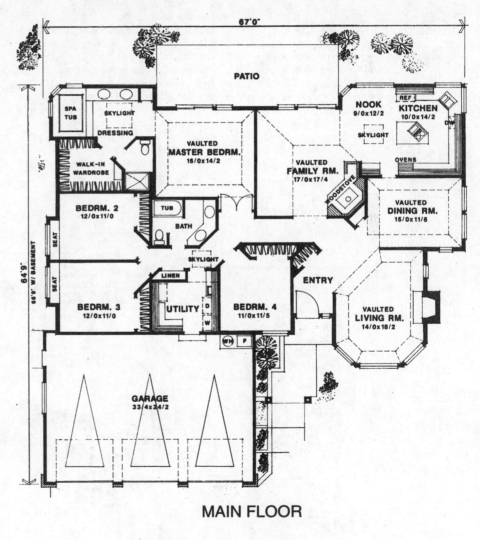

MAIN FLOOR

BASEMENT STAIRWAY LOCATION

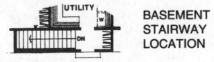

Enjoyable Four-Season Porch

- Outdoor lovers will enjoy the exciting four-season porch and expansive deck this stylish home has to offer.
- Round-top and transom windows adorn the exterior and bring light into the spacious interior. The 14-ft.-high foyer is especially light and airy, offering a view into nearly all of the living areas.
- The huge sunken Great Room has a dramatic see-through fireplace, a stunning back window wall and a 13-ft.-high vaulted ceiling.
- The spacious corner kitchen is highlighted by a functional cooktop island and is open to both the casual and the formal dining areas. Double doors access the porch and deck.
- Two bedrooms and two baths occupy the sleeping wing. The master bedroom is enhanced by a tray ceiling as well as the see-through fireplace. The stunning master bath features a dual-sink vanity and a whirlpool tub under glass.
- The den off the foyer can be used for reading or sleeping overnight guests.

Plan PI-92-535	
Bedrooms: 2	**Baths:** 2½
Living Area:	
Main floor	2,302 sq. ft.
Four-season porch	208 sq. ft.
Total Living Area:	**2,510 sq. ft.**
Daylight basement	2,302 sq. ft.
Garage	912 sq. ft.
Exterior Wall Framing:	2x6
Foundation Options:	

Daylight basement
(All plans can be built with your choice of foundation and framing. A generic conversion diagram is available. See order form.)

BLUEPRINT PRICE CODE: D

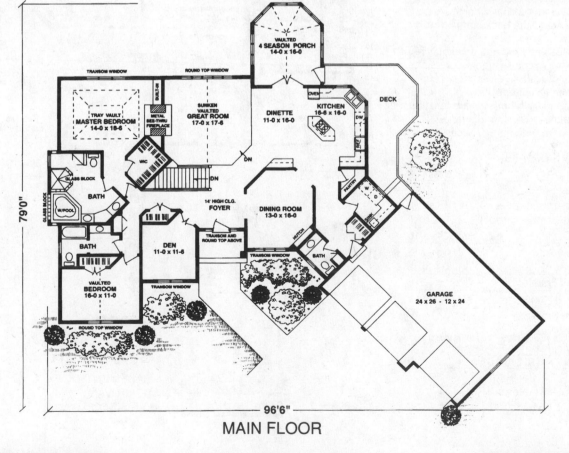

MAIN FLOOR

TO ORDER THIS BLUEPRINT, CALL TOLL-FREE 1-800-547-5570

Plan PI-92-535

PRICES AND DETAILS ON PAGES 12-15

Facade is Best on the Block

- This stylish facade will dress up any neighborhood with its symmetrical bay windows and dramatic rooflines.
- At the center of the interior is a spacious living room with a 10-ft. ceiling, a corner fireplace and a window wall that adjoins a pair of sliders leading to the rear deck.
- The powder room off the hall could also open to the deck, serving as a pool bath.
- Across the hall are the kitchen and morning room, which feature a cooktop island, a step-in pantry and a bayed eating area. The opening above the sink provides a view into the living room as well as access to a handy serving/snack counter.
- The formal dining room is located opposite the foyer.
- The bayed master suite overlooks the rear deck and offers two walk-in closets and a large private bath with a garden tub, separate vanities and an isolated toilet.
- The home also offers two additional bedrooms and a large three-car garage.

Plan DD-2513

Bedrooms: 3	Baths: 2½
Living Area:	
Main floor	2,513 sq. ft.
Total Living Area:	**2,513 sq. ft.**
Standard basement	2,513 sq. ft.
Garage	529 sq. ft.
Exterior Wall Framing:	2x4

Foundation Options:
Standard basement
Crawlspace
Slab
(Typical foundation & framing conversion diagram available—see order form.)

BLUEPRINT PRICE CODE:	D

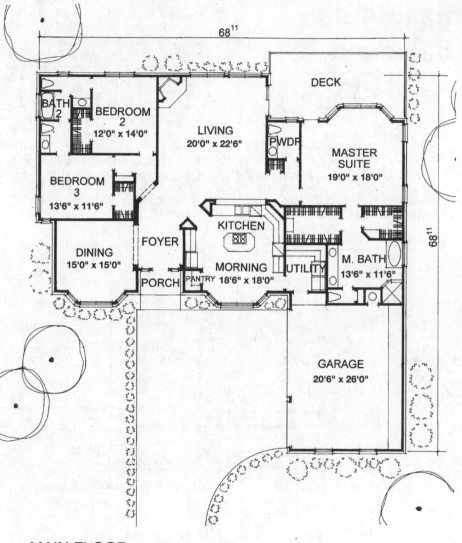

MAIN FLOOR

Beautifully Balanced

- The beautifully balanced facade of this warm one-story wraps around a central courtyard. Inside, exciting window treatments and high ceilings brighten and expand the spaces.
- The elegant front entrance leads to an impressive foyer with a 17-ft.-high ceiling and a clerestory window above. The adjoining dining room boasts a 10-ft.-high tray ceiling.
- A step down from the foyer, the living room is defined by a railing, a 10-ft.

tray ceiling and a fireplace flanked by windows. Another fireplace, this one with an extended hearth for extra seating, can be found in the neighboring family room. The family room also has French doors to the backyard.
- The efficient U-shaped kitchen is paired with a spectacular breakfast room that features a 10½-ft.-high domed ceiling and a built-in brick barbecue.
- The huge master suite boasts a 10-ft. tray ceiling, a walk-in closet and a clever compartmentalized bathroom with a dressing area and a spa tub.
- Three additional bedrooms, one of which would make an ideal office, share a hall bath.

Plan AX-93302	
Bedrooms: 3+	**Baths:** 2½
Living Area:	
Main floor	2,553 sq. ft.
Total Living Area:	**2,553 sq. ft.**
Standard basement	2,424 sq. ft.
Garage	438 sq. ft.
Exterior Wall Framing:	2x6
Foundation Options:	
Standard basement	
Slab	
(All plans can be built with your choice of foundation and framing. A generic conversion diagram is available. See order form.)	
BLUEPRINT PRICE CODE:	D

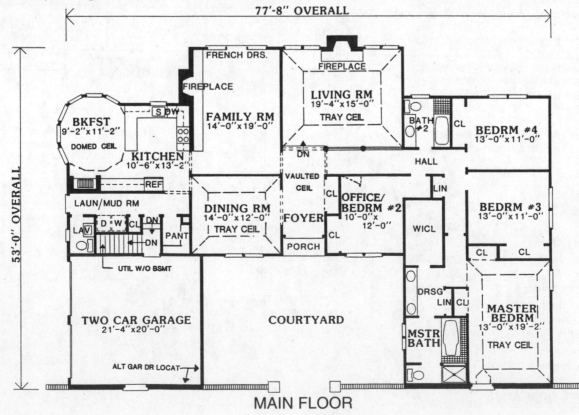

MAIN FLOOR

Plan AX-93302

PRICES AND DETAILS ON PAGES 12-15

Well-Planned Walk-Out

- A handsome exterior, combined with an excellent interior design, makes this plan a popular and smart choice.
- The tiled entry opens to the formal dining room and the Great Room, which are separated by stylish columns and heightened by vaulted ceilings.
- A see-through fireplace with an adjacent wet bar highlights the Great Room. A window wall offers wonderful views of the expansive backyard deck.
- The fantastic kitchen, which is also warmed by the fireplace, offers a built-in desk, a walk-in pantry and an angled snack bar that faces an octagonal breakfast bay.
- The spacious main-floor master suite includes a raised ceiling, a huge walk-in closet and a lavish bath.
- An elegant den, a handy half-bath and a roomy laundry complete the main floor.
- A dramatic, open stairway overlooking an eye-catching planter leads to the walk-out basement. Included are two bedrooms and a full bath, plus an optional bonus room or family room.

Plan AG-9105

Bedrooms: 3+	Baths: 2½
Living Area:	
Main floor	1,838 sq. ft.
Daylight basement (finished)	800 sq. ft.
Total Living Area:	**2,638 sq. ft.**
Daylight basement (unfinished)	1,038 sq. ft.
Garage	462 sq. ft.
Exterior Wall Framing:	2x6

Foundation Options:

Daylight basement

(All plans can be built with your choice of foundation and framing. A generic conversion diagram is available. See order form.)

BLUEPRINT PRICE CODE:	D

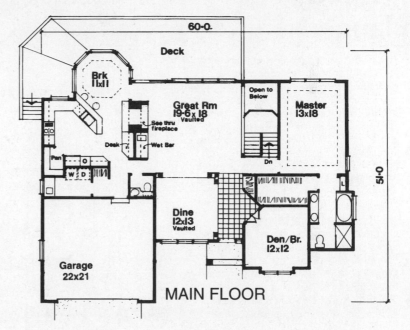

MAIN FLOOR

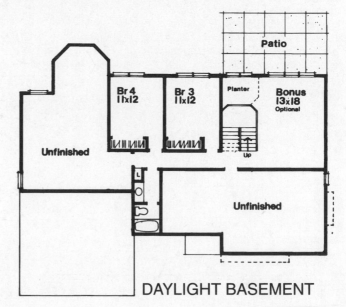

DAYLIGHT BASEMENT

Perfectly Planned

- This home's dramatic architecture and thoughtful room arrangement are a perfect combination.
- Seen from the stunning foyer, the dining room is enhanced by a 17-ft. ceiling. Double doors introduce the den or study, which also has a volume ceiling.
- Straight ahead is the living room, with its 16-ft., 9-in. vaulted ceiling. One set of doors leads to an expansive covered patio and another set leads to the informal region of the home.
- The island kitchen boasts a 16-ft., 9-in. vaulted ceiling, as well as a nice pantry and a sunny breakfast area.
- The family room displays a gorgeous fireplace, built-in shelving and a ceiling that vaults to 15 feet.
- The three secondary bedrooms have easy access to a full bath and a large laundry room.
- On the opposite side of the home, the stunning master suite opens to the patio and features his-and-hers walk-in closets and a private bath with a step-up tub, a separate shower and a bright solarium. Each of the four bedrooms has a 10-ft. ceiling.

MAIN FLOOR

Plan HDS-99-171

Bedrooms: 4+	Baths: 3

Living Area:

Main floor	2,799 sq. ft.
Total Living Area:	**2,799 sq. ft.**
Garage	575 sq. ft.

Exterior Wall Framing:

8-in. concrete block

Foundation Options:

Slab

(All plans can be built with your choice of foundation and framing. A generic conversion diagram is available. See order form.)

BLUEPRINT PRICE CODE:	D

Super Features!

- Super indoor/outdoor living features are the main ingredients of this sprawling one-story home.
- Beyond the columned entry, the foyer features a 16-ft.-high ceiling and is brightened by a fantail transom. The dining room and the living room enjoy ceilings that vault to nearly 11 feet.
- The family room, with a 15-ft. vaulted ceiling, sits at the center of the floor plan and extends to the outdoor living spaces. A handsome fireplace flanked by built-in shelves adds excitement.
- The adjoining kitchen shares the family room's vaulted ceiling and offers a cooktop island, a large pantry and a breakfast nook that opens to the patio.
- The master suite is intended to offer the ultimate in comfort. A double-door entry, a 10-ft. tray ceiling and private patio access are featured in the bedroom. The master bath shares a see-through fireplace with the bedroom.
- Three secondary bedrooms share two full baths at the other end of the home.

Plan HDS-99-164

Bedrooms: 4	Baths: 3
Living Area:	
Main floor	2,962 sq. ft.
Total Living Area:	**2,962 sq. ft.**
Garage	567 sq. ft.

Exterior Wall Framing:
2x4 and 8-in. concrete block

Foundation Options:
Slab
(All plans can be built with your choice of foundation and framing. A generic conversion diagram is available. See order form.)

BLUEPRINT PRICE CODE: D

MAIN FLOOR

Master Suite
Fit for a King

- This sprawling one-story features an extraordinary master suite that stretches from the front of the home to the back.
- Eye-catching windows and columns introduce the foyer, which flows back to the Grand Room. French doors open to the covered veranda, which offers a fabulous summer kitchen.
- The kitchen and bayed morning room are nestled between the Grand Room and a warm Gathering Room. A striking fireplace, an entertainment center and an ale bar are found here. This exciting core of living spaces also offers dramatic views of the outdoors.
- The isolated master suite features a stunning two-sided fireplace and an octagonal lounge area with veranda access. His-and-hers closets, separate dressing areas and a garden tub are other amenities. Across the home, three additional bedroom suites have private access to one of two more full baths.
- The private dining room at the front of the home has a 13-ft. coffered ceiling and a niche for a china cabinet.
- An oversized laundry room is located across from the kitchen and near the entrance to the three-car garage.

Plan EOF-60

Bedrooms: 4	Baths: 3
Living Area:	
Main floor	3,002 sq. ft.
Total Living Area:	**3,002 sq. ft.**
Garage	660 sq. ft.
Exterior Wall Framing:	2x6

Foundation Options:
Slab
(All plans can be built with your choice of foundation and framing. A generic conversion diagram is available. See order form.)

BLUEPRINT PRICE CODE:　　　　E

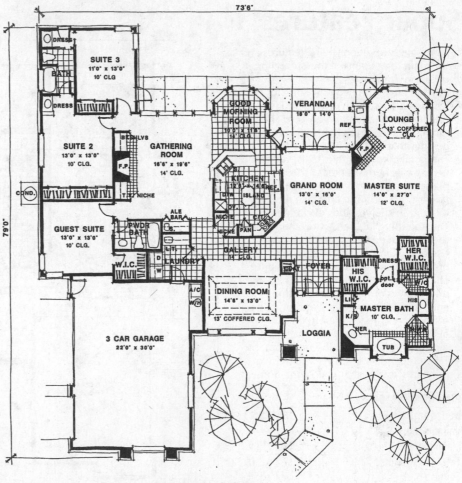

MAIN FLOOR

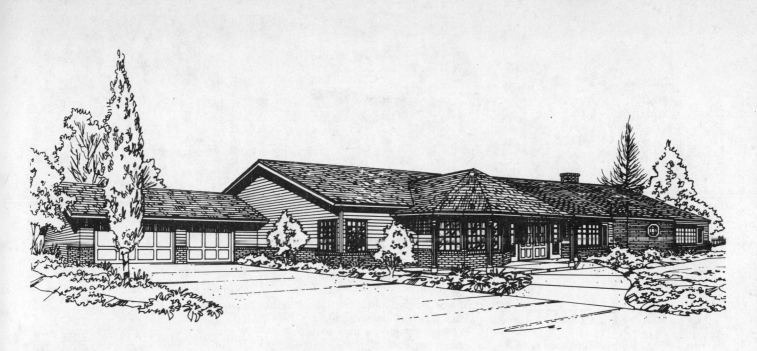

Room for Large Family

- An expansive home, this plan puts a heap of living space for a big, busy family all on one floor.
- The formal entertaining zone, consisting of a large, bright living room and a dining room, is located at the front, to the left as guests enter the large foyer.
- The more casual areas include a huge family room with a massive fireplace, and wet bar, a huge, open kitchen and sunny breakfast area.
- The magnificent master suite is fit for royalty, with its double-door entry, corner fireplace, incredible bath and large closet.
- Bedroom 2 has a private bath, while bedrooms 3 and 4 share a compartmentalized walk-through bath with private lavatory/dressing areas.
- Note the covered porch and double-doored entry at the front, plus the covered patio at the rear.

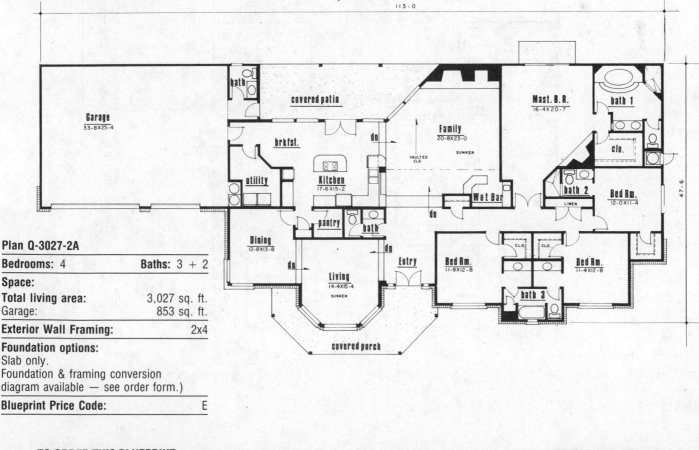

Plan Q-3027-2A

Bedrooms: 4	Baths: 3 + 2

Space:

Total living area:	3,027 sq. ft.
Garage:	853 sq. ft.

Exterior Wall Framing:	2x4

Foundation options:
Slab only.
Foundation & framing conversion diagram available — see order form.)

Blueprint Price Code:	E

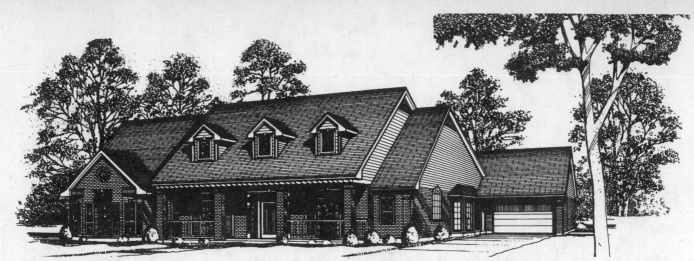

Country Sophistication

- This sophisticated country-style home features a large front porch and a handsome brick exterior.
- Guests will notice the high ceilings throughout the home. Ceilings are 9 ft. if not otherwise specified.
- The formal living areas consist of a secluded dining room and a spacious living room.
- A two-way fireplace is shared by the living room and the family room, both of which have access to a large covered rear porch.
- The bayed breakfast room flows into the kitchen, which boasts an island cooktop, a pantry, a unique window and an adjacent utility room.
- The lavish master suite offers a double shower, a huge walk-in wardrobe and a sitting area with porch access.
- Two additional bedrooms share a private, compartmentalized bath. All of the bedrooms feature large, walk-in closets.
- The good-sized study could serve as a fourth bedroom.

Plan KY-3057	
Bedrooms: 3-4	**Baths:** 3
Living Area:	
Main floor	3,057 sq. ft.
Total Living Area:	**3,057 sq. ft.**
Garage	483 sq. ft.
Exterior Wall Framing:	2x4
Foundation Options:	

Slab
(Typical foundation & framing conversion diagram available—see order form.)

BLUEPRINT PRICE CODE: E

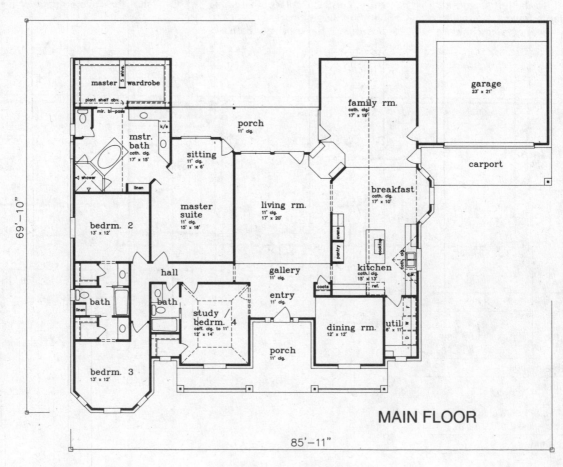

MAIN FLOOR

85'—11"

69'—10"

Plan KY-3057

PRICES AND DETAILS
ON PAGES 12-15

One-Floor Gracious Living

- An impressive roofscape, stately brick with soldier coursing and an impressive columned entry grace the exterior of this exciting single-story home.
- The entry opens to the the free-flowing interior, where the formal areas merge near the den, or guest room.
- The living room offers a window wall to a wide backyard deck, and the dining room is convenient to the kitchen.

- The octagonal island kitchen area offers a sunny breakfast nook with a large corner pantry.
- The spacious family room adjoins the kitchen and features a handsome fireplace and deck access. Laundry facilities and garage access are nearby.
- The lavish master suite with a fireplace and a state-of-the-art bath is privately situated in the left wing.
- Three secondary bedrooms have abundant closet space and share two baths on the right side of the home.
- The entire home features expansive 9-ft. ceilings.

Plan DD-3076

Bedrooms: 4+	**Baths:** 3
Living Area:	
Main floor	3,076 sq. ft.
Total Living Area:	**3,076 sq. ft.**
Standard basement	3,076 sq. ft.
Garage	648 sq. ft.
Exterior Wall Framing:	2x4

Foundation Options:

Standard basement
Crawlspace
Slab

(All plans can be built with your choice of foundation and framing. A generic conversion diagram is available. See order form.)

BLUEPRINT PRICE CODE:	E

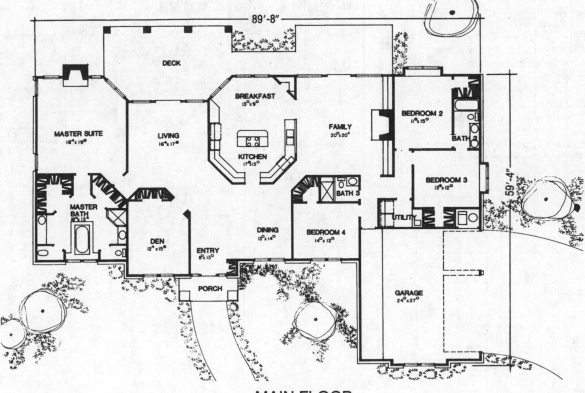

MAIN FLOOR

Distinguished Living

- Beautiful arches, sweeping rooflines and a dramatic entry court distinguish this one-story from all the rest.
- Elegant columns outline the main foyer. To the right, the dining room has a 13-ft. coffered ceiling and an ale bar with a wine rack.
- The centrally located Grand Room can be viewed from the foyer and gallery. French doors and flanking windows allow a view of the veranda as well.
- A large island kitchen and sunny morning room merge with the casual Gathering Room. The combination offers a big fireplace, a TV niche, bookshelves and a handy snack bar.
- The extraordinary master suite flaunts a 12-ft. ceiling, an exciting three-sided fireplace and a TV niche shared with the private bayed lounge. A luxurious bath, a private library and access to the veranda are also featured.
- The two smaller bedroom suites have private baths and generous closets.

Plan EOF-62

Bedrooms: 3	**Baths:** 3½
Living Area:	
Main floor	3,090 sq. ft.
Total Living Area:	**3,090 sq. ft.**
Garage	660 sq. ft.
Exterior Wall Framing:	2x6

Foundation Options:

Slab

(All plans can be built with your choice of foundation and framing. A generic conversion diagram is available. See order form.)

BLUEPRINT PRICE CODE:	E

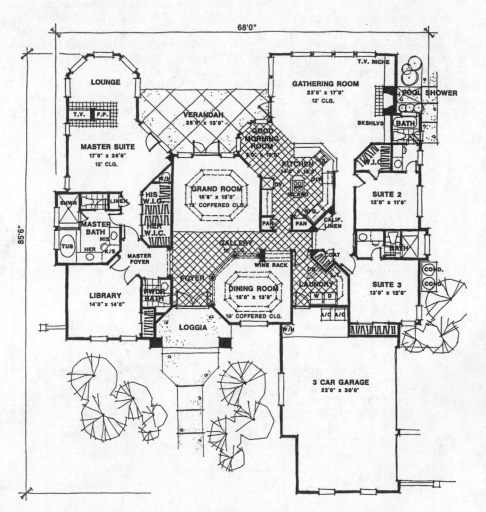

MAIN FLOOR

Spacious Contemporary with Traditional Touch

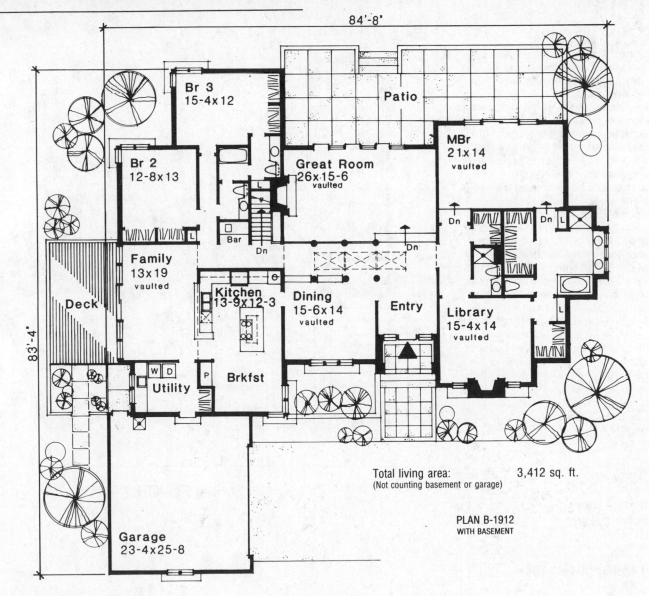

84'-8"

Br 3
15-4x12

Patio

Br 2
12-8x13

Great Room
26x15-6
vaulted

MBr
21x14
vaulted

Family
13x19
vaulted

Deck

83'-4"

Bar

Dn

Kitchen
13-9x12-3

Dining
15-6x14
vaulted

Entry

Dn

Dn

Library
15-4x14
vaulted

W D

P

Utility

Brkfst

Total living area: 3,412 sq. ft.
(Not counting basement or garage)

PLAN B-1912
WITH BASEMENT

Garage
23-4x25-8

Blueprint Price Code E
Plan B-1912

TO ORDER THIS BLUEPRINT,
CALL TOLL-FREE 1-800-547-5570

PRICES AND DETAILS
ON PAGES 12-15   183

Design Excellence

- This stunning one-story home features dramatic detailing and an exceptionally functional floor plan.
- The brick exterior and exciting window treatments beautifully hint at the spectacular interior design.
- High ceilings, a host of built-ins and angled window walls are just some of the highlights.
- The family room showcases a curved wall of windows and a three-way fireplace that can be enjoyed from the adjoining kitchen and breakfast room.
- The octagonal breakfast room offers access to a lovely porch and a handy half-bath. The large island kitchen boasts a snack bar and a unique butler's pantry that connects with the dining room. The sunken living room includes a second fireplace and a window wall.
- The master suite sports a coffered ceiling, a private sitting area and a luxurious bath with a gambrel ceiling.
- Each of the four possible bedrooms has private access to a bath.

Plan KLF-922

Bedrooms: 3+	Baths: 3½

Living Area:

Main floor	3,450 sq. ft.
Total Living Area:	**3,450 sq. ft.**
Garage	698 sq. ft.
Exterior Wall Framing:	2x4

Foundation Options:

Slab

(All plans can be built with your choice of foundation and framing. A generic conversion diagram is available. See order form.)

BLUEPRINT PRICE CODE: E

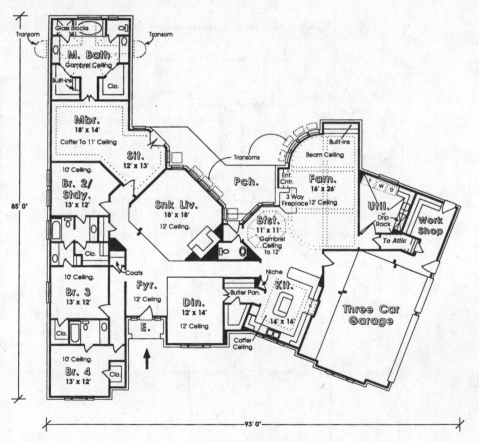

MAIN FLOOR

Plan KLF-922

Bright Design

- Sweeping rooflines, arched transom windows and a stucco exterior give this exciting design a special flair.
- Inside the high, dramatic entry, guests are greeted with a stunning view of the living room, which is expanded by a 12-ft. volume ceiling. This formal expanse is augmented by an oversized bay that looks out onto a covered patio and possible pool area.
- To the left of the foyer is the formal dining room, accented by columns and a 14-ft. receding tray ceiling.
- The island kitchen overlooks a sunny breakfast nook and a large family room, each with 12-ft.-high ceilings. A handy pass-through transports food to the patio, which offers a summer kitchen.
- The master wing includes a large bedroom with a 10-ft.-high coffered ceiling, a sitting area with patio access, a massive walk-in closet and a sun-drenched garden bath.
- The private den/study could also serve as an extra bedroom.
- Two to three more bedrooms share two full baths. The front bedrooms boast 12-ft. ceilings and the rear bedroom is accented by a 10-ft. ceiling.

Plan HDS-90-814

Bedrooms: 3+	**Baths:** 3½

Living Area:

Main floor	3,743 sq. ft.
Total Living Area:	**3,743 sq. ft.**
Garage	725 sq. ft.

Exterior Wall Framing:
2x4 and 8-in. concrete block

Foundation Options:
Slab
(All plans can be built with your choice of foundation and framing. A generic conversion diagram is available. See order form.)

BLUEPRINT PRICE CODE: F

MAIN FLOOR

Plan HDS-90-814

Luxuries Galore

- Ideally suited for a scenic site, this deluxe walk-out design offers panoramic views of the outdoors and a long list of luxuries.
- Warm brick accents highlight the exterior, where a covered porch leads to a large entry. Straight ahead, the sunken living room and the spacious family room feature window walls overlooking a huge covered deck.
- The strategically placed woodstove warms the family room as well as the adjoining kitchen and nook. The island kitchen boasts deck access, a large walk-in pantry, a glass-filled nook and a top-notch laundry room.
- The formal dining room is just across the hall and features a charming window seat.
- The master bedroom features private deck access, a roomy walk-in closet and a superb bath that offers a bayed step-up spa tub, a separate shower and a built-in desk or makeup table.
- Another bedroom and an innovative hall bath complete the main floor.
- Downstairs, you'll find two more bedrooms, a large bath, two storage areas and a recreation room with a woodstove and a full-service wet bar. The storage areas are not included in the basement square footage.

Plan NW-744

Bedrooms: 4	Baths: 3½
Living Area:	
Main floor	2,539 sq. ft.
Daylight basement	1,461 sq. ft.
Total Living Area:	**4,000 sq. ft.**
Garage	904 sq. ft.
Storage	948 sq. ft.
Exterior Wall Framing:	2x6

Foundation Options:

Daylight basement

(All plans can be built with your choice of foundation and framing. A generic conversion diagram is available. See order form.)

BLUEPRINT PRICE CODE: G

MAIN FLOOR

110' x 75'6"

DAYLIGHT BASEMENT

TO ORDER THIS BLUEPRINT, CALL TOLL-FREE 1-800-547-5570

Plan NW-744

PRICES AND DETAILS ON PAGES 12-15

Luscious and Luxurious

- This stately home's appealing exterior gives way to a luxurious and impressive interior.
- The step-down parlour is the centerpiece of the home, and boasts a 13-ft.-high flat ceiling and a full-wall fireplace and entertainment center.
- The master suite features a step-down sitting room and a corner fireplace. The opulent master bath has a linen island, a morning kitchen and a bidet.
- The library offers private access to the main hall bath.
- Graceful arches and a high, coffered ceiling adorn the formal dining room.
- The spacious kitchen includes a cooktop island, a walk-in pantry, a menu desk, a vegetable sink and a bright 'good morning' room.
- Each of the three secondary suites has a large closet and direct access to a bath.
- The huge gathering room boasts wraparound glass and a full fireplace and entertainment wall.

Plan EOF-58	
Bedrooms: 4-5	**Baths:** 4
Living Area:	
Main floor	4,021 sq. ft.
Total Living Area:	**4,021 sq. ft.**
Garage	879 sq. ft.
Exterior Wall Framing:	2x4
Foundation Options:	
Slab	
(Typical foundation & framing conversion diagram available—see order form.)	
BLUEPRINT PRICE CODE:	**G**

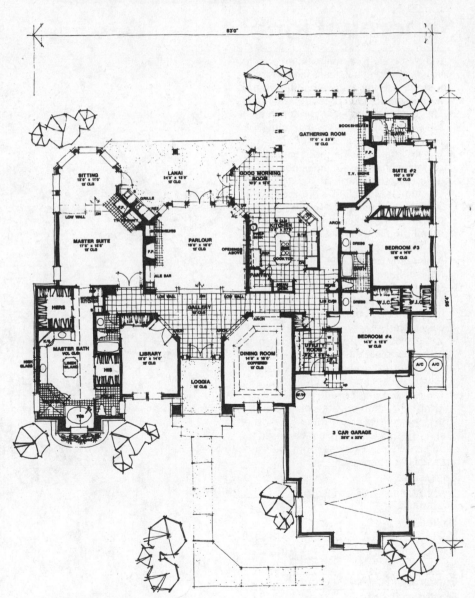

MAIN FLOOR

Superbly Done!

- A durable tile roof, magnificent concrete columns and extravagant fixed glass are a prelude to the many amenities found in this sensational contemporary home.
- The raised foyer offers a breathtaking view of the spectacular lanai and pool area through French doors.
- The fascinating living room has a high ceiling with exposed rafters and a dramatic curved wall of glass!
- The full-sized kitchen is equipped with a cooktop island and a serving counter that faces the gallery and family room. A walk-in pantry and a beautiful morning room are other features.
- An inviting fireplace, a TV center and a refreshing ale bar beckon guests into the spacious family room, which has dual access to the pool deck. The bar's handy pass-through window provides easy beverage service to the pool area.
- Three secondary bedrooms and two full baths complete this wing of the home. Each bedroom has a walk-in closet and private access to one of the baths.
- The isolated master suite is exquisitely furnished with a private sitting area, a three-way fireplace, his-and-hers closets and dressing areas, a glass-enclosed tub and a personal exercise room, plus a raised deck and spa.

Plan EOF-70

Bedrooms: 4	Baths: 3½
Living Area:	
Main floor	5,013 sq. ft.
Total Living Area:	**5,013 sq. ft.**
Garage	902 sq. ft.
Exterior Wall Framing:	concrete block

Foundation Options:

Slab

(All plans can be built with your choice of foundation and framing. A generic conversion diagram is available. See order form.)

BLUEPRINT PRICE CODE: G

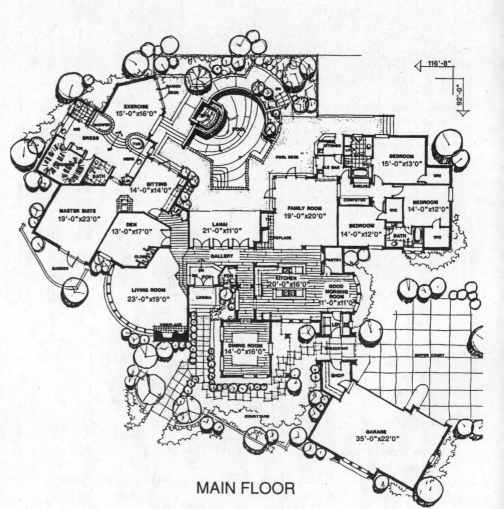

MAIN FLOOR

Plan EOF-70

PRICES AND DETAILS ON PAGES 12-15

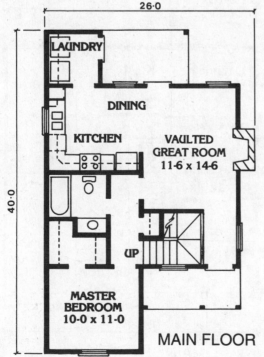

Open Design in Compact Traditional

- An instant feeling of spaciousness and openness is created in this hospitable home with a vaulted Great Room and open-railed stairway.
- Additional appeal comes from a wood-burning fireplace, visible from the adjoining kitchen and dining area.
- The spacious kitchen has a pantry and attached walk-in laundry room.
- The main-level master bedroom is well isolated from the living areas, yet easily accessible to the children's bedrooms on the upper level.

UPPER FLOOR

BEDROOM 10-0 x 11-0

DOWN

BEDROOM 10-0 x 11-0

MAIN FLOOR

26-0

40-0

LAUNDRY

DINING

KITCHEN

VAULTED GREAT ROOM 11-6 x 14-6

UP

MASTER BEDROOM 10-0 x 11-0

Plan V-1098	
Bedrooms: 3	**Baths:** 2
Space:	
Upper floor	396 sq. ft.
Main floor	702 sq. ft.
Total Living Area	**1,098 sq. ft.**
Exterior Wall Framing	2x6
Foundation options:	
Crawlspace	
(Foundation & framing conversion diagram available—see order form.)	
Blueprint Price Code	**A**

Compact Three-Bedroom

- Both openness and privacy are possible in this economical three-bedroom home design.
- The bright living room boasts a 17-ft. vaulted ceiling, a warming fireplace and a corner window. A high clerestory window lets in additional natural light.
- The modern, U-shaped kitchen features a handy corner pantry and a versatile snack bar.
- The adjacent open dining area provides access to a backyard deck through sliding glass doors.
- A lovely corner window brightens the secluded master bedroom, which also includes a roomy walk-in closet and private access to a compartmentalized hall bath.
- Upstairs, two good-sized bedrooms share a second split bath.

Plan B-101-8501

Bedrooms: 3	Baths: 2
Living Area:	
Upper floor	400 sq. ft.
Main floor	846 sq. ft.
Total Living Area:	**1,246 sq. ft.**
Garage	400 sq. ft.
Standard basement	846 sq. ft.
Exterior Wall Framing:	2x4

Foundation Options:

Standard basement

(All plans can be built with your choice of foundation and framing. A generic conversion diagram is available. See order form.)

BLUEPRINT PRICE CODE:	A

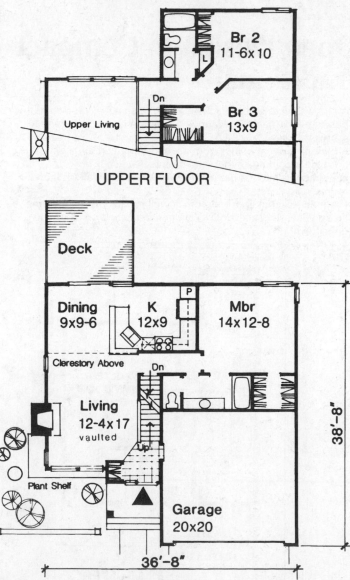

UPPER FLOOR

MAIN FLOOR

TO ORDER THIS BLUEPRINT, CALL TOLL-FREE 1-800-547-5570   Plan B-101-8501   *PRICES AND DETAILS ON PAGES 12-15*

CONTEMPORARY EXTERIOR

TRADITIONAL EXTERIOR

Economical Attraction

- This great-looking three-bedroom home is as economical as it is attractive. Two exterior styles (both are included in the blueprints) offer you the choice of a bold contemporary look or a more traditional facade.
- The exciting space-saving floor plan incorporates an open living area and a main-floor master suite with a dual-access bath.
- The vaulted living room is brightened by tall windows and warmed by a fireplace. A clerestory window lies between the living room and the dining room, which has sliding glass doors to a rear deck. The kitchen features an angled sink set into a snack bar.
- Upstairs, the balcony hall overlooks the living room. Two nice-sized bedrooms, one of which has a walk-in closet, and a full bath are found here.

Plan B-8323

Bedrooms: 3	Baths: 2
Living Area:	
Upper floor	400 sq. ft.
Main floor	846 sq. ft.
Total Living Area:	**1,246 sq. ft.**
Standard basement	846 sq. ft.
Garage	400 sq. ft.
Exterior Wall Framing:	2x4

Foundation Options:

Standard basement

(All plans can be built with your choice of foundation and framing. A generic conversion diagram is available. See order form.)

BLUEPRINT PRICE CODE:	A

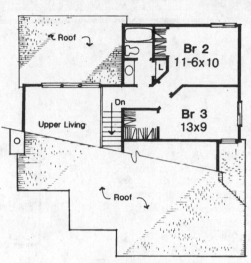

UPPER FLOOR

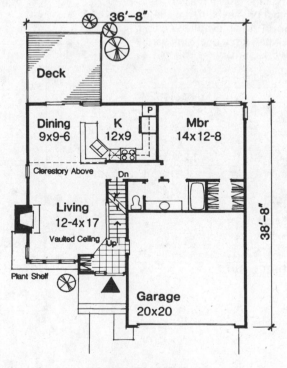

MAIN FLOOR

Plan B-8323

PRICES AND DETAILS ON PAGES 12-15 191

Fancy Country Styling

- With a covered front porch and gables above, this affordable two-story home fancies country styling.
- Off the lovely covered porch is a soaring entry, open to the upper level and featuring an angled stairway focal point.
- A large living area with a fireplace and a patio view adjoins the dining room, which opens to the outdoors.
- Convenient main-floor laundry facilities and a half-bath are located near the garage entrance.
- The upper level includes a master bedroom with a private bath, a walk-in closet and an 11-ft.-high vaulted ceiling. Another full bath with a dual-sink vanity serves the two secondary bedrooms.

Plan AG-1201

Bedrooms: 3	Baths: 2½
Living Area:	
Upper floor	668 sq. ft.
Main floor	620 sq. ft.
Total Living Area:	**1,288 sq. ft.**
Standard basement	620 sq. ft.
Garage	420 sq. ft.
Exterior Wall Framing:	2x4
Foundation Options:	

Standard basement
(All plans can be built with your choice of foundation and framing. A generic conversion diagram is available. See order form.)

BLUEPRINT PRICE CODE:	**A**

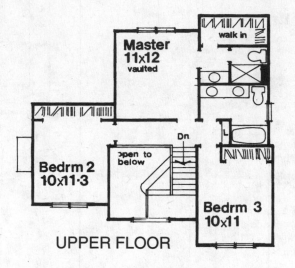

UPPER FLOOR

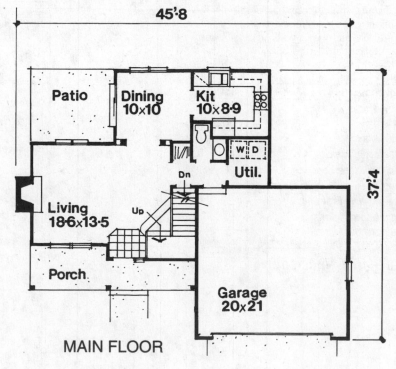

MAIN FLOOR

Plan AG-1201

PRICES AND DETAILS
ON PAGES 12-15

Charming and Space-Efficient

- Perfectly sized for a narrow lot, this charming modern cottage boasts space efficiency and affordability.
- The inviting raised foyer steps down into the two-story-high vaulted living room. Brightened by lovely front windows with high transoms, the living room also offers a handsome fireplace.
- The adjoining dining area is highlighted by overhead plant shelves and features sliding glass doors to a backyard deck.
- The cleverly designed, space-saving kitchen includes a stylish snack counter and a pantry shelf.
- Enhanced by a bright boxed-out bay with a window seat, the master bedroom also has a roomy walk-in closet and private bathroom access.
- Upstairs, a second bedroom and a loft or third bedroom share a convenient full bath with a linen closet.

Plan B-133-8510

Bedrooms: 2+	Baths: 2
Living Area:	
Upper floor	405 sq. ft.
Main floor	891 sq. ft.
Total Living Area:	**1,296 sq. ft.**
Standard basement	891 sq. ft.
Garage	402 sq. ft.
Exterior Wall Framing:	2x4

Foundation Options:

Standard basement

(All plans can be built with your choice of foundation and framing. A generic conversion diagram is available. See order form.)

BLUEPRINT PRICE CODE: A

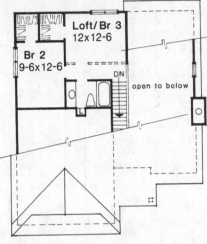

UPPER FLOOR

MAIN FLOOR

Off to a Great Start!

- Perfectly sized for families starting out, this charming feature-filled country home is a great choice!
- The entry, which flows directly into the Great Room, is graced by overhead plant shelves and a 10-ft.-high ceiling.
- Warmed by a fireplace, the Great Room boasts a soaring 15-ft. vaulted ceiling. Sliding glass doors open to a sunny backyard patio.
- The adjacent formal dining room is easily serviced by the bright and airy kitchen, which includes a bay-windowed breakfast area, a pantry and a laundry closet. Access to the two-car garage is conveniently nearby.
- Upstairs, a railed balcony overlooks the Great Room. The charming master suite is secluded for privacy and features a roomy walk-in closet and its own bath.
- Two additional bedrooms and a hallway bath complete the upper floor.

Plan AG-1301-A

Bedrooms: 3	Baths: 2½
Living Area:	
Upper floor	652 sq. ft.
Main floor	673 sq. ft.
Total Living Area:	**1,325 sq. ft.**
Standard basement	620 sq. ft.
Garage	406 sq. ft.
Exterior Wall Framing:	2x4

Foundation Options:

Standard basement
Crawlspace
(All plans can be built with your choice of foundation and framing. A generic conversion diagram is available. See order form.)

BLUEPRINT PRICE CODE:	**A**

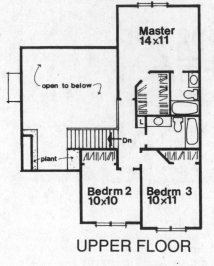

UPPER FLOOR

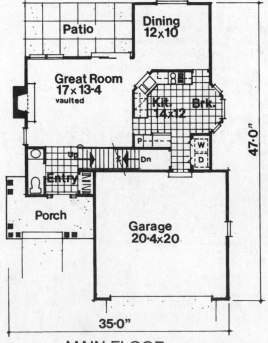

MAIN FLOOR

TO ORDER THIS BLUEPRINT, CALL TOLL-FREE 1-800-547-5570

Plan AG-1301-A

PRICES AND DETAILS ON PAGES 12-15

Striking Stone Chimney

- With tall windows and a rustic stone chimney, the striking facade of this home demands attention.
- The sheltered entry leads into a raised foyer, which steps down to the sunny living room and its dramatic 16-ft. vaulted ceiling.
- A handsome fireplace warms the living room and the adjoining dining room, which offers access to an inviting deck.
- A cozy breakfast nook is included in the efficient, open-design kitchen. A special feature is the convenient pass-through to the dining room.
- A skylighted staircase leads upstairs to the master suite, with its private bath and large walk-in closet.
- A second bedroom shares another full bath with a loft or third bedroom.
- A dramatic balcony overlooks the living room below.

Plan B-224-8512

Bedrooms: 2+	**Baths: 2½**
Living Area:	
Upper floor	691 sq. ft.
Main floor	668 sq. ft.
Total Living Area:	**1,359 sq. ft.**
Standard basement	668 sq. ft.
Garage	458 sq. ft.
Exterior Wall Framing:	**2x4**

Foundation Options:

Standard basement

(All plans can be built with your choice of foundation and framing. A generic conversion diagram is available. See order form.)

BLUEPRINT PRICE CODE:	**A**

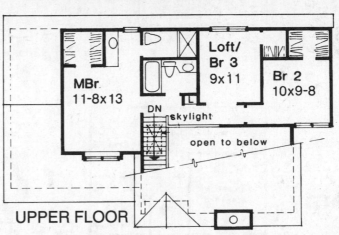

UPPER FLOOR

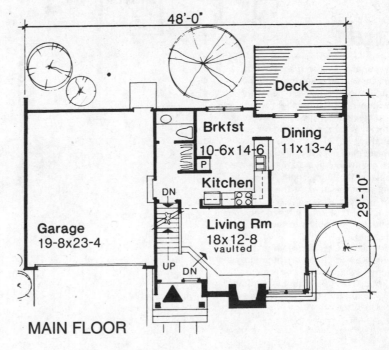

MAIN FLOOR

Economy and Beauty

Measuring in at only 1,410 sq. ft., this home will be very economical to build. What you'll also discover are beautiful arched windows which highlight the exterior, underscoring the fact that small doesn't mean you have to settle for less design quality.

The traffic plan is efficiently laid out to maximize the usable living area. Accented by a fireplace, the living room flows into the dining room to increase the visual feeling of spaciousness.

The practical U-shaped kitchen includes a handy pantry and opens to the nook for informal dining.

Upstairs, the master bedroom includes a convenient walk-in closet brightened by an illuminating skylight and a convenient vanity. Notice how the main bath adjoins the master bedroom via a pocket door for easy accessibility.

skylite **skylite**

arch

Bedrm. 2
10/0x11/8

Master
12/4x13/6

dn.

open to below

Bedrm. 3
10/0x11/0

seat

PLAN R-2099
WITHOUT BASEMENT
(CRAWLSPACE FOUNDATION)

39'-0"

Dining
10/0x10/0

Kit.
ref.

Nook
8/10x11/10

d.w.

pan

Living
12/4x17/4

up

w.h.

f.

Garage
19/4x21/8

42'-0"

Main floor:	730 sq. ft.
Upper floor:	680 sq. ft.
Total living area: (Not counting garage)	1,410 sq. ft.

Starter Home Offers Options

- Country styling adds to the appeal of this ideal starter home.
- Open living areas and little wasted hall space maximize the main-floor layout.
- A large living room sits off the foyer. Two front windows overlook the covered front porch.
- The roomy kitchen and dining area share the rear of the home. Sliders in the dining area lead outdoors.
- The homeowner will enjoy the convenient and generous-sized laundry room on the main floor, which features a folding counter that could double as a work desk.
- Three bedrooms are located on the upper level which offers a choice of one or two baths.
- An optional two-car garage is also available, adding four feet to the overall width of the home.

Plan GL-1430-P

Bedrooms: 3	Baths: 1½-2½
Space:	
Upper floor	720 sq. ft.
Main floor	710 sq. ft.
Total Living Area	**1,430 sq. ft.**
Basement	710 sq. ft.
Garage	341 sq. ft.
Optional two-car garage	427 sq. ft.
Exterior Wall Framing	**2x4**
Foundation options:	
Standard Basement	
(Foundation & framing conversion diagram available—see order form.)	
Blueprint Price Code	**A**

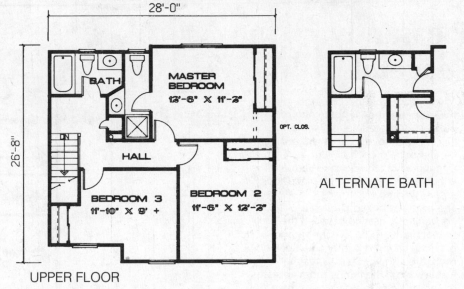

28'-0"

26'-8"

BATH

MASTER BEDROOM
12'-6" X 11'-2"

OPT. CLOS.

DN

HALL

BEDROOM 3
11'-10" X 9' +

BEDROOM 2
11'-6" X 12'-2"

UPPER FLOOR

ALTERNATE BATH

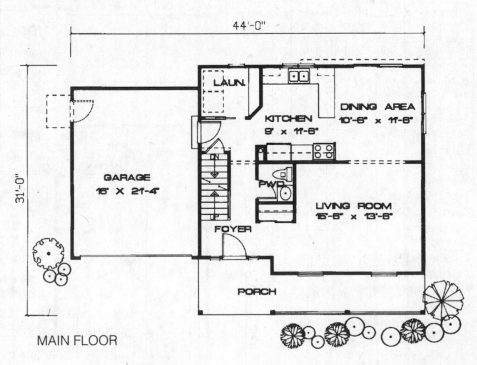

44'-0"

31'-0"

LAUN.

DINING AREA
10'-6" x 11'-6"

KITCHEN
9' x 11'-6"

GARAGE
16' X 21'-4"

DN

PWR.

LIVING ROOM
15'-6" X 13'-6"

FOYER

PORCH

MAIN FLOOR

Pleasantly Peaceful

- The covered front porch of this lovely two-story traditional home offers a pleasant and peaceful welcome.
- Off the open foyer is an oversized family room, drenched with sunlight through a French door and surrounding windows. A handsome fireplace adds further warmth.
- The neatly arranged kitchen is conveniently nestled between the formal dining room and the sunny breakfast room. A pantry and a powder room are also within easy reach.
- A stairway off the family room accesses the upper floor, which houses three bedrooms. The isolated master bedroom features a 10-ft. tray ceiling, a huge walk-in closet and a private bath offering a vaulted ceiling, an oval garden tub and a separate shower.
- The two secondary bedrooms share another full bath.

Plan FB-1466

Bedrooms: 3	Baths: 2½
Living Area:	
Upper floor	703 sq. ft.
Main floor	763 sq. ft.
Total Living Area:	**1,466 sq. ft.**
Daylight basement	763 sq. ft.
Garage	426 sq. ft.
Storage	72 sq. ft.
Exterior Wall Framing:	2x4

Foundation Options:

Daylight basement

Crawlspace

(All plans can be built with your choice of foundation and framing. A generic conversion diagram is available. See order form.)

BLUEPRINT PRICE CODE: A

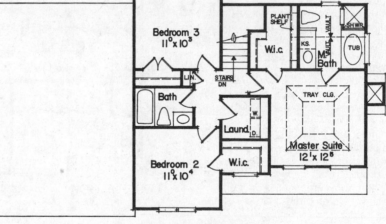

UPPER FLOOR

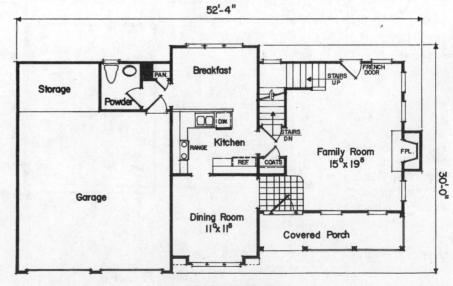

MAIN FLOOR

TO ORDER THIS BLUEPRINT, CALL TOLL-FREE 1-800-547-5570   Plan FB-1466   *PRICES AND DETAILS ON PAGES 12-15*

Carefree and Comfortable

- A dramatic 17-ft.-high entry with an illuminating clerestory window and an overhead balcony highlights this home's open and carefree interior.
- The airy, spacious feeling continues into the adjoining den with corner windows and a 17-ft. vaulted ceiling.

- The central living room is warmed by a handsome fireplace. The adjacent dining room offers sliding glass doors to a backyard patio.
- The cozy country kitchen boasts a pantry and a high 10-ft. ceiling.
- Upstairs, the master suite features a spacious walk-in closet, which frees up additional wall space and allows for a flexible furniture arrangement.
- Measuring just 30 ft. wide, this home is well suited for a narrow lot.

Plan R-2097	
Bedrooms: 3	**Baths:** 2½
Living Area:	
Upper floor	698 sq. ft.
Main floor	768 sq. ft.
Total Living Area:	**1,466 sq. ft.**
Garage	410 sq. ft.
Exterior Wall Framing:	2x6

Foundation Options:

Crawlspace
(All plans can be built with your choice of foundation and framing. A generic conversion diagram is available. See order form.)

BLUEPRINT PRICE CODE:	**A**

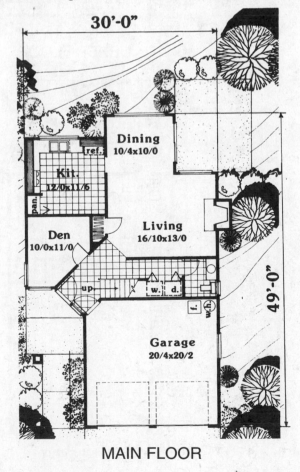

MAIN FLOOR

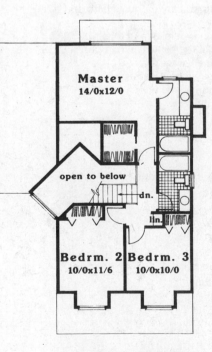

UPPER FLOOR

FRONT VIEW

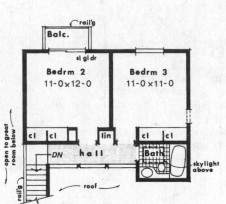

REAR VIEW

More for Less

- Big in function but small in square footage, this passive-solar plan can be built as a single-family home or as part of a multiple-unit complex.
- The floor plan flows visually from its open foyer to its high-ceilinged Great Room, where a high-efficiency fireplace is flanked by glass. Sliding glass doors open to a brilliant south-facing sun room that overlooks a backyard terrace.
- The eat-in kitchen has a pass-through to a bright dining area that opens to a nice side terrace.
- The master bedroom boasts a pair of tall windows, a deluxe private bath and two roomy closets.
- A handy laundry closet and a half-bath are located at the center of the floor plan, near the garage.
- Upstairs, a skylighted bath serves two more bedrooms, one with a private, rear-facing balcony.

Plan K-507-S

Bedrooms: 3	Baths: 2½
Living Area:	
Upper floor	397 sq. ft.
Main floor	915 sq. ft.
Sun room	162 sq. ft.
Total Living Area:	**1,474 sq. ft.**
Standard basement	915 sq. ft.
Garage	400 sq. ft.
Exterior Wall Framing:	2x4 or 2x6

Foundation Options:

Standard basement
Slab

(All plans can be built with your choice of foundation and framing. A generic conversion diagram is available. See order form.)

BLUEPRINT PRICE CODE:	A

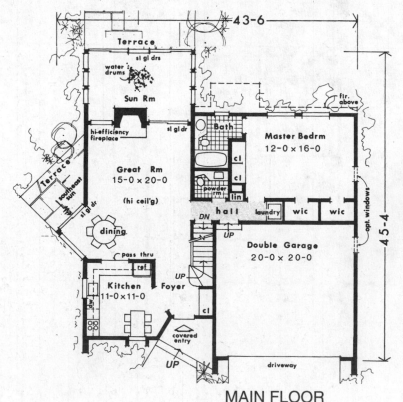

UPPER FLOOR

MAIN FLOOR

Plan K-507-S

Attractive, Sunny Design

- This versatile plan features a striking exterior and numerous energy-saving extras, like passive-solar heating, glazed roof panels with adjustable shades, and operable skylights.
- An air-lock vestibule, which minimizes heat loss, leads into the spacious living room. This room has a stone fireplace, an operable clerestory window, a 14½-ft. sloped ceiling and sliding doors to the glass-roofed solar room.
- The adjacent dining room also has a sloped ceiling and offers sliding glass doors to a backyard terrace.
- The U-shaped kitchen features a laundry closet, a handy pantry and an eating bar for informal dining.
- The skylighted upper-floor hallway leads to the master suite, which offers a private balcony and a personal bath with a whirlpool tub.
- Two additional bedrooms, one with a bay window, share a second full bath.

Plan K-521-C	
Bedrooms: 3	**Baths:** 2½
Living Area:	
Upper floor	686 sq. ft.
Main floor	690 sq. ft.
Solar room	106 sq. ft.
Total Living Area:	**1,482 sq. ft.**
Standard basement	690 sq. ft.
Garage	437 sq. ft.
Exterior Wall Framing:	2x4 or 2x6
Foundation Options:	

Standard basement
Slab
(All plans can be built with your choice of foundation and framing. A generic conversion diagram is available. See order form.)

BLUEPRINT PRICE CODE:	A

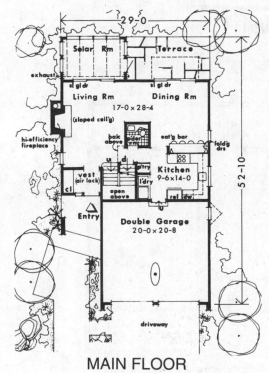

MAIN FLOOR

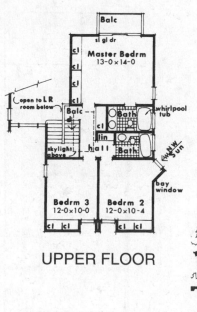

UPPER FLOOR

VIEW INTO LIVING ROOM AND SOLAR ROOM

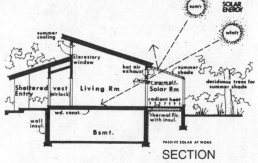

SECTION

Compact, Cozy, Inviting

- Full-width porches at the front and the rear of this home add plenty of space for outdoor living and entertaining.
- The huge, centrally located living room is the core of this three-bedroom home. The room features a corner fireplace, a 16-ft. sloped, open-beam ceiling and access to the back porch.
- The dining room combines with the kitchen to create an open, more spacious atmosphere. A long, central work island and a compact laundry closet are other space-saving features.
- The main-floor master suite offers a private bath with dual vanities and a large walk-in closet. Two additional bedrooms, a full bath and an intimate sitting area that overlooks the living room and entry are upstairs.
- A separate two-car garage is included with the blueprints.

Plan E-1421

Bedrooms: 3	Baths: 2
Living Area:	
Upper floor	561 sq. ft.
Main floor	924 sq. ft.
Total Living Area:	**1,485 sq. ft.**
Standard basement	924 sq. ft.
Exterior Wall Framing:	2x6

Foundation Options:
Standard basement
Crawlspace
Slab
(All plans can be built with your choice of foundation and framing. A generic conversion diagram is available. See order form.)

BLUEPRINT PRICE CODE: A

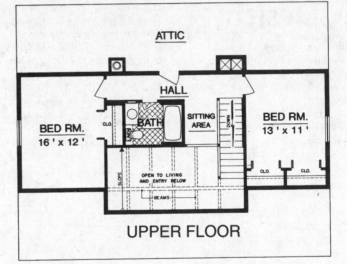

UPPER FLOOR

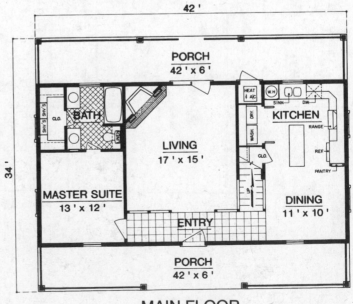

MAIN FLOOR

TO ORDER THIS BLUEPRINT, CALL TOLL-FREE 1-800-547-5570

Plan E-1421

PRICES AND DETAILS ON PAGES 12-15

Country Kitchen Centerpiece

- This charming home features a rustic combination of stone and wood, which is offset by two half-round windows in the attention-getting gables.
- The centerpiece of the floor plan is the spacious country kitchen, featuring ample work surfaces, a nice-sized eating area with built-in bookshelves and access to a large backyard deck.
- The formal dining area is highlighted by a dramatic three-sided fireplace that is shared with the adjoining living room. The living room is enhanced by a dramatic 17-ft. vaulted ceiling.
- A powder room and a deluxe laundry room are easily reached from all of the main-floor rooms as well as the garage.
- Upstairs, the master bedroom boasts a 12-ft. vaulted ceiling that reveals a plant shelf above the entrance to the private bath and the walk-in closet.
- The two smaller bedrooms are separated by a full bath. The front-facing bedroom features an arched window set into a high-ceilinged area.

Plan B-87107

Bedrooms: 3	Baths: 2½
Living Area:	
Upper floor	722 sq. ft.
Main floor	834 sq. ft.
Total Living Area:	**1,556 sq. ft.**
Standard basement	834 sq. ft.
Garage	470 sq. ft.
Exterior Wall Framing:	2x4

Foundation Options:

Standard basement

(All plans can be built with your choice of foundation and framing. A generic conversion diagram is available. See order form.)

BLUEPRINT PRICE CODE: B

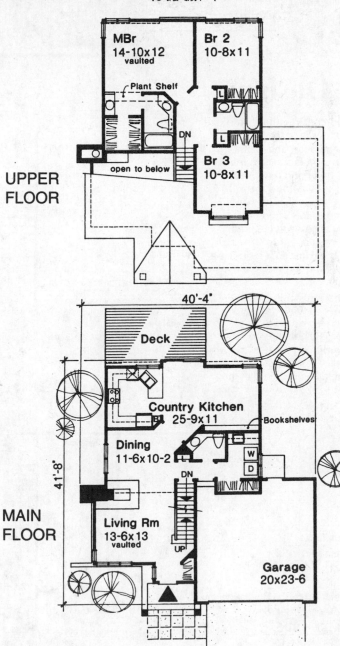

Classy Design

- Brick and wood construction, combined with traditional design overtones, gives this two-story character and class.
- A covered entry porch opens to the two-story-high foyer and the formal dining room. To the left lies the full-service kitchen, which features an angled serving bar, lots of counter space and easy access to the laundry room and the two-car garage.
- The adjoining breakfast area includes a pantry closet, a built-in desk and a French door to the backyard.
- The heart of the home is the spacious Great Room, which features an inviting fireplace framed by windows.
- The upper floor is highlighted by a spectacular overlook and an equally stunning master suite. The succulent master bath includes a vaulted ceiling and a corner spa tub.

Plan FB-1563

Bedrooms: 3	Baths: 2½
Living Area:	
Upper floor	766 sq. ft.
Main floor	797 sq. ft.
Total Living Area:	**1,563 sq. ft.**
Daylight basement	766 sq. ft.
Garage	440 sq. ft.
Exterior Wall Framing:	2x4

Foundation Options:

Daylight basement
Slab
(Typical foundation & framing conversion diagram available—see order form.)

BLUEPRINT PRICE CODE: B

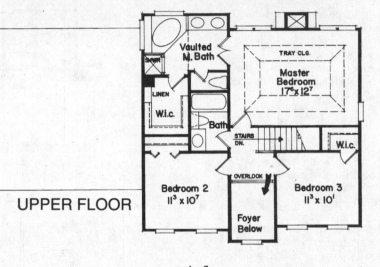

UPPER FLOOR

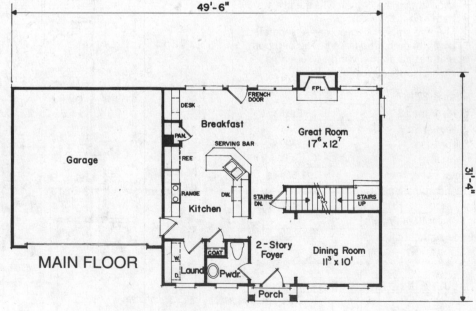

MAIN FLOOR

*TO ORDER THIS BLUEPRINT,
CALL TOLL-FREE 1-800-547-5570*

Plan FB-1563

*PRICES AND DETAILS
ON PAGES 12-15*

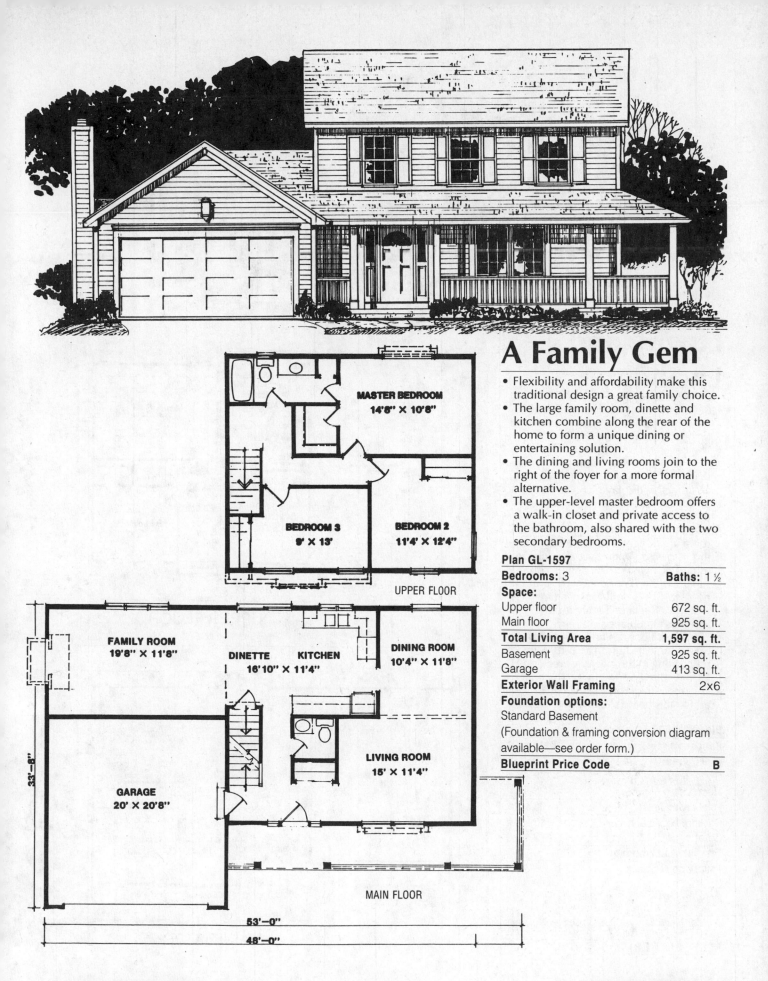

A Family Gem

- Flexibility and affordability make this traditional design a great family choice.
- The large family room, dinette and kitchen combine along the rear of the home to form a unique dining or entertaining solution.
- The dining and living rooms join to the right of the foyer for a more formal alternative.
- The upper-level master bedroom offers a walk-in closet and private access to the bathroom, also shared with the two secondary bedrooms.

Plan GL-1597

Bedrooms: 3	Baths: 1 ½
Space:	
Upper floor	672 sq. ft.
Main floor	925 sq. ft.
Total Living Area	**1,597 sq. ft.**
Basement	925 sq. ft.
Garage	413 sq. ft.
Exterior Wall Framing	2x6

Foundation options:

Standard Basement

(Foundation & framing conversion diagram available—see order form.)

Blueprint Price Code	B

MASTER BEDROOM 14'8" × 10'8"

BEDROOM 3 9' × 13'

BEDROOM 2 11'4" × 12'4"

UPPER FLOOR

FAMILY ROOM 19'8" × 11'8"

DINETTE KITCHEN 16'10" × 11'4"

DINING ROOM 10'4" × 11'8"

LIVING ROOM 15' × 11'4"

GARAGE 20' × 20'8"

33'-8"

53'-0"

48'-0"

MAIN FLOOR

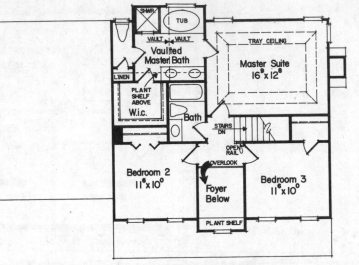

Luxury and Livability

- Big on style, this modest-sized home features a quaint Colonial exterior and an open interior.
- The covered front porch leads to a two-story foyer that opens to the formal living and dining rooms. A coat closet, an attractive display niche and a powder room are centrally located, as is the stairway to the upper floor.
- The kitchen, breakfast nook and family room are designed so that each room has its own definition yet also functions as part of a whole. The angled sink separates the kitchen from the breakfast nook, which is outlined by a bay window. The large family room includes a fireplace.
- The upper floor has an exceptional master suite, featuring an 8-ft., 6-in. tray ceiling in the sleeping area and an 11-ft. vaulted ceiling in the spa bath.
- Two more bedrooms and a balcony hall add to this home's luxury and livability.

Plan FB-1600	
Bedrooms: 3	**Baths:** 2½
Living Area:	
Upper floor	772 sq. ft.
Main floor	828 sq. ft.
Total Living Area:	**1,600 sq. ft.**
Daylight basement	828 sq. ft.
Garage	473 sq. ft.
Exterior Wall Framing:	2x4

Foundation Options:

Daylight basement
Crawlspace
Slab

(All plans can be built with your choice of foundation and framing. A generic conversion diagram is available. See order form.)

BLUEPRINT PRICE CODE:	**B**

UPPER FLOOR

MAIN FLOOR

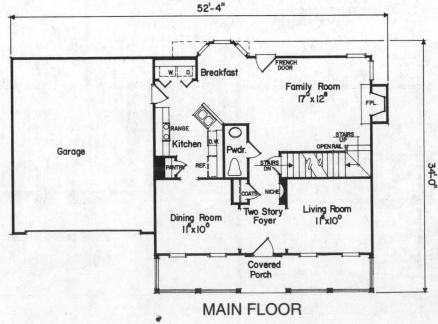

TO ORDER THIS BLUEPRINT, CALL TOLL-FREE 1-800-547-5570

Plan FB-1600

PRICES AND DETAILS ON PAGES 12-15

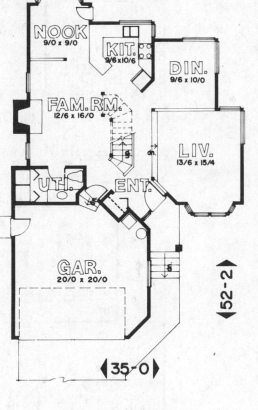

Appealing Narrow-Lot Design

This home blends both French and English design elements to create an appealing narrow lot design. Inside, an open plan adds a sense of contemporary grandeur not found in many small homes. With few walls and only the stair for division between the family room, living room, and dining area, the atmosphere is warm and homey. Visitors to this very appealing residence will be envious of the compact but spacious feeling.

The upstairs hallway is lined above with a unique vaulted skylight planting ledge. An indoor/outdoor feeling follows the hall to the spacious Master Suite. Featured in the master bath is a step-up tile tub, double vanity, and separate shower, all providing a luxurious feeling. A walk-in closet and bay window are added fine touches for this suite. The hall bath is located for easy access to the two secondary upstairs bedrooms.

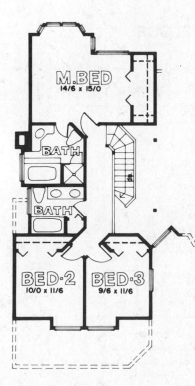

PLAN SD-8709
WITH BASEMENT

Total living area: 1,625 sq. ft.
(Not counting basement or garage)

Blueprint Price Code B
Plan SD-8709

PRICES AND DETAILS
ON PAGES 12-15

Modern Country Life

- Classic country features like a wrap-around porch, round louvered vents and a covered entry accent the exterior of this modern home.
- Just past the inviting entry, the spacious two-story-high living room is separated from the dining room by a see-through fireplace. All other first-floor rooms have 9-ft. ceilings.
- The dining room features a bright bay window. The adjacent kitchen, which serves the family room over a stylish counter, has a pantry and corner windows over the sink.
- The family room is brightened by sliding glass doors to a backyard patio. A convenient half-bath and a laundry room are nearby.
- Upstairs, the master bedroom boasts a 10-ft.-high vaulted ceiling. The master bath has a double-sink vanity, a walk-in closet and a linen closet.

Plan AG-1603

Bedrooms: 4	Baths: 2½
Living Area:	
Upper floor	853 sq. ft.
Main floor	789 sq. ft.
Total Living Area:	**1,642 sq. ft.**
Standard basement	760 sq. ft.
Garage	440 sq. ft.
Exterior Wall Framing:	2x4

Foundation Options:

Standard basement

(All plans can be built with your choice of foundation and framing. A generic conversion diagram is available. See order form.)

BLUEPRINT PRICE CODE:	B

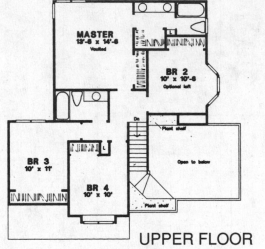

UPPER FLOOR

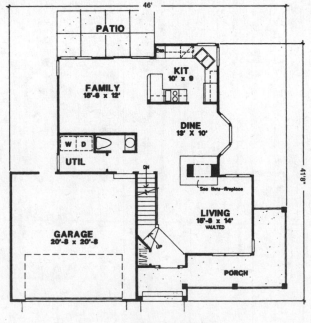

MAIN FLOOR

　　Plan AG-1603　　*PRICES AND DETAILS*
ON PAGES 12-15

Comfortable, Compact Home

- This clever home design maximizes comfort by combining luxurious extras with a modest square footage.
- The fabulous facade features a sleek roofline and rustic wood siding.
- A railing in the sidelighted entry provides views into the impressive sunken living room, which is warmed by a striking fireplace. A 17-ft. vaulted ceiling soars from the triple front windows to a railed balcony above.
- The efficient kitchen also has a railing overlooking the living room. French doors in the adjacent dining room open to a lovely backyard patio. The washer and dryer are neatly tucked in a nearby laundry closet.
- The secluded master bedroom boasts a private dressing area and direct access to the main-floor bath.
- Upstairs, the balcony provides dramatic views of the living room below. A second bath and a linen closet serve the two remaining bedrooms.

Plans P-6543-2A & -2D

Bedrooms: 3	Baths: 2
Living Area:	
Upper floor	317 sq. ft.
Main floor	780 sq. ft.
Total Living Area:	**1,097 sq. ft.**
Daylight basement	780 sq. ft.
Garage	441 sq. ft.
Exterior Wall Framing:	2x4
Foundation Options:	**Plan #**
Daylight basement	P-6543-2D
Crawlspace	P-6543-2A

(All plans can be built with your choice of foundation and framing. A generic conversion diagram is available. See order form.)

BLUEPRINT PRICE CODE:	**A**

UPPER FLOOR

BDRM. 3
10/0 x 10/0

BDRM. 2
10/6 x 10/0

TUB

LIN.   RAILING   DN.

OPEN TO LIVING BELOW

MAIN FLOOR

55'0"

24'0"

PATIO

GARAGE
20/8 x 21/4

KITCHEN
10/0 x 9/0

DINING
9/0 x 9/0

MASTER
10/8 x 11/4

WH

F

VAULTED SUNKEN LIVING RM.
15/4 x 14/0

DN.

UP

ENTRY

RAIL'G.

DRSS'G.

TUB

BASEMENT STAIRWAY LOCATION

DINING   MASTER
DN

Photo courtesy of Piercy & Barclay Designers.

Quality Design for a Narrow, Sloping Lot

Multi-pitched rooflines, custom window treatments and beveled board siding add a distinctive facade to this two-level home of only 1,516 sq. ft. Its slim 34' width allows it to fit nicely on a narrow lot while offering ample indoor and outdoor living areas.

The enclosed entry courtyard is a pleasant area for al fresco breakfasts or spill-over entertaining. The wide, high-ceilinged entry hall opens directly into the sweeping Great Room and dining area. This room is warmed by a large fireplace and has a door to a large wood deck. Also off the entry hall is the morning room with a vaulted ceiling and a matching arched window overlooking the courtyard. A half-bath and utility room is on the other side of the entry.

An open-railed stairway leads from the entry to the bedrooms on the second level. The master suite has a high dormer with peaked windows, a walk-in closet and a private bathroom. The larger of the other bedrooms could be used as a den, and it also overlooks the morning room and entry hall. If additional room is required, this plan is available with a daylight basement.

NOTE:
The above photographed home may have been modified by the homeowner. Please refer to floor plan and/or drawn elevation shown for actual blueprint details.

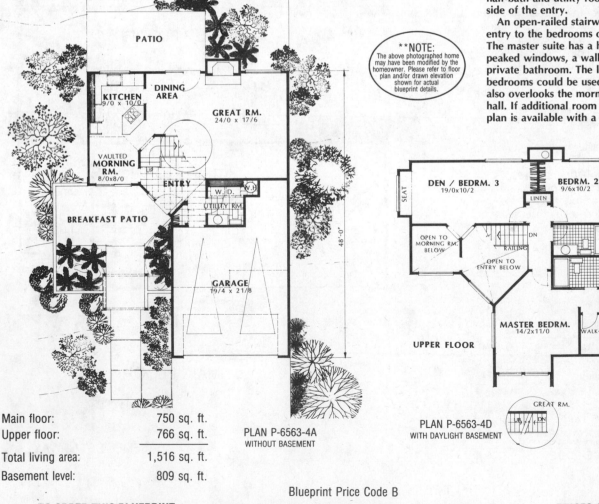

PLAN P-6563-4A
WITHOUT BASEMENT

PLAN P-6563-4D
WITH DAYLIGHT BASEMENT

Main floor:	750 sq. ft.
Upper floor:	766 sq. ft.
Total living area:	1,516 sq. ft.
Basement level:	809 sq. ft.

Blueprint Price Code B

TO ORDER THIS BLUEPRINT, CALL TOLL-FREE 1-800-547-5570

Plans P-6563-4A & -4D

PRICES AND DETAILS ON PAGES 12-15

Photo courtesy of Breland & Farmer Designers, Inc.

Stylish and Compact

- This country-style home has a classic exterior and a space-saving and compact interior.
- A quaint covered porch extends along the front of the home. The oval-glassed front door opens to the entry, which leads to the spacious living room with a handsome fireplace, windows at either end and access to a big screened porch.
- The formal dining room flows from the living room and is easily served by the convenient U-shaped kitchen.
- A nice-sized laundry room and a full bath are nearby. The two-car garage offers a super storage area.
- The deluxe master suite features a huge walk-in closet. A separate dressing area leads to an adjoining, dual-access bath.
- The upper floor offers two more bedrooms and another full bath. Each bedroom has generous closet space and independent access to attic space.

Plan E-1626

Bedrooms: 3	Baths: 2
Living Area:	
Upper floor	464 sq. ft.
Main floor	1,136 sq. ft.
Total Living Area:	**1,600 sq. ft.**
Garage	462 sq. ft.
Exterior Wall Framing:	2x6

Foundation Options:

Crawlspace

Slab

(All plans can be built with your choice of foundation and framing. A generic conversion diagram is available. See order form.)

BLUEPRINT PRICE CODE: B

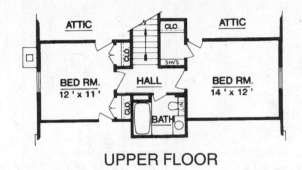

UPPER FLOOR

NOTE: The above photographed home may have been modified by the homeowner. Please refer to floor plan and/or drawn elevation shown for actual blueprint details.

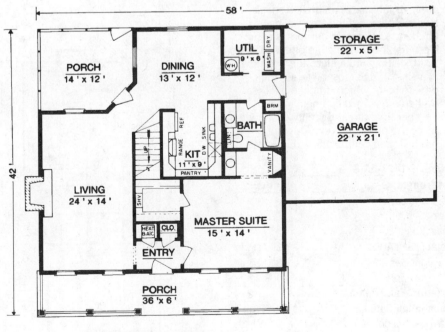

MAIN FLOOR

Instant Impact

- Bold rooflines, interesting angles and unusual window treatments give this stylish home lots of impact.
- Inside, high ceilings and an open floor plan maximize the home's square footage. At only 28 ft. wide, the home also is ideal for a narrow lot.
- A covered deck leads to the main entry, which features a sidelighted door, angled glass walls and a view of the striking open staircase.
- The Great Room is stunning, with its 16-ft. vaulted ceiling, energy-efficient woodstove and access to a large deck.
- A flat ceiling distinguishes the dining area, which shares an angled snack bar/cooktop with the step-saving kitchen. A laundry/mudroom is nearby.
- Upstairs, the master suite offers a sloped 13-ft. ceiling and a clerestory window. A walk-through closet leads to the private bath, which is enhanced by a skylighted, sloped ceiling.
- Another full bath and plenty of storage serve the other bedrooms, one of which has a sloped ceiling and a dual closet.

Plans H-1427-3A & -3B

Bedrooms: 3	Baths: 2½
Living Area:	
Upper floor	880 sq. ft.
Main floor	810 sq. ft.
Total Living Area:	**1,690 sq. ft.**
Daylight basement	810 sq. ft.
Garage	409 sq. ft.
Exterior Wall Framing:	2x4
Foundation Options:	**Plan #**
Daylight basement	H-1427-3B
Crawlspace	H-1427-3A

(All plans can be built with your choice of foundation and framing. A generic conversion diagram is available. See order form.)

BLUEPRINT PRICE CODE: B

GENERAL USE

DAYLIGHT BASEMENT

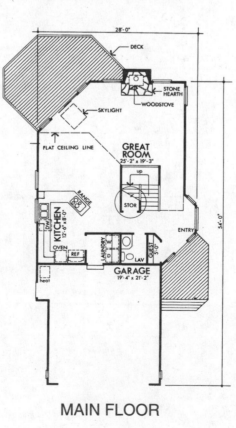

MAIN FLOOR

UPPER FLOOR

STAIRWAY AREA IN CRAWLSPACE VERSION

Affordable Victorian

- This compact Victorian design incorporates four bedrooms and three full baths into an attractive, affordable home that's only 30 ft. wide.
- In from the covered front porch, the spacious parlor includes a fireplace, and the formal dining room has a beautiful bay window.
- The galley-style kitchen offers efficient service to the breakfast nook. A laundry closet and a pantry are nearby.
- The main-floor bedroom makes a great office or guest bedroom, with a convenient full bath nearby.
- Upstairs, the master suite features an adjoining sitting room with a 14-ft. cathedral ceiling. The luxurious master bath includes a dual-sink vanity and a whirlpool tub with a shower. Two more large bedrooms share another full bath.
- An attached two-car garage off the kitchen is available upon request.

Plan C-8347-A

Bedrooms: 3+	Baths: 3
Living Area:	
Upper floor	783 sq. ft.
Main floor	954 sq. ft.
Total Living Area:	**1,737 sq. ft.**
Exterior Wall Framing:	2x4

Foundation Options:

Crawlspace
Slab
(All plans can be built with your choice of foundation and framing. A generic conversion diagram is available. See order form.)

BLUEPRINT PRICE CODE:	**B**

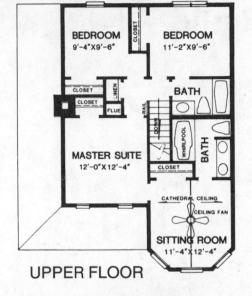

UPPER FLOOR

MAIN FLOOR

Warm, Rustic Appeal

- This quaint home has a warm, rustic appeal with a stone fireplace, paned windows and a covered front porch.
- Just off the two-story-high foyer, the living room hosts a raised-hearth fireplace and flows into the kitchen.
- The open L-shaped kitchen offers a pantry closet and a bright sink as it merges with the bayed dining room.
- The secluded master bedroom boasts a walk-in closet and a private bath with a dual-sink vanity. A laundry closet and access to a backyard deck are nearby.
- Upstairs, a hall balcony overlooks the foyer. A full bath serves two secondary bedrooms, each with a walk-in closet and access to extra storage space.
- Just off the dining room, a stairway descends to the daylight basement that contains the tuck-under garage.

Plan C-8339

Bedrooms: 3	Baths: 2
Living Area:	
Upper floor	660 sq. ft.
Main floor	1,100 sq. ft.
Total Living Area:	**1,760 sq. ft.**
Daylight basement/garage	1,100 sq. ft.
Exterior Wall Framing:	2x4

Foundation Options:
Daylight basement
(All plans can be built with your choice of foundation and framing. A generic conversion diagram is available. See order form.)

BLUEPRINT PRICE CODE: B

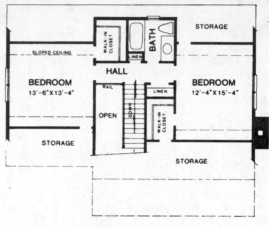

UPPER FLOOR

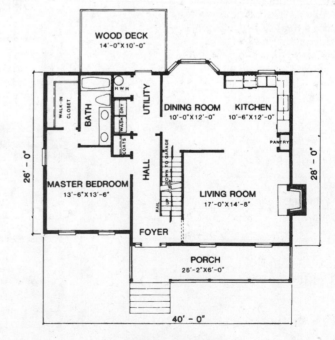

MAIN FLOOR

TO ORDER THIS BLUEPRINT, CALL TOLL-FREE 1-800-547-5570

Plan C-8339

PRICES AND DETAILS ON PAGES 12-15

New Traditional

- A lovely front porch and an open floor plan give this new traditional its modern appeal.
- The foyer opens to a fabulous living room with a 16-ft. vaulted ceiling, a fireplace and an open staircase. Railings introduce the bayed breakfast area. The efficient galley-style kitchen leads to a covered back porch.
- The sizable master suite is enhanced by a 10-ft. raised ceiling and a cozy bay window. The compartmentalized bath includes a dual-sink vanity and a walk-in closet. Another bedroom is nearby, along with a convenient laundry closet.
- Upstairs, a third bedroom has private access to a full bath. A large future area provides expansion space.

Plan J-8636

Bedrooms: 3	Baths: 3
Living Area:	
Upper floor	270 sq. ft.
Main floor	1,253 sq. ft.
Bonus room	270 sq. ft.
Total Living Area:	**1,793 sq. ft.**
Standard basement	1,287 sq. ft.
Garage	390 sq. ft.
Exterior Wall Framing:	2x4

Foundation Options:

Standard basement

Crawlspace

Slab

(All plans can be built with your choice of foundation and framing. A generic conversion diagram is available. See order form.)

BLUEPRINT PRICE CODE: B

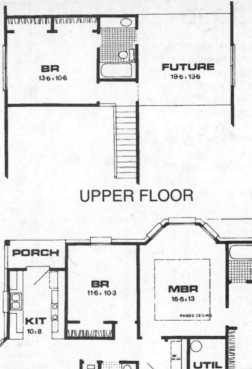

UPPER FLOOR

MAIN FLOOR

Attractive and Cozy Cottage

- This cozy country cottage is attractive, economical and easy to build.
- A striking front door with oval glass and sidelights opens directly into the huge living room, which is warmed by a nice fireplace. French doors provide access to the expansive covered front porch.
- The dining room is brightened by a boxed-out area with lots of glass.
- The efficient kitchen includes a snack bar, a windowed sink and a lazy Susan.
- The quiet main-floor master bedroom offers porch access through French doors. The master bath boasts a garden tub, a separate shower, two vanities and a walk-in closet.
- A powder room and a convenient laundry room round out the main floor.
- Upstairs, two bedrooms share another full bath. Hall closets provide additional storage space.
- A storage area for outdoor equipment is offered in the secluded carport.

Plan J-86131

Bedrooms: 3	Baths: 2½
Living Area:	
Upper floor	500 sq. ft.
Main floor	1,369 sq. ft.
Total Living Area:	**1,869 sq. ft.**
Standard basement	1,369 sq. ft.
Carport and storage	540 sq. ft.
Exterior Wall Framing:	2x4

Foundation Options:

Standard basement
Crawlspace
Slab
(All plans can be built with your choice of foundation and framing. A generic conversion diagram is available. See order form.)

BLUEPRINT PRICE CODE: B

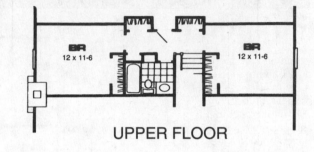

UPPER FLOOR

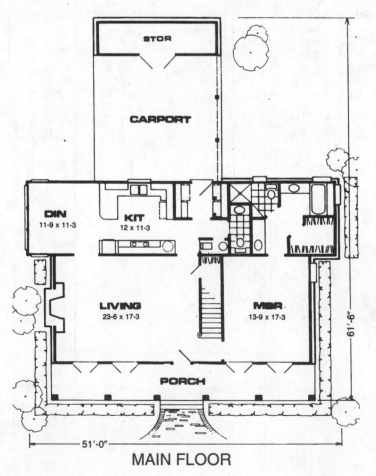

MAIN FLOOR

TO ORDER THIS BLUEPRINT, CALL TOLL-FREE 1-800-547-5570   Plan J-86131   *PRICES AND DETAILS ON PAGES 12-15*

Photo by Strode Photography

Nicely Sized and Styled

- Eye-catching entry columns and varying rooflines accent this versatile two-story.
- The 16-ft.-high vaulted entry and living room are open to the upper level. Decorative columns, a lovely corner window and a front window seat are found in the living room, which is open to the hall and the stairway.
- The roomy kitchen and breakfast area at the rear of the home offers a pantry and a bayed window that overlooks a rear patio. The kitchen also has easy access to the formal dining room and a handy pass-through to the casual family room.
- Sliding glass doors in the family room open to the patio; an optional fireplace may also be added.
- A nice-sized laundry room is convenient to the garage entrance, and a powder room is centrally located.
- All four bedrooms are found on the upper level, where a balcony overlooks the living room below. The master suite includes built-in shelves and a luxurious private bath.

Plan AG-1801

Bedrooms: 4	**Baths:** 2½
Living Area:	
Upper floor	890 sq. ft.
Main floor	980 sq. ft.
Total Living Area:	**1,870 sq. ft.**
Standard basement	980 sq. ft.
Garage	480 sq. ft.
Exterior Wall Framing:	2x6
Foundation Options:	
Standard basement	

(All plans can be built with your choice of foundation and framing. A generic conversion diagram is available. See order form.)

BLUEPRINT PRICE CODE:	B

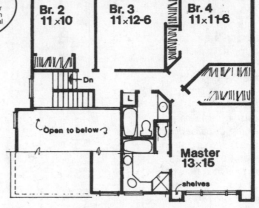

NOTE:
The above photographed home may have been modified by the homeowner. Please refer to floor plan and/or drawn elevation shown for actual blueprint details.

UPPER FLOOR

MAIN FLOOR

Photo by Mark Englund/HomeStyles

Family Charmer

- Designed with families in mind, this charming two-story packs plenty of excitement in its modest square footage.
- Dual bay windows grace the exterior, adding traditional appeal.
- A skylight bathes the 16½-ft.-high vaulted entry and the open-railed stairway with light.
- The living room features a 14½-ft. vaulted ceiling leading up to a cased-opening overlook in the third bedroom.
- The formal dining room is mere steps away from the kitchen, for serving convenience, and opens to a rear patio.
- The efficient kitchen features a corner garden sink. The bright breakfast nook boasts sliding glass doors to the patio.
- The inviting family room includes a cozy fireplace and a handy wet bar.
- The main floor also has a laundry room off the garage and a powder room.
- The three bedrooms upstairs include a master suite with a walk-in closet and a private bath. The second bedroom features a bayed window seat that overlooks the front yard.

Plans P-7681-3A & -3D

Bedrooms: 3	Baths: 2½
Living Area:	
Upper floor	875 sq. ft.
Main floor	1,020 sq. ft.
Total Living Area:	**1,895 sq. ft.**
Daylight basement	925 sq. ft.
Garage	419 sq. ft.
Exterior Wall Framing:	**2×4**
Foundation Options:	**Plan #**
Daylight basement	P-7681-3D
Crawlspace	P-7681-3A

(All plans can be built with your choice of foundation and framing. A generic conversion diagram is available. See order form.)

BLUEPRINT PRICE CODE:	**B**

UPPER FLOOR

**NOTE:
The above photographed home may have been modified by the homeowner. Please refer to floor plan and/or drawn elevation shown for actual blueprint details.

WALK IN WARDROBE · SHWR · STOR · BATH · LIN · DRESSING · TUB · BEDRM. 3 11/8x11/0 · CEILING LINE · SEAT · 36" HIGH WALL · OPEN TO BELOW · SKYLIGHT · BUILDING LINE BELOW · MASTER 13/6x15/0 · RAILING · BEDRM. 2 11/6x11/8 · SEAT

MAIN FLOOR

42'0" · 46'0" · PATIO · BUILDING LINE ABOVE · BUILDING LINE ABOVE · NOOK 8/0x10/0 · KITCHEN 9/0x12/0 · DW · DINING 11/8x11/6 · FAMILY RM. 17/0x13/4 · STOR · REF · FLOOR LINE ABOVE · RAILING · CEILING LINE · BAR · W · D · BATH · VAULTED ENTRY · WH · F · VAULTED LIVING RM. 13/4x17/6 · GARAGE 19/4x21/8

BASEMENT STAIRWAY LOCATION

NOOK · KITCHEN · DW · UP · RAILING · ENTRY

Photo by Mark Englund/HomeStyles

Irresistible Master Suite

- This traditional three-bedroom home features a main-floor master suite that is hard to resist, with an inviting window seat and a delightful bath.
- The home is introduced by a covered front entry, topped by a dormer with a half-round window.
- Just off the front entry, the formal dining room is distinguished by a tray ceiling and a large picture window overlooking the front porch.
- Straight back, the Great Room features a 16-ft.-high vaulted ceiling with a window wall facing the backyard. The fireplace can be enjoyed from the adjoining kitchen and breakfast area.
- The gourmet kitchen includes a corner sink, an island cooktop and a walk-in pantry. A 12-ft. vaulted ceiling expands the breakfast nook, which features a built-in desk and backyard deck access.
- The spacious master suite offers a 14-ft. vaulted ceiling and a luxurious private bath with a walk-in closet, a garden tub, a separate shower and a dual-sink vanity with a sit-down makeup area.
- An open-railed stairway leads up to another full bath that serves two additional bedrooms.

Plan B-89061

Bedrooms: 3	Baths: 2½
Living Area:	
Upper floor	436 sq. ft.
Main floor	1,490 sq. ft.
Total Living Area:	**1,926 sq. ft.**
Standard basement	1,490 sq. ft.
Garage	400 sq. ft.
Exterior Wall Framing:	2x4
Foundation Options:	

Standard basement
(All plans can be built with your choice of foundation and framing. A generic conversion diagram is available. See order form.)

BLUEPRINT PRICE CODE:	B

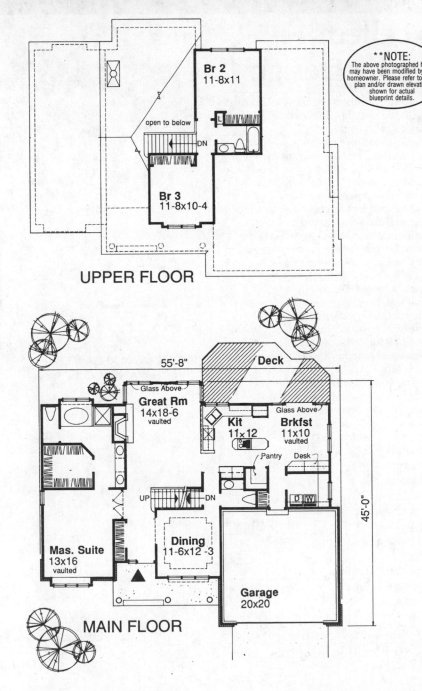

NOTE: The above photographed home may have been modified by the homeowner. Please refer to floor plan and/or drawn elevation shown for actual blueprint details.

UPPER FLOOR

Br 2
11-8x11

open to below

Br 3
11-8x10-4

MAIN FLOOR

Deck

55'-8"

Glass Above

Great Rm
14x18-6
vaulted

Kit
11x12

Brkfst
11x10
vaulted

Glass Above

Pantry

Desk

45'-0"

Mas. Suite
13x16
vaulted

Dining
11-6x12 -3

Garage
20x20

Excellent Family Design

- Long, sloping rooflines and bold design features make this home attractive in any neighborhood.
- The vaulted entry ushers visitors into the impressive Great Room with its 12½-ft. vaulted ceiling, clerestory windows and warm woodstove. A rear window wall overlooks an expansive deck.
- The magnificent kitchen opens to the informal dining area and includes a functional work island and a wet bar.
- A skylighted laundry room, a skylighted bath and two bedrooms complete the main floor. The rear-facing bedroom opens to the deck, and the front bedroom boasts a lovely window seat.
- The upstairs consists of a master bedroom retreat with a 10½-ft. vaulted ceiling. Highlights include a walk-in closet and a luxurious private bath with a spa tub.
- The optional daylight basement adds lots of space for recreation and entertaining, plus a fourth bedroom and a large shop/storage area.

Plans P-528-2A & -2D

Bedrooms: 3+	Baths: 2-3
Living Area:	
Upper floor	498 sq. ft.
Main floor	1,456 sq. ft.
Daylight basement	1,410 sq. ft.
Total Living Area:	**1,954/3,364 sq. ft.**
Garage	502 sq. ft.
Exterior Wall Framing:	2x6
Foundation Options:	**Plan #**
Daylight basement	P-528-2D
Crawlspace	P-528-2A

(All plans can be built with your choice of foundation and framing. A generic conversion diagram is available. See order form.)

BLUEPRINT PRICE CODE:	B/E

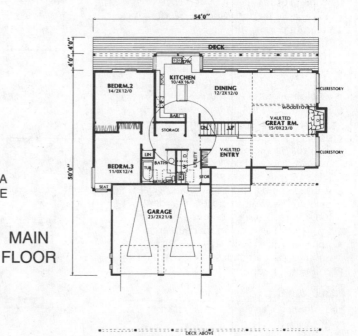

UPPER FLOOR

STAIRWAY AREA IN CRAWLSPACE VERSION

MAIN FLOOR

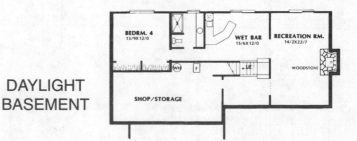

DAYLIGHT BASEMENT

TO ORDER THIS BLUEPRINT, CALL TOLL-FREE 1-800-547-5570

Plans P-528-2A & -2D

PRICES AND DETAILS ON PAGES 12-15

Photo by Mark Englund/HomeStyles

Farmhouse with Style

- A covered porch, dormer windows and a rear deck give this farmhouse the style and function demanded by today's homeowners.
- Inside, the 16-ft.-high vaulted foyer leads directly to the living room and flaunts a beautiful open-railed staircase.
- The living room flows into the formal dining room, which has a French door opening to the front porch.
- A pocket door reveals the informal areas, where the kitchen offers a snack bar to the sunny nook, and the adjoining family room accesses a rear deck. The space is enhanced by a warm fireplace.
- Upstairs, an arched opening adorns the entrance to the master bedroom's private bath. Three more bedrooms share another full bath, and a laundry closet is handy to all the bedrooms.

Plan CDG-2002

Bedrooms: 4	Baths: 2½
Living Area:	
Upper floor	1,077 sq. ft.
Main floor	888 sq. ft.
Total Living Area:	**1,965 sq. ft.**
Daylight basement	682 sq. ft.
Garage	441 sq. ft.
Exterior Wall Framing:	2x6

Foundation Options:

Daylight basement

Crawlspace

(All plans can be built with your choice of foundation and framing. A generic conversion diagram is available. See order form.)

BLUEPRINT PRICE CODE:	B

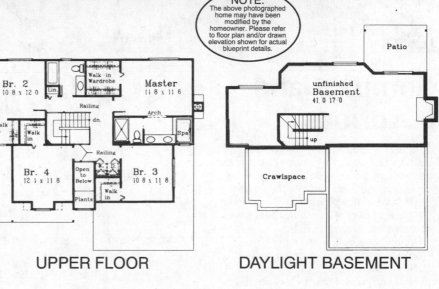

NOTE: The above photographed home may have been modified by the homeowner. Please refer to floor plan and/or drawn elevation shown for actual blueprint details.

UPPER FLOOR

DAYLIGHT BASEMENT

MAIN FLOOR

Compact and Luxurious

- The best from the past and the present is bundled up in this compact design, reminiscent of a New England saltbox.
- The cozy kitchen has a center island with a breakfast counter and a built-in range and oven. The corner sink saves on counter space.
- A decorative railing separates the formal dining room from the sunken living room.
- The living room features a vaulted ceiling, built-in shelves, a central fireplace and access to a large rear deck.
- The upper-floor master suite boasts a spa bath, a separate shower and a walk-in closet.

Plan H-1453-1A

Bedrooms: 3	Baths: 2
Living Area:	
Upper floor	386 sq. ft.
Main floor	1,385 sq. ft.
Total Living Area:	**1,771 sq. ft.**
Garage	409 sq. ft.
Exterior Wall Framing:	2x6

Foundation Options:
Crawlspace
(Typical foundation & framing conversion diagram available—see order form.)

BLUEPRINT PRICE CODE: B

UPPER FLOOR

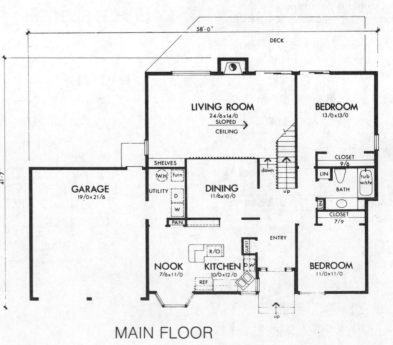

MAIN FLOOR

TO ORDER THIS BLUEPRINT, CALL TOLL-FREE 1-800-547-5570

Plan H-1453-1A

PRICES AND DETAILS ON PAGES 12-15

Up-to-Date Country Styling

- Nearly surrounded by a covered wood porch, this traditional 1,860-sq.-ft. farm-styled home is modernized for today's active, up-to-date family.
- Inside, the efficient floor plan promotes easy mobility with vast openness and a minimum of cross-traffic.
- The spacious living and dining area is warmed by a fireplace with a stone hearth; sliding glass doors off the dining room open to the porch.
- The U-shaped country kitchen is centrally located and overlooks a bright breakfast nook and a big family room with a woodstove and its own sliding glass doors to a patio.
- On the upper floor is a large master bedroom with corner windows, a dressing area and a private bath. Two secondary bedrooms share a second bath with a handy dual-sink vanity.

Plans P-7677-2A & -2D

Bedrooms: 3	Baths: 2½
Living Area:	
Upper floor	825 sq. ft.
Main floor	1,035 sq. ft.
Total Living Area:	**1,860 sq. ft.**
Daylight basement	1,014 sq. ft.
Garage	466 sq. ft.
Exterior Wall Framing:	2x6
Foundation Options:	**Plan #**
Daylight basement	P-7677-2D
Crawlspace	P-7677-2A

(All plans can be built with your choice of foundation and framing. A generic conversion diagram is available. See order form.)

BLUEPRINT PRICE CODE: B

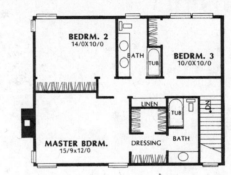

UPPER FLOOR

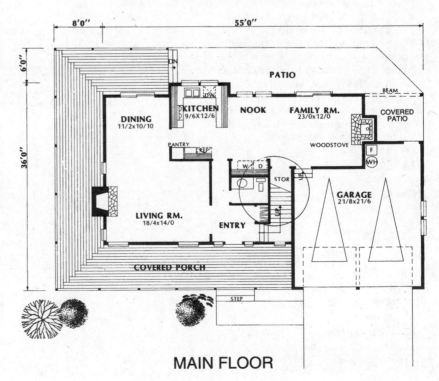

MAIN FLOOR

TO ORDER THIS BLUEPRINT,
CALL TOLL-FREE 1-800-547-5570

Plans P-7677-2A & -2D

PRICES AND DETAILS
ON PAGES 12-15

223

Unique Inside and Out

- This delightful design is as striking on the inside as it is on the outside.
- The focal point of the home is the huge Grand Room, which features a vaulted ceiling, plant shelves and lots of glass, including a clerestory window. French doors flanking the fireplace lead to the covered porch and the two adjoining sun decks.
- The centrally located kitchen offers easy access from any room in the house, and a full bath, a laundry area and the garage entrance are nearby.
- The two main-floor master suites are another unique design element of the home. Both of the suites showcase a volume ceiling, a sunny window seat, a walk-in closet, a private bath and French doors that open to a sun deck.
- Upstairs, two guest suites overlook the vaulted Grand Room below.

Plan EOF-13

Bedrooms: 4	Baths: 3
Living Area:	
Upper floor	443 sq. ft.
Main floor	1,411 sq. ft.
Total Living Area:	**1,854 sq. ft.**
Garage	264 sq. ft.
Storage	50 sq. ft.
Exterior Wall Framing:	2x6

Foundation Options:

Crawlspace

(Typical foundation & framing conversion diagram available—see order form.)

BLUEPRINT PRICE CODE:	**B**

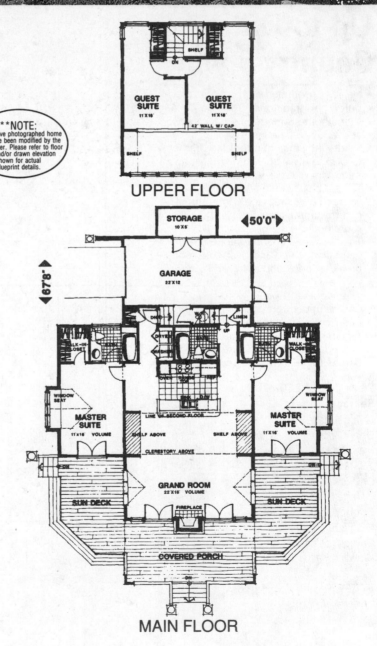

NOTE:
The above photographed home may have been modified by the homeowner. Please refer to floor plan and/or drawn elevation shown for actual blueprint details.

UPPER FLOOR

MAIN FLOOR

TO ORDER THIS BLUEPRINT, CALL TOLL-FREE 1-800-547-5570

Plan EOF-13

PRICES AND DETAILS ON PAGES 12-15

Front Porch Dresses Up Facade

- A covered front porch adorns the facade of this updated two-story.
- Opposite the foyer are the formal living and dining rooms.
- Oriented to the rear of the home are the family room with fireplace and skylights, the dinette and a U-shaped kitchen.
- A powder room and convenient main-floor washer/dryer intercept incoming traffic from the garage.
- Three generous-sized bedrooms occupy the upper floor.

Plan A-2237-DS

Bedrooms: 3	Baths: 1 ½
Space:	
Upper floor	672 sq. ft.
Main floor	972 sq. ft.
Total Living Area	**1,644 sq. ft.**
Basement	972 sq. ft.
Garage	484 sq. ft.
Exterior Wall Framing	**2x6**

Foundation options:

Standard Basement

(Foundation & framing conversion diagram available—see order form.)

Blueprint Price Code	**B**

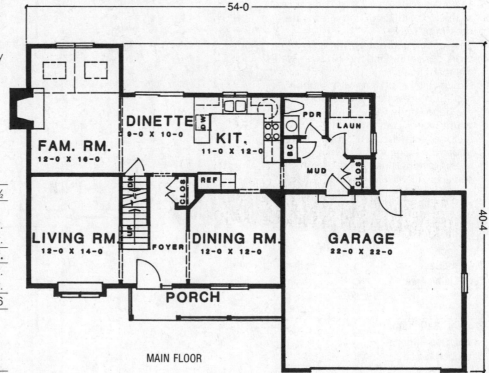

UPPER FLOOR

MAIN FLOOR

Efficient Split-Entry

- Space is used efficiently and effectively in this bright split-entry home.
- Just off the inviting foyer is the sun-filled living room, with its 15-ft.-high vaulted ceiling, nice fireplace and tall windows.
- A railed stairway leads up to the dining area, which offers views into the living room below. Outdoor meals may be served on the large backyard deck.
- The adjacent U-shaped kitchen features a handy eating bar for quick breakfasts or afternoon snacks.
- The main-floor master bedroom boasts a spacious walk-in closet, private access to the hall's full bath and a separate dressing vanity.
- The second bedroom, with its built-in work desk and window seat, completes the main floor.
- Downstairs, a full bath with laundry facilities serves the third bedroom and the huge family room, which boasts a warm woodstove.
- A storage crawlspace occupies the area under the living room. With a few modifications, this storage area could serve as a darkroom or wine cellar.

Plan U-8503-SL

Bedrooms: 3	Baths: 2
Living Area:	
Main floor	1,091 sq. ft.
Daylight basement	555 sq. ft.
Total Living Area:	**1,646 sq. ft.**
Storage area (low clearance)	220 sq. ft.
Garage	440 sq. ft.
Exterior Wall Framing:	2x4

Foundation Options:

Daylight basement

(All plans can be built with your choice of foundation and framing. A generic conversion diagram is available. See order form.)

BLUEPRINT PRICE CODE:	**B**

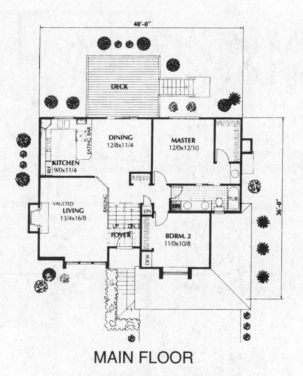

MAIN FLOOR

DAYLIGHT BASEMENT

Bedrooms on Walkout Level

DECK

OPEN TO DINING

KITCHEN 9/0x11/0

VAULTED **LIVING RM.** 22/0x13/4

DINING

FAMILY RM. 12/0x15/4

NOOK

F WH

BATH

STEP RAIL VAULTED **ENTRY**

GARAGE 19/10x22/8

DN

SKYLIGHTS

44'0"

39'0"

MAIN FLOOR

PLAN P-7676-2D
WITH DAYLIGHT BASEMENT

FLOOR LINE ABOVE

BEDRM. 2 11/2x11/10

W D

BEDRM. 3 10/8x10/2

MASTER 12/8x13/8

LIN

UP

BATH

TUB

BATH

SH

STOR

LOWER LEVEL

Main floor:	898 sq. ft.
Lower floor:	754 sq. ft.
Total living area: (Not counting garage)	1,652 sq. ft.

Blueprint Price Code B

Plan P-7676-2D

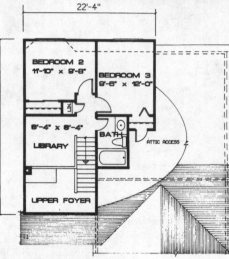

Single-Level Conveniences

- This modern-day Cape Cod offers the convenience of single-level living with the secondary bedrooms and a separate bath located on the upper level.
- The open floor plan allows a view of the family room fireplace from the kitchen and the bayed dining area.
- Pocket doors between the family room and the living room provide the modest-sized home flexibility. They may be closed for a cozy, private sitting area or opened for frequent traffic flow or entertaining.
- The generous-sized master bedroom is convenient to the kitchen and the laundry room. It features a large walk-in closet and a private bath.
- Joining the two bedrooms on the upper level is a skylighted library loft that overlooks the foyer below. A larger alternate bath may replace the smaller bath, adding 48 sq. feet.

Plan GL-1654-P

Bedrooms: 3	Baths: 2½
Living Area:	
Upper floor	462 sq. ft.
Main floor	1,192 sq. ft.
Total Living Area:	**1,654 sq. ft.**
Standard basement	1,192 sq. ft.
Garage	448 sq. ft.
Exterior Wall Framing:	2x4

Foundation Options:

Standard basement

(All plans can be built with your choice of foundation and framing. A generic conversion diagram is available. See order form.)

BLUEPRINT PRICE CODE: **B**

ALTERNATE BATH
ADD 48 SQ.FT.

UPPER FLOOR

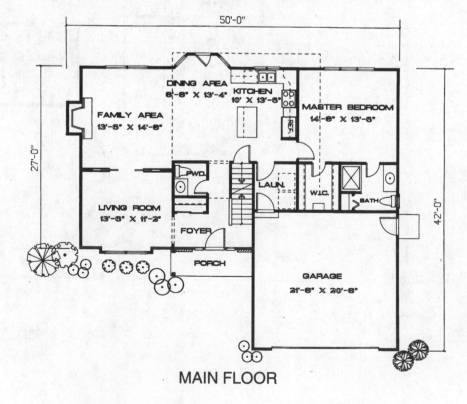

MAIN FLOOR

TO ORDER THIS BLUEPRINT,
CALL TOLL-FREE 1-800-547-5570

Plan GL-1654-P

PRICES AND DETAILS
ON PAGES 12-15

Plenty of Presence

- A stucco facade complemented by fieldstone, a dramatic roofline and handsome keystones accenting the window treatments gives this home plenty of presence.
- Inside, the two-story foyer boasts an open stairway with a balcony overlook. Straight ahead, the huge family room is expanded by a 16½-ft. vaulted ceiling, plus a tall window and a French door that frame the fireplace.
- The adjoining dining room flows into the kitchen and breakfast room, which feature an angled serving bar, a bright window wall and a French door that opens to a covered patio.
- The main-floor master suite is the pride of the floor plan, offering a 10-ft. tray ceiling. The deluxe master bath has a 14-ft. vaulted ceiling, a garden tub and a spacious walk-in closet.
- The upper floor offers two more bedrooms, a full bath and attic space.

Plan FB-1681

Bedrooms: 3	Baths: 2½
Living Area:	
Upper floor	449 sq. ft.
Main floor	1,232 sq. ft.
Total Living Area:	**1,681 sq. ft.**
Daylight basement	1,232 sq. ft.
Garage and storage	435 sq. ft.
Exterior Wall Framing:	2x4

Foundation Options:
Daylight basement
Crawlspace
(All plans can be built with your choice of foundation and framing. A generic conversion diagram is available. See order form.)

BLUEPRINT PRICE CODE:	**B**

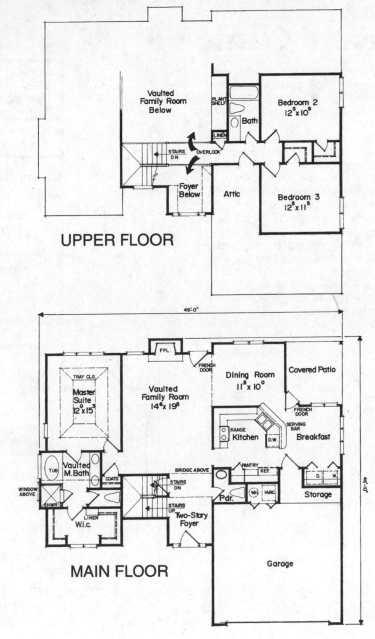

UPPER FLOOR

MAIN FLOOR

Updated Classic

- An interesting blend of exterior styles and a modern floor plan combine to make this home an American favorite.
- A covered front porch ushers guests into the inviting foyer, which leads to a half-bath and and an open-railed staircase.
- To the left of the foyer, the sunken living room features a soaring 17½-ft.-high ceiling and French doors to a patio.
- The formal dining room flows into the kitchen, which incorporates a casual eating area with sliders to the backyard.
- A laundry closet and a pantry are conveniently located at the intersection of the kitchen, the garage entrance and the family room.
- The spacious family room hosts a handsome fireplace, a built-in audio/visual cabinet and a bay window.
- Upstairs, the roomy master suite offers two closets and a private bath. Another full bath serves the remaining bedrooms.

Plan PH-1707

Bedrooms: 3	Baths: 2½
Living Area:	
Upper floor	692 sq. ft.
Main floor	1,015 sq. ft.
Total Living Area:	**1,707 sq. ft.**
Basement	994 sq. ft.
Garage	419 sq. ft.
Exterior Wall Framing:	2x6

Foundation Options:
Daylight basement
Standard basement
Crawlspace
Slab
(All plans can be built with your choice of foundation and framing. A generic conversion diagram is available. See order form.)

BLUEPRINT PRICE CODE: B

UPPER FLOOR

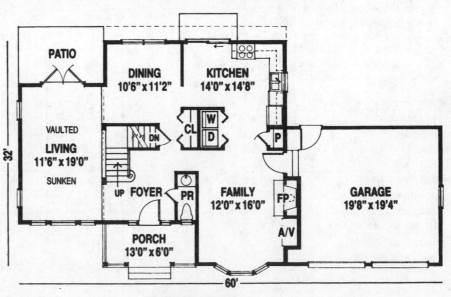

MAIN FLOOR

TO ORDER THIS BLUEPRINT, CALL TOLL-FREE 1-800-547-5570

Plan PH-1707

PRICES AND DETAILS ON PAGES 12-15

Spanish Flair

- A clay tiled roof and a stucco facade give this compact two-story home a Spanish flair.
- Guests are welcomed through double doors into the two-story entry.
- Straight ahead is the beautiful living room, which boasts a 13½-ft. vaulted ceiling, a wet bar and a cozy fireplace.
- The adjacent dining room is highlighted by a huge bay window and offers backyard access through an elegant French door.
- Quick meals can be enjoyed at the breakfast bar that extends from the

modern gourmet kitchen. A closet pantry and a green-house window above the sink are also featured.
- Rounding out the first floor is a handsome study. With a closet and a nearby bath, the study could be modified as an extra bedroom.
- Upstairs, the railed balcony provides a lovely view into the living room below.
- Entered through double doors, the romantic master bedroom showcases a private balcony, a huge walk-in closet and a compartmentalized bath with a separate dressing area.
- The two remaining bedrooms share another full bath.

Plan Q-1707-1A	
Bedrooms: 3	**Baths:** 3
Living Area:	
Upper floor	831 sq. ft.
Main floor	876 sq. ft.
Total Living Area:	**1,707 sq. ft.**
Garage	466 sq. ft.
Exterior Wall Framing:	2x4
Foundation Options:	

Slab
(All plans can be built with your choice of foundation and framing. A generic conversion diagram is available. See order form.)

BLUEPRINT PRICE CODE:	B

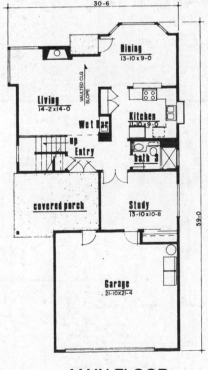

MAIN FLOOR

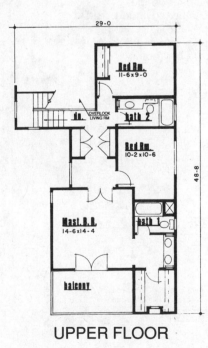

UPPER FLOOR

Family Farmhouse

- There's more to this house than its charming front porch, steeply pitched roof and dormer windows.
- A feeling of spaciousness is emphasized by the open floor plan, with the living room adjoining the kitchen and bayed breakfast area. A snack bar allows easy service to the living room.
- The back door leads from the carport to the utility room, which is convenient to the kitchen and half-bath.
- The secluded main-floor master bedroom offers a large walk-in closet and a private bathroom.
- Upstairs, two bedrooms share another full bath. One includes dormer windows and the other a window seat. A door at the top of the stairs provides access to attic space that could be turned into an extra bedroom.

Plan J-86133

Bedrooms: 3	Baths: 2½
Living Area:	
Upper floor	559 sq. ft.
Main floor	1,152 sq. ft.
Total Living Area:	**1,711 sq. ft.**
Standard basement	1,152 sq. ft.
Carport	387 sq. ft.
Storage	85 sq. ft.
Exterior Wall Framing:	2x4

Foundation Options:
Standard basement
Crawlspace
Slab
(All plans can be built with your choice of foundation and framing. A generic conversion diagram is available. See order form.)

BLUEPRINT PRICE CODE: B

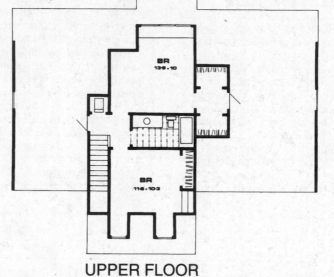

UPPER FLOOR

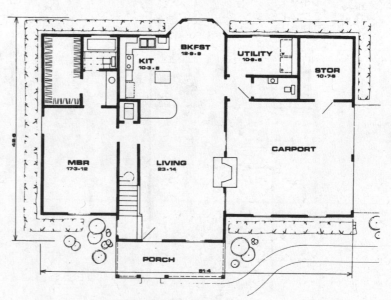

MAIN FLOOR

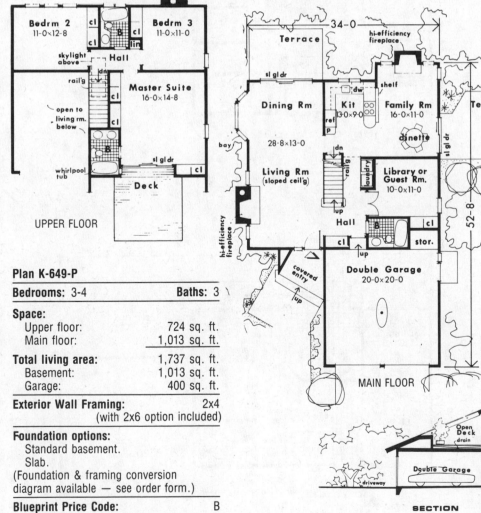

UPPER FLOOR

Bedrm 2
11-0×12-8

Bedrm 3
11-0×11-0

skylight above

rail'g

Master Suite
16-0×14-8

open to living rm. below

whirlpool tub

Deck

MAIN FLOOR

34-0

Terrace

hi-efficiency fireplace

Dining Rm
28-8×13-0

Kit
13-0×9-0

Family Rm
16-0×11-0

dinette

Living Rm
(sloped ceil'g)

Library or Guest Rm.
10-0×11-0

Hall

stor.

hi-efficiency fireplace

covered entry

Double Garage
20-0×20-0

52-8

Plan K-649-P

Bedrooms: 3-4	**Baths:** 3

Space:

Upper floor:	724 sq. ft.
Main floor:	1,013 sq. ft.

Total living area:	**1,737 sq. ft.**
Basement:	1,013 sq. ft.
Garage:	400 sq. ft.

Exterior Wall Framing: 2x4
(with 2x6 option included)

Foundation options:
Standard basement.
Slab.
(Foundation & framing conversion diagram available — see order form.)

Blueprint Price Code: B

Contemporary Features Unusual Roof Deck

- Upstairs master suite includes a private deck, sunken into a cavity in the garage roof.
- Balance of the plan is also designed to be open and airy.
- The living room has a sloped ceiling and an impressive fireplace, and flows into the dining area.
- The kitchen, family room and dinette area function well together for family dining and other activities.
- A library or guest bedroom with a full bath also offers the option of becoming a home office.

Open Deck

Master Suite

Bedrm 3

Double Garage

Bath

Library or Guest Rm.

Family Rm

driveway

SECTION

Bsmt.

Country-Style Colonial

- The timeless exterior of this country-style Colonial is complemented by a trendy interior floor plan.
- The stairs in this split-entry design are out of sight, tucked around the corner from the entry.
- The living room has an arched opening to the dining room and an optional fireplace.
- The sunny kitchen is open to the breakfast room, which features sliding glass doors to the backyard patio and a built-in pantry closet. The kitchen also overlooks the family room, which features a fireplace surrounded by three windows.
- An open stairway adorned with a plant shelf and a round window leads to the second floor.
- Angled walls and generous proportions typify the three children's bedrooms. The deluxe master suite includes an oversized sleeping area, two walk-in closets and a private bath with a spa tub and a dual-sink vanity.

Plan AG-1701

Bedrooms: 4	Baths: 2½
Living Area:	
Upper floor	850 sq. ft.
Main floor	912 sq. ft.
Total Living Area:	**1,762 sq. ft.**
Standard basement	912 sq. ft.
Garage	413 sq. ft.
Exterior Wall Framing:	2x4

Foundation Options:

Standard basement
(Typical foundation & framing conversion diagram available—see order form.)

BLUEPRINT PRICE CODE: B

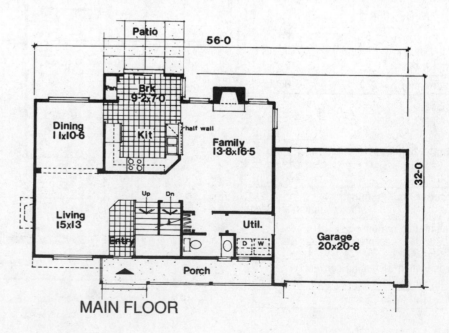

UPPER FLOOR

MAIN FLOOR

Plan AG-1701

PRICES AND DETAILS
ON PAGES 12-15

Cottage Suits Small Lot

- Designed to fit on a sloping or small lot, this compact country-style cottage has the amenities of a much larger home.
- The large front porch opens to the home's surprising two-story-high foyer, which views into the living room.
- The spacious living room is warmed by a handsome fireplace that is centered between built-in bookshelves.
- Enhanced by a sunny bay that opens to a backyard deck, the dining room offers a comfortable eating area that is easily served by the island kitchen.
- The secluded main-floor master bedroom includes a roomy walk-in closet. The spectacular master bath showcases a corner garden tub, a designer shower, a built-in bench and a dual-sink vanity.
- Upstairs, a railed balcony overlooks the foyer. Two secondary bedrooms with walk-in closets share a central bath.

Plan C-8870

Bedrooms: 3	Baths: 2
Living Area:	
Upper floor	664 sq. ft.
Main floor	1,100 sq. ft.
Total Living Area:	**1,764 sq. ft.**
Daylight basement/garage	1,100 sq. ft.
Exterior Wall Framing:	2x4

Foundation Options:

Daylight basement

(All plans can be built with your choice of foundation and framing. A generic conversion diagram is available. See order form.)

BLUEPRINT PRICE CODE:	**B**

UPPER FLOOR

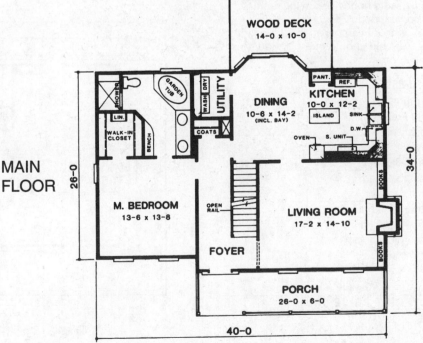

MAIN FLOOR

Casual Country Living

- With its covered wraparound porch, this gracious design is ideal for warm summer days or starry evenings.
- The spacious living room boasts a handsome brick-hearth fireplace and built-in book and gun storage. A French door accesses the backyard.
- The open kitchen design provides plenty of space for food storage and preparation with its pantry and oversized central island.
- Two mirror-imaged baths service the three bedrooms on the upper floor. Each secondary bedroom features a window seat and two closets. The master bedroom has a large walk-in closet and a private bath.
- A versatile hobby or sewing room is also included.
- An optional carport off the dining room is available upon request. Please specify when ordering.

Plan J-8895

Bedrooms: 3	Baths: 2½
Living Area:	
Upper floor	860 sq. ft.
Main floor	919 sq. ft.
Total Living Area:	**1,779 sq. ft.**
Standard basement	919 sq. ft.
Optional carport	462 sq. ft.
Exterior Wall Framing:	2x4

Foundation Options:

Standard basement
Crawlspace
Slab

(All plans can be built with your choice of foundation and framing. A generic conversion diagram is available. See order form.)

BLUEPRINT PRICE CODE:	B

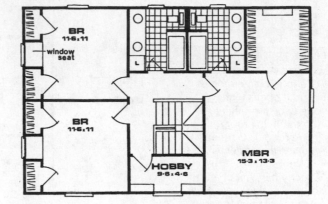

UPPER FLOOR

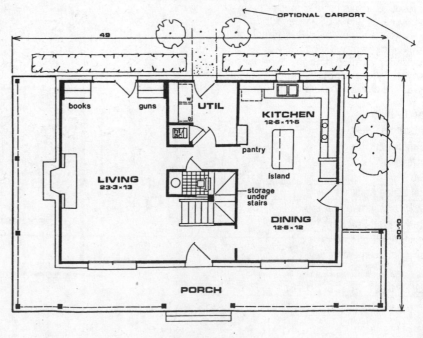

MAIN FLOOR

Plan J-8895

PRICES AND DETAILS
ON PAGES 12-15

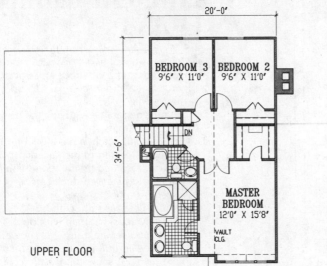

20'-0'

BEDROOM 3
9'6' X 11'0'

BEDROOM 2
9'6' X 11'0'

34'-6'

DN

MASTER
BEDROOM
12'0' X 15'8'

VAULT
CLG.

UPPER FLOOR

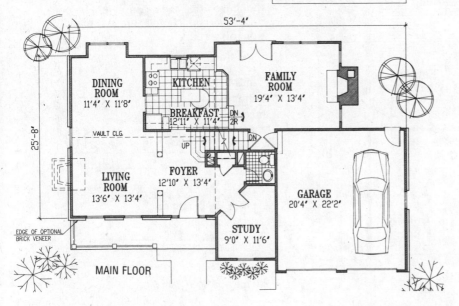

53'-4'

DINING
ROOM
11'4' X 11'8'

KITCHEN

FAMILY
ROOM
19'4' X 13'4'

25'-8'

BREAKFAST
12'11' X 11'4'

DN
2R

VAULT CLG.

UP

DN

LIVING
ROOM
13'6' X 13'4'

FOYER
12'10' X 13'4'

GARAGE
20'4' X 22'2'

EDGE OF OPTIONAL
BRICK VENEER

STUDY
9'0' X 11'6'

MAIN FLOOR

Country Comfort

- The traditional exterior of this two-story contrasts comfortably with its modern, open and airy interior.
- For family activities and entertaining, the living room and dining room combine, both with vaulted ceilings.
- The large, eat-in kitchen offers a combination breakfast bar and work island; adjoined is a sunken family room with fireplace and double doors to an optional outdoor alternative.
- A lovely front study could also serve as a fourth bedroom.
- A beautiful front window wall and vaulted ceiling accent the upstairs master bedroom, also with generous luxury bath.

Plan CH-220-A	
Bedrooms: 3-4	**Baths: 2 ½**
Space:	
Upper floor	700 sq. ft.
Main floor	1,082 sq. ft.
Total Living Area	**1,782 sq. ft.**
Basement	980 sq. ft.
Garage	451 sq. ft.
Exterior Wall Framing	**2x4**

Foundation options:

Standard Basement
Daylight Basement
Crawlspace

(Foundation & framing conversion diagram available—see order form.)

Blueprint Price Code	**B**

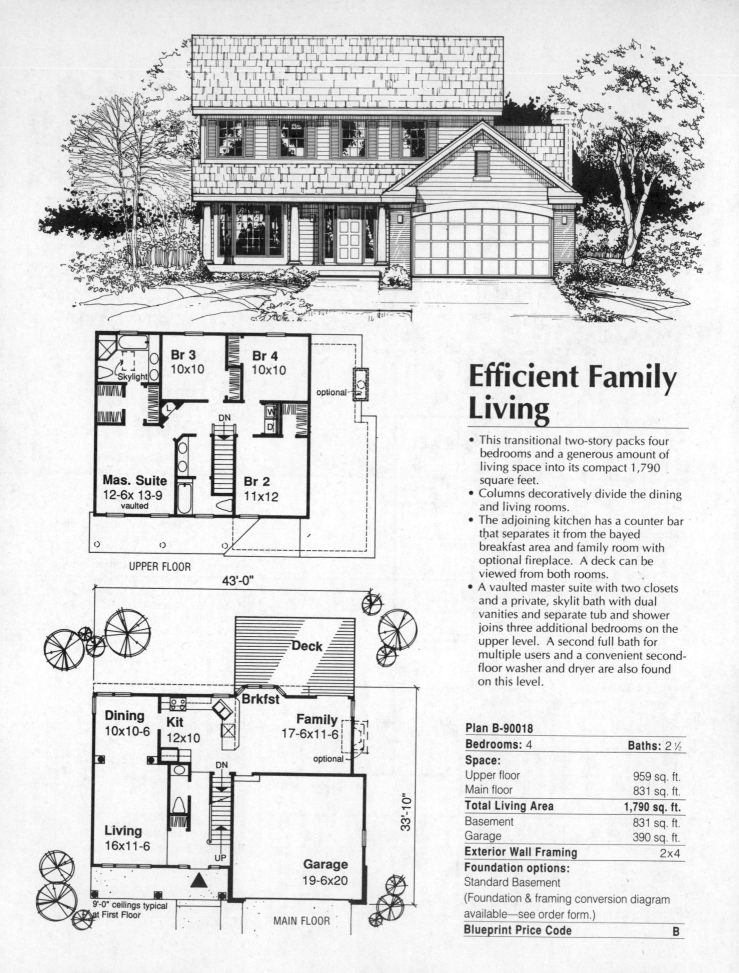

UPPER FLOOR

43'-0"

Deck

Brkfst

Dining
10x10-6

Kit
12x10

Family
17-6x11-6
optional

DN

Living
16x11-6

UP

Garage
19-6x20

33'-10"

9'-0" ceilings typical
at First Floor

MAIN FLOOR

Br 3
10x10

Br 4
10x10

optional

Skylight

DN

W
D

Mas. Suite
12-6x 13-9
vaulted

Br 2
11x12

Efficient Family Living

- This transitional two-story packs four bedrooms and a generous amount of living space into its compact 1,790 square feet.
- Columns decoratively divide the dining and living rooms.
- The adjoining kitchen has a counter bar that separates it from the bayed breakfast area and family room with optional fireplace. A deck can be viewed from both rooms.
- A vaulted master suite with two closets and a private, skylit bath with dual vanities and separate tub and shower joins three additional bedrooms on the upper level. A second full bath for multiple users and a convenient second-floor washer and dryer are also found on this level.

Plan B-90018	
Bedrooms: 4	**Baths: 2 ½**
Space:	
Upper floor	959 sq. ft.
Main floor	831 sq. ft.
Total Living Area	**1,790 sq. ft.**
Basement	831 sq. ft.
Garage	390 sq. ft.
Exterior Wall Framing	**2x4**
Foundation options:	
Standard Basement	
(Foundation & framing conversion diagram available—see order form.)	
Blueprint Price Code	**B**

TO ORDER THIS BLUEPRINT, CALL TOLL-FREE 1-800-547-5570

Plan B-90018

PRICES AND DETAILS ON PAGES 12-15

Attention to Tradition

- This unique design combines contemporary exterior styling with traditional elements.
- The covered front porch flows into a two-story-high foyer, highlighted by a window above.
- Decorative columns and open railings define the adjoining living room, also accented with a lovely corner window, a front-facing window seat and a vaulted ceiling open to the upper floor.
- Conveniently located on the main floor yet out of sight is an oversized laundry room near the garage entrance.
- The sunny, bayed eat-in kitchen is nestled between the formal dining room and the informal family room. A handy serving counter extends from the kitchen into the family room, which also offers a two-story volume ceiling, an optional fireplace and patio access.
- Three nice-sized bedrooms and two full baths share the upper floor.

Plan AG-1605

Bedrooms: 3	Baths: 2½
Living Area:	
Upper floor	821 sq. ft.
Main floor	980 sq. ft.
Total Living Area:	**1,801 sq. ft.**
Standard basement	980 sq. ft.
Garage	480 sq. ft.
Exterior Wall Framing:	2x4

Foundation Options:

Standard basement

(All plans can be built with your choice of foundation and framing. A generic conversion diagram is available. See order form.)

BLUEPRINT PRICE CODE:	**B**

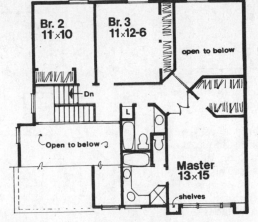

UPPER FLOOR

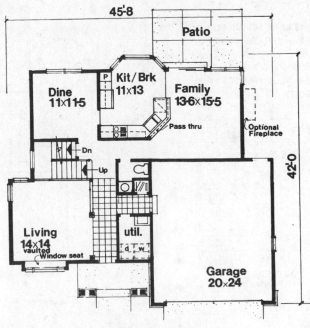

MAIN FLOOR

Windows of Opportunity

- This handsome home features a wide assortment of windows, flooding the interior with light and accentuating the open, airy atmosphere.
- The two-story-high entry is brightened by a beautiful Palladian window above. Just ahead, the vaulted Great Room also showcases a Palladian window. The adjoining dining area offers sliding glass doors that open to a large deck.
- The centrally located kitchen includes a boxed-out window over the sink, providing a nice area for plants.
- The family/breakfast area hosts a snack bar and a wet bar, in addition to a fireplace that warms the entire area.
- Upstairs, the master suite boasts corner windows, a large walk-in closet and a compartmentalized bath with a dual-sink vanity. A balcony overlooking the foyer and the Great Room leads to two more bedrooms and a full bath.

Plan B-129-8510

Bedrooms: 3	Baths: 2½
Living Area:	
Upper floor	802 sq. ft.
Main floor	922 sq. ft.
Total Living Area:	**1,724 sq. ft.**
Standard basement	924 sq. ft.
Garage	579 sq. ft.
Exterior Wall Framing:	2x4

Foundation Options:

Standard basement

(All plans can be built with your choice of foundation and framing. A generic conversion diagram is available. See order form.)

BLUEPRINT PRICE CODE:	B

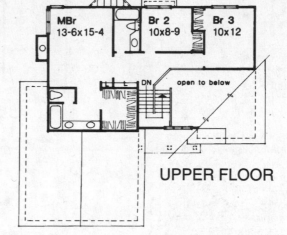

UPPER FLOOR

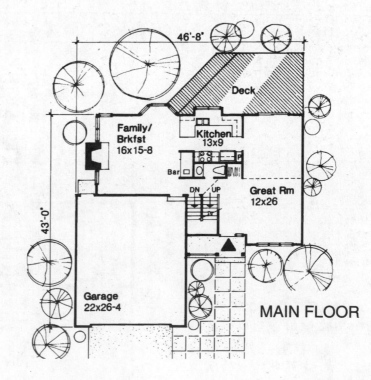

MAIN FLOOR

Plan B-129-8510

PRICES AND DETAILS ON PAGES 12-15

Spirited Split

- A lovely front porch, expressed timber and ascending exterior stairs create an anticipation that is well rewarded inside this three-bedroom split-level.
- The vaulted living room off the foyer has a handsome fireplace and front window; it joins the formal dining room with wet bar.
- Also vaulted are the kitchen and breakfast room, with pantry and entrance to the wrapping rear deck.
- Up several steps is the elegant vaulted master bedroom and private skylit bath with plant shelf above the tub and walk-in closet; two additional bedrooms and a second bath are also included.
- The lower level offers a half bath, laundry room and a bonus area with bar.

MAIN FLOOR

43'-0"

48'-0"

- Mas. Suite 12-6x15-6 vaulted
- Skylight
- Plant Shelf
- Br 2 11x13-4
- Br 3 10x13
- Deck
- Brkfst 8-6x8-4 vaulted
- Kit vaulted
- Dining 12x8 vaulted
- Bar
- P
- DN
- UP
- Plant Shelf
- Living Rm 14-6x16-6 vaulted

LOWER FLOOR

- Bonus Space 19x13
- Bar
- Mechanical
- UP
- DN
- D W
- Basement
- Garage 21-4x19-4

Plan B-89032

Bedrooms: 3	Baths: 2½

Living Area:

Main floor	1,424 sq. ft.
Lower floor	150 sq. ft.
Bonus space	273 sq. ft.
Total Living Area:	**1,847 sq. ft.**
Partial basement	575 sq. ft.
Garage	412 sq. ft.

Exterior Wall Framing: 2x4

Foundation Options:

Partial basement

(Typical foundation & framing conversion diagram available—see order form.)

BLUEPRINT PRICE CODE: B

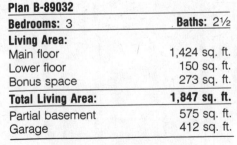

Intriguing Two-Story Home

- An unusual roofline and a rustic stone chimney grace the exterior of this intriguing two-story, four-bedroom home.
- The covered entryway opens to a reception hall that offers a strking view of the open, airy living spaces.
- The living room is enhanced by a high-efficiency fireplace and a skylighted, sloped ceiling. An upper-level balcony and a circular dining room are other eye-catching design features of the formal living areas.
- Folding doors open to the informal living areas, which consist of the family room, another circular dinette and a U-shaped kitchen. The kitchen is equipped with a snack bar, and the family room has sliding glass doors leading to an isolated terrace.
- The blueprints offer the option of reversing the locations of the kitchen and the family room.
- The secluded master bedroom suite offers many amenities, such as a private terrace, a walk-in closet and a wonderful bath with garden whirlpool tub. A main-floor laundry and a powder room are close by.
- An open stairway rises to a balcony, three additional bedrooms and a compartmentalized bath. Lots of closet space plus attic storage areas add to the efficiency of this plan.

Plan K-662-NA

Bedrooms: 4	Baths: 2 ½
Space:	
Upper floor	670 sq. ft.
Main floor	1,196 sq. ft.
Total Living Area	**1,866 sq. ft.**
Basement	1,196 sq. ft.
Garage	418 sq. ft.
Exterior Wall Framing	2x4 or 2x6

Foundation options:
Standard Basement
Slab
(Foundation & framing conversion diagram available—see order form.)

Blueprint Price Code	**B**

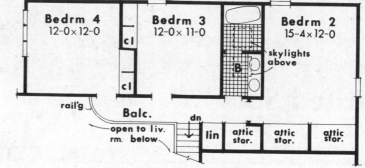

UPPER FLOOR

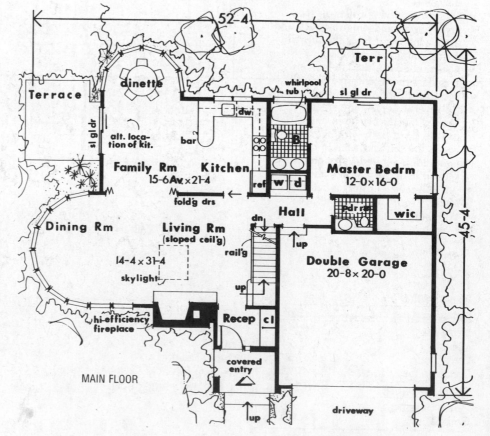

MAIN FLOOR

Plan K-662-NA

PRICES AND DETAILS ON PAGES 12-15

Octagonal Dining Bay

- Classic traditional styling is recreated with a covered front porch and triple dormers with half-round windows.
- Off the entry porch, double doors reveal the reception area, with a walk-in closet and a half-bath.

- The living room features a striking fireplace and leads to the dining room, with its octagonal bay.
- The island kitchen overlooks the dinette and the family room, which features a second fireplace and sliding glass doors to a rear deck.
- Upstairs, the master suite boasts a walk-in closet and a whirlpool bath. A skylighted hallway connects three more bedrooms and another full bath.

Plan K-680-R	
Bedrooms: 4	**Baths:** 2½
Living Area:	
Upper floor	853 sq. ft.
Main floor	1,047 sq. ft.
Total Living Area:	**1,900 sq. ft.**
Standard basement	1,015 sq. ft.
Garage and storage	472 sq. ft.
Exterior Wall Framing:	2x4 or 2x6

Foundation Options:

Standard basement

Slab

(All plans can be built with your choice of foundation and framing. A generic conversion diagram is available. See order form.)

BLUEPRINT PRICE CODE:	B

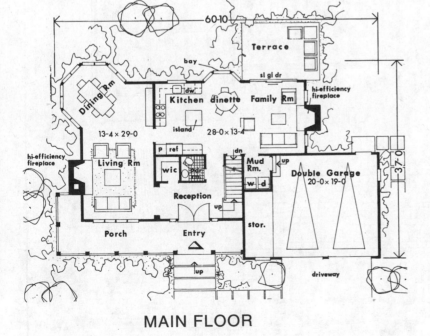

MAIN FLOOR

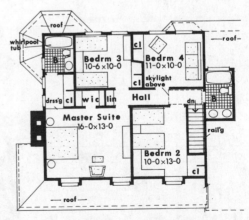

UPPER FLOOR

VIEW INTO LIVING ROOM AND DINING ROOM

CH-210-B

Alternate Exteriors

- Timeless exterior detailing and a functional, cost-effective interior are found in this traditional home.
- The kitchen, bayed breakfast room and vaulted family room with skylights and fireplace flow together to form the heart of the home.
- Lots of light filters into the front-facing formal living room.
- Upstairs, the master suite boasts a vaulted ceiling, large walk-in closet and private luxury bath.
- For the flavor of a full, covered front porch, Plan CH-210-B should be your choice.

BEDROOM 2 10'0" X 11'4"

BEDROOM 3 10'0" X 11'4"

MASTER BEDROOM 13'0" X 17'8"

DN

VAULT CLG.

EDGE OF OPTIONAL BRICK VENEER

UPPER FLOOR

44'-0"

DINING ROOM 10'6" X 13'0"

KITCHEN 10'0" X 12'8"

BREAKFAST 9'1" X 7'4"

VAULT CLG.

FAMILY ROOM 13'0" X 16'4"

EDGE OF OPTIONAL BRICK VENEER

LIVING ROOM 13'0" X 15'0"

DN

UP

FOYER

GARAGE 19'4" X 20'8"

38'-0"

MAIN FLOOR

Plan CH-210-A & -B

Bedrooms: 3	**Baths:** 2½

Space:

Upper floor	823 sq. ft.
Main floor	1,079 sq. ft.
Total Living Area	**1,902 sq. ft.**
Basement	978 sq. ft.
Garage	400 sq. ft.
Exterior Wall Framing	2x4

Foundation options:

Standard Basement
Daylight Basement
Crawlspace
(Foundation & framing conversion diagram available—see order form.)

Blueprint Price Code	B

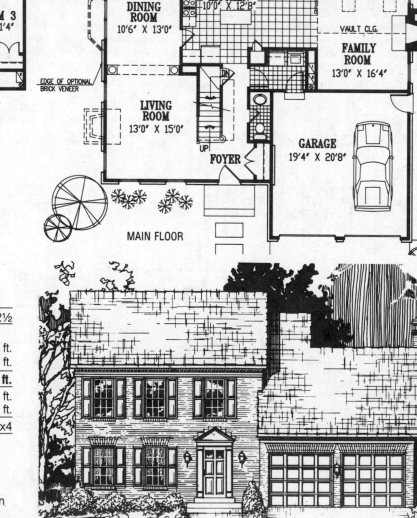

CH-210-A

Spacious and Open

- A brilliant wall of windows invites guests into the two-story-high foyer of this striking traditional home.
- At the center of this open floor plan, the sunken family room boasts a 21-ft. vaulted ceiling and a striking fireplace with flanking windows.
- The cozy dinette merges with the family room and the island kitchen, creating a spacious, open atmosphere. A pantry closet, a laundry room, a half-bath and garage access are all nearby.
- The formal living and dining rooms are found at the front of the home. The living room boasts a 10½-ft. cathedral ceiling and a lovely window arrangement.
- The main-floor master bedroom has a 10-ft., 10-in. tray ceiling, a walk-in closet and a lush bath designed for two.
- Upstairs, two bedrooms share another full bath and a balcony landing that overlooks the family room and foyer.

Plan A-2207-DS

Bedrooms: 3	**Baths:** 2½

Living Area:	
Upper floor	518 sq. ft.
Main floor	1,389 sq. ft.
Total Living Area:	**1,907 sq. ft.**
Standard basement	1,389 sq. ft.
Garage	484 sq. ft.
Exterior Wall Framing:	**2x6**

Foundation Options:

Standard basement

(All plans can be built with your choice of foundation and framing. A generic conversion diagram is available. See order form.)

BLUEPRINT PRICE CODE: **B**

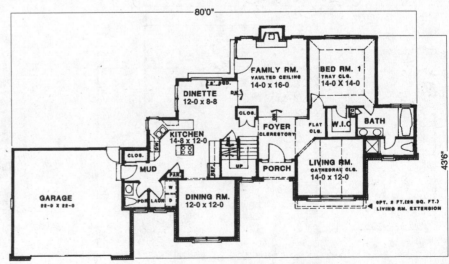

UPPER FLOOR

MAIN FLOOR

TO ORDER THIS BLUEPRINT,
CALL TOLL-FREE 1-800-547-5570

Plan A-2207-DS

PRICES AND DETAILS
ON PAGES 12-15

245

Quality Space in Compact Four-Bedroom Design

- This well-planned design makes good use of a small lot by putting 1,909 sq. ft. of space on a foundation less than 1,000 sq. ft. in size.
- A large family room/breakfast/kitchen area is great for family dining and other activities.
- Roomy, vaulted living room

includes an impressive fireplace, a feature not often found in homes of this modest size.
- Upstairs, you'll find four bedrooms and a balcony overlooking the living room below.
- The master bedroom includes a private bath and large walk-in closet.

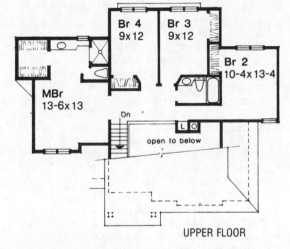

UPPER FLOOR

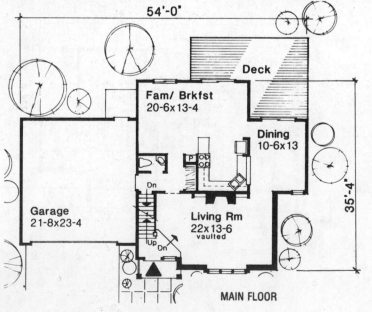

MAIN FLOOR

Plan B-117-8506

Bedrooms: 4	Baths: 2½
Space:	
Upper floor:	915 sq. ft.
Main floor:	994 sq. ft.
Total living area:	1,909 sq. ft.
Basement:	994 sq. ft.
Garage:	505 sq. ft.
Exterior Wall Framing:	2x4

Foundation options:
Standard basement only.
(Foundation & framing conversion diagram available — see order form.)

Blueprint Price Code:	B

TO ORDER THIS BLUEPRINT, CALL TOLL-FREE 1-800-547-5570

Plan B-117-8506

PRICES AND DETAILS ON PAGES 12-15

Balcony Overlooks Living Room

First floor: 1,018 sq. ft.
Second floor: 900 sq. ft.

Total living area: 1,918 sq. ft.
(Not counting garage)

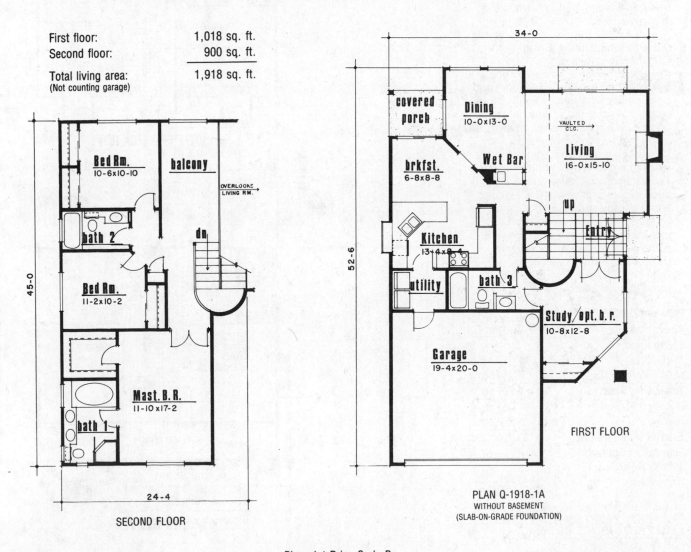

Bed Rm.
10-6x10-10

balcony

OVERLOOKS
LIVING RM.

bath 2

dn

Bed Rm.
11-2x10-2

Mast. B. R.
11-10 x 17-2

bath 1

45-0

24-4

SECOND FLOOR

34-0

covered porch

Dining
10-0x13-0

VAULTED
CLG.

brkfst.
6-8x8-8

Wet Bar

Living
16-0x15-10

Kitchen
13-4x8-4

up

Entry

52-6

utility

bath 3

Study/opt. b.r.
10-8x12-8

Garage
19-4x20-0

FIRST FLOOR

PLAN Q-1918-1A
WITHOUT BASEMENT
(SLAB-ON-GRADE FOUNDATION)

Blueprint Price Code B
Plan Q-1918-1A

Farmhouse for Today

- An inviting covered porch and decorative dormer windows lend traditional warmth and charm to this attractive design.
- The up-to-date interior includes ample space for entertaining as well as for daily family activities.
- The elegant foyer is flanked on one side by the formal, sunken living room and on the other by a sunken family room with a fireplace and an entertainment center. Each room features an 8½-ft. tray ceiling and views of the porch.
- The dining room flows from the living room to increase the entertaining space.
- The kitchen/nook/laundry area forms a large expanse for casual family living and domestic chores.
- Upstairs, the grand master suite includes a large closet and a private bath with a garden tub, a designer shower and a private deck.
- A second full bath serves the two secondary bedrooms.

Plan U-87-203

Bedrooms: 3	**Baths:** 2½

Living Area:	
Upper floor	857 sq. ft.
Main floor	1,064 sq. ft.
Total Living Area:	**1,921 sq. ft.**
Standard basement	1,064 sq. ft.
Garage	552 sq. ft.

Exterior Wall Framing: 2x4 or 2x6

Foundation Options:
Standard basement
Crawlspace
Slab
(All plans can be built with your choice of foundation and framing. A generic conversion diagram is available. See order form.)

BLUEPRINT PRICE CODE: B

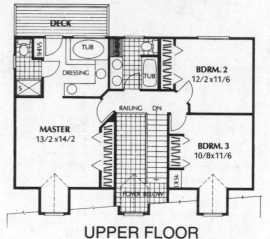

UPPER FLOOR

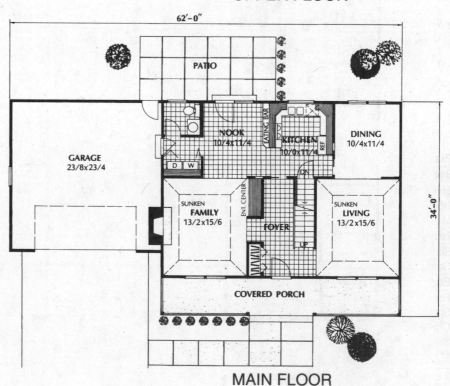

MAIN FLOOR

Country Living

- A covered porch, half-round transom windows and three dormers give this home its warm, nostalgic appeal. Shuttered windows and a louvered vent beautify the side-entry, two-car garage.
- Designed for the ultimate in country living, the floor plan starts off with a dynamic Great Room that flows to a bayed dining area. A nice fireplace adds warmth, while a French door provides access to a backyard covered porch. A powder room is just steps away.
- A 12-ft., 4-in. vaulted ceiling presides over the large country kitchen, which offers a bayed nook, an oversized breakfast bar and a convenient pass-through to the rear porch.
- The exquisite master suite boasts a tray ceiling, a bay window and an alcove for built-in shelves or extra closet space. Other amenities include a large walk-in closet and a compartmentalized bath.
- Upstairs, 9-ft. ceilings enhance two more bedrooms and a second full bath. Each bedroom boasts a cozy dormer window and two closets.

Plan AX-93311

Bedrooms: 3	Baths: 2½
Living Area:	
Upper floor	570 sq. ft.
Main floor	1,375 sq. ft.
Total Living Area:	**1,945 sq. ft.**
Standard basement	1,280 sq. ft.
Garage	450 sq. ft.
Exterior Wall Framing:	2x4

Foundation Options:

Standard basement
Crawlspace
Slab
(All plans can be built with your choice of foundation and framing. A generic conversion diagram is available. See order form.)

BLUEPRINT PRICE CODE: **B**

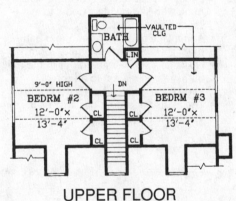

UPPER FLOOR

VIEW INTO GREAT ROOM

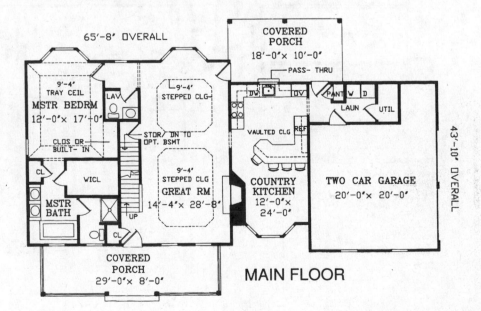

MAIN FLOOR

Living on a Sloping Lot

- The interesting roofline, attractive front deck and dramatic windows of this stylish family home give it lasting contemporary appeal.
- The two-story entry opens up to the spacious living room, which boasts floor-to-ceiling windows and an 11½-ft. vaulted ceiling with exposed beams.

- The adjoining dining area provides access to a wraparound railed deck.
- The updated kitchen offers a walk-in pantry, an eating bar and a breakfast nook with sliding glass doors to a second railed deck.
- A fireplace and access to a rear patio highlight the attached family room.
- Upstairs, a washer and dryer in the hall bath are convenient to all three bedrooms, making laundry a breeze.
- The master bedroom has an 11½-ft. vaulted ceiling and a private bath.

Plan P-7737-4D	
Bedrooms: 3	**Baths:** 2½
Living Area:	
Upper floor	802 sq. ft.
Main floor	1,158 sq. ft.
Total Living Area:	**1,960 sq. ft.**
Tuck-under garage	736 sq. ft.
Exterior Wall Framing:	2x6
Foundation Options:	
Crawlspace	

(All plans can be built with your choice of foundation and framing. A generic conversion diagram is available. See order form.)

BLUEPRINT PRICE CODE:	B

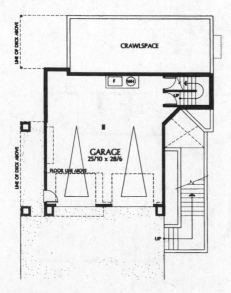

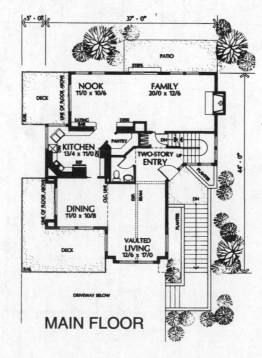

MAIN FLOOR

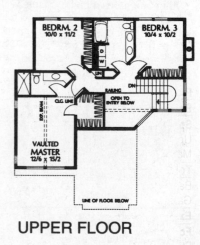

UPPER FLOOR

Plan P-7737-4D

PRICES AND DETAILS ON PAGES 12-15

Attractive, Open Interior

- Multiple rooflines and an articulate facade generate an attractive curb appeal.
- Inside, sloped ceilings and jutting bays heighten the open, airy atmosphere.
- The formal living and dining rooms are highlighted by an angled fireplace.
- The informal living areas at the rear of the home include a modern, open kitchen flanked by a cozy family room with fireplace and a bright dinette.
- A den or fourth bedroom and a main-floor laundry room complete this level.
- An angled stairway leads to the three additional bedrooms on the upper level.

Plan K-684-D

Bedrooms: 3-4	Baths: 3
Space:	
Upper floor	702 sq. ft.
Main floor	1,273 sq. ft.
Total Living Area	**1,975 sq. ft.**
Basement	1,225 sq. ft.
Garage	440 sq. ft.
Exterior Wall Framing	2x4 or 2x6

Foundation options:
Standard Basement
Slab
(Foundation & framing conversion diagram available—see order form.)

Blueprint Price Code	B

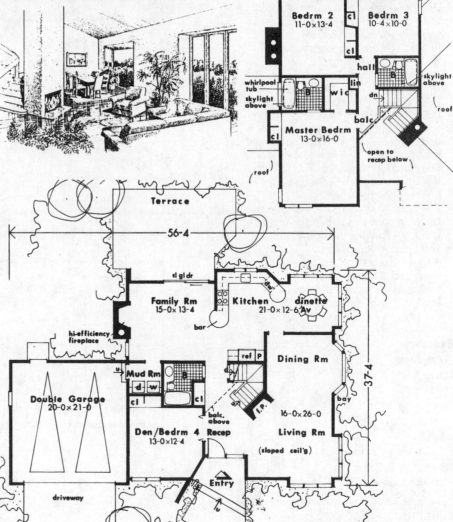

TO ORDER THIS BLUEPRINT,
CALL TOLL-FREE 1-800-547-5570

Plan K-684-D

PRICES AND DETAILS
ON PAGES 12-15
251

Relax on the Front Porch

- With its wraparound covered porch, this quaint two-story home makes summer evenings a breeze.
- Inside, a beautiful open stairway welcomes guests into the vaulted foyer, which connects the formal areas. The front-facing living and dining rooms have views of the covered front porch.
- French doors open from the living room to the family room, where a fireplace and corner windows warm and brighten this spacious activity area.
- The breakfast nook, set off by a half-wall, hosts a handy work desk and opens to the back porch.
- The country kitchen offers an oversized island, a pantry closet and illuminating windows flanking the corner sink.
- The upper-floor master suite boasts two walk-in closets and a private bath with a tub and a separate shower. Two more bedrooms, another full bath and a laundry room are also included.

Plan AGH-1997

Bedrooms: 3	Baths: 2½
Living Area:	
Upper floor	933 sq. ft.
Main floor	1,064 sq. ft.
Total Living Area:	**1,997 sq. ft.**
Standard basement	1,064 sq. ft.
Garage	662 sq. ft.
Exterior Wall Framing:	2x6

Foundation Options:

Standard basement
(All plans can be built with your choice of foundation and framing. A generic conversion diagram is available. See order form.)

BLUEPRINT PRICE CODE: B

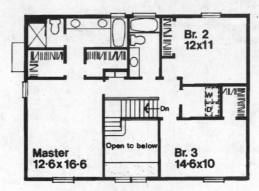

UPPER FLOOR

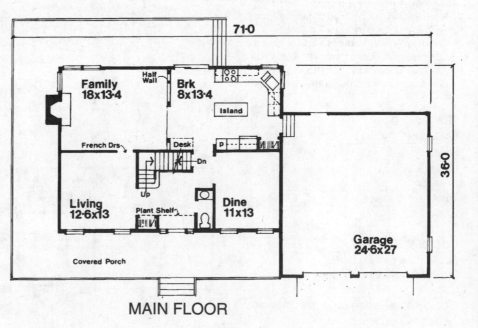

MAIN FLOOR

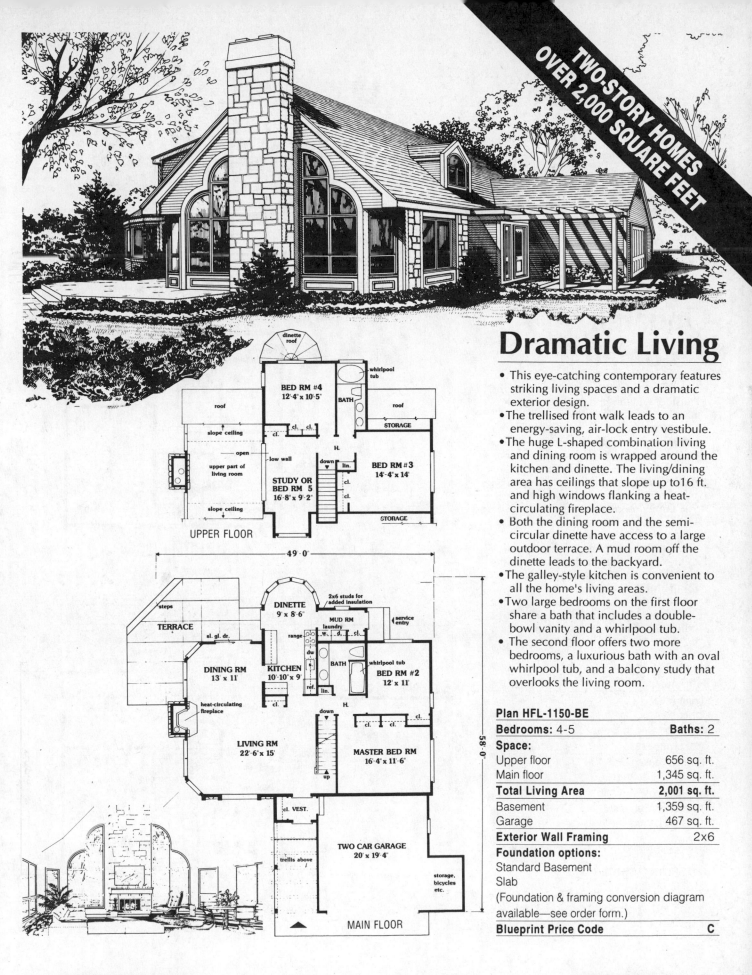

UPPER FLOOR

- dinette roof
- BED RM #4 12'-4" x 10'-5"
- whirlpool tub
- BATH
- roof
- roof
- STORAGE
- cl.   cl.
- cl.
- open
- low wall
- H.
- down
- lin.
- BED RM #3 14'-4" x 14'
- cl.
- cl.
- STORAGE
- upper part of living room
- slope ceiling
- STUDY OR BED RM 5 16'-8" x 9'-2"
- slope ceiling

MAIN FLOOR

- 49'-0"
- 58'-0"
- steps
- TERRACE
- sl. gl. dr.
- DINETTE 9' x 8'-6"
- 2x6 studs for added insulation
- MUD RM
- laundry
- w.   d.   cl.
- service entry
- range
- DINING RM 13' x 11'
- KITCHEN 10'-10" x 9'
- dw
- ref.
- lin.
- BATH
- whirlpool tub
- BED RM #2 12' x 11'
- heat-circulating fireplace
- cl.
- H.
- down
- cl.   cl.   cl.
- LIVING RM 22'-6" x 15'
- MASTER BED RM 16'-4" x 11'-6"
- up
- cl. VEST.
- trellis above
- TWO CAR GARAGE 20' x 19'-4"
- storage, bicycles etc.

Dramatic Living

- This eye-catching contemporary features striking living spaces and a dramatic exterior design.
- The trellised front walk leads to an energy-saving, air-lock entry vestibule.
- The huge L-shaped combination living and dining room is wrapped around the kitchen and dinette. The living/dining area has ceilings that slope up to 16 ft. and high windows flanking a heat-circulating fireplace.
- Both the dining room and the semi-circular dinette have access to a large outdoor terrace. A mud room off the dinette leads to the backyard.
- The galley-style kitchen is convenient to all the home's living areas.
- Two large bedrooms on the first floor share a bath that includes a double-bowl vanity and a whirlpool tub.
- The second floor offers two more bedrooms, a luxurious bath with an oval whirlpool tub, and a balcony study that overlooks the living room.

Plan HFL-1150-BE	
Bedrooms: 4-5	**Baths:** 2
Space:	
Upper floor	656 sq. ft.
Main floor	1,345 sq. ft.
Total Living Area	**2,001 sq. ft.**
Basement	1,359 sq. ft.
Garage	467 sq. ft.
Exterior Wall Framing	2x6
Foundation options:	
Standard Basement	
Slab	
(Foundation & framing conversion diagram available—see order form.)	
Blueprint Price Code	C

Updated Colonial

- This home offers Colonial styling on the outside, with an updated, ultra-modern floor plan inside.
- Guests are welcomed into a formal gallery that leads to all of the main-floor living areas. The large living room and the formal dining room flank the gallery. Optional folding doors open the living room to the family room.
- The family room features an inviting fireplace as its hub and sliding-door access to a backyard terrace.
- The kitchen is located for easy service to the formal dining room as well as the bayed dinette. A mudroom/laundry room and a powder room are nearby.
- Upstairs, the master suite boasts a private bath and a wall of closets. Three unique secondary bedrooms share a hall bath, which has a dual-sink vanity.

Plan K-274-M

Bedrooms: 4	Baths: 2½
Living Area:	
Upper floor	990 sq. ft.
Main floor	1,025 sq. ft.
Total Living Area:	**2,015 sq. ft.**
Standard basement	983 sq. ft.
Garage and storage	520 sq. ft.
Exterior Wall Framing:	2x4 or 2x6

Foundation Options:

Standard basement

Slab

(All plans can be built with your choice of foundation and framing. A generic conversion diagram is available. See order form.)

BLUEPRINT PRICE CODE:	C

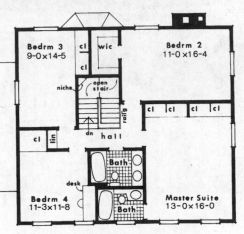

UPPER FLOOR

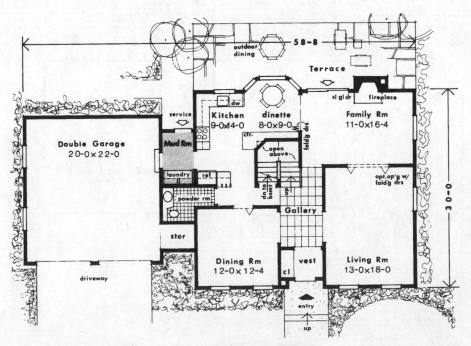

MAIN FLOOR

Plan K-274-M

PRICES AND DETAILS ON PAGES 12-15

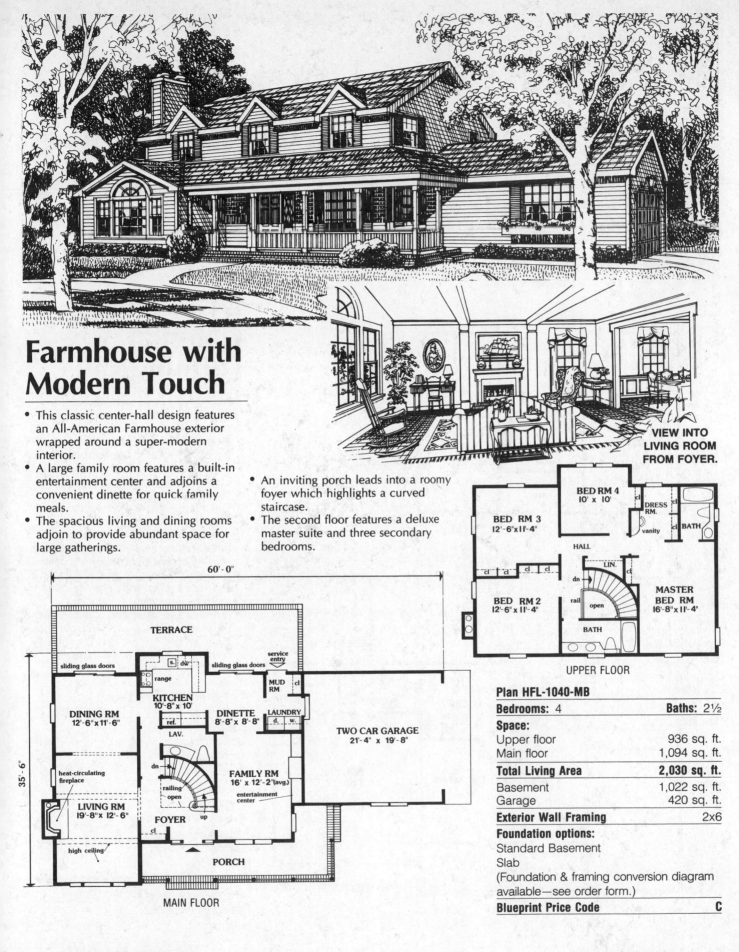

Farmhouse with Modern Touch

- This classic center-hall design features an All-American Farmhouse exterior wrapped around a super-modern interior.
- A large family room features a built-in entertainment center and adjoins a convenient dinette for quick family meals.
- The spacious living and dining rooms adjoin to provide abundant space for large gatherings.
- An inviting porch leads into a roomy foyer which highlights a curved staircase.
- The second floor features a deluxe master suite and three secondary bedrooms.

VIEW INTO LIVING ROOM FROM FOYER.

UPPER FLOOR

BED RM 4 — 10' x 10'
DRESS. RM.
BATH
BED RM 3 — 12'-6" x 11'-4"
HALL
LIN.
BED RM 2 — 12'-6" x 11'-4"
MASTER BED RM — 16'-8" x 11'-4"
BATH

MAIN FLOOR

60'-0"
35'-6"
TERRACE
sliding glass doors
sliding glass doors
service entry
s. dw
range
KITCHEN 10'-8" x 10'
ref.
MUD RM
cl
DINING RM 12'-6" x 11'-6"
DINETTE 8'-8" x 8'-8"
LAUNDRY d. w.
TWO CAR GARAGE 21'-4" x 19'-8"
LAV.
heat-circulating fireplace
dn
railing open
up
FAMILY RM 16' x 12'-2" (avg.)
entertainment center
LIVING RM 19'-8" x 12'-6"
FOYER
cl
high ceiling
PORCH

Plan HFL-1040-MB

Bedrooms: 4	**Baths:** 2½

Space:	
Upper floor	936 sq. ft.
Main floor	1,094 sq. ft.
Total Living Area	**2,030 sq. ft.**
Basement	1,022 sq. ft.
Garage	420 sq. ft.
Exterior Wall Framing	2x6

Foundation options:
Standard Basement
Slab
(Foundation & framing conversion diagram available—see order form.)

Blueprint Price Code	C

Distinctive Colonial Farmhouse

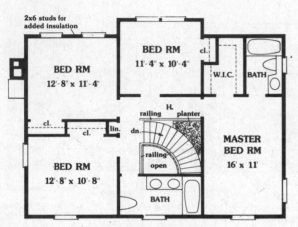

2x6 studs for added insulation

BED RM 12'-8" x 11'-4"

BED RM 11'-4" x 10'-4"

cl.

W.I.C.

BATH

cl.

cl.

lin.

H.

railing planter

dn.

railing open

BED RM 12'-8" x 10'-8"

MASTER BED RM 16' x 11'

BATH

UPPER FLOOR

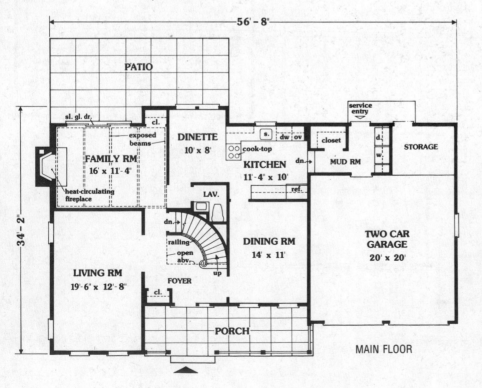

56'-8"

PATIO

34'-2"

sl. gl. dr.

cl.

exposed beams

FAMILY RM 16' x 11'-4"

heat-circulating fireplace

DINETTE 10' x 8'

s.

dw ov

cook-top

KITCHEN 11'-4" x 10'

dn.

ref.

service entry

closet

MUD RM

d.

w.

STORAGE

LAV.

dn.

railing open abv.

up

FOYER

DINING RM 14' x 11'

TWO CAR GARAGE 20' x 20'

LIVING RM 19'-6" x 12'-8"

cl.

PORCH

MAIN FLOOR

- Although a casual living theme flows throughout this farmhouse, elegance is not forgotten.
- A beautiful circular stair ascends from the central foyer to the bedrooms on the upper level.
- Formal living and dining rooms flank the foyer.
- The informal family room at the rear captures an Early American style with exposed beams, wood paneling and a brick fireplace wall. Sliding glass doors provide access to the adjoining patio.
- A sunny dinette opens to an efficiently arranged kitchen with a handy laundry room near the garage entrance.
- A decorative railing and a planter adorn the second-floor balcony that overlooks the foyer below. Four generous-sized bedrooms and two baths share this level.

Plan HFL-1010-CR

Bedrooms: 4	Baths: 2 ½
Space:	
Upper floor	932 sq. ft.
Main floor	1,099 sq. ft.
Total Living Area	**2,031 sq. ft.**
Basement	998 sq. ft.
Garage and storage	476 sq. ft.
Exterior Wall Framing	2x4

Foundation options:
Standard Basement
Slab
(Foundation & framing conversion diagram available—see order form.)

Blueprint Price Code	C

Open, Flowing Floor Plan

- Open, flowing rooms punctuated with wonderful windows enhance this spacious four-bedroom home.
- The two-story-high foyer is brightened by an arched window above. To the left lies the living room, which flows into the family room. An inviting fireplace and windows overlooking a rear terrace highlight the family room.
- The centrally located kitchen serves both the formal dining room and the dinette, with a view of the family room beyond. Sliding glass doors in the dinette open to a lovely terrace.
- Upstairs, the master suite features an arched window and a walk-in closet with a dressing area. The private master bath includes a dual-sink vanity, a skylighted whirlpool tub and a separate shower.
- The three remaining bedrooms share another skylighted bath.

Plan AHP-9020

Bedrooms: 4	Baths: 2½
Living Area:	
Upper floor	1,021 sq. ft.
Main floor	1,125 sq. ft.
Total Living Area:	**2,146 sq. ft.**
Standard basement	1,032 sq. ft.
Garage	480 sq. ft.
Exterior Wall Framing:	2x6

Foundation Options:

Standard basement

Crawlspace

Slab

(All plans can be built with your choice of foundation and framing. A generic conversion diagram is available. See order form.)

BLUEPRINT PRICE CODE: C

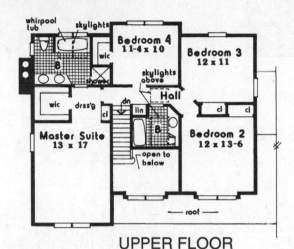

UPPER FLOOR

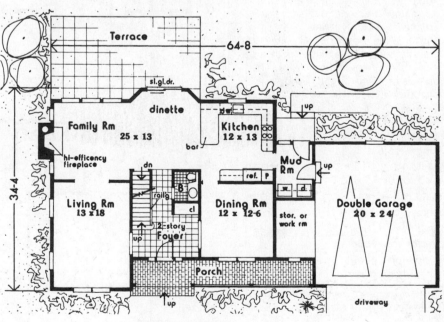

MAIN FLOOR

Front Porch Invites Visitors

- This neat and well-proportioned design exudes warmth and charm.
- The roomy foyer connects the formal dining room and living room for special occasions, and the living and family rooms join together to create abundant space for large gatherings.
- The large kitchen, dinette and family room flow from one to the other for great casual family living.
- Upstairs, the roomy master suite is complemented by a master bath available in two configurations. The unique library is brightened by a beautiful arched window.

Plan GL-2161

Bedrooms: 3	**Baths:** 2½
Living Area:	
Upper floor	991 sq. ft.
Main floor	1,170 sq. ft.
Total Living Area	**2,161 sq. ft.**
Standard basement	1,170 sq. ft.
Garage	462 sq. ft.
Exterior Wall Framing	2x6

Foundation Options:

Standard basement

(All plans can be built with your choice of foundation and framing. A generic conversion diagram is available. See order form.)

BLUEPRINT PRICE CODE	**C**

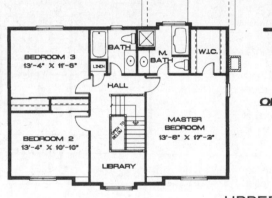

UPPER FLOOR

OPT. MSTR. BATH

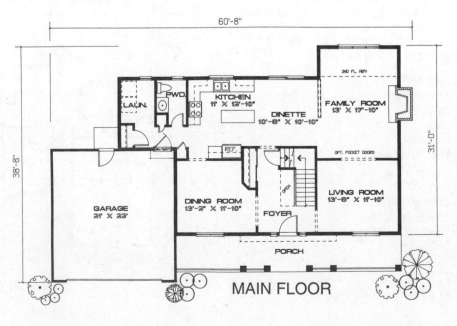

MAIN FLOOR

TO ORDER THIS BLUEPRINT, CALL TOLL-FREE 1-800-547-5570

Plan GL-2161

PRICES AND DETAILS ON PAGES 12-15

Country Kitchen

- A lovely front porch, dormers and shutters give this home a country-style exterior and complement its comfortable and informal interior.
- The roomy country kitchen connects with the sunny breakfast nook and the formal dining room.
- The central portion of the home consists of a large family room with a handsome fireplace and easy access to a backyard deck.
- The main-floor master suite, particularly impressive for a home of this size, features a majestic master bath with a corner garden tub, two walk-in closets and a dual-sink vanity with knee space.
- Upstairs, you will find two more good-sized bedrooms, a double bath and a large storage area.

Plan C-8645

Bedrooms: 3	**Baths:** 2½

Living Area:	
Upper floor	704 sq. ft.
Main floor	1,477 sq. ft.
Total Living Area:	**2,181 sq. ft.**
Standard basement	1,400 sq. ft.
Garage and storage	561 sq. ft.
Exterior Wall Framing:	2x4

Foundation Options:

Standard basement
Crawlspace
Slab
(All plans can be built with your choice of foundation and framing.
A generic conversion diagram is available. See order form.)

BLUEPRINT PRICE CODE:	C

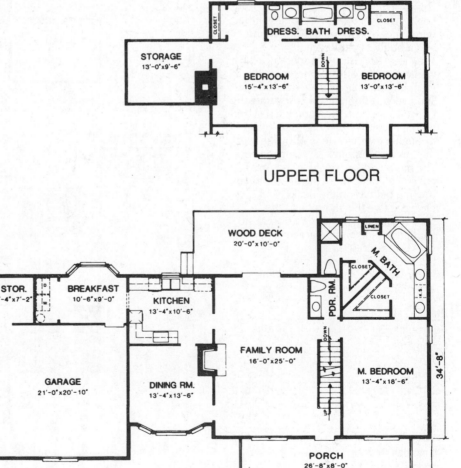

UPPER FLOOR

MAIN FLOOR

TO ORDER THIS BLUEPRINT,
CALL TOLL-FREE 1-800-547-5570

Plan C-8645

PRICES AND DETAILS
ON PAGES 12-15

259

Photo by Mark Englund/HomeStyles

State-of-the-Art Floor Plan

- This design's state-of-the-art floor plan begins with a two-story-high foyer that introduces a stunning open staircase and a bright Great Room.
- The Great Room is expanded by a 17-ft. vaulted ceiling and a window wall with French doors that open to a rear deck.
- Short sections of half-walls separate the Great Room from the open kitchen and dining room. Natural light streams in through a greenhouse window above the sink and lots of glass facing the deck.
- The main-floor master suite has a 9-ft. coved ceiling and private access to an inviting hot tub on the deck. Walk-in closets frame the entrance to the luxurious bath, highlighted by a 10-ft. vaulted ceiling and an arched window above a raised spa tub.
- Upstairs, a balcony hall leads to two bedrooms and a continental bath, plus a den and a storage room.

Plan S-2100

Bedrooms: 3+	**Baths:** 2½

Living Area:	
Upper floor	660 sq. ft.
Main floor	1,440 sq. ft.
Total Living Area:	**2,100 sq. ft.**
Standard basement	1,440 sq. ft.
Garage	552 sq. ft.
Exterior Wall Framing:	2x6

Foundation Options:

Standard basement

Crawlspace

Slab

(All plans can be built with your choice of foundation and framing. A generic conversion diagram is available. See order form.)

BLUEPRINT PRICE CODE: C

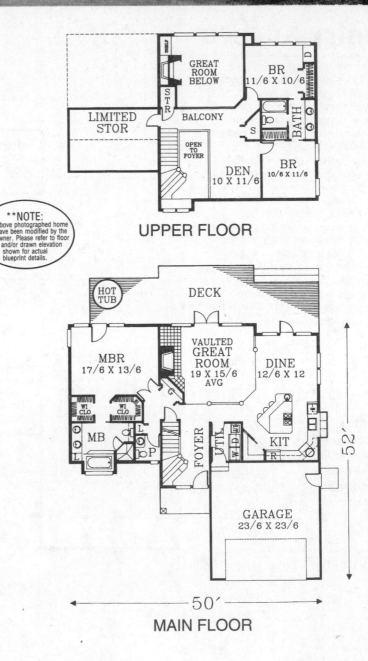

NOTE:
The above photographed home may have been modified by the homeowner. Please refer to floor plan and/or drawn elevation shown for actual blueprint details.

UPPER FLOOR

MAIN FLOOR

Fantastic Floor Plan!

- Featured on "Hometime," the popular PBS television program, this unique design combines a dynamic exterior with a fantastic floor plan.
- The barrel-vaulted entry leads into the vaulted foyer, which is outlined by elegant columns. To the left, the living room features a 13-ft. vaulted ceiling, a curved wall and corner windows. To the right, the formal dining room is enhanced by a tray ceiling.
- Overlooking a large backyard deck, the island kitchen includes a corner pantry and a built-in desk. The breakfast room shares a columned snack bar with the family room, which has a fireplace and a 17-ft., 8-in. vaulted ceiling.
- The master suite boasts a 15-ft. vaulted ceiling and private access to a romantic courtyard. The sunken master bath features an enticing spa tub and a separate shower, both encased by a curved glass-block wall.
- The two upstairs bedrooms have private access to a large full bath.

Plan B-88015

Bedrooms: 3	Baths: 2½
Living Area:	
Upper floor	534 sq. ft.
Main floor	1,689 sq. ft.
Total Living Area:	**2,223 sq. ft.**
Standard basement	1,689 sq. ft.
Garage	455 sq. ft.
Exterior Wall Framing:	2x4

Foundation Options:

Standard basement
(All plans can be built with your choice of foundation and framing. A generic conversion diagram is available. See order form.)

BLUEPRINT PRICE CODE: C

NOTE:
The above photographed home may have been modified by the homeowner. Please refer to floor plan and/or drawn elevation shown for actual blueprint details.

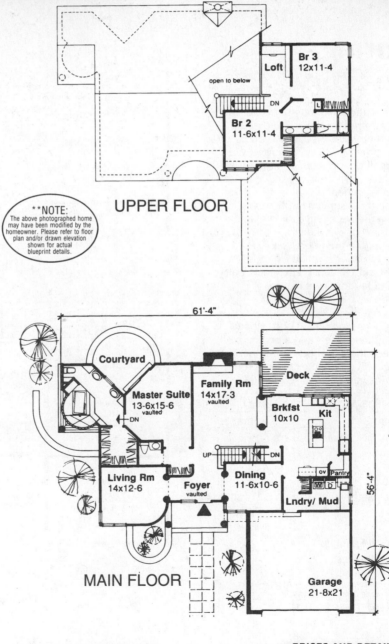

UPPER FLOOR

MAIN FLOOR

Loft

Br 3 12x11-4

Br 2 11-6x11-4

Courtyard

Master Suite 13-6x15-6 vaulted

Family Rm 14x17-3 vaulted

Deck

Brkfst 10x10

Kit

Living Rm 14x12-6

Foyer vaulted

Dining 11-6x10-6

Pantry

Lndry/ Mud

Garage 21-8x21

61'-4"

56'-4"

Alluring Two-Story

- This dramatic contemporary is adorned with staggered rooflines that overlap and outline large expanses of glass.
- Flanking the two-story-high foyer are the formal dining room and the sunken living room, which is expanded by an airy 16-ft. cathedral ceiling.
- The adjoining sunken family room boasts a fireplace and sliding glass doors to a backyard patio.
- A step up, the bright breakfast area enjoys an eating bar that extends from the efficient U-shaped kitchen. A half-bath and laundry facilities are convenient.
- The second level features a spacious master bedroom with a 12-ft. sloped ceiling, dual closets and a private bath. Two secondary bedrooms, another full bath and an optional expansion room above the garage are also included.

Plan AX-8596-A

Bedrooms: 3+	Baths: 2½
Living Area:	
Upper floor	738 sq. ft.
Main floor	1,160 sq. ft.
Bonus room	226 sq. ft.
Total Living Area:	**2,124 sq. ft.**
Standard basement	1,160 sq. ft.
Garage	465 sq. ft.
Exterior Wall Framing:	2x4

Foundation Options:

Standard basement
(All plans can be built with your choice of foundation and framing. A generic conversion diagram is available. See order form.)

BLUEPRINT PRICE CODE: C

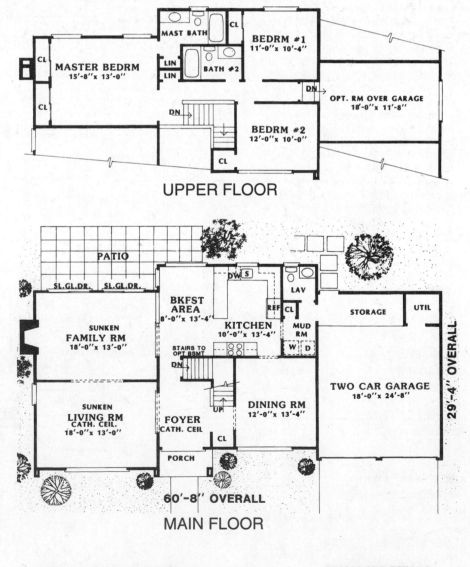

UPPER FLOOR

MAIN FLOOR

Plan AX-8596-A

PRICES AND DETAILS ON PAGES 12-15

Distinctive
Two-Story

- The playful and distinctive exterior of this two-story encloses a functional, contemporary interior.
- The living areas unfold from the skylighted foyer, which is open to the upper-floor balcony. The formal sunken living room features a soaring 17-ft. cathedral ceiling. The adjoining step-down family room offers a fireplace and sliding glass doors to a wonderful deck.
- A low partition allows a view of the family room's fireplace from the breakfast area and the island kitchen.
- A luxurious master suite with a 13-ft. cathedral ceiling and room for three additional bedrooms are found on the upper floor, in addition to a dramatic view of the foyer below.

Plan AX-8922-A

Bedrooms: 3+	Baths: 2½
Living Area:	
Upper floor	840 sq. ft.
Main floor	1,213 sq. ft.
Fourth bedroom	240 sq. ft.
Total Living Area:	**2,293 sq. ft.**
Standard basement	1,138 sq. ft.
Garage	470 sq. ft.
Exterior Wall Framing:	2x4

Foundation Options:

Standard basement
Slab
(All plans can be built with your choice of foundation and framing. A generic conversion diagram is available. See order form.)

BLUEPRINT PRICE CODE:	C

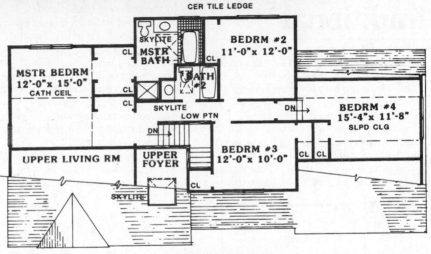

UPPER FLOOR

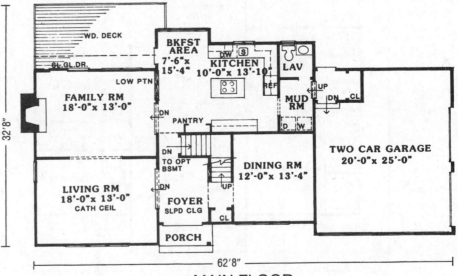

MAIN FLOOR

Gracious Traditional

- This traditional home is perfect for a corner lot, with a quaint facade and an attached garage around back.
- Tall windows, elegant dormers and a covered front porch welcome guests to the front entry and into the foyer.
- Just off the foyer, the formal dining room boasts a built-in hutch and views to the front porch.
- The expansive, skylighted Great Room features a wet bar, a 16-ft. vaulted ceiling, a stunning fireplace and access to the screened back porch.
- The kitchen includes a large pantry and an eating bar to the bayed breakfast nook. A large utility room with garage access is nearby.
- The master bedroom offers a walk-in closet and a bath with a large corner tub and his-and-hers vanities.
- Two additional bedrooms have big walk-in closets, built-in desks and easy access to another full bath.
- Upstairs, a loft overlooks the Great Room and is perfect as an extra bedroom or a recreation area.

Plan C-8920

Bedrooms: 3+	Baths: 3
Living Area:	
Upper floor	305 sq. ft.
Main floor	1,996 sq. ft.
Total Living Area:	**2,301 sq. ft.**
Daylight basement	1,996 sq. ft.
Garage	469 sq. ft.
Exterior Wall Framing:	2x4

Foundation Options:
Daylight basement
Crawlspace
(All plans can be built with your choice of foundation and framing. A generic conversion diagram is available. See order form.)

BLUEPRINT PRICE CODE:	C

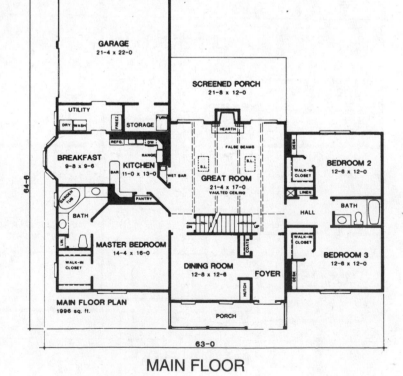

MAIN FLOOR

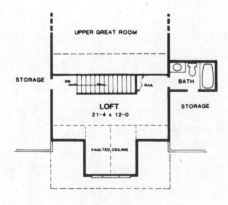

UPPER FLOOR

TO ORDER THIS BLUEPRINT, CALL TOLL-FREE 1-800-547-5570   Plan C-8920   *PRICES AND DETAILS ON PAGES 12-15*

You Asked for It!

- Our most popular plan in recent years, E-3000, has now been downsized for affordability, without sacrificing character or excitement.
- Exterior appeal is created with a covered front porch with decorative columns, triple dormers and rail-topped corner windows.
- The floor plan has combined the separate living and family rooms available in E-3000 into one spacious family room with a corner fireplace and a 17-ft.-high vaulted ceiling. The area flows into the dining room through a columned gallery.
- The kitchen serves the breakfast room over an angled snack bar, and features a huge pantry.
- The stunning main-floor master suite offers a private sitting area, a walk-in closet and a dramatic, angled bath.
- There are two large bedrooms upstairs accessible via a curved staircase with a bridge balcony.

Plan E-2307

Bedrooms: 3	Baths: 2½
Living Area:	
Upper floor	595 sq. ft.
Main floor	1,765 sq. ft.
Total Living Area:	**2,360 sq. ft.**
Standard basement	1,765 sq. ft.
Garage	484 sq. ft.
Storage	44 sq. ft.
Exterior Wall Framing:	2x6

Foundation Options:

Standard basement
Crawlspace
Slab
(All plans can be built with your choice of foundation and framing. A generic conversion diagram is available. See order form.)

BLUEPRINT PRICE CODE: C

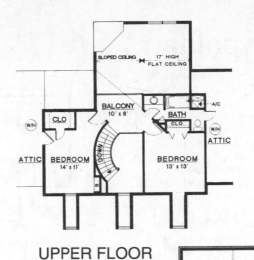

UPPER FLOOR

MAIN FLOOR

TO ORDER THIS BLUEPRINT,
CALL TOLL-FREE 1-800-547-5570

Plan E-2307

PRICES AND DETAILS
ON PAGES 12-15
265

Striking Countrypolitan

- This home's eye-catching exterior encloses a modern interior to provide a great family plan for any setting.
- A pleasant covered porch leads into the entry, which adjoins a half-bath.
- Around the corner, the spacious living room boasts a 14-ft.-high vaulted ceiling with an exposed beam, plus a handsome stone fireplace and a wet bar. A French door opens to a covered back porch.
- A large eating area and country kitchen are the focal point of the home. The roomy kitchen offers an oversized island work counter and a handy pantry. The formal dining room and a neatly organized laundry/utility room are conveniently nearby.
- The secluded master bedroom includes three wardrobe closets. Double doors access the private master bath, which shows off a spa tub, a separate shower and a stylish dual-sink vanity.
- Upstairs, three additional bedrooms are serviced by a second full bath.

Plan E-2303

Bedrooms: 4	Baths: 2½
Living Area:	
Upper floor	814 sq. ft.
Main floor	1,553 sq. ft.
Total Living Area:	**2,367 sq. ft.**
Standard basement	1,553 sq. ft.
Garage and storage	626 sq. ft.
Exterior Wall Framing:	2x6

Foundation Options:

Standard basement

Crawlspace

Slab

(All plans can be built with your choice of foundation and framing. A generic conversion diagram is available. See order form.)

BLUEPRINT PRICE CODE: C

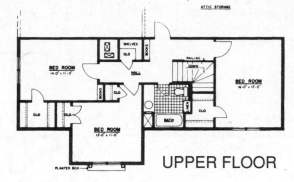

UPPER FLOOR

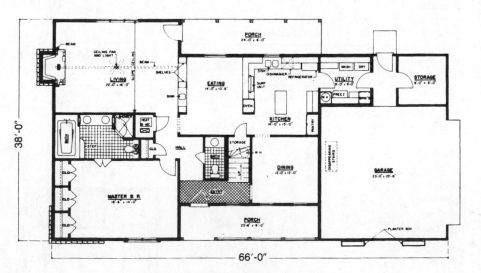

MAIN FLOOR

TO ORDER THIS BLUEPRINT, CALL TOLL-FREE 1-800-547-5570   Plan E-2303   *PRICES AND DETAILS ON PAGES 12-15*

Simple and Comfortable

- It's hard to beat a design like this for simple comfort.
- The wide, welcoming front porch dresses up the home's basic rectangular shape, adding grace and eye appeal.
- Inside, the formal dining room opens off the foyer, which leads to a spacious living room with a handsome fireplace.
- The open country kitchen includes a cooktop island and a spacious, sunny breakfast area. A utility room and access to the carport are nearby.
- The deluxe master-bedroom suite includes a luxurious master bath with two walk-in closets and double sinks.
- Upstairs, two dormered bedrooms share a double bath and are connected by a balcony loft overlooking the living room below.

Plan J-86113

Bedrooms: 3	Baths: 2½
Living Area:	
Upper floor	658 sq. ft.
Main floor	1,740 sq. ft.
Total Living Area:	**2,398 sq. ft.**
Standard basement	1,740 sq. ft.
Carport	440 sq. ft.
Exterior Wall Framing:	2x4
Foundation Options:	
Standard basement	
Crawlspace	
Slab	

(All plans can be built with your choice of foundation and framing. A generic conversion diagram is available. See order form.)

BLUEPRINT PRICE CODE:	C

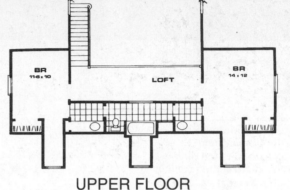

UPPER FLOOR

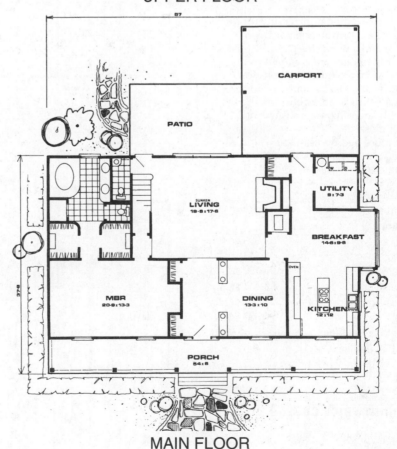

MAIN FLOOR

Photo by Mark Englund/HomeStyles

Old-Fashioned Charm

- A trio of dormers add old-fashioned charm to this modern design.
- Both the living room and the dining room offer 12-ft.-high vaulted ceilings and flow together to create a sense of even more spaciousness.
- The open kitchen/nook/family room features a sunny alcove, a walk-in pantry and a woodstove.
- A first-floor den and a walk-through utility room are other big bonuses.
- Upstairs, the master suite includes a walk-in closet and a deluxe bath with a spa tub and a separate shower and water closet.
- Two more bedrooms, each with a window seat, and a bonus room complete this stylish design.

Plan CDG-2004

Bedrooms: 3+	Baths: 2½
Living Area:	
Upper floor	928 sq. ft.
Main floor	1,317 sq. ft.
Bonus area	192 sq. ft.
Total Living Area:	**2,437 sq. ft.**
Partial daylight basement	780 sq. ft.
Garage	537 sq. ft.
Exterior Wall Framing:	2x6

Foundation Options:

Partial daylight basement

Crawlspace

(All plans can be built with your choice of foundation and framing. A generic conversion diagram is available. See order form.)

BLUEPRINT PRICE CODE: C

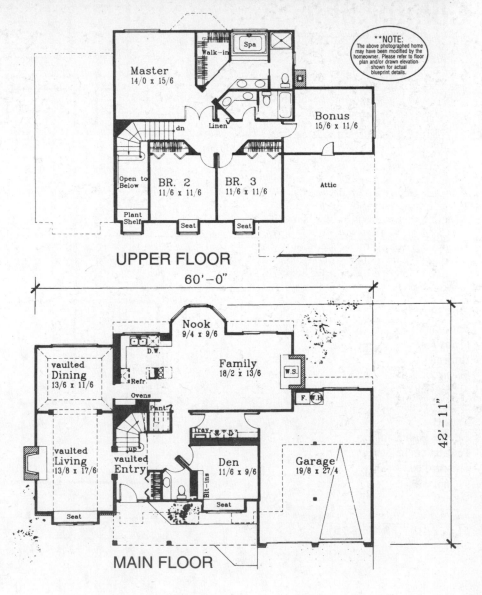

NOTE:
The above photographed home may have been modified by the homeowner. Please refer to floor plan and/or drawn elevation shown for actual blueprint details.

UPPER FLOOR

MAIN FLOOR

Plan CDG-2004

PRICES AND DETAILS ON PAGES 12-15

Photo by Karlis Grants

Dramatic Interior Spaces

- This home's design utilizes unique shapes and angles to create a dramatic and dynamic interior.
- Skylights brighten the impressive two-story entry from high above, as it flows to the formal living areas.
- The sunken Great Room features a massive stone-hearthed fireplace with flanking windows, plus a 19-ft. vaulted ceiling. Sliding glass doors open the formal dining room to a backyard patio.
- The spacious kitchen features an oversized island, plenty of counter space and a sunny breakfast nook.
- A den or third bedroom shares a full bath with another secondary bedroom to complete the main floor.
- An incredible bayed master suite takes up the entire upper floor of the home. The skylighted master bath features a bright walk-in closet, a dual-sink vanity, a sunken tub and a separate shower.

Plans P-6580-3A & -3D

Bedrooms: 2+	Baths: 2
Living Area:	
Upper floor	705 sq. ft.
Main floor	1,738 sq. ft.
Total Living Area:	**2,443 sq. ft.**
Daylight basement	1,738 sq. ft.
Garage	512 sq. ft.
Exterior Wall Framing:	2x4
Foundation Options:	**Plan #**
Daylight basement	P-6580-3D
Crawlspace	P-6580-3A

(All plans can be built with your choice of foundation and framing. A generic conversion diagram is available. See order form.)

BLUEPRINT PRICE CODE:	C

MASTER SUITE 20/0X15/0

SKYLIGHT

OPEN TO GREAT RM. BELOW

WALK-IN W'ROBE

SKYLIGHT

SKYLIGHTS

SUNKEN TUB

ENTRY BELOW

UPPER FLOOR

NOTE:
The above photographed home may have been modified by the homeowner. Please refer to floor plan and/or drawn elevation shown for actual blueprint details.

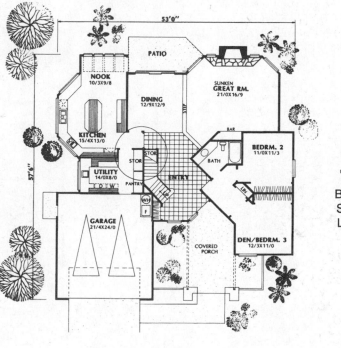

53'0"

PATIO

NOOK 10/3X9/8

DINING 12/9X12/9

SUNKEN GREAT RM. 21/0X16/9

KITCHEN 15/4X13/0

BAR

BEDRM. 2 11/0X11/3

BATH

STOR

STOR

57'6"

UTILITY 14/0X8/0

STOR

ENTRY

PANTRY

WH

F

GARAGE 21/4X24/0

COVERED PORCH

DEN/BEDRM. 3 12/3X11/0

STOR

UTILITY

BASEMENT STAIRWAY LOCATION

MAIN FLOOR

Tasteful Style

- Traditional lines and a contemporary floor plan combine to make this home a perfect choice for the '90s.
- The two-story-high entry introduces the formal living room, which is warmed by a fireplace and brightened by a round-top window arrangement. The living room's ceiling rises to 13 ft., 9 inches.
- A handy pocket door separates the formal dining room from the kitchen for special occasions. The U-shaped kitchen features an eating bar, a work desk and a bayed nook with access to an outdoor patio.
- The spacious family room includes a second fireplace and outdoor views.
- Ceilings in all main-floor rooms are at least 9 ft. high for added spaciousness.
- Upstairs, the master suite features a 12-ft. vaulted ceiling, two walk-in closets and a compartmentalized bath with a luxurious tub in a window bay.
- Two additional bedrooms share a split bath. A versatile bonus room could serve as an extra bedroom or as a sunny area for hobbies or paperwork.

Plan S-8389

Bedrooms: 3+	Baths: 2½
Living Area:	
Upper floor	932 sq. ft.
Main floor	1,290 sq. ft.
Bonus room	228 sq. ft.
Total Living Area:	**2,450 sq. ft.**
Standard basement	1,290 sq. ft.
Garage	429 sq. ft.
Exterior Wall Framing:	2x6

Foundation Options:

Standard basement
Crawlspace
Slab

(All plans can be built with your choice of foundation and framing. A generic conversion diagram is available. See order form.)

BLUEPRINT PRICE CODE: C

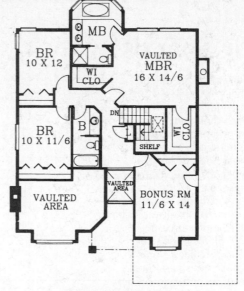

UPPER FLOOR

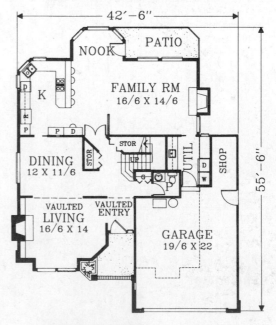

MAIN FLOOR

TO ORDER THIS BLUEPRINT, CALL TOLL-FREE 1-800-547-5570   Plan S-8389   *PRICES AND DETAILS ON PAGES 12-15*

Panoramic Porch

- A gracious, ornately rounded front porch and a two-story turreted bay lend Victorian charm to this home.
- A two-story foyer with round-top transom windows and a plant ledge above greets guests at the entry.
- The living room enjoys a 13-ft.-high ceiling and a panoramic view overlooking the front porch and yard.
- The formal dining room and den each feature a bay window for added style.
- The sunny kitchen incorporates an angled island cooktop with a eating bar to the bayed breakfast room.
- A step down, the family room offers a corner fireplace that may be enjoyed throughout the casual living spaces.
- The upper floor is highlighted by a stunning master suite, which flaunts an octagonal sitting area with a 10-ft. tray ceiling and turreted bay. The master bath offers a corner spa tub and a separate shower. Two additional bedrooms share another full bath.

Plan AX-90307

Bedrooms: 3+	Baths: 3
Living Area:	
Upper floor	956 sq. ft.
Main floor	1,499 sq. ft.
Total Living Area:	**2,455 sq. ft.**
Standard basement	1,499 sq. ft.
Garage	410 sq. ft.
Exterior Wall Framing:	2x4

Foundation Options:

Standard basement

Slab

(All plans can be built with your choice of foundation and framing. A generic conversion diagram is available. See order form.)

BLUEPRINT PRICE CODE: C

UPPER FLOOR

MAIN FLOOR

All-American Country Home

- The covered wraparound porch of this popular all-American home creates an old-fashioned country appeal.
- Off the entryway is the generous-sized living room, which offers a fireplace and French doors that open to the porch.
- The large adjoining dining room further expands the entertaining area.
- The country kitchen has a handy island and flows into the cozy family room, which is enhanced by exposed beams. A handsome fireplace warms the entire informal area, while windows overlook the porch.
- The quiet upper floor hosts four good-sized bedrooms and two baths. The master suite includes a walk-in closet, a dressing area and a private bath with a sit-down shower.
- This home is available with or without a basement and with or without a garage.

PLANS H-3711-1 & -1A WITH GARAGE

NOTE:
The above photographed home may have been modified by the homeowner. Please refer to floor plan and/or drawn elevation shown for actual blueprint details.

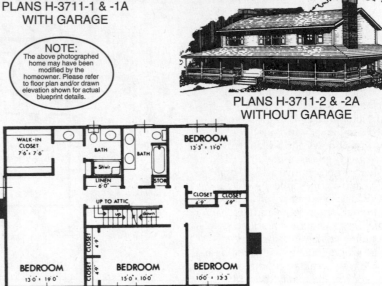

PLANS H-3711-2 & -2A WITHOUT GARAGE

UPPER FLOOR

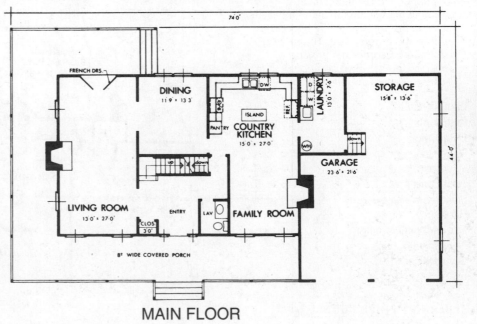

MAIN FLOOR

Plans H-3711-1, -1A, -2 & -2A

Bedrooms: 4	Baths: 2½
Living Area:	
Upper floor	1,176 sq. ft.
Main floor	1,288 sq. ft.
Total Living Area:	**2,464 sq. ft.**
Standard basement	1,176 sq. ft.
Garage	505 sq. ft.
Exterior Wall Framing:	2x6
Foundation Options:	**Plan #**
Basement with garage	H-3711-1
Basement without garage	H-3711-2
Crawlspace with garage	H-3711-1A
Crawlspace without garage	H-3711-2A

(All plans can be built with your choice of foundation and framing. A generic conversion diagram is available. See order form.)

BLUEPRINT PRICE CODE:	C

Big, Bright Country Kitchen

- Decorative dormers, shuttered windows and a large covered front porch give this charming two-story home a pleasant country flavor.
- Inside, the central Great Room is warmed by a handsome fireplace. The adjoining dining room offers sliding glass doors to a backyard deck.
- The enormous country kitchen features a sunny bay-windowed eating area and a convenient island counter. The nearby laundry/utility area accesses the garage and the backyard.
- The main-floor master bedroom boasts a roomy walk-in closet and private access to a compartmentalized bath with an oversized linen closet.
- Upstairs, two bedrooms with window seats share a full bath. An easy-to-access storage area is above the garage. Another convenient storage area can be reached from the garage.

Plan C-8040

Bedrooms: 3	Baths: 2
Living Area:	
Upper floor	718 sq. ft.
Main floor	1,318 sq. ft.
Total Living Area:	**2,036 sq. ft.**
Daylight basement	1,221 sq. ft.
Garage	436 sq. ft.
Exterior Wall Framing:	2x4

Foundation Options:

Daylight basement
Crawlspace
Slab
(All plans can be built with your choice of foundation and framing. A generic conversion diagram is available. See order form.)

BLUEPRINT PRICE CODE:	**C**

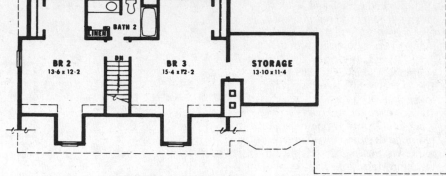

UPPER FLOOR

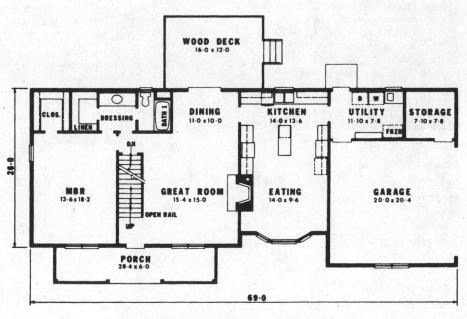

MAIN FLOOR

French Beauty

- High-pitched gables and a stucco facade accent this French beauty.
- Off the two-story-high foyer, the sunken living room features a warm fireplace, a front-facing bay window and a vaulted ceiling that soars to 14½ feet.
- The formal dining room is a quiet spot for special occasions.
- The gourmet kitchen offers an island work area, a roomy pantry, a handy planning desk and a corner sink under windows. Sliding glass doors open from the sunny breakfast nook to an inviting backyard deck.
- Three steps below the main level, the family room is visible from the nook through an open railing. The spacious family room boasts a second fireplace and easy access to a large patio.
- A bedroom, a full bath and a utility room with garage access are nearby.
- Three bedrooms are housed on the upper floor. The master bedroom includes a private bath.
- A skylighted bath serves the two secondary bedrooms, one of which is highlighted by a 12½-ft. vaulted ceiling and a Palladian window arrangement.

Plan U-89-403

Bedrooms: 4	**Baths:** 3

Living Area:	
Upper floor	656 sq. ft.
Main floor	1,385 sq. ft.
Total Living Area:	**2,041 sq. ft.**
Partial basement	704 sq. ft.
Garage	466 sq. ft.
Exterior Wall Framing:	2x4

Foundation Options:

Partial basement
Crawlspace
Slab

(All plans can be built with your choice of foundation and framing. A generic conversion diagram is available. See order form.)

BLUEPRINT PRICE CODE: C

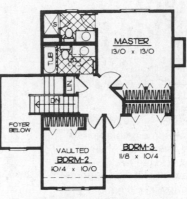

UPPER FLOOR

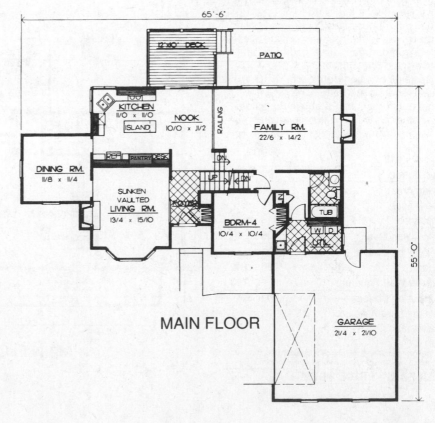

MAIN FLOOR

TO ORDER THIS BLUEPRINT, CALL TOLL-FREE 1-800-547-5570

Plan U-89-403

PRICES AND DETAILS ON PAGES 12-15

Arresting Angles

- This arresting design, with its towering windows and vertical angles, is filled with light and luxurious spaces.
- A bridge on the upper floor visually separates the soaring reception area from the living room, which features a cathedral ceiling. The floor-to-ceiling stone-faced fireplace is framed by glass, starting with sliding glass doors and rising to triangular-shaped windows.
- The kitchen is flanked by the casual dinette and the formal dining room. The dining room is open to the living room, and both rooms view out to a partially covered backyard terrace.
- A den overlooking a side terrace and a library/guest room with a nearby bath add to the main floor's versatility.
- The upper floor is highlighted by great views and a superb master suite. The spacious sleeping area overlooks the living room below and accesses a private deck. The luxurious master bath includes a whirlpool tub, a separate dressing area and a walk-in closet.

Plan K-653-U

Bedrooms: 3+	Baths: 3
Living Area:	
Upper floor	844 sq. ft.
Main floor	1,208 sq. ft.
Total Living Area:	**2,052 sq. ft.**
Standard basement	1,208 sq. ft.
Garage	427 sq. ft.
Exterior Wall Framing:	2x4 or 2x6

Foundation Options:

Standard basement
Slab
(All plans can be built with your choice of foundation and framing. A generic conversion diagram is available. See order form.)

BLUEPRINT PRICE CODE: C

UPPER FLOOR

MAIN FLOOR

Great Spaces

- Open, airy casual living spaces and intimate formal areas are the hallmarks of this intriguing home.
- A two-story-high foyer introduces the living room, where French doors open to a veranda. On the opposite side of the foyer is a spacious dining room with a delightful bay window.
- The casual areas combine at the back of the home. The family room features a two-story-high ceiling and a fireplace framed with glass, including a French door that opens to the backyard.
- A half-wall is all that separates the family room from the inviting bay-windowed nook. An angled serving counter/snack bar keeps the kitchen open to the activity areas.
- A walk-in pantry and a laundry room are nearby, just off the garage entrance.
- Upstairs, the luxurious master suite features an elegant 9-ft. tray ceiling. The master bath boasts a 12-ft. vaulted ceiling, an oval garden tub, a private toilet compartment and a walk-in closet adorned with a plant shelf.
- Two more bedrooms, a versatile loft and a hall bath complete the upper floor.

Plan FB-5056-MAGU

Bedrooms: 3+	**Baths:** 2½
Living Area:	
Upper floor	1,019 sq. ft.
Main floor	1,034 sq. ft.
Total Living Area:	**2,053 sq. ft.**
Daylight basement	1,034 sq. ft.
Garage	415 sq. ft.
Exterior Wall Framing:	2x4

Foundation Options:

Daylight basement

(All plans can be built with your choice of foundation and framing. A generic conversion diagram is available. See order form.)

BLUEPRINT PRICE CODE: C

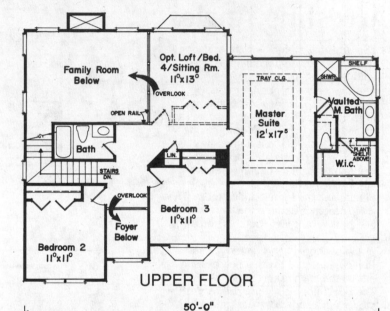

UPPER FLOOR

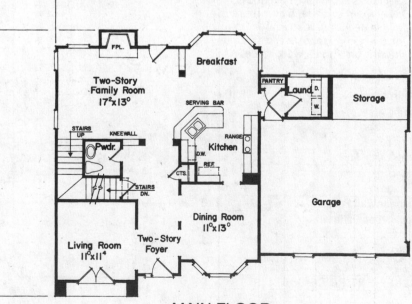

MAIN FLOOR

Plan FB-5056-MAGU

PRICES AND DETAILS ON PAGES 12-15

Fluid Floor Plan

- This updated 1½-story home features cathedral ceilings and a fluid floor plan that combine for easy family living.
- Several design options are offered, including a hutch space in the formal dining room, a 30-sq.-ft. extension off the family room, a window seat in the master bedroom, an alternate master bath layout and an alternate mudroom/entry design.
- A handsome fireplace and an 11½-ft. cathedral ceiling highlight the large family room, which opens to the dinette and the island kitchen. An 11-ft. cathedral ceiling is also found in the adjoining living room.
- The master suite features a 9-ft. tray ceiling, a large walk-in closet, a dressing area and a private bath.
- Upstairs, two more bedrooms share a hall bath. A window seat in the front bedroom offers storage space below.
- The blueprints also include an alternate upper-floor layout that adds another bedroom. The ceiling in the family room is lowered to 8 ft. to allow for a bedroom overhead.

Plan GL-2070

Bedrooms: 3	Baths: 2½
Living Area:	
Upper floor	509 sq. ft.
Main floor	1,561 sq. ft.
Total Living Area:	**2,070 sq. ft.**
Standard basement	1,561 sq. ft.
Garage	462 sq. ft.
Exterior Wall Framing:	2x6

Foundation Options:

Standard basement

(All plans can be built with your choice of foundation and framing. A generic conversion diagram is available. See order form.)

BLUEPRINT PRICE CODE: C

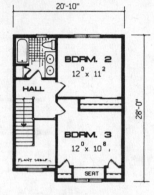

UPPER FLOOR

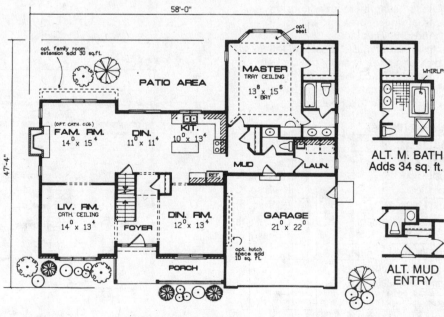

MAIN FLOOR

Distinctive Family Design

- This beautiful, time-tested traditional design packs many features into a highly livable floor plan.
- To the left of the foyer, the 16½-ft. vaulted living room flows into the dining room, providing a huge space for both formal entertaining and family gatherings.
- The big kitchen includes a handy work island and a sunny dinette, which opens to the backyard. A half-bath, laundry facilities and garage access are nearby.
- The large family room adjoins the casual dinette area and boasts a handsome fireplace.
- Upstairs, the master bedroom features two large closets and a private bath. Three additional bedrooms share another full bath. A central balcony overlooks the foyer below.

Plan A-2109-DS

Bedrooms: 4	Baths: 2½
Living Area:	
Upper floor	942 sq. ft.
Main floor	1,148 sq. ft.
Total Living Area:	**2,090 sq. ft.**
Standard basement	1,148 sq. ft.
Garage	484 sq. ft.
Exterior Wall Framing:	2x4

Foundation Options:

Standard basement

(All plans can be built with your choice of foundation and framing. A generic conversion diagram is available. See order form.)

BLUEPRINT PRICE CODE:	C

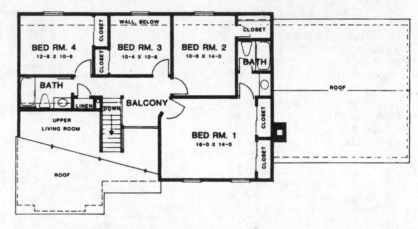

UPPER FLOOR

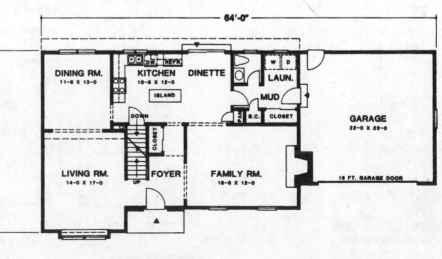

MAIN FLOOR

TO ORDER THIS BLUEPRINT, CALL TOLL-FREE 1-800-547-5570

Plan A-2109-DS

PRICES AND DETAILS ON PAGES 12-15

Easy to Build

- The basic rectangular shape of this two-story home makes it economical to build. The well-zoned interior isolates all four bedrooms on the upper floor.
- Off the covered porch, the airy foyer reveals the open stairway and unfolds to each of the living areas.
- The formal rooms are positioned at the front of the home and overlook the porch. The large living room boasts a handsome fireplace and extends to a rear porch through sliding glass doors.
- The central family room hosts casual family activities and shows off a rustic wood-beam ceiling. This room also opens to the porch and integrates with the kitchen and the bright dinette for a big, open atmosphere.
- A half-bath, a laundry area and a handy service porch are located near the entrance from the garage.
- Two dual-sink bathrooms serve the bedrooms upstairs. The spacious master bedroom has a private bath and a big walk-in closet.

Plan HFL-1070-RQ

Bedrooms: 4	Baths: 2½
Living Area:	
Upper floor	1,013 sq. ft.
Main floor	1,082 sq. ft.
Total Living Area:	**2,095 sq. ft.**
Standard basement	889 sq. ft.
Garage and storage	481 sq. ft.
Exterior Wall Framing:	2x6

Foundation Options:

Standard basement

Slab

(All plans can be built with your choice of foundation and framing. A generic conversion diagram is available. See order form.)

BLUEPRINT PRICE CODE:	C

VIEW INTO FAMILY ROOM, KITCHEN AND DINETTE

UPPER FLOOR

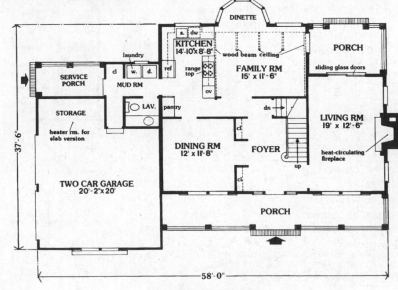

MAIN FLOOR

Sleek Exterior, Exciting Interior

- The sleek lines of this dynamic design are punctuated by the brick pillars of the beautiful covered entrance.
- Angled walls, varied ceiling heights and unusual room arrangements give the interior spaces intrigue.
- The 17-ft.-high skylighted entry leads to the living room on the right and the formal dining room on the left. Each of these rooms has a bright bay window and a 9-ft., 3-in. tray ceiling.
- A pocket door connects the dining room to the efficient kitchen, which shares an eating bar with the 12-ft. vaulted breakfast nook.
- The big family room features a 16½-ft. vaulted ceiling, a corner fireplace and patio access through a French door.
- Double doors introduce the gorgeous master suite, which boasts a luxurious bath with a skylighted, step-up spa tub.
- Two bedrooms share a skylighted bath on the upper floor.

Plans P-7747-3A & -3D

Bedrooms: 3	Baths: 2½
Living Area:	
Upper floor	444 sq. ft.
Main floor	1,662 sq. ft.
Total Living Area:	**2,106 sq. ft.**
Daylight basement	1,662 sq. ft.
Garage	746 sq. ft.
Exterior Wall Framing:	2x6
Foundation Options:	**Plan #**
Daylight basement	P-7747-3D
Crawlspace	P-7747-3A

(All plans can be built with your choice of foundation and framing. A generic conversion diagram is available. See order form.)

BLUEPRINT PRICE CODE:	C

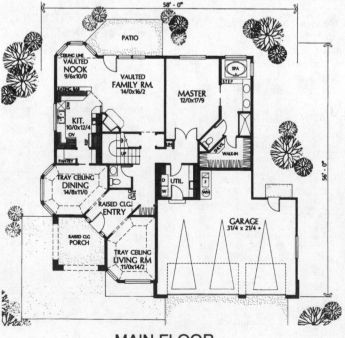

UPPER FLOOR

MAIN FLOOR

BASEMENT STAIRWAY LOCATION

Classic Victorian

- This classic exterior is built around an interior that offers all the amenities desired by today's families.
- In from the covered front porch, the entry features a curved stairway and a glass-block wall to the dining room.
- A step down from the entry, the Great Room boasts a dramatic 24½-ft. cathedral ceiling and provides ample space for large family gatherings.
- The formal dining room is available for special occasions, while the 13-ft.-high breakfast nook serves everyday needs.
- The adjoining island kitchen offers plenty of counter space and opens to a handy utility room and a powder room.
- The deluxe main-floor master suite features a 14½-ft. cathedral ceiling and an opulent private bath with a garden spa tub and a separate shower.
- Upstairs, two secondary bedrooms share a full bath and a balcony overlooking the Great Room below.
- Detached two-car garage plans available upon request.

Plan DW-2112

Bedrooms: 3	Baths: 2½
Living Area:	
Upper floor	514 sq. ft.
Main floor	1,598 sq. ft.
Total Living Area:	**2,112 sq. ft.**
Standard basement	1,598 sq. ft.
Exterior Wall Framing:	2x4

Foundation Options:
Standard basement
Crawlspace
Slab

(All plans can be built with your choice of foundation and framing. A generic conversion diagram is available. See order form.)

BLUEPRINT PRICE CODE: **C**

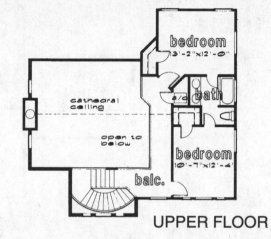

UPPER FLOOR

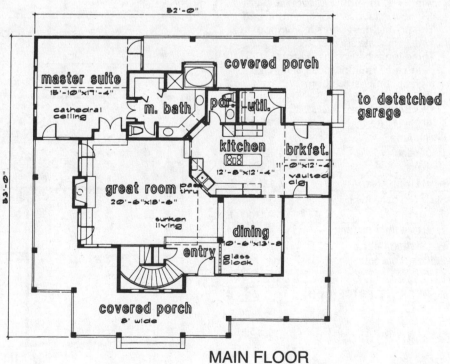

MAIN FLOOR

Comfortable Country Home

- A central gable and a wide, welcoming front porch with columns give this design comfortable country charm.
- The large living room is open to the dining room, which features a tray ceiling and views to the backyard.
- The kitchen offers an oversized island counter with a snack bar. The adjoining breakfast area has a sliding glass door to the backyard and a half-wall that separates it from the family room. This inviting room includes a fireplace and a bay window with a cozy seat.
- Upstairs, the master suite boasts three windows, including a lovely arched window, that overlook the front yard. The private bath offers a whirlpool tub and a separate shower.
- Three more bedrooms, a second full bath and a multipurpose den make this a great family-sized home.

Plan OH-165

Bedrooms: 4+	**Baths: 2½**
Living Area:	
Upper floor	1,121 sq. ft.
Main floor	1,000 sq. ft.
Total Living Area:	**2,121 sq. ft.**
Standard basement	1,000 sq. ft.
Garage	400 sq. ft.
Exterior Wall Framing:	2x4

Foundation Options:

Standard basement
(All plans can be built with your choice of foundation and framing. A generic conversion diagram is available. See order form.)

BLUEPRINT PRICE CODE: **C**

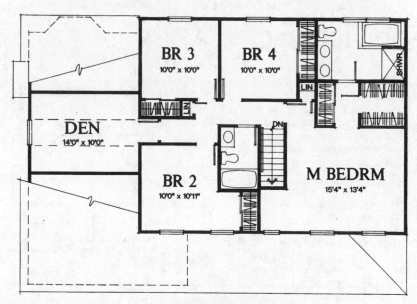

UPPER FLOOR

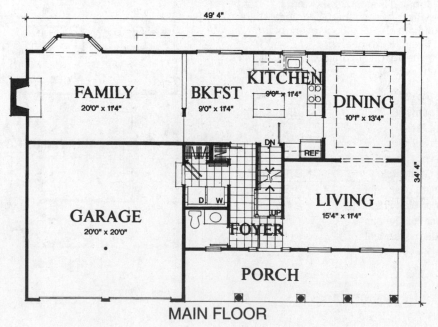

MAIN FLOOR

Plan OH-165

PRICES AND DETAILS ON PAGES 12-15

Visual Surprises

- The exterior of this home is accented with a dramatic roof cavity, while the inside uses angles to enhance the efficiency and variety of the floor plan.
- The double-door entry opens to a reception area, which unfolds to the spacious living room. A 16½-ft. sloped ceiling and an angled fireplace add drama to the living room and the adjoining bayed dining room, where sliding doors access a backyard terrace.
- The efficient kitchen easily serves both the formal dining room and the cheerful dinette, which offers sweeping outdoor views. A fireplace in the adjoining family room warms the entire area. A second terrace is accessible via sliding glass doors.
- The oversized laundry room could be finished as a nice hobby room.
- A skylighted stairway leads up to the sleeping areas. The master suite is fully equipped with a private bath, a separate dressing area, a walk-in closet and an exciting sun deck alcoved above the garage. Three additional bedrooms share another full bath.

Plan K-540-L

Bedrooms: 4	Baths: 2½
Living Area:	
Upper floor	884 sq. ft.
Main floor	1,238 sq. ft.
Total Living Area:	**2,122 sq. ft.**
Standard basement	1,106 sq. ft.
Garage	400 sq. ft.
Storage	122 sq. ft.
Exterior Wall Framing:	2x4 or 2x6
Foundation Options:	
Standard basement	
Slab	

(All plans can be built with your choice of foundation and framing. A generic conversion diagram is available. See order form.)

BLUEPRINT PRICE CODE: C

UPPER FLOOR

Bedrm 2
10-0×11-4

Bedrm 3
11-0×10-0

Bedrm 4
11-0×10-0

Master Suite
13-0×16-0

Hall

Balc.

rail'g

open to liv'g room below

skylights above

roof

dn

dress'g

vanity

sl gl dr

whirlpool tub

w i c

Open Deck

MAIN FLOOR

58-4

43-0

Terrace

Terrace

sl gl dr

dinette

sl gl dr

Dining Rm
14-0×12-0

Kitchen

dw

ref

Family Rm
13-0×27-0

hi-efficiency fireplace

d

w

sl gl dr

stor.

L'dry & Hobby
11-8×11-4

stor.

bay

hi-efficiency fireplace

(sloped ceil'g)

Living Rm
14-0×25-0

Recep

Entry

up

up

dn

pdr rm

Double Garage
20-0×20-0

driveway

Dramatic Family Room

- An impressive porch and simple, balanced rooflines make this warm and friendly farmhouse a classic beauty.
- The two-story foyer and formal living and dining rooms maintain the feeling of generous hospitality.
- The large and open country kitchen, with its big, bright breakfast area, pantry, wall oven and pass-through to the family room, is the perfect host for informal family gatherings.
- The step-down family room at the back of the home features a 15-ft. cathedral ceiling and a prominent fireplace.
- Three bedrooms and two full baths occupy the upper floor. The spacious and luxurious master suite has a big private bath and inherits a huge walk-in closet through the efficient use of the space above the garage.

Plan OH-163

Bedrooms: 3	Baths: 2½
Living Area:	
Upper floor	852 sq. ft.
Main floor	1,270 sq. ft.
Total Living Area:	**2,122 sq. ft.**
Partial basement	934 sq. ft.
Garage	576 sq. ft.
Exterior Wall Framing:	2x4

Foundation Options:

Partial basement

(All plans can be built with your choice of foundation and framing. A generic conversion diagram is available. See order form.)

BLUEPRINT PRICE CODE:	C

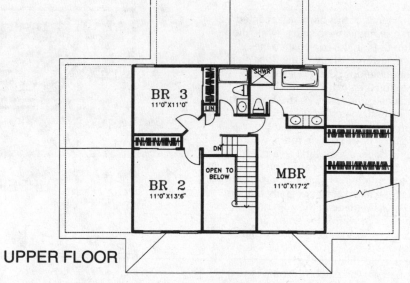

UPPER FLOOR

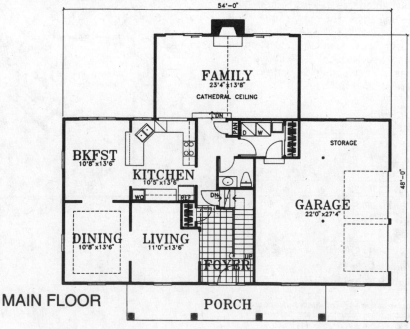

MAIN FLOOR

Classic Country Beauty

- This distinctive home boasts a classic facade, highlighted by triple dormers and an expansive covered front porch.
- An airy central gallery introduces the interior. The living room flows into the adjacent formal dining room, which features a 10-ft., 4-in. cathedral ceiling and sliding French doors to a covered back porch.
- The kitchen includes an island work counter and a sunny dinette nestled within a semi-circular glass wall.
- A wood-burning fireplace with a slate hearth accents the spacious family room. French doors lead to a lovely backyard terrace.
- Upstairs, the master suite has a 10-ft., 4-in. cathedral ceiling, two closets and a skylighted bath with dual sinks, a whirlpool tub and a separate shower.
- Two of the three remaining bedrooms offer 11-ft.-high sloped ceilings and dormers that are large enough to accommodate built-in desks.

Plan K-695-T

Bedrooms: 4	Baths: 2½
Living Area:	
Upper floor	1,030 sq. ft.
Main floor	1,100 sq. ft.
Total Living Area:	**2,130 sq. ft.**
Standard basement	1,100 sq. ft.
Garage	450 sq. ft.
Exterior Wall Framing:	2x4 or 2x6
Foundation Options:	
Standard basement	
Slab	

(All plans can be built with your choice of foundation and framing. A generic conversion diagram is available. See order form.)

BLUEPRINT PRICE CODE: C

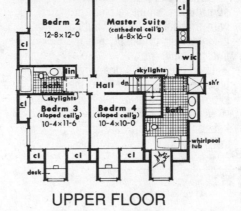

UPPER FLOOR

VIEW INTO FAMILY ROOM

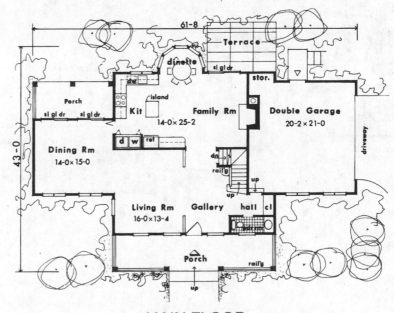

MAIN FLOOR

TO ORDER THIS BLUEPRINT,
CALL TOLL-FREE 1-800-547-5570

Plan K-695-T

PRICES AND DETAILS
ON PAGES 12-15

285

Upstairs Suite Creates Adult Retreat

● This multi-level design is ideal for a gently sloping site with a view to the rear.

● Upstairs master suite is a sumptuous "adult retreat" complete with magnificent bath, vaulted ceiling, walk-in closet, private deck and balcony loft.
● Living room includes wood stove area and large windows to the rear. Wood bin can be loaded from outside.
● Main floor also features roomy kitchen and large utility area.

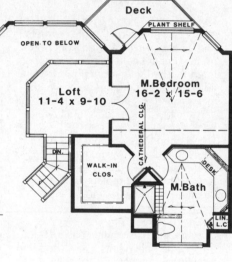

Deck
OPEN TO BELOW
PLANT SHELF
Loft
11-4 x 9-10
M.Bedroom
16-2 x 15-6
CATHEDRAL CLG.
WALK-IN CLOS.
DN.
DESK
M.Bath
LIN. L.C.

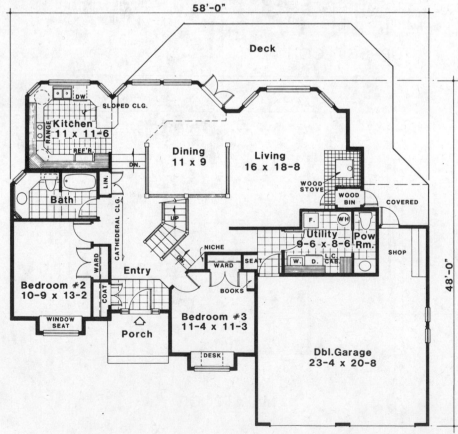

58'-0"

Deck

Kitchen 11 x 11-6
SLOPED CLG.
DW
RANGE
REF'R.
DN.
Dining 11 x 9
Living 16 x 18-8
WOOD STOVE
WOOD BIN
COVERED
Bath
LIN.
CATHEDRAL CLG.
UP
Utility 9-6 x 8-6
F.
WH
Pow. Rm.
SHOP
W. D. CAB
L.C.
NICHE
SEAT
WARD
BOOKS
Bedroom #2 10-9 x 13-2
WARD
COAT
Entry
DN.
WINDOW SEAT
Porch
Bedroom #3 11-4 x 11-3
DESK
Dbl.Garage 23-4 x 20-8

48'-0"

Plan NW-544-S	
Bedrooms: 3	Baths: 2½
Space:	
Upper floor:	638 sq. ft.
Main floor:	1,500 sq. ft.
Total living area:	2,138 sq. ft.
Garage:	545 sq. ft.
Exterior Wall Framing:	2x6
Foundation options: Crawlspace only. (Foundation & framing conversion diagram available — see order form.)	
Blueprint Price Code:	C

TO ORDER THIS BLUEPRINT, CALL TOLL-FREE 1-800-547-5570

Plan NW-544-S

PRICES AND DETAILS ON PAGES 12-15

Classy Country-Style Home

- Modest in size but big on living space, this home has lots of class.
- The classic country exterior is refined by the archway leading to the front porch and the elegant entry door topped by an arched window.
- The vaulted foyer opens to the formal dining room, framed by stylish columns. Straight ahead are the living room, breakfast nook and kitchen, which are fashioned using the open Great Room concept.
- The living room focuses on a central fireplace with a French door on one side and a window on the other. The breakfast nook overlooks the rear patio and is open to both the living room and the kitchen. The walk-through kitchen also provides easy access to the formal dining room.
- The main-floor master suite includes two walk-in closets, a double vanity, a luxurious garden tub and a separate shower.
- The upper level features two spacious bedrooms that share a hall bath. The optional bonus room above the garage is reached by back stairs located off the laundry area on the main level.

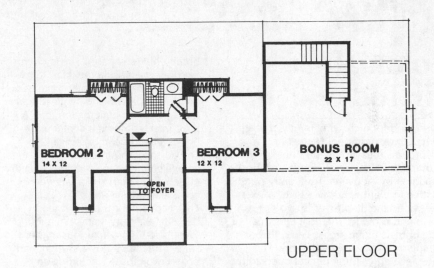

UPPER FLOOR

Plan APS-1712

Bedrooms: 3-4	Baths: 2 ½
Space:	
Upper floor	532 sq. ft.
Main floor	1,215 sq. ft.
Optional Bonus Room	398 sq. ft.
Total Living Area	**2,145 sq. ft.**
Garage	440 sq. ft.
Exterior Wall Framing	2x4
Foundation options:	
Crawlspace	
Slab	
(Foundation & framing conversion diagram available—see order form.)	
Blueprint Price Code	C

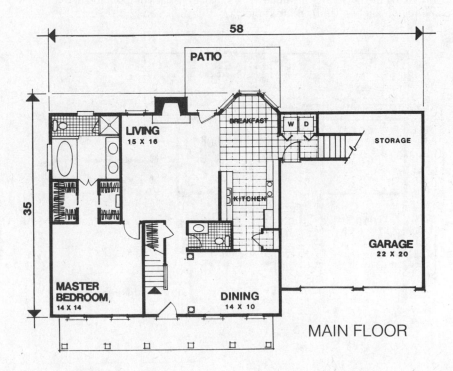

MAIN FLOOR

TO ORDER THIS BLUEPRINT,
CALL TOLL-FREE 1-800-547-5570

Plan APS-1712

PRICES AND DETAILS
ON PAGES 12-15

287

Colonial for Today

- Designed for a growing family, this handsome traditional home offers four bedrooms plus a den and three complete baths. The Colonial exterior is updated by a covered front entry porch with a fanlight window above.
- The dramatic tiled foyer is two stories high and provides direct access to all of the home's living areas. The spacious living room has an inviting brick fireplace and sliding pocket doors to the adjoining dining room.
- Overlooking the backyard, the huge combination kitchen/family room is the home's hidden charm. The kitchen features a peninsula breakfast bar with seating for six. The family room has a window wall with sliding glass doors that open to an enticing terrace. A built-in entertainment center and bookshelves line another wall.
- The adjacent mudroom is just off the garage entrance and includes a pantry closet. A full bath and a large den complete the first floor.
- The second floor is highlighted by a beautiful balcony that is open to the foyer below. The luxurious master suite is brightened by a skylight and boasts two closets, including an oversized walk-in closet. The master bath has a whirlpool tub and a dual-sink vanity.

Plan AHP-7050	
Bedrooms: 4+	**Baths: 3**
Living Area:	
Upper floor	998 sq. ft.
Main floor	1,153 sq. ft.
Total Living Area:	**2,151 sq. ft.**
Standard basement	1,067 sq. ft.
Garage	439 sq. ft.
Exterior Wall Framing:	2x6
Foundation Options:	
Standard basement	
Crawlspace	
Slab	

(All plans can be built with your choice of foundation and framing. A generic conversion diagram is available. See order form.)

BLUEPRINT PRICE CODE:	C

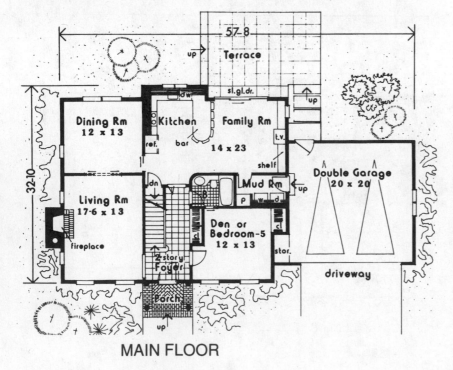

MAIN FLOOR

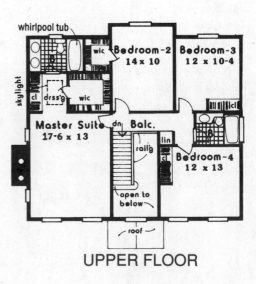

UPPER FLOOR

TO ORDER THIS BLUEPRINT, CALL TOLL-FREE 1-800-547-5570

Plan AHP-7050

PRICES AND DETAILS ON PAGES 12-15

Down-Home Country Flavor!

- Open living areas, decorative dormers and a spacious wraparound porch give this charming home its country feel.
- The main entrance opens into an enormous living room, which boasts a handsome fireplace flanked by bright windows and built-in cabinets.
- The adjoining dining room is brightened by windows on three sides. A rear French door opens to the porch.
- The modern kitchen serves the dining room over an eating bar. A half-bath and a laundry/utility area with access to the garage and porch are nearby.
- The removed master bedroom includes a roomy walk-in closet and a private bath with a corner shower and a dual-sink vanity with knee space.
- All main-floor rooms have 9-ft. ceilings.
- Two upper-floor bedrooms share a hallway bath, which is enhanced by one of three dormer windows.

Plan J-90013

Bedrooms: 3	Baths: 2½
Living Area:	
Upper floor	823 sq. ft.
Main floor	1,339 sq. ft.
Total Living Area:	**2,162 sq. ft.**
Standard basement	1,339 sq. ft.
Garage	413 sq. ft.
Storage	106 sq. ft.
Exterior Wall Framing:	2x4

Foundation Options:

Standard basement

Crawlspace

Slab

(All plans can be built with your choice of foundation and framing. A generic conversion diagram is available. See order form.)

BLUEPRINT PRICE CODE: C

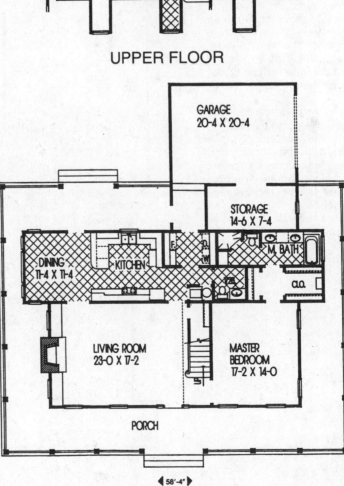

UPPER FLOOR

MAIN FLOOR

TO ORDER THIS BLUEPRINT,
CALL TOLL-FREE 1-800-547-5570

Plan J-90013

PRICES AND DETAILS
ON PAGES 12-15

289

Welcoming Curb Appeal

- A covered porch, a bay window and decorative trim create a pleasant curb appeal for this country-style home.
- Inside, a formal living room and dining room flank the two-story foyer with its central open-railed stairway.
- A spectacular sunken family room with a masonry fireplace and a three-sided backyard view sits at the rear of the home.
- At the center of the floor plan, the roomy island kitchen and dinette combine for a spacious setting. A closet pantry, a work desk and outdoor access through sliding glass doors are featured.
- A handy main-floor laundry closet is located near the powder room at the garage entrance.
- Three nice-sized secondary bedrooms and a big master bedroom with a personal bath and a walk-in closet are included in the upper level.

Plan GL-2164-P

Bedrooms: 4	Baths: 2½
Living Area:	
Upper floor	1,062 sq. ft.
Main floor	1,102 sq. ft.
Total Living Area:	**2,164 sq. ft.**
Standard basement	1,102 sq. ft.
Garage	525 sq. ft.
Exterior Wall Framing:	2x6

Foundation Options:

Standard basement

(All plans can be built with your choice of foundation and framing. A generic conversion diagram is available. See order form.)

BLUEPRINT PRICE CODE:	C

UPPER FLOOR

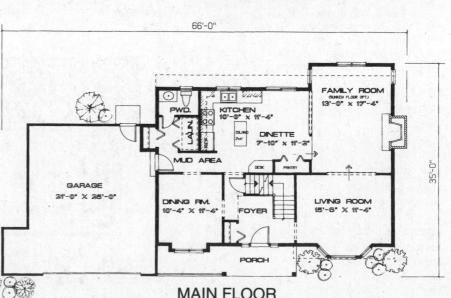

MAIN FLOOR

Plan GL-2164-P

PRICES AND DETAILS ON PAGES 12-15

Updated Classic

- Light-filled and airy, this classic country-style home is filled with modern amenities.
- Brightened by high transom windows, the inviting two-story-high foyer flows into the spacious living room and the formal dining room.
- The efficient kitchen features a breakfast bar and a window over the sink. The adjoining dinette offers sliding glass doors to a backyard terrace. The nearby mudroom/laundry room has garage and backyard access.
- The friendly family room enjoys a view of the backyard through a row of three windows. The handsome fireplace is flanked by glass.
- Upstairs, the spectacular master bedroom boasts a 10-ft. cathedral ceiling and a roomy walk-in closet. The skylighted master bath showcases a whirlpool tub, a separate shower and a dual-sink vanity.
- Another skylighted bath services the three remaining bedrooms.

Plan AHP-9402

Bedrooms: 4	Baths: 2½
Living Area:	
Upper floor	1,041 sq. ft.
Main floor	1,129 sq. ft.
Total Living Area:	**2,170 sq. ft.**
Standard basement	1,129 sq. ft.
Garage and storage	630 sq. ft.
Exterior Wall Framing:	2x4 or 2x6

Foundation Options:

Standard basement
Crawlspace
Slab
(All plans can be built with your choice of foundation and framing. A generic conversion diagram is available. See order form.)

BLUEPRINT PRICE CODE: C

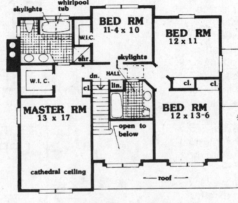

UPPER FLOOR

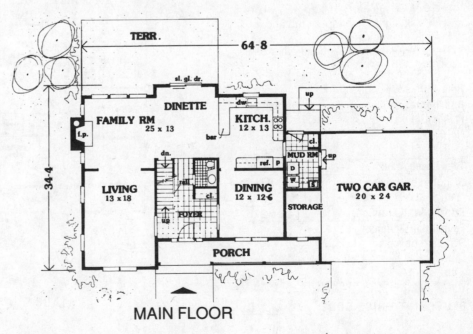

MAIN FLOOR

TO ORDER THIS BLUEPRINT, CALL TOLL-FREE 1-800-547-5570

Plan AHP-9402

A Move Up

- Narrow lap siding and repeated half-round windows with divided panes give this traditional home a different look.
- The roomy interior offers space for the upwardly mobile family, with four to five bedrooms and large activity areas.
- The two-story foyer welcomes guests into a spacious formal living expanse that combines the living and dining rooms. A handsome fireplace and a dramatic cathedral ceiling are featured.
- Behind double doors is a cozy study or an optional fifth bedroom.
- A big family room with a fireplace and a media center is the focus of the informal areas. Lovely French doors open to the backyard terrace.
- Adjoining the family room is a well-designed kitchen and a bayed dinette.
- The master suite is secluded in a quiet corner of the main floor. The suite boasts a private terrace, a personal bath with a skylighted whirlpool tub and a large walk-in closet.
- Three more bedrooms and another bath occupy the upper floor.

Plan AHP-9396

Bedrooms: 4+	Baths: 2½
Living Area:	
Upper floor	643 sq. ft.
Main floor	1,553 sq. ft.
Total Living Area:	**2,196 sq. ft.**
Standard basement	1,553 sq. ft.
Garage and storage	502 sq. ft.
Exterior Wall Framing:	2x4 or 2x6

Foundation Options:

Standard basement

Crawlspace

Slab

(All plans can be built with your choice of foundation and framing. A generic conversion diagram is available. See order form.)

BLUEPRINT PRICE CODE: C

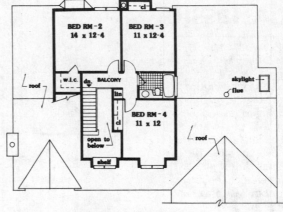

UPPER FLOOR

MAIN FLOOR

   Plan AHP-9396   *PRICES AND DETAILS ON PAGES 12-15*

Artful Arches

- This home's wonderful windows and gorgeous gables are accentuated by artful brickwork arches.
- A covered porch with columns leads into the tiled entry, brightened by sidelights and a half-round transom.
- The entry flows into the tray-ceilinged formal dining room, lighted by a stunning arch-top window arangement.
- The sunny island kitchen features a bay window in the breakfast area, a nifty planning desk and corner windows over the sink. Laundry facilities and garage access are also nearby.
- The vaulted Great Room, highlighted by tall casement windows, opens to a rear patio through sliding doors. A unique fireplace warms the entire area.
- The luxurious vaulted master suite, which walks out to its own patio, boasts a large walk-in closet and a generous bath with dual vanities, a whirlpool tub and a separate shower.
- On the upper floor, a balcony with a plant shelf overlooks the Great Room below and three nice bedrooms share two full baths.

Plan AG-2201

Bedrooms: 4	Baths: 3½
Living Area:	
Upper floor	716 sq. ft.
Main floor	1,496 sq. ft.
Total Living Area:	**2,212 sq. ft.**
Standard basement	1,450 sq. ft.
Garage	484 sq. ft.
Exterior Wall Framing:	2x6

Foundation Options:

Standard basement
(All plans can be built with your choice of foundation and framing. A generic conversion diagram is available. See order form.)

BLUEPRINT PRICE CODE: C

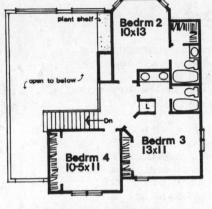

UPPER FLOOR

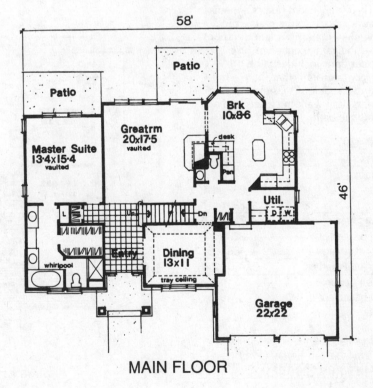

MAIN FLOOR

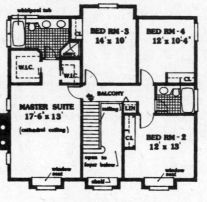

Tradition Recreated

- Classic traditional styling is recreated in this home with its covered porch, triple dormers and half-round windows.
- A central hall stems from the two-story-high foyer and accesses each of the main living areas.
- A large formal space is created with the merging of the living room and the dining room. The living room boasts a fireplace and a view of the front porch.
- The informal spaces merge at the rear of the home. The kitchen features an oversized cooktop island. The sunny dinette is enclosed with a circular glass wall. The family room boasts a media center and access to the rear terrace.
- A convenient main-floor laundry room sits near the garage entrance.
- The upper floor includes three secondary bedrooms that share a full bath, and a spacious master bedroom that offers dual walk-in closets and a large private bath.

Plan AHP-9393

Bedrooms: 4+	Baths: 3
Living Area:	
Upper floor	989 sq. ft.
Main floor	1,223 sq. ft.
Total Living Area:	**2,212 sq. ft.**
Standard basement	1,223 sq. ft.
Garage and storage	488 sq. ft.
Exterior Wall Framing:	2x4 or 2x6

Foundation Options:
Standard basement
Crawlspace
Slab
(Typical foundation & framing conversion diagram available—see order form.)

BLUEPRINT PRICE CODE: C

UPPER FLOOR

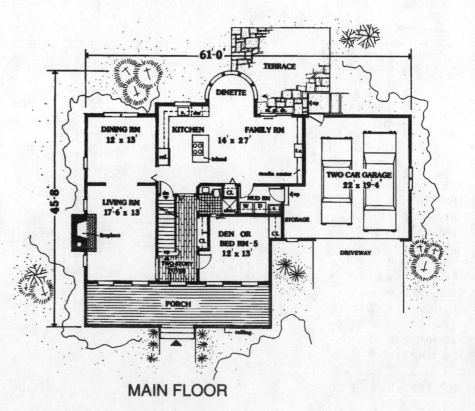

MAIN FLOOR

Plan AHP-9393

PRICES AND DETAILS
ON PAGES 12-15

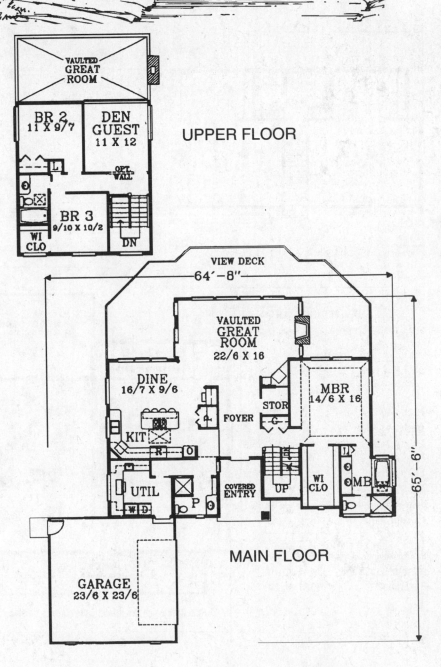

A Custom Contemporary

- Clean lines and custom design touches are found throughout this contemporary home.
- A spectacular vaulted Great Room enclosed in windows offers a fireplace and a wraparound deck.
- Open to the Great Room is a cozy dining area and kitchen with island cooktop/eating bar, pantry and view of the adjoining deck.
- The secluded master suite has a coved ceiling, large walk-in closet and private bath with dual vanities, garden tub and separate shower.
- Two additional bedrooms, plus a guest room or den that can be enclosed or informally open, are found on the upper level.

Plan LRD-51391

Bedrooms: 3+	Baths: 3
Living Area:	
Upper floor	550 sq. ft.
Main floor	1,671 sq. ft.
Total Living Area:	**2,221 sq. ft.**
Standard basement	1,671 sq. ft.
Garage	552 sq. ft.
Exterior Wall Framing:	2x6

Foundation Options:
Standard basement
Crawlspace
(Foundation & framing conversion diagram available — see order form.)

BLUEPRINT PRICE CODE:	C

UPPER FLOOR

VAULTED GREAT ROOM

BR 2 11 X 9/7

DEN GUEST 11 X 12

OPT. WALL

BR 3 9/10 X 10/2

WI CLO

DN

MAIN FLOOR

VIEW DECK

64'-8"

65'-6"

VAULTED GREAT ROOM 22/6 X 16

DINE 16/7 X 9/6

KIT

FOYER

STOR

MBR 14/6 X 16

UTIL

COVERED ENTRY

UP

WI CLO

MB

GARAGE 23/6 X 23/6

Informal Living in a Cozy Cottage

An informal floor plan complements the Cape Cod exterior of this home. The 1,499 sq. ft. of heated living area on the main floor is divided into three sections. The master suite features a walk-in closet and an unusual bath-and-a-half arrangement. A second bedroom makes an excellent nursery or can be used as a den.

The middle section is the living room with an inside fireplace and a door opening onto the rear deck. An eat-in country kitchen with island counter, breakfast bay and utility nook make up the third section.

An additional 728 sq. ft. of heated living area on the upper floor consists of a second full bath and two bedrooms with ample closet space. A storage area is provided over the garage. All or part of the basement can be used to supplement the main living area.

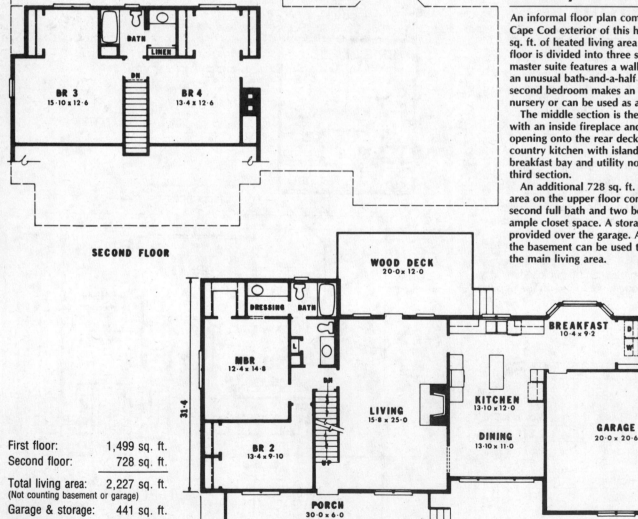

SECOND FLOOR

BR 3
15·10 x 12·6

BATH

LINEN

DN

BR 4
13·4 x 12·6

FIRST FLOOR

WOOD DECK
20·0 x 12·0

DRESSING   BATH

MBR
12·4 x 14·8

BREAKFAST
10·4 x 9·2

STORAGE

KITCHEN
13·10 x 12·0

LIVING
15·8 x 25·0

DINING
13·10 x 11·0

GARAGE
20·0 x 20·6

BR 2
13·4 x 9·10

PORCH
30·0 x 6·0

31·4

29·0

71·4

Specify daylight basement, crawlspace or slab foundation.

First floor: 1,499 sq. ft.
Second floor: 728 sq. ft.

Total living area: 2,227 sq. ft.
(Not counting basement or garage)
Garage & storage: 441 sq. ft.
Basement: 1,381 sq. ft.

Blueprint Price Code C

Plan C-8030

*PRICES AND DETAILS
ON PAGES 12-15*

Family-Oriented Home Design

- From the two-story foyer to the separate guest and family areas, this striking home was designed for formal entertaining and casual family living.
- The heart of the family gathering area is the large family room with a nice fireplace and outdoor access.
- Kneewalls and an angled eating bar visually separate the kitchen, breakfast room and family room without sacrificing the light, open feeling of the entire area.
- The home's three bedrooms are located on the upper floor. The master suite is highlighted with a tray ceiling and a private bath with a vaulted ceiling and an oval tub. Knee space allows the vanity to be used as a makeup table.
- The optional bonus room can be used as a study or playroom.

Plan FB-5055-MANS

Bedrooms: 3+	Baths: 2½
Living Area:	
Upper floor	874 sq. ft.
Main floor	1,008 sq. ft.
Optional bonus room	378 sq. ft.
Total Living Area:	**2,260 sq. ft.**
Daylight basement	1,008 sq. ft.
Garage	415 sq. ft.
Exterior Wall Framing:	2x4

Foundation Options:
Daylight basement
Slab
(Typical foundation & framing conversion diagram available–see order form.)

BLUEPRINT PRICE CODE: C

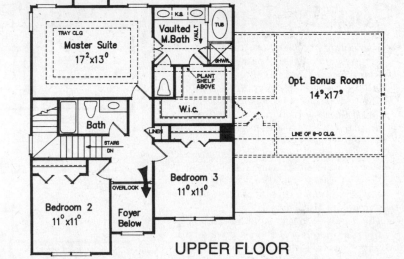

UPPER FLOOR

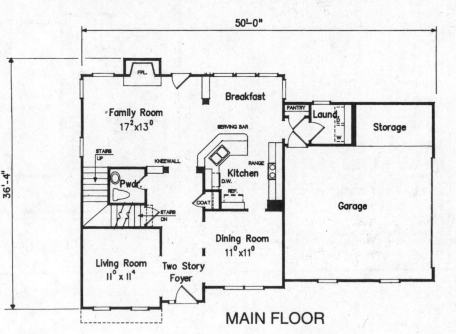

MAIN FLOOR

Luxurious Country Home

- This country cottage hosts many luxuries, such as an expansive Great Room, good-sized sleeping areas and a large screened back porch.
- The rustic front porch opens into the Great Room, which offers a handsome fireplace and access to the large screened back porch.
- The bright kitchen features a huge work island, and unfolds to both the formal dining room and the breakfast bay. A handy laundry closet and access to the garage are also offered.
- The removed master suite has views of the front porch and offers a private bath with two walk-in closets, a dual-sink vanity, a spa tub and a separate shower.
- Upstairs are two oversized bedrooms, each with a dressing room that accesses a common bath.

Plan C-8535

Bedrooms: 3	Baths: 2½
Living Area:	
Upper floor	765 sq. ft.
Main floor	1,535 sq. ft.
Total Living Area:	**2,300 sq. ft.**
Daylight basement	1,535 sq. ft.
Garage	424 sq. ft.
Exterior Wall Framing:	2x4

Foundation Options:

Daylight basement

(All plans can be built with your choice of foundation and framing. A generic conversion diagram is available. See order form.)

BLUEPRINT PRICE CODE:	C

UPPER FLOOR

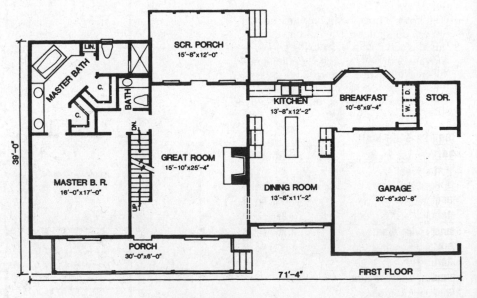

MAIN FLOOR

TO ORDER THIS BLUEPRINT, CALL TOLL-FREE 1-800-547-5570

Plan C-8535

PRICES AND DETAILS ON PAGES 12-15

Grand Colonial Home

- This grand Colonial home boasts a porch entry framed by bay windows and gable towers.
- The two-story foyer flows to the dining room on the left and adjoins the bayed living room on the right, with its warm fireplace and flanking windows.
- At the rear, the family room features a 17-ft. ceiling, a media wall, a bar and terrace access through French doors.
- Connected to the family room is a high-tech kitchen with an island work area, a pantry, a work desk and a circular dinette.
- A private terrace, a romantic fireplace, a huge walk-in closet and a lavish bath with a whirlpool tub are featured in the main-floor master suite.
- Three bedrooms and two full baths share the upper floor.

Plan AHP-9120

Bedrooms: 4	Baths: 3
Living Area:	
Upper floor	776 sq. ft.
Main floor	1,551 sq. ft.
Total Living Area:	**2,327 sq. ft.**
Standard basement	1,580 sq. ft.
Garage	440 sq. ft.
Exterior Wall Framing:	2x4 or 2x6

Foundation Options:

Standard basement
Crawlspace
Slab
(All plans can be built with your choice of foundation and framing. A generic conversion diagram is available. See order form.)

BLUEPRINT PRICE CODE: C

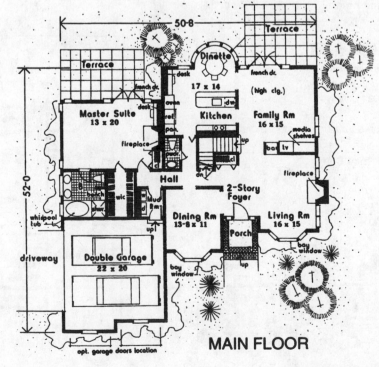

UPPER FLOOR

MAIN FLOOR

TO ORDER THIS BLUEPRINT,
CALL TOLL-FREE 1-800-547-5570

Plan AHP-9120

PRICES AND DETAILS
ON PAGES 12-15
299

Flamboyant Floor Plan

- A host of architectural styles went into the making of this interesting design, from country and Victorian to contemporary. A mixture of gable and hip roofs, a bayed front porch and several differently shaped windows give the exterior plenty of impact.
- A dramatic open floor plan combines to make the home stylishly up to date. High ceilings throughout much of the main level add to the flamboyant floor plan.
- The fantastic family room features a soaring ceiling, a fireplace and an abundance of windows. The adjoining breakfast room has a cathedral ceiling and is open to the kitchen. The attached sun porch is enclosed in glass, with skylights in the sloped ceiling. Formal dining is reserved for the unusual dining room at the front of the home.
- The first-floor master suite boasts a cathedral ceiling, lots of closet space and an irresistible garden tub.
- Three bedrooms and a full bath make up the second level. Each of the bedrooms has a walk-in closet.

Plan AX-1318

Bedrooms: 4	Baths: 2 ½
Space:	
Upper floor	697 sq. ft.
Main floor	1,642 sq. ft.
Total Living Area	**2,339 sq. ft.**
Basement	1,384 sq. ft.
Garage	431 sq. ft.
Exterior Wall Framing	2x4

Foundation options:
Standard Basement
Crawlspace
Slab
(Foundation & framing conversion diagram available—see order form.)

Blueprint Price Code	C

UPPER FLOOR

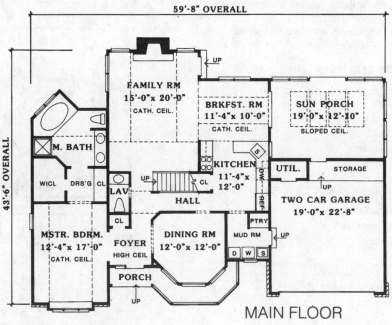

MAIN FLOOR

TO ORDER THIS BLUEPRINT, CALL TOLL-FREE 1-800-547-5570

Plan AX-1318

PRICES AND DETAILS ON PAGES 12-15

Loaded with Livability

- The attractive exterior of this home packages a marvelous floor plan that provides the utmost in livability.
- The gorgeous entry sports a 17-ft.-high vaulted ceiling. A 12-ft. vaulted ceiling presides over the spacious living room, which is enhanced by a dramatic boxed-out window. The adjoining dining room opens to a delightful covered patio.
- The kitchen features an island cooktop, a bright angled sink and a sunny nook that accesses another patio. A woodstove in the family room radiates warmth to the entire area.
- A half-bath, laundry facilities and garage access are nearby.
- Upstairs, the sumptuous master suite includes a deluxe bath and a large wardrobe closet.
- Two secondary bedrooms share a compartmentalized bath. A large bonus room above the garage offers a myriad of possible uses.

Plan R-2111

Bedrooms: 3+	Baths: 2½
Living Area:	
Upper floor	945 sq. ft.
Main floor	1,115 sq. ft.
Bonus room	285 sq. ft.
Total Living Area:	**2,345 sq. ft.**
Garage	851 sq. ft.
Exterior Wall Framing:	2x6
Foundation Options:	

Crawlspace
(All plans can be built with your choice of foundation and framing. A generic conversion diagram is available. See order form.)

BLUEPRINT PRICE CODE: C

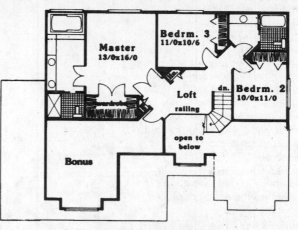

UPPER FLOOR

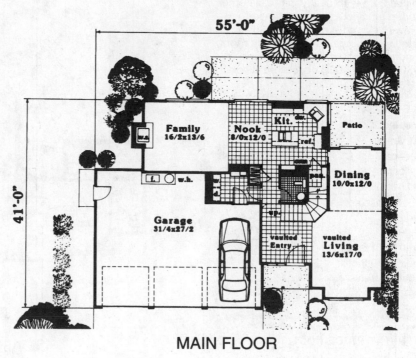

MAIN FLOOR

Plan R-2111

PRICES AND DETAILS
ON PAGES 12-15

One More Time!

- The character and excitement of our most popular plan in recent years, E-3000, have been recaptured in this smaller version of the design.
- The appealing facade is distinguished by a covered front porch and accented with decorative columns, triple dormers and rail-topped corner windows.
- Off the foyer, a central gallery leads to the spacious family room, where a corner fireplace and a 17-ft. vaulted ceiling are highlights. Columns in the gallery introduce the kitchen and the dining areas.
- The kitchen showcases a walk-in pantry, a built-in desk and a long snack bar that serves the eating nook and the dining room.
- The stunning main-floor master suite offers a quiet sitting area and a private angled bath with dual vanities, a corner garden tub and a separate shower.
- A lovely curved stairway leads to a balcony that overlooks the family room and the foyer. Two large bedrooms, a split bath and easily accessible attics are also found upstairs.

Plan E-2307-A

Bedrooms: 3	Baths: 2½
Living Area:	
Upper floor	595 sq. ft.
Main floor	1,765 sq. ft.
Total Living Area:	**2,360 sq. ft.**
Standard basement	1,765 sq. ft.
Garage	484 sq. ft.
Storage	44 sq. ft.
Exterior Wall Framing:	2x6

Foundation Options:

Standard basement
Crawlspace
Slab
(All plans can be built with your choice of foundation and framing. A generic conversion diagram is available. See order form.)

BLUEPRINT PRICE CODE: C

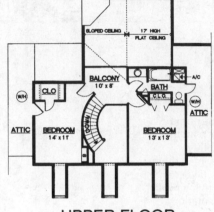

UPPER FLOOR

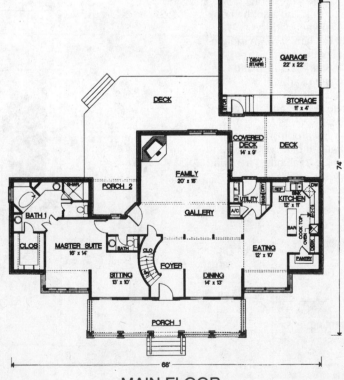

MAIN FLOOR

Great Spaces

- The dynamic exterior of this unique home includes an eye-catching arched window and a cutout in the roof above the covered walkway.
- The impressive entry features a dramatic 15½-ft. vaulted ceiling and opens to the stunning sunken Great Room. A 9-ft. ceiling with wood beams and floor-to-ceiling windows enhance the sunken Great Room. A warm woodstove with a built-in wood bin and a nearby wet bar are other attractions found here.
- The skylighted kitchen offers a convenient snack bar, a greenhouse sink and an adjoining breakfast area.
- The main-floor master suite boasts a large walk-in closet, a private bath with a garden tub and private access to a covered patio or deck.
- A balcony hall upstairs leads to two more bedrooms and another bath.

Plan LRD-22884

Bedrooms: 3	Baths: 2½
Living Area:	
Upper floor	674 sq. ft.
Main floor	1,686 sq. ft.
Total Living Area:	**2,360 sq. ft.**
Standard basement	1,686 sq. ft.
Garage	450 sq. ft.
Exterior Wall Framing:	2x6

Foundation Options:

Standard basement
Crawlspace

(All plans can be built with your choice of foundation and framing. A generic conversion diagram is available. See order form.)

BLUEPRINT PRICE CODE: C

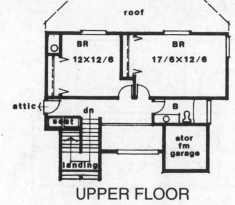

UPPER FLOOR

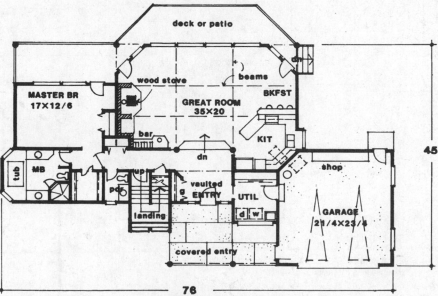

MAIN FLOOR

TO ORDER THIS BLUEPRINT,
CALL TOLL-FREE 1-800-547-5570

Plan LRD-22884

PRICES AND DETAILS
ON PAGES 12-15

303

Spacious Kitchen/Family Room Area

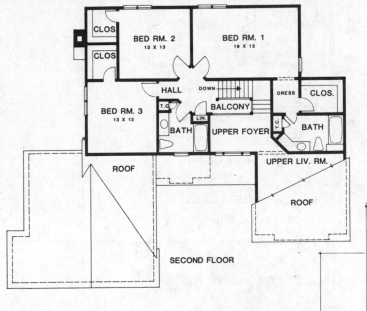

PLAN A-2181-DS
WITH BASEMENT

First floor: 1,356 sq. ft.
Second floor: 1,015 sq. ft.
Total living area: 2,371 sq. ft.
(Not counting basement or garage)

SECOND FLOOR

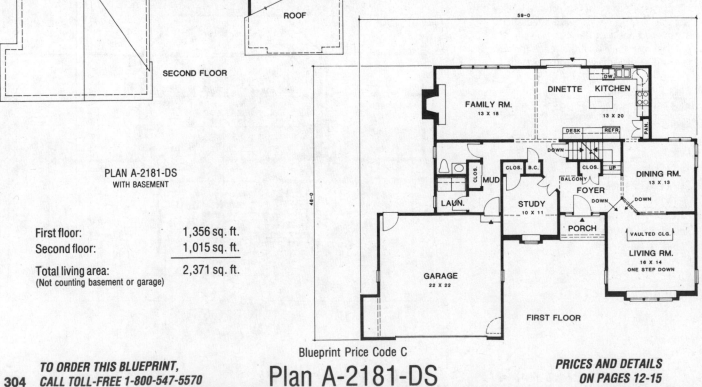

FIRST FLOOR

Blueprint Price Code C

Plan A-2181-DS

Large-Scale Living

- Eye-catching windows and an appealing wraparound porch highlight the exterior of this outstanding home.
- Inside, high ceilings and large-scale living spaces prevail, beginning with the foyer, which has an 18-ft. ceiling.
- The spacious living room flows into the formal dining room, which opens to the porch and to an optional rear deck.
- The island kitchen extends to a bright breakfast room with deck access. The family room offers an 18-ft. vaulted ceiling and a corner fireplace.
- Unless otherwise noted, every main-floor room boasts a 9-ft. ceiling.
- Upstairs, the lushs master bedroom boasts an 11-ft. vaulted ceiling and two walk-in closets. The skylighted master bath features a spa tub, a separate shower and a dual-sink vanity.
- Three more bedrooms are reached by a balcony, which overlooks the family room. In one bedroom, the ceiling jumps to 10 ft. at the beautiful window.

Plan AX-93309

Bedrooms: 4	Baths: 2½
Living Area:	
Upper floor	1,180 sq. ft.
Main floor	1,290 sq. ft.
Total Living Area:	**2,470 sq. ft.**
Basement	1,290 sq. ft.
Garage and storage	421 sq. ft.
Exterior Wall Framing:	2x4

Foundation Options:

Daylight basement
Standard basement
Slab

(All plans can be built with your choice of foundation and framing. A generic conversion diagram is available. See order form.)

BLUEPRINT PRICE CODE: C

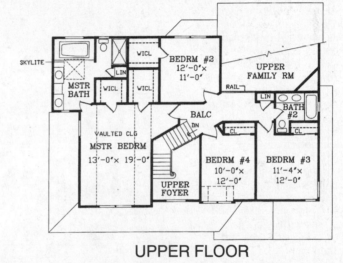

UPPER FLOOR

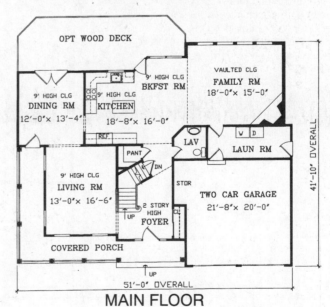

MAIN FLOOR

TO ORDER THIS BLUEPRINT,
CALL TOLL-FREE 1-800-547-5570

Plan AX-93309

PRICES AND DETAILS
ON PAGES 12-15

305

Pillars of Success

- A stunning two-story entry porch with heavy support pillars creates a look of success for this exciting new design.
- The covered entrance gives way to an open entry foyer with closets for coats and general storage. A powder room is just steps away.
- Straight ahead, the Great Room features a fireplace, a TV niche and a 16-ft. vaulted ceiling. A French door gives access to a view deck that wraps around much of the home.
- The kitchen's island boasts a cooktop and a convenient snack counter. The adjacent dining bay offers great views.
- The main-floor master suite has a 10-ft. coved ceiling, private deck access, built-in shelves, a dressing area and a private skylighted bath.
- A den or guest room includes a 9-ft. vaulted ceiling and deck access.
- The upper floor has a central hobby area with a 13-ft. vaulted ceiling. Two bedrooms feature views to the Great Room below.

Plan LRD-32190

Bedrooms: 3+	Baths: 3
Living Area:	
Upper floor	606 sq. ft.
Main floor	1,865 sq. ft.
Total Living Area:	**2,471 sq. ft.**
Standard basement	1,865 sq. ft.
Garage	529 sq. ft.
Exterior Wall Framing:	2x6

Foundation Options:

Standard basement
Crawlspace
Slab

(All plans can be built with your choice of foundation and framing. A generic conversion diagram is available. See order form.)

BLUEPRINT PRICE CODE: C

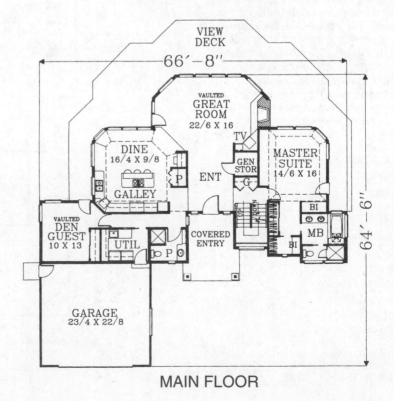

UPPER FLOOR

MAIN FLOOR

Dynamic Design

- Angled walls, vaulted ceilings and lots of glass set the tempo for this dynamic home.
- The covered front entry opens to a raised foyer and a beautiful staircase with a bayed landing.
- One step down, a spectacular see-through fireplace with a raised hearth and built-in wood storage is visible from both the bayed dining room and the stunning Great Room.
- The Great Room also showcases an 18-ft.-high vaulted ceiling, wraparound windows and access to a deck or patio.
- The adjoining nook has a door to the deck and is served by the kitchen's snack bar. The kitchen is enhanced by a 9-ft. ceiling, corner windows and a pass-through to the dining room.
- Upstairs, the master suite offers a 10-ft.-high coved ceiling, a splendid bath, a large walk-in closet and a private deck.

Plan S-41587

Bedrooms: 3+	Baths: 3
Living Area:	
Upper floor	1,001 sq. ft.
Main floor	1,550 sq. ft.
Total Living Area:	**2,551 sq. ft.**
Basement	1,550 sq. ft.
Garage (three-car)	773 sq. ft.
Exterior Wall Framing:	**2x6**

Foundation Options:
Daylight basement
Standard basement
Crawlspace
Slab
(All plans can be built with your choice of foundation and framing. A generic conversion diagram is available. See order form.)

BLUEPRINT PRICE CODE: **D**

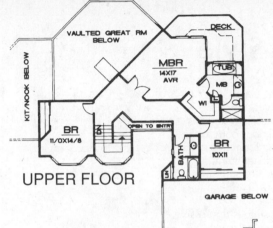

UPPER FLOOR

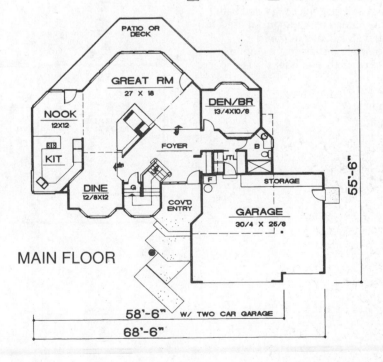

MAIN FLOOR

58'-6" w/ TWO CAR GARAGE
68'-6"
55'-6"

TO ORDER THIS BLUEPRINT,
CALL TOLL-FREE 1-800-547-5570

Plan S-41587

PRICES AND DETAILS
ON PAGES 12-15

307

Classic Country-Style

- Almost completely surrounded by an expansive porch, this classic plan exudes warmth and grace.
- The foyer is liberal in size and leads guests to a formal dining room to the left or the large living room to the right.
- The open country kitchen includes a sunny, bay-windowed breakfast nook. A utility area, a full bath and garage access are nearby.
- Upstairs, the master suite is impressive, with its large sleeping area, walk-in closet and magnificent garden bath.
- Three secondary bedrooms share a full bath with a dual-sink vanity.
- Also note the stairs leading up to an attic, which is useful for storage space.

Plan J-86134

Bedrooms: 4	Baths: 3
Living Area:	
Upper floor	1,195 sq. ft.
Main floor	1,370 sq. ft.
Total Living Area:	**2,565 sq. ft.**
Standard basement	1,370 sq. ft.
Garage	576 sq. ft.
Exterior Wall Framing:	2x4

Foundation Options:

Standard basement
Crawlspace
Slab

(All plans can be built with your choice of foundation and framing. A generic conversion diagram is available. See order form.)

BLUEPRINT PRICE CODE:	D

NOTE:
The above photographed home may have been modified by the homeowner. Please refer to floor plan and/or drawn elevation shown for actual blueprint details.

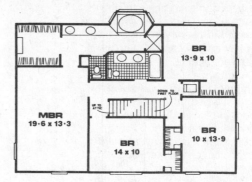

UPPER FLOOR

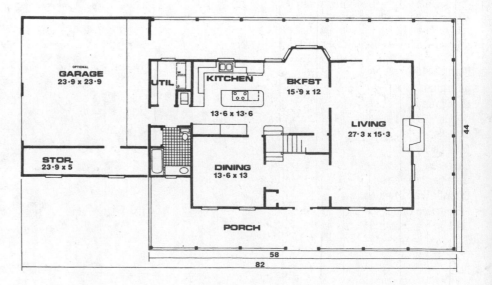

MAIN FLOOR

Photo by Kevin Haslip

Privacy and Luxury

- This home's large roof planes and privacy fences enclose a thoroughly modern, open floor plan.
- A beautiful courtyard greets guests on their way to the secluded entrance. Inside, a two-story-high entry area leads directly into the living and dining rooms, which boast an 11-ft. vaulted ceiling, plus floor-to-ceiling windows and a fireplace with a stone hearth.
- The angular kitchen features a snack bar to the adjoining family room and a passive-solar sun room that offers natural brightness.
- A 14½-ft. vaulted ceiling presides over the family room. Sliding glass doors access a backyard patio with a sun deck and a hot tub.
- The luxurious master suite opens to both the front courtyard and the backyard hot tub area. The 11-ft.-high vaulted bath includes a dual-sink vanity, a raised garden tub, a separate shower and a corner walk-in closet.
- Two secondary bedrooms and another bath share the upper floor, which boasts commanding views of main-floor areas.

Plans P-7663-3A & -3D

Bedrooms: 3+	Baths: 3
Living Area:	
Upper floor	569 sq. ft.
Main floor	2,039 sq. ft.
Total Living Area:	**2,608 sq. ft.**
Daylight basement	2,039 sq. ft.
Garage	799 sq. ft.
Exterior Wall Framing:	2x4
Foundation Options:	**Plan #**
Daylight basement	P-7663-3D
Crawlspace	P-7663-3A

(All plans can be built with your choice of foundation and framing. A generic conversion diagram is available. See order form.)

BLUEPRINT PRICE CODE:	D

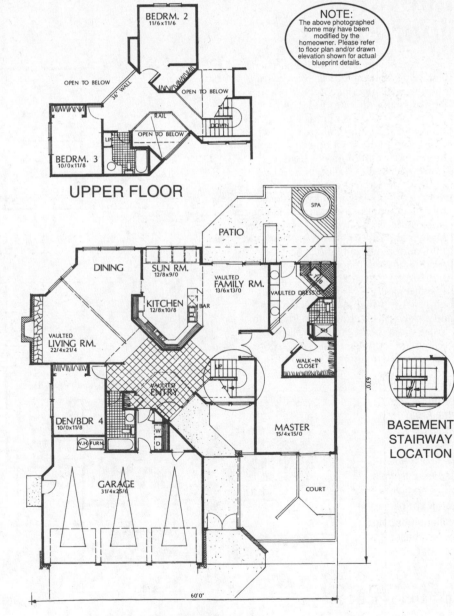

NOTE: The above photographed home may have been modified by the homeowner. Please refer to floor plan and/or drawn elevation shown for actual blueprint details.

UPPER FLOOR

MAIN FLOOR

BASEMENT STAIRWAY LOCATION

Innovative Floor Plan

- The wide, covered front porch, arched windows and symmetrical lines of this traditional home conceal the modern, innovative floor plan found within.
- A two-story-high foyer guides guests to the front-oriented formal areas, which have views to the front porch.
- The hotspot of the home is the Great Room, with one of the home's three fireplaces and a media wall. Flanking doors open to a large backyard deck.
- The island kitchen and glassed-in eating nook overlook the deck and access a handy mudroom. High 9-ft. ceilings add to the aura of warmth and hospitality found on the main floor of this home.
- Another of the fireplaces is offered in the master suite. This private oasis also boasts a 13-ft.-high cathedral ceiling and a delicious bath with a garden tub.
- Upstairs, one bedroom has a sloped ceiling and a private bath. Three more bedrooms share another full bath.

Plan AHP-9360

Bedrooms: 5	Baths: 3½
Living Area:	
Upper floor	970 sq. ft.
Main floor	1,735 sq. ft.
Total Living Area:	**2,705 sq. ft.**
Standard basement	1,550 sq. ft.
Garage and utility area	443 sq. ft.
Exterior Wall Framing:	2x6

Foundation Options:
Standard basement
Crawlspace
Slab
(All plans can be built with your choice of foundation and framing. A generic conversion diagram is available. See order form.)

BLUEPRINT PRICE CODE:	D

UPPER FLOOR

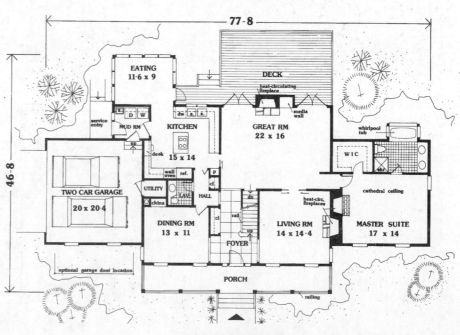

MAIN FLOOR

Plan AHP-9360

Home with Sparkle

- This dynamite design simply sparkles, with the main living areas geared toward a gorgeous greenhouse at the back of the home.
- At the front of the home, a sunken foyer introduces the formal dining room, which is framed by a curved half-wall. The sunken living room boasts a 17-ft. vaulted ceiling and a nice fireplace.
- The spacious kitchen features a bright, two-story skywell above the island. The family room's ceiling rises to 17 feet. These rooms culminate at a solar greenhouse with an indulgent hot tub and a 12-ft. vaulted ceiling. The neighboring bath has a raised spa tub.
- Upstairs, the impressive master suite includes its own deck and a stairway to the greenhouse. A vaulted library with a woodstove augments the suite. Ceilings soar to 16 ft. in both areas.

Plan S-8217

Bedrooms: 3+	Baths: 2
Living Area:	
Upper floor	789 sq. ft.
Main floor	1,709 sq. ft.
Bonus room	336 sq. ft.
Total Living Area:	**2,834 sq. ft.**
Partial basement	1,242 sq. ft.
Garage	441 sq. ft.
Exterior Wall Framing:	2x6

Foundation Options:

Partial basement
Crawlspace
Slab

(All plans can be built with your choice of foundation and framing. A generic conversion diagram is available. See order form.)

BLUEPRINT PRICE CODE: D

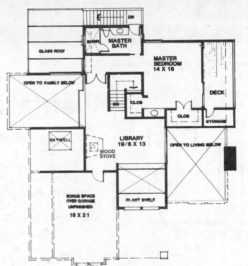

UPPER FLOOR

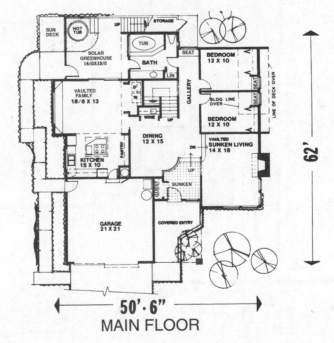

MAIN FLOOR

Photo by Mark Englund/HomeStyles

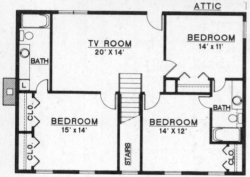

TV ROOM
20' X 14'

BEDROOM
14' x 11'

BATH

BEDROOM
15' x 14'

BEDROOM
14' x 12'

STAIRS

BATH

ATTIC

CLO.

CLO.

CLO.

CLO.

UPPER FLOOR

Plantation Perfected

- The stately plantation style with two-story columns, triple dormers, full-width porch and shuttered windows, is perfected with a modern, exciting floor plan.
- A vast living room lies to the left of the entry and stairs, complete with

a fireplace and access to the rear porch and deck.
- The formal dining room is located to the right of the entry.
- The island kitchen overlooks the eating bay, and has glimpses of the living room through columns.
- The stunning main floor master suite features sloped ceilings, a garden bath overlooking a private courtyard, and a bay windowed sitting room.
- The three bedrooms upstairs share a large TV/playroom.

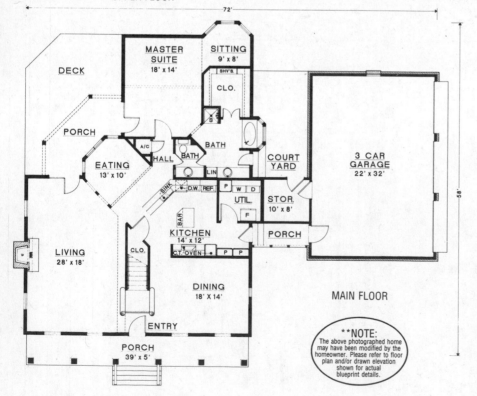

72'

58'

DECK

PORCH

MASTER SUITE
18' x 14'

SITTING
9' x 8'

SHV'S.

CLO.

A/C

HALL

BATH

BATH

LIN

COURT YARD

3 CAR GARAGE
22' x 32'

EATING
13' x 10'

SINK

D.W. REF.

P

W   D

UTIL.

F

STOR.
10' x 8'

PORCH

BAR

LIVING
28' x 18'

KITCHEN
14' x 12'

CLO.

CT. OVEN

P   P

DINING
18' X 14'

ENTRY

PORCH
39' x 5'

MAIN FLOOR

**NOTE:
The above photographed home may have been modified by the homeowner. Please refer to floor plan and/or drawn elevation shown for actual blueprint details.

Plan E-2800

Bedrooms: 4	**Baths:** 3
Space:	
Upper floor:	1,120 sq. ft.
Main floor:	1,768 sq. ft.
Total living area:	2,888 sq. ft.
Basement:	1,768 sq. ft.
Garage:	726 sq. ft.
Exterior Wall Framing:	2x6
Ceiling Heights:	
Upper floor:	8'
Main floor:	9'

Foundation options:
Crawlspace.
Standard basement.
Slab.
(Foundation & framing conversion diagram available — see order form.)

Blueprint Price Code: D

Dramatic Rear Views

- Columned front and rear porches offer country styling to this elegant two-story.
- The formal dining room and living room flank the two-story-high foyer.
- A dramatic array of windows stretches along the informal, rear-oriented living areas, where the central family room features a 17-ft.-high vaulted ceiling and a striking fireplace.
- The modern kitchen features an angled snack counter, a walk-in pantry and a work island, in addition to the bayed morning room.
- The exciting and secluded master suite has a sunny bayed sitting area with its own fireplace. Large walk-in closets lead to a luxurious private bath with angled dual vanities, a garden spa tub and a separate shower.
- The centrally located stairway leads to three extra bedrooms and two full baths on the upper floor.

Plan DD-2912

Bedrooms: 4	Baths: 3½
Living Area:	
Upper floor	916 sq. ft.
Main floor	2,046 sq. ft.
Total Living Area:	**2,962 sq. ft.**
Standard basement	1,811 sq. ft.
Garage	513 sq. ft.
Exterior Wall Framing:	2x4

Foundation Options:

Standard basement

Crawlspace

Slab

(All plans can be built with your choice of foundation and framing. A generic conversion diagram is available. See order form.)

BLUEPRINT PRICE CODE: D

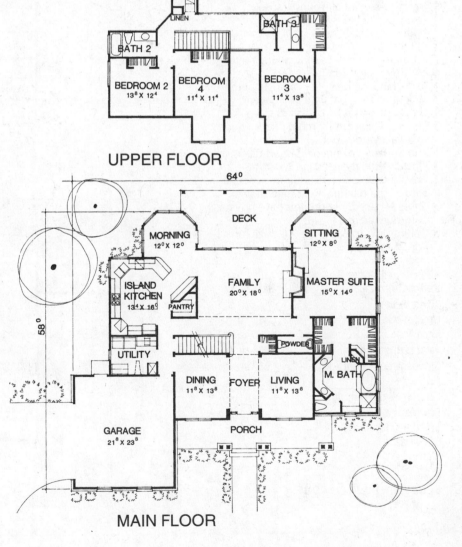

UPPER FLOOR

MAIN FLOOR

Photo by Mark Englund/HomeStyles

Stately Elegance

- The elegant interior of this home is introduced by a dramatic barrel-vaulted entry with stately columns.
- Double doors open to the 19-ft.-high foyer, where a half-round transom window brightens an attractive open-railed stairway.
- Off the foyer, the living room is separated from the sunny dining room by impressive columns.
- The island kitchen offers a bright corner sink, a walk-in pantry and a bayed breakfast area with backyard views.
- The adjoining family room offers a door to a backyard patio, while a wet bar and a fireplace enhance the whole area.
- Upstairs, the master suite boasts a private bath with two walk-in closets, a garden spa tub and a separate shower.
- Three secondary bedrooms have private bathroom access.
- Ceilings in all rooms are 9 ft. high for added spaciousness.

**NOTE:
The above photographed home may have been modified by the homeowner. Please refer to floor plan and/or drawn elevation shown for actual blueprint details.

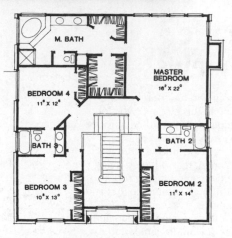

UPPER FLOOR

Plan DD-2968-A

Bedrooms: 4+	Baths: 3½
Living Area:	
Upper floor	1,382 sq. ft.
Main floor	1,586 sq. ft.
Total Living Area:	**2,968 sq. ft.**
Standard basement	1,586 sq. ft.
Garage	521 sq. ft.
Exterior Wall Framing:	2x4

Foundation Options:
Standard basement
Crawlspace
Slab
(All plans can be built with your choice of foundation and framing. A generic conversion diagram is available. See order form.)

BLUEPRINT PRICE CODE:	D

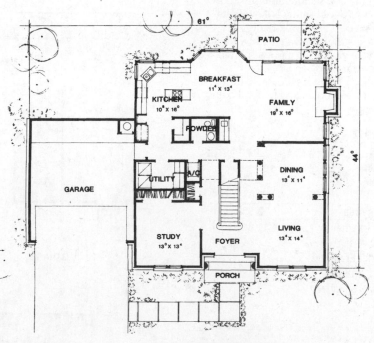

MAIN FLOOR

TO ORDER THIS BLUEPRINT, CALL TOLL-FREE 1-800-547-5570

Plan DD-2968-A

PRICES AND DETAILS ON PAGES 12-15

Photo by Gil Ford

Spacious and Stately

- This popular home design boasts a classic Creole exterior and a symmetrical layout, with 9-ft.-high ceilings on the main floor.
- French doors lead from the formal living and dining rooms to the large family room. The central fireplace is flanked by French doors that open to a covered rear porch and an open-air deck.
- The kitchen is reached easily from the family room, the dining room and the rear entrance. An island cooktop and a window-framed eating area are other features found here.
- The real seller, though, is the main-floor master suite with its spectacular bath. Among its many extras are a built-in vanity, a spa tub and a 16-ft. sloped ceiling with a skylight.
- Three upstairs bedrooms, each with double closets and private bath access, make this the perfect family-sized home.

Plan E-3000

Bedrooms: 4	Baths: 3½
Living Area:	
Upper floor	1,027 sq. ft.
Main floor	2,008 sq. ft.
Total Living Area:	**3,035 sq. ft.**
Standard basement	2,008 sq. ft.
Garage	484 sq. ft.
Storage	96 sq. ft.
Exterior Wall Framing:	2x6

Foundation Options:

Standard basement
Crawlspace
Slab

(All plans can be built with your choice of foundation and framing. A generic conversion diagram is available. See order form.)

BLUEPRINT PRICE CODE: E

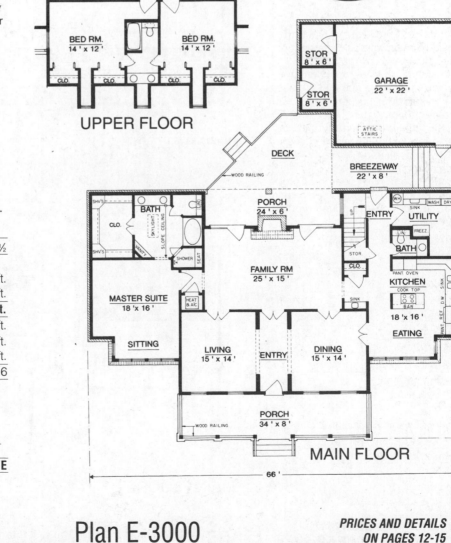

NOTE:
The above photographed home may have been modified by the homeowner. Please refer to floor plan and/or drawn elevation shown for actual blueprint details.

UPPER FLOOR

MAIN FLOOR

Photo by Mark Englund/HomeStyles

Master Suite with Fireplace, Deck

- This brick-accented two-story has front stacked bay windows, a three-car garage and staggered rooflines.
- Inside you'll find large, open living areas oriented to the rear and fireplaces in the living room, sunken family room and master bedroom.
- Both the family room and study open out to a rear patio; the island kitchen and bayed nook join the family room, which also offers a wet bar.
- Room for two to three bedrooms plus the master suite with private deck and lavish, skylit spa bath is found on the upper level.

Plan P-7751-3A and P-7751-3D

Bedrooms: 3-4	Baths: 2 ½
Space:	
Upper floor	1,411 sq. ft.
Main floor	1,737 sq. ft.
Total Living Area	**3,148 sq. ft.**
Basement	1,737 sq. ft.
Garage	677 sq. ft.
Exterior Wall Framing	**2x6**
Foundation options:	**Plan #**
Daylight Basement	P-7751-3D
Crawlspace	P-7751-3A
(Foundation & framing conversion diagram available—see order form.)	
Blueprint Price Code	**E**

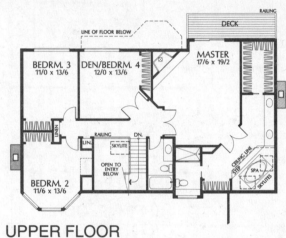

UPPER FLOOR

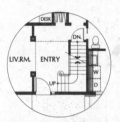

BASEMENT STAIR LOCATION-P-7751-3D

**NOTE: The above photographed home may have been modified by the homeowner. Please refer to floor plan and/or drawn elevation shown for actual blueprint details.

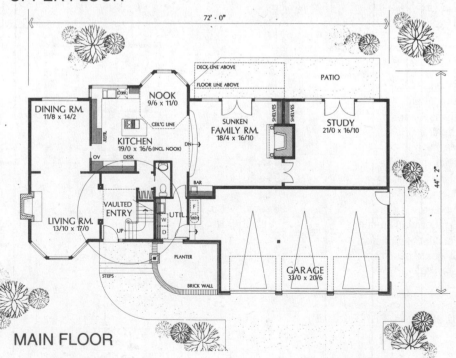

MAIN FLOOR

Victorian Farmhouse

- Fish-scale shingles and horizontal siding team up with the detailed front porch to create a look of yesterday. Brickwork enriches the sides and rear of the home.
- The main level features 10-ft.-high ceilings throughout the central living space. The front-oriented formal areas merge with the family room via three sets of French doors.

- The island kitchen and skylighted eating area have 16-ft. sloped ceilings.
- A breezeway off the deck connects the house to a roomy workshop. A two-car garage is located under the workshop and a large utility room is just inside the rear entrance.
- The main-floor master suite offers an opulent skylighted bath with a garden vanity, a spa tub, a separate shower and an 18-ft.-high sloped ceiling.
- The upper floor offers three more bedrooms, two full baths and a balcony that looks to the backyard.

Plan E-3103

Bedrooms: 4	Baths: 3½
Living Area:	
Upper floor	1,113 sq. ft.
Main floor	2,040 sq. ft.
Total Living Area:	**3,153 sq. ft.**
Daylight basement	2,040 sq. ft.
Tuck-under garage and storage	580 sq. ft.
Workshop and storage	580 sq. ft.
Exterior Wall Framing:	2x6

Foundation Options:

Daylight basement
Crawlspace
Slab
(All plans can be built with your choice of foundation and framing. A generic conversion diagram is available. See order form.)

BLUEPRINT PRICE CODE:	E

MAIN FLOOR

UPPER FLOOR

Oriented for Scenic Rear View

- That elegant look of the past is found in this expansive post-modern design.
- A two-story vaulted entry leads to spacious formal entertaining areas.
- A dining room with built-in China closet is to the left.
- To the right is a formal living room with a strikingly elegant bow window.
- The family room and living room share an interesting corner fireplace.
- A convenient powder room is tucked away behind the sweeping curved staircase.
- A see-through wine rack is an eye-catcher in the kitchen, along with its green-house window, island chopping block and abundant counter space.
- The living and family rooms are defined by decorative columns and arches and are a step-down from the foyer/hallway.
- Upstairs, a luxurious master suite boasts a sunny bow window, deluxe bath and enormous closet.
- Three other bedrooms, a full bath and a large unfinished "bonus space" complete the second floor.

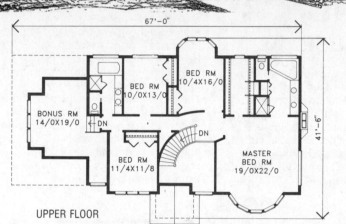

UPPER FLOOR

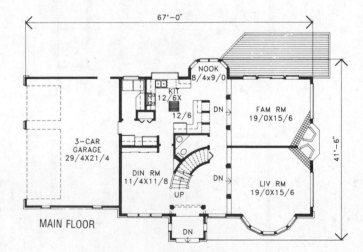

MAIN FLOOR

Plan SD-8819

Bedrooms: 4-5	Baths: 2½

Space:

Upper floor:	1,500 sq. ft.
Main floor:	1,476 sq. ft.

Total living area:	**2,976 sq. ft.**
Bonus area:	266 sq. ft.
Basement:	approx. 1,476 sq. ft.
Garage:	626 sq. ft.

Exterior Wall Framing: 2x6

Foundation options:
Standard basement.
Crawlspace.
(Foundation & framing conversion diagram available — see order form.)

Blueprint Price Code: D

Truly Nostalgic

- Designed after "Monteigne," an Italianate home near Natchez, Mississippi, this reproduction utilizes modern stucco finishes for the exterior.
- Columns and arched windows give way to a two-story-high foyer, which is accented by a striking, curved stairwell.
- The foyer connects the living room and the study, each boasting a 14-ft. ceiling and a cozy fireplace or woodstove.
- Adjacent to the formal dining room, the kitchen offers a snack bar and a bayed eating room. A unique entertainment center is centrally located to serve the main activity rooms of the home.
- A gorgeous sun room stretches across the rear of the main floor and overlooks a grand terrace.
- The plush master suite and bath boast his-and-hers vanities, large walk-in closets and a glassed-in garden tub.
- A main-floor guest bedroom features a walk-in closet and private access to another full main-floor bath.
- Two more bedrooms with private baths are located on the upper level. They share a sitting area and a veranda.

Plan E-3200

Bedrooms: 4	Baths: 4
Living Area:	
Upper floor	629 sq. ft.
Main floor	2,655 sq. ft.
Total Living Area:	**3,284 sq. ft.**
Standard basement	2,655 sq. ft.
Garage	667 sq. ft.
Exterior Wall Framing:	2x6

Foundation Options:

Standard basement

Crawlspace

Slab

(All plans can be built with your choice of foundation and framing. A generic conversion diagram is available. See order form.)

BLUEPRINT PRICE CODE: E

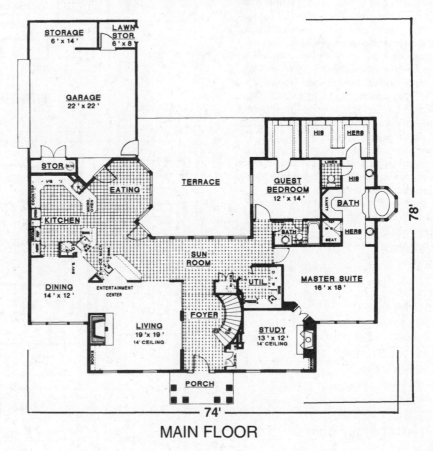

UPPER FLOOR

MAIN FLOOR

TO ORDER THIS BLUEPRINT,
CALL TOLL-FREE 1-800-547-5570

Plan E-3200

PRICES AND DETAILS
ON PAGES 12-15

319

Deluxe Master Suite

- This traditional home has an enticing style all its own, with a deluxe main-floor master suite.
- In from the covered porch, the front entry flows into the main living areas.
- Straight ahead, the family room features a handsome fireplace flanked by doors to a screened back porch.
- The kitchen easily services the formal dining room and offers a snack bar to the bayed breakfast nook. A nice utility room with a pantry and a half-bath is just off the nook and the garage entry.
- The secluded master suite boasts a 9-ft. tray ceiling and a luxurious bath with a garden tub, a separate shower and two vanities, one with knee space.
- Upstairs, each of the two additional bedrooms has a walk-in closet and a private bath. The optional bonus room can be finished as a large game room, a bedroom or an office.

Plan C-8915

Bedrooms: 3+	Baths: 3½
Living Area:	
Upper floor	832 sq. ft.
Main floor	1,927 sq. ft.
Bonus room	624 sq. ft.
Total Living Area:	**3,383 sq. ft.**
Daylight basement	1,674 sq. ft.
Garage	484 sq. ft.
Exterior Wall Framing:	2x4

Foundation Options:

Daylight basement

Crawlspace

(All plans can be built with your choice of foundation and framing. A generic conversion diagram is available. See order form.)

BLUEPRINT PRICE CODE: E

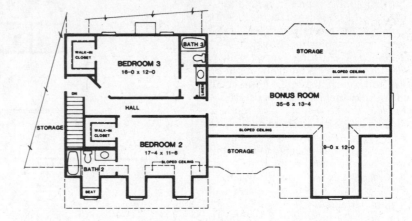

UPPER FLOOR

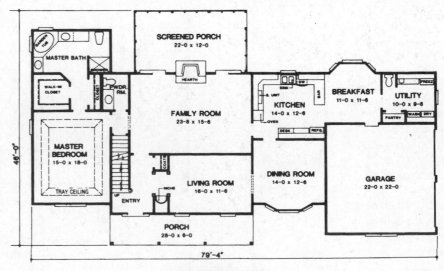

MAIN FLOOR

TO ORDER THIS BLUEPRINT, CALL TOLL-FREE 1-800-547-5570   Plan C-8915   *PRICES AND DETAILS ON PAGES 12-15*

Traditional Treat

- A covered front porch with ornamental columns and brackets provides a traditional treat on the exterior of this four-bedroom two-story home.
- Entering the front door, a dramatic view awaits guests of a vaulted foyer with double-back stairs leading up to a bridge overlook above.
- To the left of the foyer, through an arched, columned opening, lies the formal living room with fireplace and formal dining room beyond.
- To the right of the foyer is a double-doored den/guest room with built-in desk.
- The rear-facing family room opens to the island kitchen and breakfast nook.
- The four upstairs bedrooms include an exciting master suite with private bath highlighted by a spa tub.

UPPER FLOOR

Br. 4
13/4 x 9/10

Br. 2
10/2 x 11/2

Spa
Lin.

dn.

Lin.

Master
13/4 x 15/6

Open to Below

Br. 3
11/0 x 12/2

Plan CDG-2026

Bedrooms: 4-5	**Baths: 2½**

Space:	
Upper floor:	1,089 sq. ft.
Main floor:	1,295 sq. ft.

Total living area:	2,384 sq. ft.
Garage:	452 sq. ft.

Exterior Wall Framing:	2x4

Foundation options:
Crawlspace.
(Foundation & framing conversion diagram available — see order form.)

Blueprint Price Code:	C

MAIN FLOOR

66'-0"

39'-0"

Nook
7/0 x 8/0

Patio

Dining
11/2 x 11/6

Ovens

Refr.

Pan.

Arch

Family
15/4 x 15/6

W.S.

W.H.

F.

Blt-in

Garage
21 2 x 21 4

Living
13/4 x 15/2

Arch

vaulted Foyer

Den/Guest
11 0 x 10/2
Blt-in

up

Porch

Spectacular Great Room!

- Open, light-filled spaces centered around a spectacular Great Room mark this updated traditional design.
- The tiled foyer opens to the dining room, which is defined by columns and an overhead plant shelf and enhanced by a 9½-ft.-high flat ceiling.
- The huge central Great Room features a wall of windows, a 17-ft.-high vaulted ceiling and a see-through fireplace with an adjacent wet bar. Sliding glass doors access a delightful deck.
- The kitchen offers a built-in desk, a large pantry, an angled snack bar and a gazebo-like breakfast nook.
- The master suite boasts a 9½-ft. ceiling and a spa bath that includes a separate shower and a huge walk-in closet.
- Double doors open to a quiet den or extra bedroom. The vaulted ceiling soars to a height of 12 ft. above a gorgeous arched window.
- An open, skylighted stairway leads to the upper floor, where two more bedrooms share another full bath.

Plan AG-2401

Bedrooms: 3+	Baths: 2½
Living Area:	
Upper floor	550 sq. ft.
Main floor	1,855 sq. ft.
Total Living Area:	**2,405 sq. ft.**
Standard basement	1,815 sq. ft.
Garage	441 sq. ft.
Exterior Wall Framing:	2x6

Foundation Options:

Standard basement

(All plans can be built with your choice of foundation and framing. A generic conversion diagram is available. See order form.)

BLUEPRINT PRICE CODE:	C

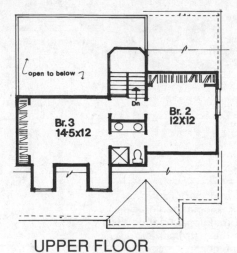

UPPER FLOOR

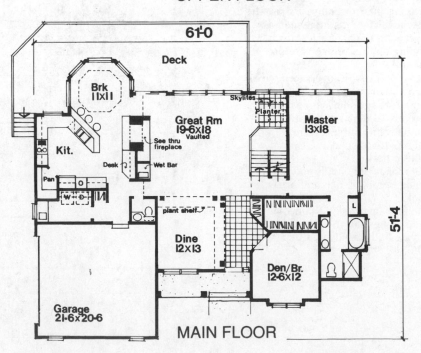

MAIN FLOOR

Open Spaces, Elegant Places

- Past its inviting columned entry, the stunning 19-ft.-high foyer of this beautiful modern home is brightened by high transom windows.
- Off the foyer, the vaulted dining room opens to a backyard patio through sliding glass doors. A decorative rail provides views into the sunken and vaulted living room.
- The spacious island kitchen offers a sunny bay-windowed breakfast nook, a roomy walk-in pantry and a corner sink.
- The adjacent family room features a handsome fireplace and patio access. A French door leads into a quiet den.
- Up the skylighted staircase, double doors lead into the luxurious master bedroom. The elegant master bath is highlighted by skylights and boasts a step-up spa tub, a separate shower and a sit-down, dual-sink vanity.
- Two additional bedrooms have private access to a shared skylighted bath. Both rooms also include separate dressing areas with walk-in closets and individual vanities.

Plan CDG-2047

Bedrooms: 3+	Baths: 3
Living Area:	
Upper floor	1,112 sq. ft.
Main floor	1,295 sq. ft.
Total Living Area:	**2,407 sq. ft.**
Garage	620 sq. ft.
Exterior Wall Framing:	2x6

Foundation Options:

Crawlspace

(All plans can be built with your choice of foundation and framing. A generic conversion diagram is available. See order form.)

BLUEPRINT PRICE CODE: **C**

UPPER FLOOR

Spa
Skylight
Arch
Master
13/0 x 19/4
Walk-in Wardrobe
Br. 2
13/0 x 11/0
dn
Skylight
Skylight
Walk-in Wardrobe
Linen
Open to Below
Walk-in Wardrobe
vaulted Br 3
11/0 x 15/2
Seat

MAIN FLOOR

54'-0" Patio
49'-0"
Nook
10/0 x 11/0
D.W.
Family
16/0 x 16/6
Ovens
Refr.
Pantry
Den
9/8 x 11/8
vaulted Dining
12/2 x 12/8
Railing
up
dn
F. W.B.
vaulted Foyer
Garage
28/4 x 21/4
sunken/ vaulted Living
12/4 x 17/4

Five-Bedroom Traditional

- This sophisticated traditional home makes a striking statement both inside and out.
- The dramatic two-story foyer is flanked by the formal living spaces. The private dining room overlooks the front porch, while the spacious living room has outdoor views on two sides.
- A U-shaped kitchen with a snack bar, a sunny dinette area and a large family room flow together at the back of the home. The family room's fireplace warms the open, informal expanse, while sliding glass doors in the dinette access the backyard terrace.
- The second floor has five roomy bedrooms and two skylighted bathrooms. The luxurious master suite has a high ceiling with a beautiful arched window, a dressing area and a huge walk-in closet. The private bath offers dual sinks, a whirlpool tub and a separate shower.
- Attic space is located above the garage.

Plan AHP-9392

Bedrooms: 5	Baths: 2½
Living Area:	
Upper floor	1,223 sq. ft.
Main floor	1,193 sq. ft.
Total Living Area:	**2,416 sq. ft.**
Standard basement	1,130 sq. ft.
Garage	509 sq. ft.
Storage	65 sq. ft.
Exterior Wall Framing:	2x4 or 2x6

Foundation Options:
Standard basement
Crawlspace
Slab
(Typical foundation & framing conversion diagram available—see order form.)

BLUEPRINT PRICE CODE: C

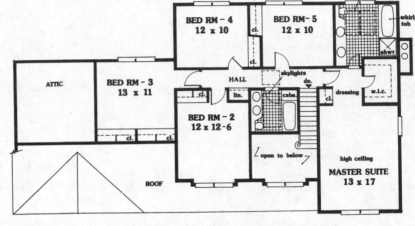

UPPER FLOOR

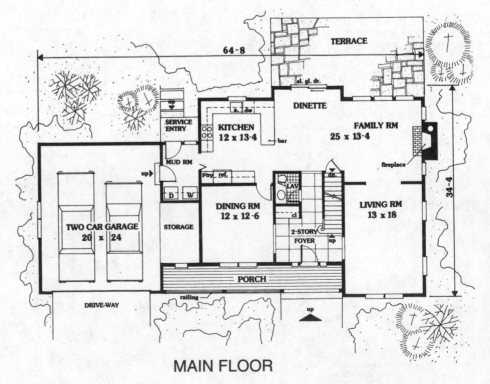

MAIN FLOOR

Plan AHP-9392

PRICES AND DETAILS ON PAGES 12-15

Classy Country

- A classy portico and a dramatic five-sided bay pique interest for this grand country-style home.
- The interior commands attention with its own delights. The two-story gallery soars to a height of 18 ft. and hosts an elegant curved stairway.
- The spectacular five-sided living room is enclosed in glass and warmed by an alluring fireplace angled into a niche off the stairway. The living room flows into the formal dining room, which is also accented by a bay window.
- A corner pantry and a circular snack bar are offered in the spacious U-shaped kitchen. The adjoining dinette opens to a backyard terrace.
- For casual comfort, the family will enjoy the open family room, complete with another fireplace.
- Four big bedrooms and two baths occupy the upper floor. The master bedroom is highlighted by a 13-ft. cathedral ceiling and a unique boxed-out window arrangement. The private master bath boasts a skylighted whirlpool tub, a dual-sink vanity and a skylighted dressing area.

Plan K-697-T

Bedrooms: 4	Baths: 2½
Living Area:	
Upper floor	1,105 sq. ft.
Main floor	1,319 sq. ft.
Total Living Area:	**2,424 sq. ft.**
Daylight basement	1,250 sq. ft.
Garage	430 sq. ft.
Exterior Wall Framing:	2x4 or 2x6

Foundation Options:
Daylight basement
Slab
(All plans can be built with your choice of foundation and framing. A generic conversion diagram is available. See order form.)

BLUEPRINT PRICE CODE:	C

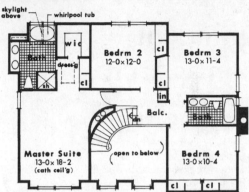

UPPER FLOOR

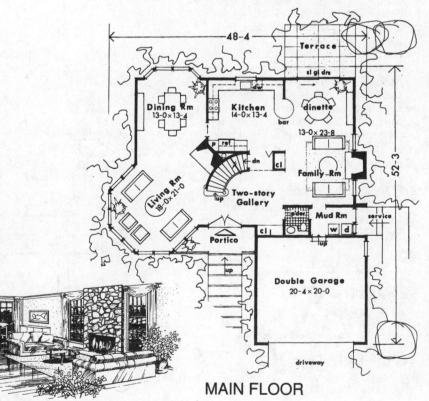

MAIN FLOOR

VIEW INTO FAMILY ROOM AND DINETTE

Magnificent Masonry Arch

- This beautiful brick home attracts the eye with its magnificent masonry arch over the recessed entry.
- The two-story-high foyer is highlighted by a huge half-round transom as it spreads between a bayed study and the formal dining room.
- The fabulous kitchen boasts a walk-in pantry closet, a snack bar, handy laundry facilities and a sunny bayed breakfast nook with backyard access.
- The adjoining family room features a soothing fireplace flanked by windows.
- The main-floor master suite includes a cathedral-ceilinged bath with a walk-in closet, a garden tub, a separate shower and two vanities, one with knee space.
- Another full bath serves the study, which may also be used as a bedroom.
- An upper-floor balcony leads to two additional bedrooms, each with private access to a common full bath.

Plan KLF-9309

Bedrooms: 3+	Baths: 3
Living Area:	
Upper floor	574 sq. ft.
Main floor	1,863 sq. ft.
Total Living Area:	**2,437 sq. ft.**
Garage	519 sq. ft.
Exterior Wall Framing:	2x4

Foundation Options:

Slab

(All plans can be built with your choice of foundation and framing. A generic conversion diagram is available. See order form.)

BLUEPRINT PRICE CODE: C

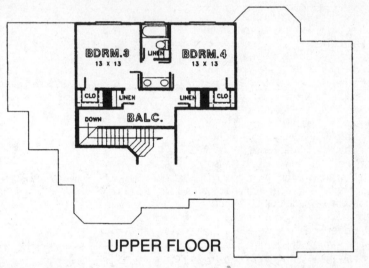

UPPER FLOOR

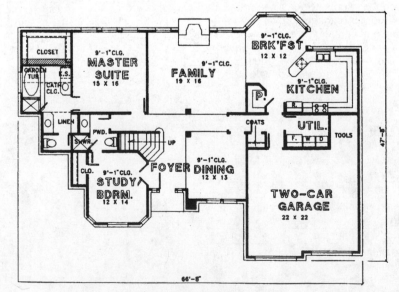

MAIN FLOOR

TO ORDER THIS BLUEPRINT, CALL TOLL-FREE 1-800-547-5570   Plan KLF-9309   *PRICES AND DETAILS* ON PAGES 12-15

Spacious Home for Scenic Lots

- Vertical wood siding, stone accents, large windows and a spectacular deck make this home ideal for a mountain, lake, golf course or other scenic site.
- The front porch opens to a spacious foyer, which unfolds to the formal dining room.
- The sunken family room is set off from the hall with an open rail and boasts a 20-ft. cathedral ceiling, a stone fireplace and access to a large deck.

- The U-shaped kitchen opens to a bright breakfast room with deck access.
- A laundry/utility room is conveniently located between the breakfast room and the two-car garage.
- The master suite is removed from the secondary bedrooms and offers a roomy walk-in closet. The compartmentalized master bath includes a separate dressing area with a dual-sink vanity.
- Two additional bedrooms share a unique bath with separate vanities and dressing areas.
- A fabulous upstairs studio is brightened by tall, angled windows and could provide extra space for guests.

Plan C-7710	
Bedrooms: 3+	**Baths:** 2
Living Area:	
Upper floor	248 sq. ft.
Main floor	2,192 sq. ft.
Total Living Area:	**2,440 sq. ft.**
Daylight basement	2,192 sq. ft.
Garage	431 sq. ft.
Storage and utility	132 sq. ft.
Exterior Wall Framing:	2x4

Foundation Options:

Daylight basement
Crawlspace
Slab

(All plans can be built with your choice of foundation and framing. A generic conversion diagram is available. See order form.)

BLUEPRINT PRICE CODE:	C

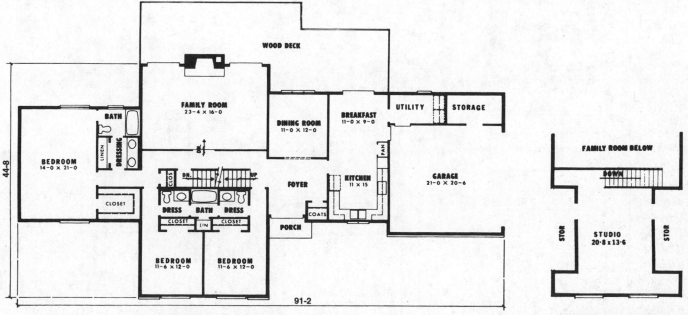

MAIN FLOOR

UPPER FLOOR

Timeless Styling

- This home's timeless gables and classic front porch conceal an expansive interior with modern styling.
- Sidelighted double doors open from the porch to the elegant two-story gallery and its curved, open-railed staircase.
- The living room boasts stylish windows, a fireplace with built-in wood storage and a 14-ft., 6-in. cathedral ceiling.
- The semi-circular dining room basks in light from a radiant arrangement of windows, offering a panoramic view.
- The kitchen features a bright sink, a nifty snack bar and a sunny half-circle dinette with views to the backyard.
- Another fireplace warms the family room, which also features sliding glass doors to a backyard terrace.
- The mudroom has laundry facilities, plus access to a half-bath and to the two-car garage.
- The upper-floor master suite offers a balcony and a private bath with a whirlpool tub and a separate shower. A skylighted bath serves the three secondary bedrooms.

Plan K-692-T

Bedrooms: 4	Baths: 2½
Living Area:	
Upper floor	950 sq. ft.
Main floor	1,498 sq. ft.
Total Living Area:	**2,448 sq. ft.**
Daylight basement	1,430 sq. ft.
Garage	440 sq. ft.
Exterior Wall Framing:	2x4 or 2x6

Foundation Options:

Daylight basement

Slab

(All plans can be built with your choice of foundation and framing. A generic conversion diagram is available. See order form.)

BLUEPRINT PRICE CODE: C

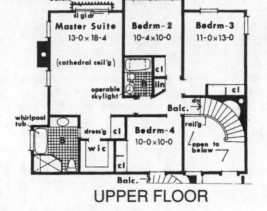

UPPER FLOOR

VIEW INTO FAMILY ROOM

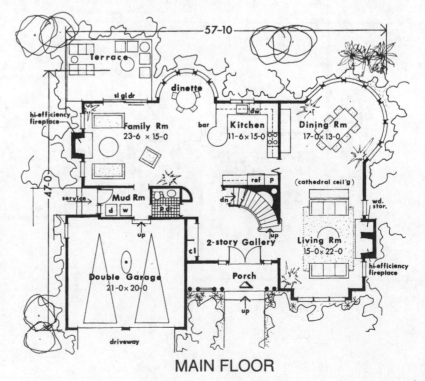

MAIN FLOOR

TO ORDER THIS BLUEPRINT,
CALL TOLL-FREE 1-800-547-5570

Plan K-692-T

PRICES AND DETAILS
ON PAGES 12-15

Modern Elegance

- Half-round transom windows and a barrel-vaulted porch with paired columns lend elegance to the facade of this post-modern design.
- Inside, the two-story-high foyer leads past a den and a diagonal, open-railed stairway to the sunken living room.
- A 17-ft. vaulted ceiling and a striking fireplace enhance the living room, while square columns introduce the adjoining formal dining room.
- The adjacent kitchen is thoroughly modern, including an island cooktop and a large pantry. A sunny bay window defines the breakfast area, where a sliding glass door opens to the angled backyard deck.
- Columns preface the sunken family room, which also sports a 17-ft.-high vaulted ceiling and easy access to the deck. A half-bath, a laundry room and access to the garage are nearby.
- Upstairs, the master suite features a 10-ft. vaulted ceiling, a private bath and a large walk-in closet.

Plan B-89005

Bedrooms: 4	Baths: 2½
Living Area:	
Upper floor	1,083 sq. ft.
Main floor	1,380 sq. ft.
Total Living Area:	**2,463 sq. ft.**
Standard basement	1,380 sq. ft.
Garage	483 sq. ft.
Exterior Wall Framing:	2x4

Foundation Options:

Standard basement

(All plans can be built with your choice of foundation and framing. A generic conversion diagram is available. See order form.)

BLUEPRINT PRICE CODE:	C

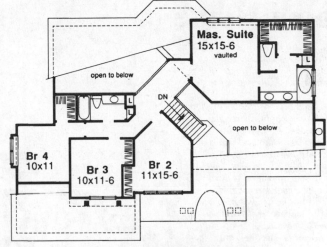

UPPER FLOOR

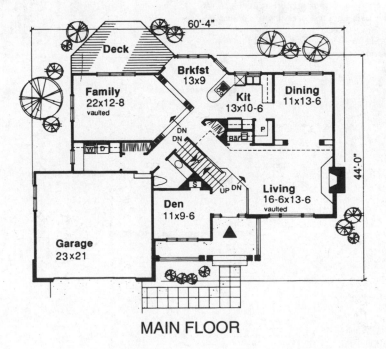

MAIN FLOOR

Rustic Four-Bedroom Home

This 2,467 sq. ft. rustic design includes a deluxe master suite with walk-in and walk-thru closets, linen closet, large double vanity and both a tub and separate shower stall.

The U-shaped kitchen features a counter bar open to the Great Room, which has a raised-hearth fireplace. A large utility room and a second bedroom and full bath with linen closet are located on the 1,694 sq. ft. main floor.

Two additional bedrooms and a third full bath with linen closet are located upstairs. A built-in bookcase, window seats and access to attic storage areas are also included on the 773 sq. ft. upper floor.

Front porch, dormers, shutters, multi-paned windows and a combination of wood and stone materials combine for a rustic exterior. The screened-in porch doubles as a covered breezeway connecting house and garage.

Specify crawlspace or daylight basement foundation when ordering.

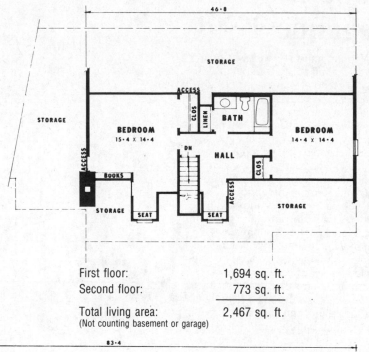

First floor: 1,694 sq. ft.

Second floor: 773 sq. ft.

Total living area: 2,467 sq. ft.
(Not counting basement or garage)

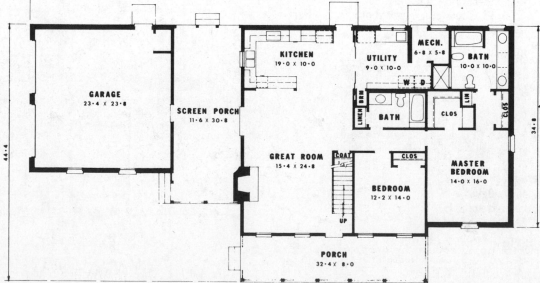

Blueprint Price Code C

Plan C-7746

Fantastic Facade, Stunning Spaces

- Matching dormers and a generous covered front porch give this home its fantastic facade. Inside, the open living spaces are just as stunning.
- A two-story foyer bisects the formal living areas. The living room offers three bright windows, an inviting fireplace and sliding French doors to the Great Room. The formal dining room overlooks the front porch and has easy access to the kitchen.
- The Great Room is truly grand, featuring a fireplace and a TV center flanked by French doors that lead to a large deck.
- A circular dinette connects the Great Room to the kitchen, which is handy to a mudroom and a powder room.
- The main-floor master suite boasts a 14-ft. cathedral ceiling, a walk-in closet and a private bath with a whirlpool tub.
- Upstairs, four large bedrooms share another whirlpool bath. One bedroom offers a 12-ft. sloped ceiling.

Plan AHP-9397

Bedrooms: 5	Baths: 2½
Living Area:	
Upper floor	928 sq. ft.
Main floor	1,545 sq. ft.
Total Living Area:	**2,473 sq. ft.**
Standard basement	1,165 sq. ft.
Garage and storage	432 sq. ft.
Exterior Wall Framing:	2x4 or 2x6

Foundation Options:
Standard basement
Crawlspace
Slab
(All plans can be built with your choice of foundation and framing. A generic conversion diagram is available. See order form.)

BLUEPRINT PRICE CODE:	**C**

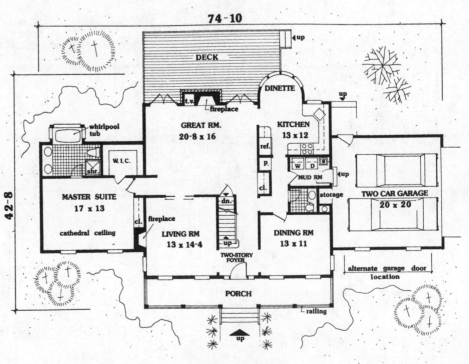

UPPER FLOOR

MAIN FLOOR

ELEVATION A

Exciting Views, Inside and Out

- Your choice of three elevations is available for this beautiful brick-accented home.
- Oriented to the rear are the vaulted family room with fireplace and deck, a study or guest bedroom with double doors and the lavish master suite with volume ceilings, plant shelf and bath with jacuzzi.
- The balcony atop the curved foyer stairway overlooks the breakfast nook and family room.
- Formal dining and living rooms to the front of the home have lovely window treatments and volume ceilings.
- Storage space and two mid-sized bedrooms are found upstairs.

ELEVATION B

ELEVATION C

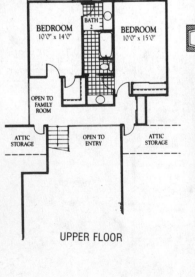

UPPER FLOOR

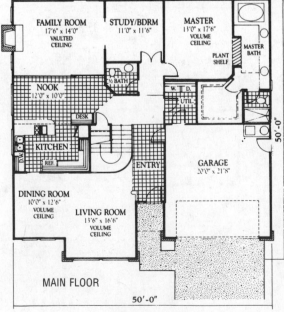

MAIN FLOOR

50'-0"

Plan R-2151

Bedrooms: 3-4	Baths: 2 ½
Space:	
Upper floor	630 sq. ft.
Main floor	1,855 sq. ft.
Total Living Area	**2,485 sq. ft.**
Garage	433 sq. ft.
Exterior Wall Framing	2 x 6

Foundation options:

Crawlspace

(Foundation & framing conversion diagram available—see order form.)

Blueprint Price Code	**C**

NOTE: Please specify elevation preference when ordering.

Fabulous Facade

- Beautiful windows, accented with columns and keystones, blanket the facade of this distinguished home.
- The interior spaces are deceptively spacious, beginning with a two-story-high entry and an open staircase.
- The right side of the home is taken up by a bayed living room that stretches to the formal dining room.
- The casual living area includes an island kitchen with a walk-in pantry and an adjoining morning room with access to a rear patio. The family room has a fireplace and plenty of windows.
- Upstairs, the master bedroom has a ceiling that slopes to 10 feet. The master bath offers two walk-in closets separated by a whirlpool bath, plus a shower and a toilet compartment.
- Walk-in closets are also found in the two remaining bedrooms. The front-facing bedroom boasts a 9-ft. ceiling and an arched window. The game room also has a 9-ft. ceiling.

Plan DD-2460

Bedrooms: 3+	Baths: 2½
Living Area:	
Upper floor	1,407 sq. ft.
Main floor	1,085 sq. ft.
Total Living Area:	**2,492 sq. ft.**
Standard basement	1,085 sq. ft.
Garage	410 sq. ft.
Exterior Wall Framing:	2x4

Foundation Options:
Standard basement
Crawlspace
Slab
(All plans can be built with your choice of foundation and framing. A generic conversion diagram is available. See order form.)

BLUEPRINT PRICE CODE: C

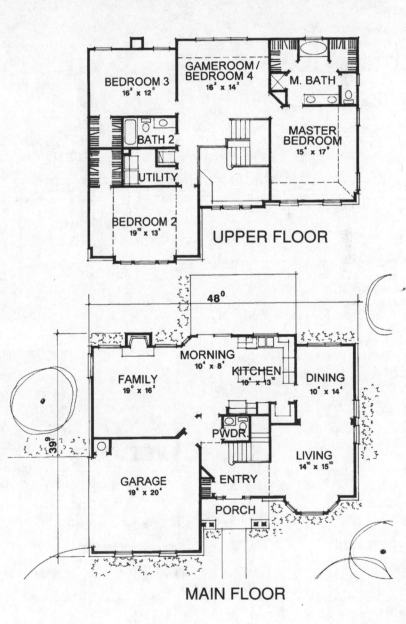

UPPER FLOOR

MAIN FLOOR

Formal Meets Informal

- The charming, columned front porch of this appealing home leads visitors into a two-story-high foyer with a beautiful turned staircase.
- The gracious formal living room shares a 15-ft. cathedral ceiling and a dramatic see-through fireplace with the adjoining family room.
- A railing separates the family room from the spacious breakfast area and the island kitchen. A unique butler's pantry joins the kitchen to the dining room, which is enhanced by a tray ceiling.
- A convenient laundry room is located between the kitchen and the entrance to the garage .
- All four bedrooms are located on the upper level. The master suite boasts an 11-ft. cathedral ceiling, a walk-in closet and a large, luxurious bath.

Plan OH-132

Bedrooms: 4	Baths: 2½
Living Area:	
Upper floor	1,118 sq. ft.
Main floor	1,396 sq. ft.
Total Living Area:	**2,514 sq. ft.**
Standard basement	1,396 sq. ft.
Garage	413 sq. ft.
Storage/workshop	107 sq. ft.
Exterior Wall Framing:	2x4

Foundation Options:

Standard basement

(All plans can be built with your choice of foundation and framing. A generic conversion diagram is available. See order form.)

BLUEPRINT PRICE CODE: D

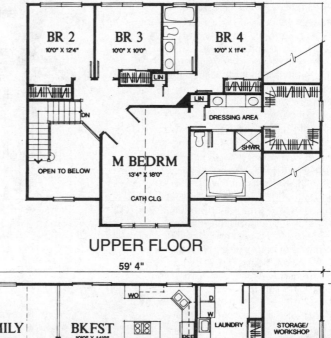

UPPER FLOOR

MAIN FLOOR

TO ORDER THIS BLUEPRINT, CALL TOLL-FREE 1-800-547-5570

Plan OH-132

PRICES AND DETAILS ON PAGES 12-15

Nostalgic Exterior Appeal

- A covered front porch, large half-round windows and Victorian gable details give this nostalgic home classic appeal.
- A stunning two-story foyer awaits guests at the entry, which is flooded with light from the half-round window above.
- The central island kitchen is brightened by the bay-windowed breakfast room, which looks into the family room over a low partition.
- Highlighted by a skylight and a corner fireplace, the cathedral-ceilinged family room is sure to be a high-traffic area. Sliding glass doors allow activities to be extended to the backyard patio.
- Upstairs, the master bedroom boasts a unique sloped ceiling and a lovely boxed-out window. The master bath has a spa tub, a corner shower and a dual-sink vanity. A dressing area and a walk-in closet are also offered.
- Three more upstairs bedrooms share two linen closets and a hallway bath. A railed balcony bridge overlooks the foyer and the family room.

Plan AX-90305

Bedrooms: 4	Baths: 2½
Living Area:	
Upper floor	1,278 sq. ft.
Main floor	1,237 sq. ft.
Total Living Area:	**2,515 sq. ft.**
Standard basement	1,237 sq. ft.
Garage	400 sq. ft.
Exterior Wall Framing:	2x4

Foundation Options:

Standard basement

Slab

(All plans can be built with your choice of foundation and framing. A generic conversion diagram is available. See order form.)

BLUEPRINT PRICE CODE: D

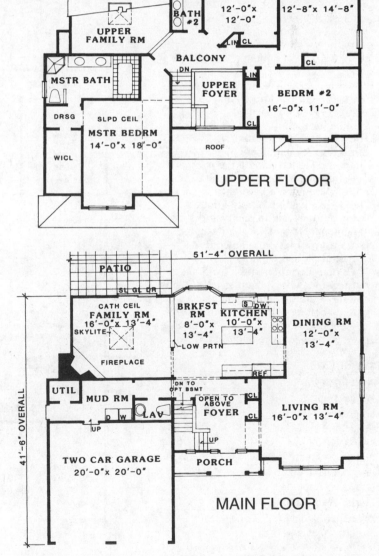

UPPER FLOOR

MAIN FLOOR

All the Best

- This unique home offers the best of both worlds, with its charming, old-time exterior and modern, luxurious interior.
- The covered front porch leads to a two-story foyer with a beautiful open staircase. To the right, the large formal dining room showcases a boxed-out window. To the left, the living room overlooks the front porch and has the option of a cased opening or a solid wall facing the family room.
- The expansive family room is brightened by a dramatic window wall and has a French door to the backyard. The fireplace is positioned so it can be enjoyed from the adjoining kitchen.
- The deluxe kitchen boasts a double oven, a huge walk-in pantry and a long serving bar. The 11½-ft.-high vaulted breakfast room is illuminated by a gorgeous arched window.
- The upper floor includes a dynamite master suite, which features a 9½-ft. tray ceiling in the sleeping area and a 16-ft. vaulted ceiling in the luxurious bath.
- The big bonus room could serve as a playroom or an extra bedroom.

Plan FB-2516

Bedrooms: 3+	Baths: 2½
Living Area:	
Upper floor	1,057 sq. ft.
Main floor	1,212 sq. ft.
Bonus room	247 sq. ft.
Total Living Area:	**2,516 sq. ft.**
Daylight basement	1,212 sq. ft.
Garage and storage	504 sq. ft.

Exterior Wall Framing: 2x4

Foundation Options:

Daylight basement

Crawlspace

(All plans can be built with your choice of foundation and framing. A generic conversion diagram is available. See order form.)

BLUEPRINT PRICE CODE: D

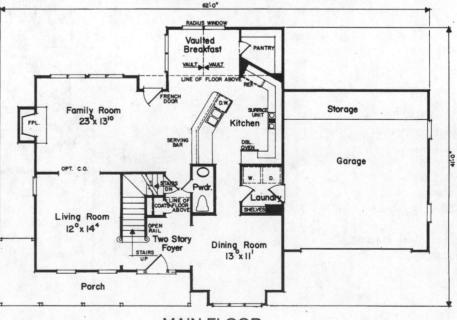

UPPER FLOOR

MAIN FLOOR

TO ORDER THIS BLUEPRINT, CALL TOLL-FREE 1-800-547-5570

Plan FB-2516

PRICES AND DETAILS ON PAGES 12-15

Solid Character

- A dramatic, stately roofline and a distinguished brick facade give a solid look to this distinctive family home.
- The impressive two-story-high foyer boasts an elegant tray ceiling.
- A columned arch introduces the formal dining room, where French doors bring the outside in.
- The central kitchen includes a pantry and features an arched opening over the sink. The nearby breakfast bay offers a built-in serving shelf with an arched pass-through to the family room.
- Flanked by tall windows, a handsome fireplace is the focal point of the two-story-high family room.
- Ceilings in all main-floor rooms are 9 ft. high unless otherwise specified.
- Upstairs, a railed balcony overlooks the family room and the foyer. The tray-ceilinged master suite boasts a morning kitchen and a vaulted sitting room. The master bath has a 13-ft. vaulted ceiling and showcases a corner garden tub, a separate shower and a dual-sink vanity.
- Three additional bedrooms, a second full bath and a laundry room complete the upper floor.

Plan FB-5048-NELS

Bedrooms: 4	Baths: 2½
Living Area:	
Upper floor	1,309 sq. ft.
Main floor	1,240 sq. ft.
Total Living Area:	**2,549 sq. ft.**
Daylight basement	1,240 sq. ft.
Garage	400 sq. ft.
Exterior Wall Framing:	2x4

Foundation Options:

Daylight basement

(All plans can be built with your choice of foundation and framing. A generic conversion diagram is available. See order form.)

BLUEPRINT PRICE CODE: D

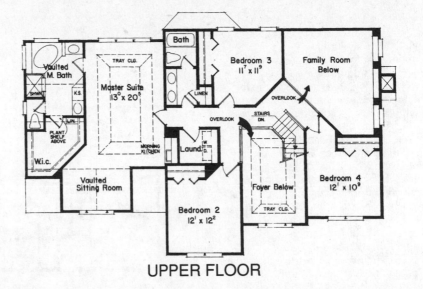

UPPER FLOOR

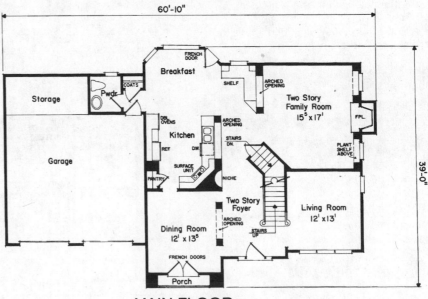

MAIN FLOOR

Stately Colonial

- This stately Colonial features a covered front entry and a secondary entry near the garage and the utility room.
- The main foyer opens to a comfortable den with elegant double doors.
- The formal living areas adjoin to the left of the foyer and culminate in a lovely bay window overlooking the backyard.
- The open island kitchen has a great central location, easily accessed from each of the living areas. Informal dining can be extended to the outdoors through sliding doors in the dinette.
- A half-wall introduces the big family room, which boasts a high 16-ft., 9-in. vaulted ceiling, an inviting fireplace and optional built-in cabinets.
- The upper floor is shared by four bedrooms, including a spacious master bedroom with a large walk-in closet, a dressing area for two and a private bath. An alternate bath layout is included in the blueprints.
- A bonus room may be added above the garage for additional space.

Plan A-2283-DS

Bedrooms: 4+	Baths: 2½
Living Area:	
Upper floor	1,137 sq. ft.
Main floor	1,413 sq. ft.
Total Living Area:	**2,550 sq. ft.**
Optional bonus room	280 sq. ft.
Standard basement	1,413 sq. ft.
Garage	484 sq. ft.
Exterior Wall Framing:	2x6

Foundation Options:

Standard basement

(All plans can be built with your choice of foundation and framing. A generic conversion diagram is available. See order form.)

BLUEPRINT PRICE CODE:	D

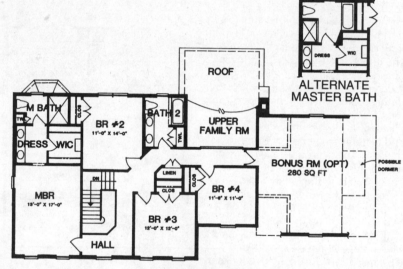

ALTERNATE MASTER BATH

UPPER FLOOR

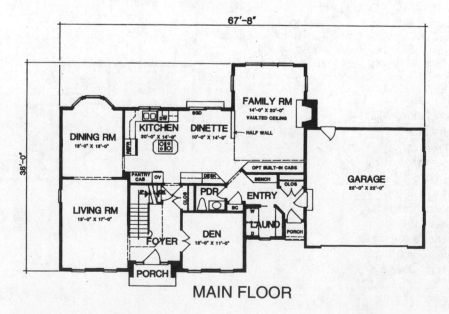

MAIN FLOOR

   Plan A-2283-DS   **PRICES AND DETAILS ON PAGES 12-15**

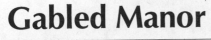

Gabled Manor

- Distinctive gables and a distinguished stone facade give a classic look to this richly detailed family home.
- The inviting entry vaults to 16 ft. and unfolds to the cozy living room and its warm fireplace.
- The intimate formal dining room is easily serviced by the island kitchen, which features a pantry and corner windows above the sink. French doors in the adjoining breakfast area open to a backyard patio.
- Under a spectacular vaulted ceiling that slopes to 18 ft., the fantastic family room boasts patio access and a handsome fireplace flanked by glass.
- The luxurious master suite is expanded by an 11-ft., 8-in.-high flat ceiling and includes a roomy walk-in closet and a relaxing sitting area with a clever juice bar. The master bath showcases a corner garden tub, a separate shower and an L-shaped dual-sink vanity.
- Three more bedrooms and a second full bath are located upstairs.

Plan B-91035

Bedrooms: 4	Baths: 2½
Living Area:	
Upper floor	583 sq. ft.
Main floor	1,982 sq. ft.
Total Living Area:	**2,565 sq. ft.**
Standard basement	1,982 sq. ft.
Garage	508 sq. ft.
Exterior Wall Framing:	2x6

Foundation Options:

Standard basement

(All plans can be built with your choice of foundation and framing. A generic conversion diagram is available. See order form.)

BLUEPRINT PRICE CODE:	D

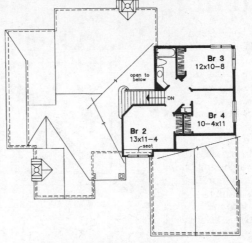

UPPER FLOOR

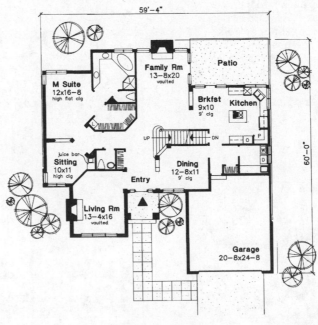

MAIN FLOOR

Elegant Interior

- An inviting covered porch welcomes guests into the elegant interior of this spectacular country home.
- Just past the entrance, the formal dining room boasts a stepped ceiling and a nearby server with a sink.
- The adjoining island kitchen has an eating bar that serves the breakfast room, which is enhanced by a 12-ft. cathedral ceiling and a bayed area of 8- and 9-ft.-high windows. Sliding glass doors lead to a covered side porch.
- Brightened by a row of 8-ft.-high windows and a glass door to the backyard, the spacious Great Room features a stepped ceiling, a built-in media center and a corner fireplace.
- The master bedroom has a tray ceiling and a cozy sitting area. The skylighted master bath boasts a whirlpool tub, a separate shower and a walk-in closet.
- A second main-floor bedroom offers private access to a compartmentalized bath. Two more bedrooms share a third bathroom on the upper floor.

Plan AX-3305-B

Bedrooms: 3+	Baths: 3
Living Area:	
Upper floor	550 sq. ft.
Main floor	2,017 sq. ft.
Total Living Area:	**2,567 sq. ft.**
Upper-floor storage	377 sq. ft.
Standard basement	2,017 sq. ft.
Garage	415 sq. ft.
Exterior Wall Framing:	2x4

Foundation Options:

Standard basement
Crawlspace
Slab

(All plans can be built with your choice of foundation and framing. A generic conversion diagram is available. See order form.)

BLUEPRINT PRICE CODE: D

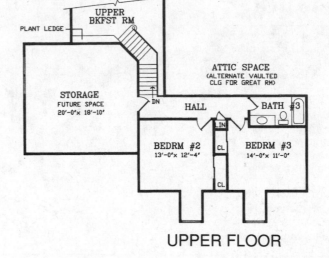

UPPER FLOOR

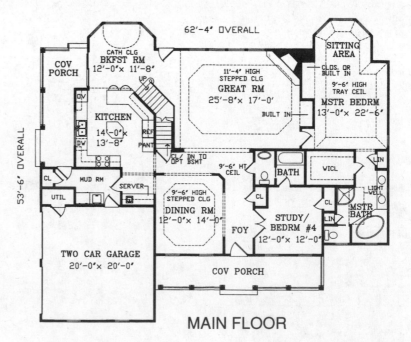

MAIN FLOOR

TO ORDER THIS BLUEPRINT, CALL TOLL-FREE 1-800-547-5570

Plan AX-3305-B

PRICES AND DETAILS ON PAGES 12-15

Tradition Reacquainted

- This home's paneled shutters, rustic columns and oval-glassed front door reacquaint passersby with traditional homes from days gone by.
- The floor plan's airy kitchen, spacious family room and distinct formal spaces are also designed for traditional ease and comfort.
- The two-story foyer features two coat closets with plant shelves above. French doors in the adjoining living room open to the front porch.

- The formal dining room unfolds from the living room, creating a large expanse for entertaining.
- The island kitchen features a handy serving bar, a sunny breakfast area and decorative half-walls leading to the adjacent family room.
- Stunning window walls highlight both the breakfast room and the family room, where a striking fireplace offers comfort and ambience.
- Upstairs, an exciting master suite offers a tray ceiling and built-in shelves. The vaulted master bath boasts a corner spa tub, a make-up table with knee space and his-and-hers walk-in closets. Three more bedrooms share a split bath.

Plan FB-5344-MADR	
Bedrooms: 4	Baths: 2½
Living Area:	
Upper floor	1,372 sq. ft.
Main floor	1,210 sq. ft.
Total Living Area:	**2,582 sq. ft.**
Daylight basement	1,210 sq. ft.
Garage and storage	450 sq. ft.
Exterior Wall Framing:	2x4

Foundation Options:

Daylight basement

(All plans can be built with your choice of foundation and framing. A generic conversion diagram is available. See order form.)

BLUEPRINT PRICE CODE: D

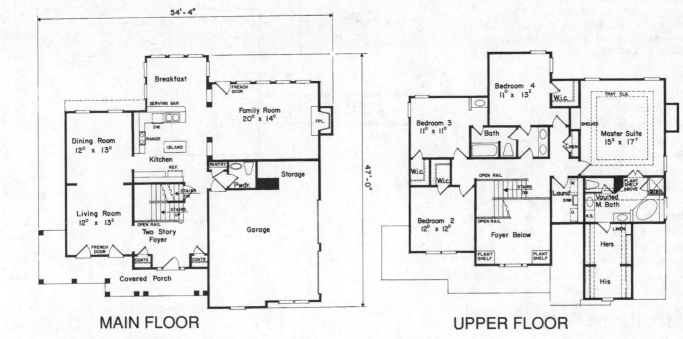

MAIN FLOOR

UPPER FLOOR

Gracious, Open Living

- An especially open floor plan gives this home a spacious, airy feeling. The full wraparound porch extends the openness to the outdoors.
- The oversized foyer offers views into the formal dining room and the study and displays a unique two-way staircase to the upper floor.
- The Great Room, breakfast area and kitchen combine at the rear of the home for a spacious, informal setting. The kitchen features an oversized work island and a view of the fireplace. Access to the porch is provided on either side of the bayed breakfast area.
- Three bedrooms, two baths and an exciting playroom are located on the upper floor. The master bedroom has a large walk-in closet and a luxury bath entered through double doors. The bath offers dual dressing areas, an isolated toilet and a beautiful bayed tub area.

Plan J-9289

Bedrooms: 3	Baths: 3
Living Area:	
Upper floor	1,212 sq. ft.
Main floor	1,370 sq. ft.
Total Living Area:	**2,582 sq. ft.**
Standard basement	1,370 sq. ft.
Garage	576 sq. ft.
Storage	144 sq. ft.
Exterior Wall Framing:	2x4

Foundation Options:
Standard basement
Crawlspace
Slab
(Typical foundation & framing conversion diagram available—see order form.)

BLUEPRINT PRICE CODE:	D

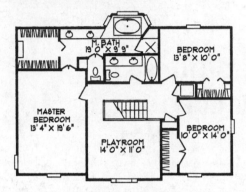

UPPER FLOOR

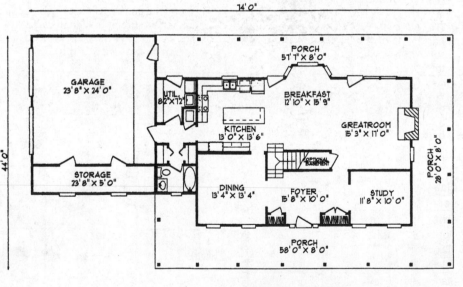

MAIN FLOOR

TO ORDER THIS BLUEPRINT,
CALL TOLL-FREE 1-800-547-5570

Plan J-9289

PRICES AND DETAILS
ON PAGES 12-15

Inside Angles

- This cleverly designed home offers a space-efficient floor plan that is well suited for building on a narrow lot.
- Past the columned porch, the vaulted entry orients guests to the home's angled interior.
- Beyond the entry, the spectacular Great Room features a 17-ft.-high vaulted ceiling, a corner fireplace and French doors to an inviting patio.
- The adjoining formal dining room is convenient to the kitchen and offers access to a sizable backyard deck.
- The kitchen serves the Great Room via a handy pass-through above the sink. The sunny morning room accesses the deck through sliding glass doors.
- A turned stairway brightened by tall windows leads to the upper floor. The elegant master bedroom is enhanced by a 10-ft. gambrel ceiling. The master bath showcases a spa tub, a separate shower, a dual-sink vanity and his-and-hers walk-in closets.

Plan DD-2594

Bedrooms: 2+	Baths: 2½
Living Area:	
Upper floor	1,127 sq. ft.
Main floor	1,467 sq. ft.
Total Living Area:	**2,594 sq. ft.**
Standard basement	1,467 sq. ft.
Garage	488 sq. ft.
Exterior Wall Framing:	2x4

Foundation Options:

Standard basement
Crawlspace
Slab
(All plans can be built with your choice of foundation and framing. A generic conversion diagram is available. See order form.)

BLUEPRINT PRICE CODE:	D

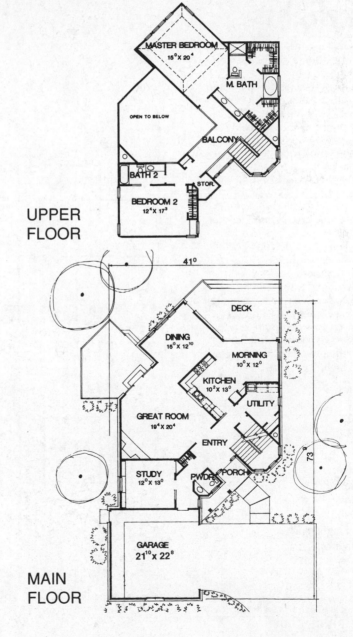

UPPER FLOOR

MAIN FLOOR

Highlighted by Skylights

- The traditional country exterior of this attractive brick home encloses an airy, light-filled interior.
- The inviting covered porch opens into the foyer, which features a 15-ft.-high sloped ceiling. Off the foyer is the sunken living room with a boxed-out bay and a window seat.
- Opposite the living room, the formal dining room boasts a 9-ft. tray ceiling.
- The skylighted island kitchen includes a bayed breakfast area. Defined by columns and half-walls, the skylighted family room enjoys a dramatic corner fireplace and French doors to a backyard deck. A 13-ft. sloped ceiling enhances the entire area.
- The master bedroom boasts a roomy walk-in closet and a spectacular skylighted bath with a 14-ft. cathedral ceiling and a corner platform tub.
- Upstairs, two more bedrooms have private access to a shared full bath.
- Plans for both a two-car and a three-car garage are included in the blueprints.

VIEW INTO FAMILY ROOM, BREAKFAST ROOM AND KITCHEN

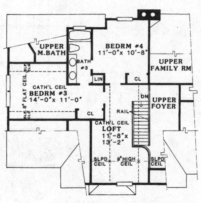

UPPER FLOOR

Plan AX-1310-B

Bedrooms: 4	Baths: 3½
Living Area:	
Upper floor	625 sq. ft.
Main floor	1,973 sq. ft.
Total Living Area:	**2,598 sq. ft.**
Standard basement	1,973 sq. ft.
Two-car garage	407 sq. ft.
Three-car garage	617 sq. ft.
Exterior Wall Framing:	2x4

Foundation Options:

Standard basement
Crawlspace
Slab

(All plans can be built with your choice of foundation and framing. A generic conversion diagram is available. See order form.)

BLUEPRINT PRICE CODE: D

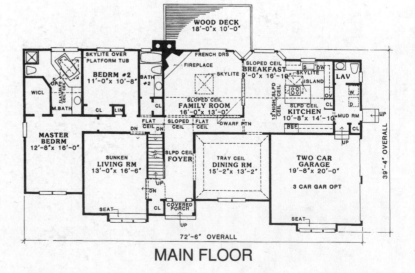

MAIN FLOOR

Plan AX-1310-B

PRICES AND DETAILS ON PAGES 12-15

Established Character

- A charming front porch with support pillars, palladian windows, dormers, and brick all give this home an established character.
- The formal living and dining rooms overlook the rear deck with plenty of glass and feature a tall fireplace rising up to meet the vaulted ceiling.
- The kitchen has a work island overlooking the octagonal morning room and the informal family living space.
- There are two bedrooms on the main floor and two more on the upper floor.
- The main floor master suite overlooks the rear yard. It features a large walk-in closet and exciting private bath with separate shower and tub under the palladian window.

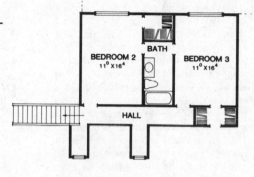

UPPER FLOOR

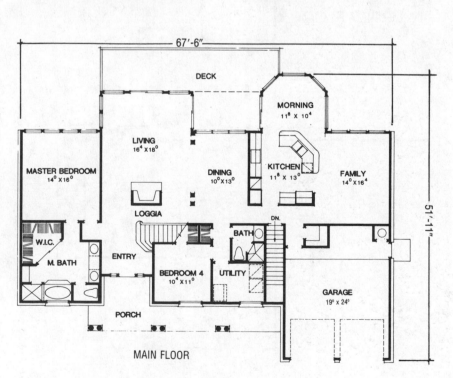

MAIN FLOOR

Plan DD-2509

Bedrooms: 4	**Baths:** 3

Space:	
Upper floor:	588 sq. ft.
Main floor:	2,011 sq. ft.
Total living area:	**2,599 sq. ft.**
Standard basement:	2,011 sq. ft.
Garage:	456 sq. ft.

Exterior Wall Framing:	2x4

Ceiling Heights:	
Upper floor:	8'
Main floor:	9'

Foundation options:
Standard basement.
Crawlspace.
Slab.
(Foundation & framing conversion diagram available — see order form.)

Blueprint Price Code:	D

Quaint Detailing

- Quaint windows accented by keystones and shutters exemplify the detailing found in this stately brick home.
- The columned front entry leads to the two-story foyer that flows between the front-oriented formal areas.
- The 18-ft. ceiling extends past an open-railed stairway to the expansive family room, which boasts a fireplace and a French door to the backyard.
- The bayed breakfast nook features an angled serving counter/desk that wraps around to the adjoining island kitchen. A pantry, a laundry room, a half-bath and the garage entrance are all nearby.
- Ceilings in all main-floor rooms are 9 ft. high unless otherwise specified.
- Upstairs, the master suite includes a 10-ft. tray ceiling, a see-through fireplace and his-and-hers walk-in closets. The posh bath flaunts a 12-ft. vaulted ceiling and a garden spa tub.
- A balcony bridge connects three more bedrooms, two with walk-in closets, and another full bath.

Plan FB-5237-NORW

Bedrooms: 4	Baths: 2½
Living Area:	
Upper floor	1,353 sq. ft.
Main floor	1,248 sq. ft.
Total Living Area:	**2,601 sq. ft.**
Daylight basement	1,248 sq. ft.
Garage	528 sq. ft.
Exterior Wall Framing:	2x4

Foundation Options:

Daylight basement

(All plans can be built with your choice of foundation and framing. A generic conversion diagram is available. See order form.)

BLUEPRINT PRICE CODE: D

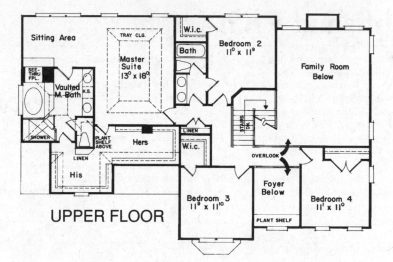

UPPER FLOOR

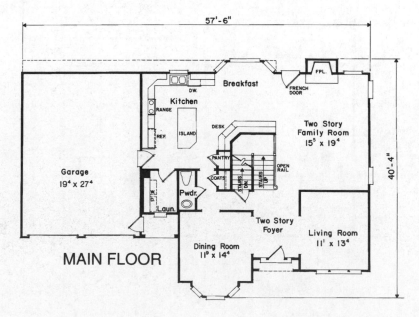

MAIN FLOOR

Comfortable Contemporary

- Contemporary lines give this home a bold facade. Its interior is both innovative and comfortable.
- Graced with a beautiful fireplace and three large windows, the living room is open to the dining room. The dining room features a sliding glass door that accesses a partially covered patio.
- The U-shaped kitchen boasts a writing desk, a pantry, a cooktop island and a breakfast nook with patio access.
- Showcasing a beautiful fireplace flanked by windows, the sunken family room is perfect for casual entertaining.
- Double doors introduce a quiet den or extra bedroom. A full bath is nearby.
- The master bedroom is highlighted by a private deck, a walk-in wardrobe, a sunken tub and a dual-sink vanity.
- The three remaining upper-floor bedrooms share another full bath.

Plans P-7644-2A & -2D

Bedrooms: 4+	Baths: 3
Living Area:	
Upper floor	1,101 sq. ft.
Main floor	1,523 sq. ft.
Total Living Area:	**2,624 sq. ft.**
Daylight basement	1,286 sq. ft.
Garage	935 sq. ft.
Exterior Wall Framing:	2x4
Foundation Options:	**Plan #**
Daylight basement	P-7644-2D
Crawlspace	P-7644-2A

(All plans can be built with your choice of foundation and framing. A generic conversion diagram is available. See order form.)

BLUEPRINT PRICE CODE:	D

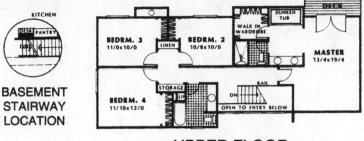

BASEMENT STAIRWAY LOCATION

UPPER FLOOR

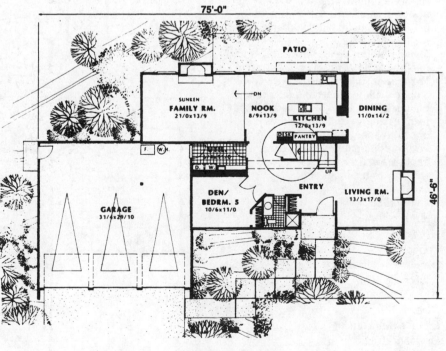

MAIN FLOOR

Fantastic Front Entry

- A fantastic arched window presides over the 18-ft.-high entry of this two-story, giving guests a bright welcome.
- The spacious living room is separated from the dining room by a pair of boxed columns with built-in shelves.
- The kitchen offers a walk-in pantry, a serving bar and a sunny breakfast room with a French door to the backyard.
- A boxed column accents the entry to the 18-ft. vaulted family room, which boasts a dramatic window bank and an inviting fireplace.
- The main-floor den is easily converted into an extra bedroom or guest room.
- The master suite has a 10-ft. tray ceiling, a huge walk-in closet and decorative plant shelves. The 15½-ft. vaulted bath features an oval tub and two vanities, one with knee space.
- Three additional bedrooms share another full bath near the second stairway to the main floor.

Plan FB-2680

Bedrooms: 4+	Baths: 3
Living Area:	
Upper floor	1,256 sq. ft.
Main floor	1,424 sq. ft.
Total Living Area:	**2,680 sq. ft.**
Daylight basement	1,424 sq. ft.
Garage	496 sq. ft.
Exterior Wall Framing:	2x4

Foundation Options:

Daylight basement

(All plans can be built with your choice of foundation and framing. A generic conversion diagram is available. See order form.)

BLUEPRINT PRICE CODE: D

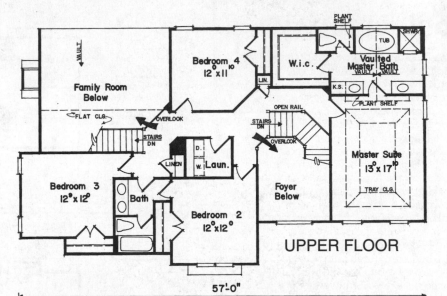

UPPER FLOOR

57'-0"

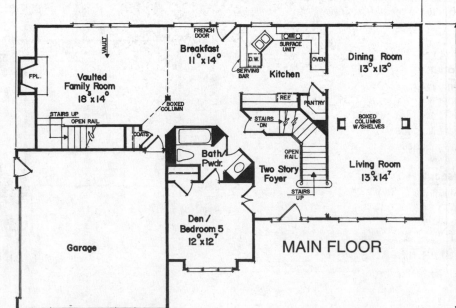

MAIN FLOOR

41'-0"

Photo by Mark Englund

Vivacious Victorian

- A traditional Victorian exterior appeal is created with a cupola room, covered front porch with dainty detailing, and bay windows with leaded glass.
- Inside, however, the house functions like a modern 1990s family home, rather than an 1890s home of yesteryear. Bright, open-feeling rooms flow into each other to allow maximum family interaction.
- The front entry opens to an octagon-shaped parlor with adjacent stairwell. To the right of the entry is the formal dining room with quaint bay window.
- The island kitchen is conveniently situated between the formal dining room and the informal breakfast eating area. Just beyond is the great room with fireplace and rear deck access.
- There are three bedrooms and two full baths upstairs, including a lavish master bedroom suite with two walk-in closets, separate shower and tub under the commanding cupola.

UPPER FLOOR

44·0

LAUNDRY

BREAKFAST

GREAT ROOM
16-0 x 20-6

KITCHEN

51·0

UP

DINING ROOM
13-0 x 14-0

MAIN FLOOR

**NOTE:
The above photographed home may have been modified by the homeowner. Please refer to floor plan and/or drawn elevation shown for actual blueprint details.

BEDROOM
12-0 x 16-0

BEDROOM
11-6 x 13-0

DOWN

MASTER
BEDROOM
13-0 x 17-0

Plan V-2440	
Bedrooms: 3	**Baths:** 2½
Space:	
Upper floor	1,266 sq. ft.
Main floor	1,482 sq. ft.
Total Living Area	**2,748 sq. ft.**
Exterior Wall Framing	2x6
Foundation options:	
Crawlspace	
(Foundation & framing conversion diagram available—see order form.)	
Blueprint Price Code	D

Distinct Design

- This home's distinct design is seen from the curvature of its covered porch to its decorative wrought-iron roof rail.
- The 17-ft.-high foyer is lighted in an oval theme, through the clerestory window, the front door and its flanking sidelights. The broad foyer stretches between the vaulted formal living areas and a casual TV room across from a full bath.
- With its unique corner design, the fireplace in the Great Room also warms the unusual rounded dining room and the breakfast area.
- The dining room boasts a 14-ft-high ceiling, while the kitchen features an angled sink, a nearby pantry and a handy wet bar facing the Great Room.
- The master suite, with its 13-ft.-high tray ceiling, offers a bath with a spa tub and a designer shower, both brightened by glass blocks.
- Upstairs, a balcony hall leads to a turreted recreation room, two bedrooms and a full bath.

Plan AX-92326

Bedrooms: 3+	Baths: 3
Living Area:	
Upper floor	736 sq. ft.
Main floor	1,960 sq. ft.
Total Living Area:	**2,696 sq. ft.**
Standard basement	1,915 sq. ft.
Garage	455 sq. ft.
Exterior Wall Framing:	2x4

Foundation Options:

Standard basement

Crawlspace

Slab

(All plans can be built with your choice of foundation and framing. A generic conversion diagram is available. See order form.)

BLUEPRINT PRICE CODE: **D**

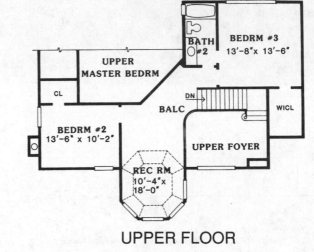

UPPER FLOOR

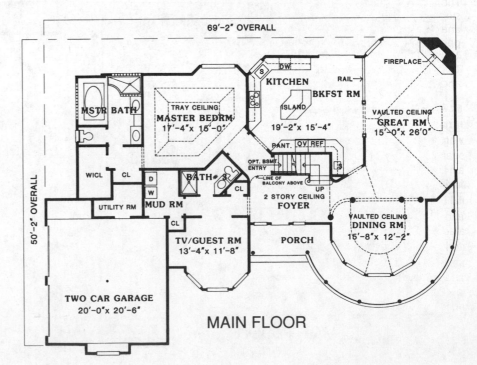

MAIN FLOOR

Sunny Spaces

- Graced by skylights and clerestory windows, this bright and airy home is filled with sunny spaces.
- The skylighted foyer boasts a 12-ft. sloped ceiling and showcases a sunstreaked open-railed stairway.
- Off the foyer, the intimate sunken living room features a 16-ft. cathedral ceiling and tall corner windows. Defined by columns and rails, the adjacent formal dining room is enhanced by an elegant 12-ft. stepped ceiling.
- The skylighted island kitchen includes a sunny breakfast space, which is separated from the family room by a half-wall. Expanded by a skylighted 16-ft. cathedral ceiling, the family room offers a handsome fireplace and access to a sunken rear sun room.
- The deluxe master suite is graced by a stepped ceiling, a bayed sitting room and a private bath. Sliding glass doors open to the sun room, which boasts an 11-ft., 7-in. vaulted ceiling.
- Two more bedrooms, a study alcove and a full bath are found upstairs.

Plan AX-91314

Bedrooms: 3+	Baths: 3
Living Area:	
Upper floor	544 sq. ft.
Main floor	1,959 sq. ft.
Sun room	202 sq. ft.
Total Living Area:	**2,705 sq. ft.**
Standard basement	1,833 sq. ft.
Garage	482 sq. ft.
Exterior Wall Framing:	2x4

Foundation Options:

Standard basement

Crawlspace

Slab

(All plans can be built with your choice of foundation and framing. A generic conversion diagram is available. See order form.)

BLUEPRINT PRICE CODE: **D**

UPPER FLOOR

MAIN FLOOR

TO ORDER THIS BLUEPRINT,
CALL TOLL-FREE 1-800-547-5570

Plan AX-91314

PRICES AND DETAILS
ON PAGES 12-15

351

Unforgettable Floor Plan

- Unusual shapes and exciting features give this home an unforgettable floor plan and a handsome facade.
- The exterior is distinguished by an arched-window entry flanked by columns. Columns are also used on the large L-shaped front porch. Arched windows in the study and in one of the second-story bedrooms echo the graceful lines of the entry.
- To the right of the tiled entry hall lies the vaulted living room, separated by half-walls and columns. To the left is the eye-catching study, with its octagonal tray ceiling. The dining room also has a tray ceiling and is tucked between the living room and the kitchen for easy yet intimate entertaining.
- The showpiece of the main floor is the spectacular kitchen, breakfast room and family room arrangement. A wonderful see-through fireplace warms the entire area. The breakfast room features large bay windows, a tray ceiling and an angled countertop snack bar facing the kitchen. The vaulted family room accesses a large rear patio.
- The crown jewel of the second floor is the stunning master suite, with its romantic fireplace, intimate sitting area and private deck. The plush master bath includes his 'n hers sinks, a garden tub and separate shower.

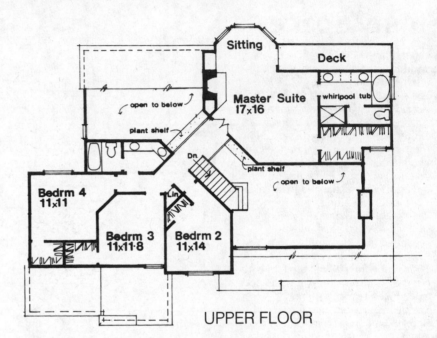

UPPER FLOOR

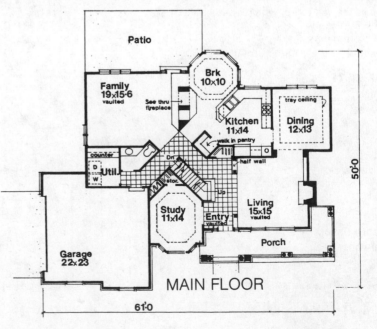

MAIN FLOOR

Plan AG-2701	
Bedrooms: 4	**Baths:** 2 ½
Space:	
Upper floor	1,195 sq. ft.
Main floor	1,572 sq. ft.
Total Living Area	**2,767 sq. ft.**
Basement	1,572 sq. ft.
Garage	506 sq. ft.
Exterior Wall Framing	2x6
Foundation options:	
Standard Basement	
(Foundation & framing conversion diagram	
available—see order form.)	
Blueprint Price Code	D

Victorian Touches

- A huge covered porch and fishscale shingles bring Victorian elements to the facade of this country-style home.
- The spacious foyer leads to the formal living and dining rooms on either side.
- The informal living areas flow together at the back of the home for easy entertaining.
- The island kitchen features a pantry and a bright corner sink. The oversized, bayed dinette offers sliding glass doors to the backyard.
- The sunken family room boasts a rear window wall and a large fireplace.
- Upstairs, the master suite offers a private bath with corner whirlpool tub, a separate shower and a dual-sink vanity. The two remaining bedrooms share a hall bath.
- A large bonus room over the garage could be used as a hobby area, home office or playroom.
- Central to the upper floor is an inviting sitting area with lovely oval window.

Plan Pl-91-567

Bedrooms: 3+	Baths: 2½
Living Area:	
Upper floor	1,194 sq. ft.
Main floor	1,258 sq. ft.
Bonus room	369 sq. ft.
Total Living Area:	**2,821 sq. ft.**
Standard basement	1,244 sq. ft.
Garage	672 sq. ft.
Exterior Wall Framing:	2x6

Foundation Options:

Standard basement

(Typical foundation & framing conversion diagram available—see order form.)

BLUEPRINT PRICE CODE:	D

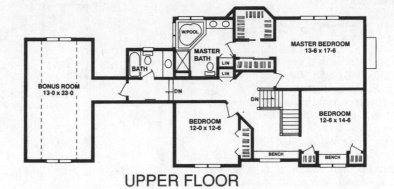

UPPER FLOOR

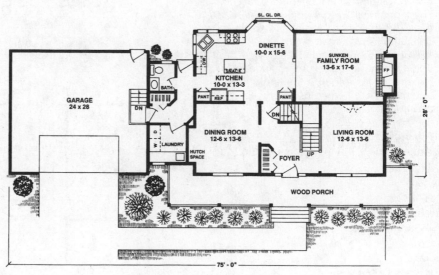

MAIN FLOOR

Spacious Country-Style

- With a minimum of four bedrooms and an open floor plan, this design is perfect for growing families.
- The covered front porch and country-style detailing give the exterior a warm, homey look.
- Inside, an arched opening in the two-story foyer provides a view into the formal dining room. Straight ahead, the vaulted family room offers a fireplace and an arched opening to the breakfast nook and kitchen.
- The spacious nook and kitchen area features a French door to the backyard, a work island and lots of counter space.
- The formal living room, reminiscent of the old-fashioned parlor, overlooks the delightful front porch.
- The upper floor is highlighted by a luxurious master suite, plus includes a balcony hall overlook, a multipurpose loft, three large bedrooms and two additional baths.

Plan FB-5016-MARY

Bedrooms: 4+	Baths: 4
Living Area:	
Upper floor	1,408 sq. ft.
Main floor	1,426 sq. ft.
Total Living Area:	**2,834 sq. ft.**
Daylight basement	1,426 sq. ft.
Garage	240 sq. ft.
Storage	40 sq. ft.
Exterior Wall Framing:	2x4

Foundation Options:

Daylight basement
(Typical foundation & framing conversion diagram available—see order form.)

BLUEPRINT PRICE CODE: D

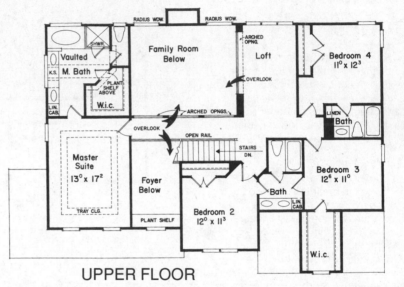

UPPER FLOOR

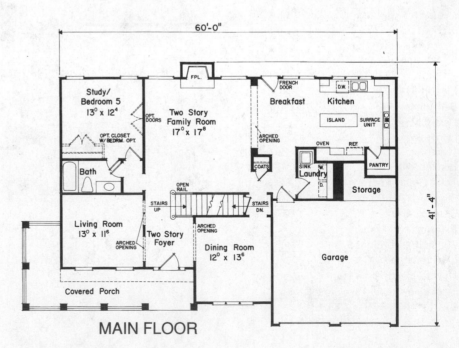

MAIN FLOOR

Plan FB-5016-MARY

PRICES AND DETAILS ON PAGES 12-15

Symmetrical Bay Windows

- This home's ornate facade proudly displays a pair of symmetrical copper-topped bay windows.
- A bright, two-story-high foyer stretches to the vaulted Great Room, with its fireplace and backyard deck access.
- The island kitchen offers a snack bar and a breakfast nook that opens to the deck and the garage.
- The main-floor master suite features private deck access, dual walk-in closets and a personal bath with a corner garden tub. A laundry room and a bayed study are nearby.
- Upstairs, three secondary bedrooms and another full bath are located off the balcony bridge, which overlooks both the Great Room and the foyer.
- A second stairway off the breakfast nook climbs to a bonus room, which adjoins an optional full bath and closet.

Plan C-9010

Bedrooms: 4+	Baths: 2½-3½
Living Area:	
Upper floor	761 sq. ft.
Main floor	1,637 sq. ft.
Bonus room	347 sq. ft.
Optional bath and closet	106 sq. ft.
Total Living Area:	**2,851 sq. ft.**
Daylight basement	1,637 sq. ft.
Garage	572 sq. ft.
Exterior Wall Framing:	2x4

Foundation Options:

Daylight basement
Crawlspace
(All plans can be built with your choice of foundation and framing. A generic conversion diagram is available. See order form.)

BLUEPRINT PRICE CODE: D

UPPER FLOOR

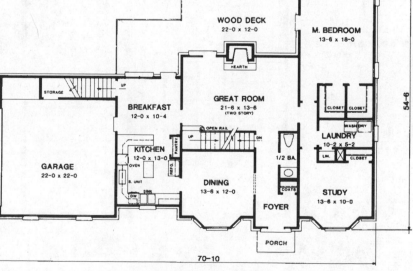

MAIN FLOOR

Brick Beauty

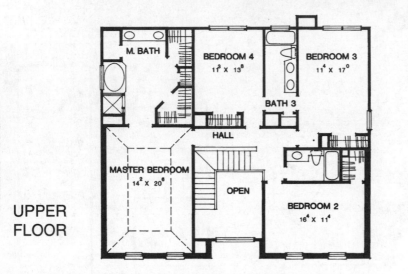

UPPER FLOOR

M. BATH

BEDROOM 4
11³ X 13⁸

BEDROOM 3
11⁴ X 17⁰

BATH 3

HALL

MASTER BEDROOM
14² X 20⁶

OPEN

BEDROOM 2
16⁴ X 11⁴

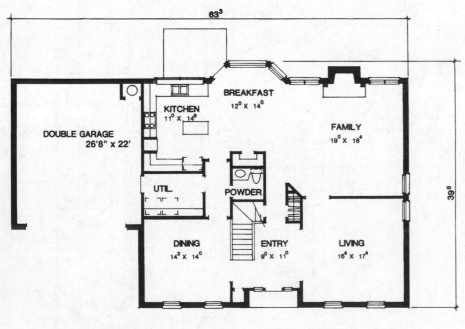

MAIN FLOOR

63³

BREAKFAST
12⁰ X 14⁰

KITCHEN
11⁰ X 14⁰

DOUBLE GARAGE
26'8" X 22'

FAMILY
19⁰ X 18⁴

UTIL.

POWDER

DINING
14² X 14⁰

ENTRY
9⁰ X 11⁰

LIVING
16⁴ X 17⁴

39⁸

- The beautiful brick exterior of this elegant home is further enriched by dormer windows and the stunning arched window above the front door.
- The large living spaces include a formal dining room and a living room, plus an open family room, breakfast room and kitchen combination. The wall of glass overlooking the backyard is interrupted only by the family room's fireplace. A built-in pantry in the breakfast area and a work island in the kitchen are other special features.
- The upper floor hosts four bedrooms, including an extravagant master suite. A tray ceiling adds drama and dimension to the suite's sleeping area, while the luxurious bathroom offers a spa bath, separate shower, dual-sink vanity and loads of closet space.
- The two rear-facing bedrooms enjoy private access to a full bath. Another bath is adjacent to the remaining bedroom.

Plan DD-2928-D

Bedrooms: 4	**Baths:** 3½

Living Area:	
Upper floor	1,381 sq. ft.
Main floor	1,518 sq. ft.
Total Living Area:	**2,899 sq. ft.**
Standard basement	1,518 sq. ft.
Garage	474 sq. ft.
Exterior Wall Framing:	2x4

Foundation Options:
Standard basement
Crawlspace
Slab
(Typical foundation & framing conversion diagram available—see order form.)

BLUEPRINT PRICE CODE:	D

A Family Tradition

- This traditional design has clean, sharp styling, with family-sized areas for formal and casual gatherings.
- The sidelighted foyer is graced with a beautiful open staircase and a wide coat closet. Flanking the foyer are the spacious formal living areas.
- The everyday living areas include an island kitchen, a bayed dinette and a large family room with a fireplace.
- Just off the entrance from the garage, double doors open to the quiet study, which boasts built-in bookshelves.
- A powder room and a deluxe laundry room with cabinets are convenient to the active areas of the home.
- Upstairs, the master suite features a roomy split bath and a large walk-in closet. Three more bedrooms share another split bath.

Plan A-118-DS

Bedrooms: 4+	Baths: 2½
Living Area:	
Upper floor	1,344 sq. ft.
Main floor	1,556 sq. ft.
Total Living Area:	**2,900 sq. ft.**
Standard basement	1,556 sq. ft.
Garage	576 sq. ft.
Exterior Wall Framing:	2x4

Foundation Options:

Standard basement
(All plans can be built with your choice of foundation and framing. A generic conversion diagram is available. See order form.)

BLUEPRINT PRICE CODE: D

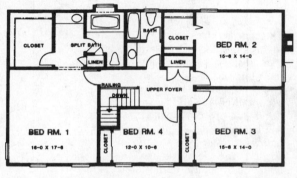

UPPER FLOOR

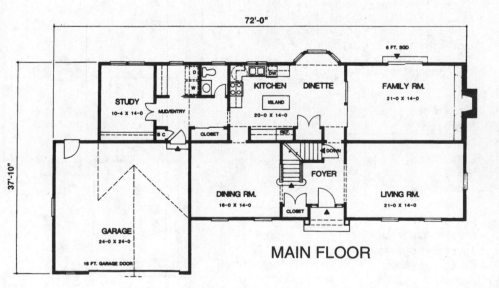

MAIN FLOOR

TO ORDER THIS BLUEPRINT,
CALL TOLL-FREE 1-800-547-5570

Plan A-118-DS

PRICES AND DETAILS
ON PAGES 12-15

357

Live in Luxury

- This luxurious home is introduced by a striking facade. Arched windows and a majestic entry accent the stucco finish. An alternate brick exterior is included with the blueprints.
- A graceful curved stairway is showcased in the grand two-story foyer, which is flanked by the formal rooms. The spacious living room flaunts an inviting fireplace. Double doors at the rear close off the adjoining study, which has functional built-in shelves.
- The central family room boasts a second fireplace and two sets of French doors that open to the backyard.
- A full pantry and a range island with an eating bar offer extra storage and work space in the roomy kitchen. The attached breakfast room is dramatically surrounded by windows.
- The spacious master suite and three secondary bedrooms are located on the upper floor. The master bedroom offers dual walk-in closets and a skylighted private bath with twin vanities and an oval spa tub. A second bath services the secondary bedrooms. The laundry room is conveniently located on the upper floor as well.

Plan CH-360-A

Bedrooms: 4	Baths: 2½
Living Area:	
Upper floor	1,354 sq. ft.
Main floor	1,616 sq. ft.
Total Living Area:	**2,970 sq. ft.**
Basement	1,616 sq. ft.
Garage	462 sq. ft.
Exterior Wall Framing:	2x4

Foundation Options:

Daylight basement

Standard basement

Crawlspace

(All plans can be built with your choice of foundation and framing. A generic conversion diagram is available. See order form.)

BLUEPRINT PRICE CODE: D

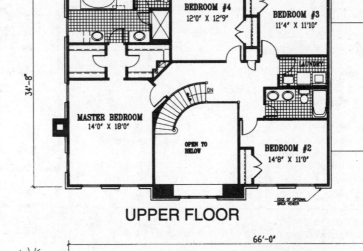

UPPER FLOOR

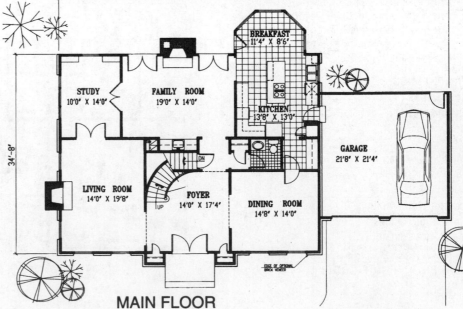

MAIN FLOOR

TO ORDER THIS BLUEPRINT, CALL TOLL-FREE 1-800-547-5570

Plan CH-360-A

PRICES AND DETAILS ON PAGES 12-15

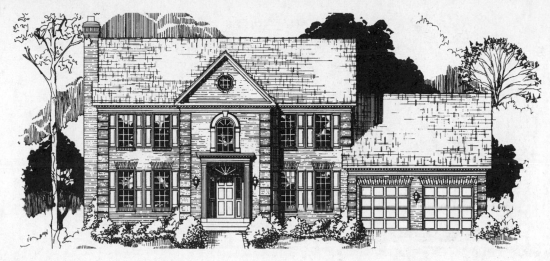

Stately and Roomy

- The exquisite exterior of this two-story home opens to a very roomy interior.
- The magnificent two-story-high foyer shows off a curved, open-railed stairway to the upper floor and opens to a study on the right and the formal living areas on the left.
- The spacious living room flows into a formal dining room that overlooks the outdoors through a lovely bay window.
- A large work island and snack counter sit at the center of the open kitchen and breakfast room. An oversized pantry closet, a powder room and a laundry room are all close at hand.
- Adjoining the breakfast room is the large sunken family room, featuring a 12-ft.-high vaulted ceiling, a cozy fireplace and outdoor access.
- The upper floor includes a stunning master bedroom with an 11-ft. vaulted ceiling and a luxurious private bath.
- Three additional bedrooms share a second full bath.

Plan CH-280-A

Bedrooms: 4+	Baths: 2½
Living Area:	
Upper floor	1,262 sq. ft.
Main floor	1,797 sq. ft.
Total Living Area:	**3,059 sq. ft.**
Basement	1,797 sq. ft.
Garage	462 sq. ft.
Exterior Wall Framing:	2x4

Foundation Options:

Daylight basement

Standard basement

Crawlspace

(All plans can be built with your choice of foundation and framing. A generic conversion diagram is available. See order form.)

BLUEPRINT PRICE CODE: **E**

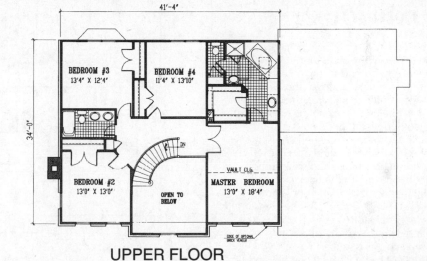

UPPER FLOOR

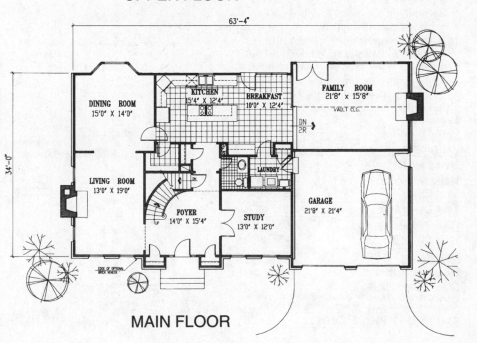

MAIN FLOOR

TO ORDER THIS BLUEPRINT,
CALL TOLL-FREE 1-800-547-5570

Plan CH-280-A

PRICES AND DETAILS
ON PAGES 12-15

359

Large and Luxurious

- This two-story home offers large, luxurious living areas with a variety of options to complement any lifestyle.
- The two-story-high foyer shows off an angled stairway and flows to the elegant formal living spaces on the right.
- The gourmet kitchen boasts a sunny sink, a walk-in pantry and an island cooktop with a serving bar. The adjoining breakfast nook has French doors opening to the backyard.
- Highlighting the main floor is a huge sunken family room, which is expanded by a 17-ft. vaulted ceiling and hosts a handy wet bar and a handsome fireplace. An open rail views to the breakfast room and kitchen beyond.
- Completing the main floor is a den or guest bedroom with private access to a full bath, making a great guest suite.
- Upstairs, the master suite boasts a 10-ft. tray ceiling in the sleeping area and a 15-ft. vaulted ceiling in the garden bath.
- Each of the three remaining bedrooms has private access to a bath.

Plan FB-3071

Bedrooms: 4+	Baths: 4
Living Area:	
Upper floor	1,419 sq. ft.
Main floor	1,652 sq. ft.
Total Living Area:	**3,071 sq. ft.**
Daylight basement	1,652 sq. ft.
Garage	456 sq. ft.
Exterior Wall Framing:	2x4

Foundation Options:

Daylight basement

(All plans can be built with your choice of foundation and framing. A generic conversion diagram is available. See order form.)

BLUEPRINT PRICE CODE: E

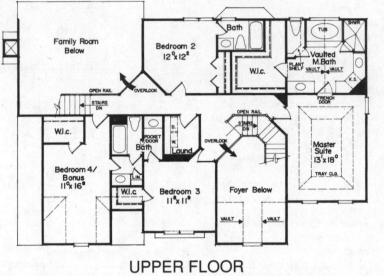

UPPER FLOOR

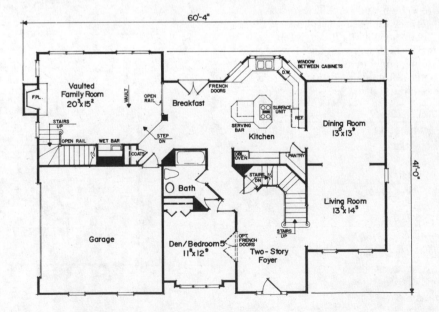

MAIN FLOOR

Striking Stucco

- The facade of this striking stucco home is adorned with elegant window treatments and eye-catching gables.
- Inside, a two-story-high foyer views to an open-railed staircase and is brightened by an arched window.
- To the right of the foyer, an arched opening connects the living room to the formal dining room.
- The casual living areas consist of an open kitchen, a sunny breakfast nook and a family room with a fireplace. The kitchen boasts a island cooktop, while the nook offers a French door leading to the backyard. A second stairway in the family room accesses the upper floor.
- Just off the foyer, a den with access to a full bath may serve as a guest room.
- Ceilings in all main-floor rooms are 9 ft. high unless otherwise specified.
- Upstairs, the master suite features a 9-ft. tray ceiling and a private bath with a 12-ft. vaulted ceiling over a garden tub.
- Three additional bedrooms, one with an 11-ft. vaulted ceiling, share two more full baths. A versatile bonus room is also included.

Plan FB-5081-AVER

Bedrooms: 4+	Baths: 4
Living Area:	
Upper floor	1,325 sq. ft.
Main floor	1,447 sq. ft.
Bonus room	301 sq. ft.
Total Living Area:	**3,073 sq. ft.**
Daylight basement	1,447 sq. ft.
Garage	465 sq. ft.
Exterior Wall Framing:	2x4

Foundation Options:

Daylight basement

(All plans can be built with your choice of foundation and framing. A generic conversion diagram is available. See order form.)

BLUEPRINT PRICE CODE: E

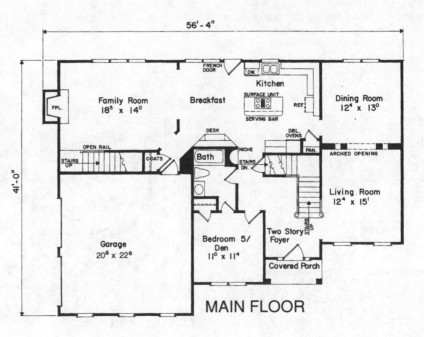

UPPER FLOOR

MAIN FLOOR

Spacious and Striking

- Alluring angles and an open, airy floor plan distinguish this impressive home, designed to take advantage of a sloping lot.
- A gorgeous covered deck and patio give guests a royal welcome.
- Designed for both entertaining and family gatherings, the home's main floor features a bright family room with an 11-ft.-high vaulted ceiling and fabulous windows. A two-way fireplace with a lovely semi-round planter is shared with the adjoining dining room.
- The combination kitchen and breakfast area features a 10-ft. vaulted ceiling, a center island and a high pot shelf.
- The roomy master suite boasts a 10-ft. vaulted ceiling and double doors to a private balcony. The sumptuous master bath includes a beautiful Jacuzzi, a separate shower and a walk-in closet.
- Three more bedrooms and three full baths are located on the lower floor.
- A second family room includes a wet bar and double doors to a large covered patio.

Plan Q-3080-1A

Bedrooms: 4	Baths: 4½
Living Area:	
Main floor	1,575 sq. ft.
Lower floor	1,505 sq. ft.
Total Living Area:	**3,080 sq. ft.**
Garage	702 sq. ft.
Exterior Wall Framing:	2x4

Foundation Options:

Slab

(All plans can be built with your choice of foundation and framing. A generic conversion diagram is available. See order form.)

BLUEPRINT PRICE CODE: E

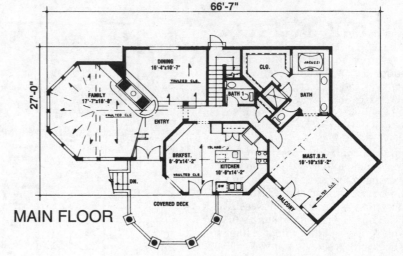

MAIN FLOOR

LOWER FLOOR

TO ORDER THIS BLUEPRINT, CALL TOLL-FREE 1-800-547-5570

Plan Q-3080-1A

PRICES AND DETAILS ON PAGES 12-15

Timeless Beauty

- Reflected in its lovely windows and stone and stucco facade, this home has timeless beauty and lasting appeal.
- Past the inviting covered front porch, the two-story-high entry is flanked by the intimate formal areas.
- Warmed by a handsome fireplace, the large family room features a window wall with views to a backyard patio.
- The good-sized kitchen includes a pantry and an angled serving bar. The adjoining morning room opens to the partially covered patio.
- The main-floor bedroom is a perfect guest or in-law suite, with easy access to the bathroom, utility room and garage. All main-floor ceilings are 10 ft. high for added spaciousness.
- Upstairs, a versatile game room boasts a 10-ft. ceiling and access to a nice deck.
- The master bedroom also has a 10-ft. ceiling and enjoys a private covered porch, a roomy walk-in closet and a luxurious bath with a garden tub.
- Three additional upper-floor bedrooms and a full bath all have 9-ft. ceilings.

Plan DD-2952

Bedrooms: 5	Baths: 3
Living Area:	
Upper floor	1,721 sq. ft.
Main floor	1,394 sq. ft.
Total Living Area:	**3,115 sq. ft.**
Standard basement	1,394 sq. ft.
Garage	442 sq. ft.
Exterior Wall Framing:	2x4

Foundation Options:
Standard basement
Crawlspace
Slab
(All plans can be built with your choice of foundation and framing. A generic conversion diagram is available. See order form.)

BLUEPRINT PRICE CODE: E

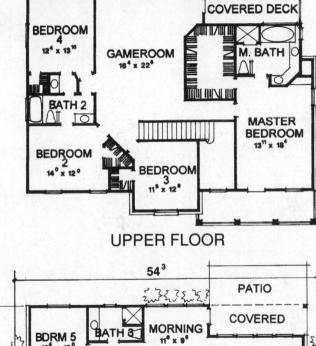

UPPER FLOOR

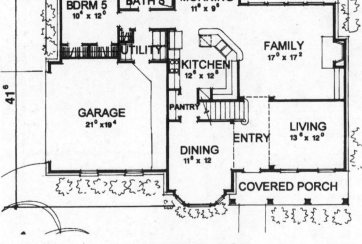

MAIN FLOOR

TO ORDER THIS BLUEPRINT,
CALL TOLL-FREE 1-800-547-5570

Plan DD-2952

PRICES AND DETAILS
ON PAGES 12-15

363

Tall Two-Story

- This gorgeous two-story is introduced by a barrel-vaulted entry and supporting columns. Inside, a spectacular curved staircase leads to a balcony overlook.
- Off the two-story-high foyer, a library with a 16-ft.-high vaulted ceiling is perfect for reading or study.
- A formal dining room opposite the library opens to the fabulous island kitchen. The kitchen offers an angled serving bar to the bayed breakfast area and adjoining living room.
- The spacious living room, with an 18-ft. vaulted ceiling, opens to a backyard patio. A fireplace flanked by built-in shelving warms the whole family area.
- The master bedroom boasts a 10-ft. gambrel ceiling, a sunny bay window and patio access. The spacious master bath offers his-and-hers walk-in closets, an oval tub and a separate shower.
- A second stairway near the utility room leads to the upper floor, where there are three more bedrooms, two baths and a bonus room above the garage. The bonus room could be finished as a game room, a media center or a hobby area.

Plan DD-3125

Bedrooms: 4+	**Baths:** 3½

Living Area:

Upper floor	982 sq. ft.
Main floor	2,147 sq. ft.
Total Living Area:	**3,129 sq. ft.**
Unfinished Bonus	196 sq. ft.
Standard basement	1,996 sq. ft.
Garage	771 sq. ft.
Exterior Wall Framing:	2x4

Foundation Options:

Standard basement
Crawlspace
Slab

(All plans can be built with your choice of foundation and framing.
A generic conversion diagram is available. See order form.)

BLUEPRINT PRICE CODE: E

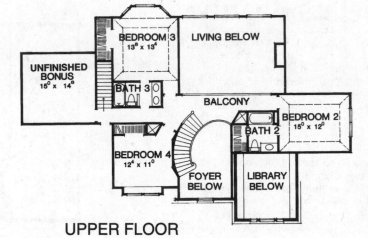

UPPER FLOOR

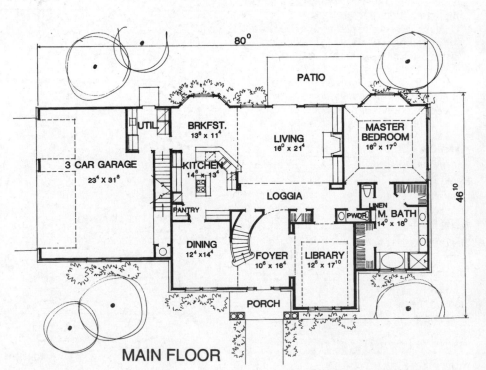

MAIN FLOOR

TO ORDER THIS BLUEPRINT, CALL TOLL-FREE 1-800-547-5570

Plan DD-3125

PRICES AND DETAILS ON PAGES 12-15

Stunning Country-Style

- A lovely front porch that encases bay windows provides a friendly welcome to this stunning country-style home.
- Inside, the main living areas revolve around the large country kitchen and dinette, complete with an island worktop, a roomy built-in desk and access to a backyard deck.
- A raised-hearth fireplace, French doors and a 12-ft., 4-in. cathedral ceiling highlight the casual family room.
- The formal dining room is open to the living room and features an inviting window seat and a tray ceiling. A French door in the bay-windowed living room opens to the relaxing porch.
- A quiet den and a large laundry area/mudroom complete the main floor.
- The upper floor showcases a super master suite with a bay window, an 11-ft., 8-in. tray ceiling, two walk-in closets and a private bath with a garden tub and its own dramatic ceiling.
- Three additional bedrooms share a full bath designed for multiple users.

Plan A-538-R

Bedrooms: 4+	Baths: 2½
Living Area:	
Upper floor	1,384 sq. ft.
Main floor	1,755 sq. ft.
Total Living Area:	**3,139 sq. ft.**
Standard basement	1,728 sq. ft.
Garage	576 sq. ft.
Exterior Wall Framing:	2x4

Foundation Options:

Standard basement

(All plans can be built with your choice of foundation and framing. A generic conversion diagram is available. See order form.)

BLUEPRINT PRICE CODE:	E

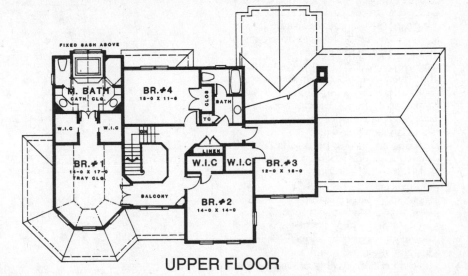

UPPER FLOOR

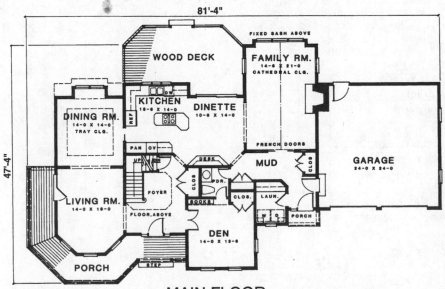

MAIN FLOOR

TO ORDER THIS BLUEPRINT,
CALL TOLL-FREE 1-800-547-5570

Plan A-538-R

PRICES AND DETAILS
ON PAGES 12-15

365

Creative Spaces

- This expansive home uses vaulted ceilings and multiple levels to create a functional, airy floor plan.
- The broad, vaulted entry foyer leads to the bayed living room, which is warmed by a striking fireplace. A few steps down, the dining room opens to a wide backyard deck.
- The island kitchen features a sunny sink area and a breakfast nook with deck access. A laundry room, a half-bath and a den or extra bedroom are also found on this level.
- Adjacent to the nook, the sunken family room boasts a wet bar, a second fireplace and a bright window wall with sliding glass doors to a lovely patio.
- Upstairs, the master suite includes a sunken bedroom with a private deck. The lavish master bath offers a sunken garden tub, a dual-sink vanity and a skylight near the private shower.
- Three large secondary bedrooms share another skylighted bath. Each bedroom has its own unique design feature.

Plans P-7664-4A & -4D

Bedrooms: 4+	Baths: 2½
Living Area:	
Upper floor	1,301 sq. ft.
Main floor	1,853 sq. ft.
Total Living Area:	**3,154 sq. ft.**
Daylight basement	1,486 sq. ft.
Garage	668 sq. ft.
Exterior Wall Framing:	2x4
Foundation Options:	**Plan #**
Daylight basement	P-7664-4D
Crawlspace	P-7664-4A

(All plans can be built with your choice of foundation and framing. A generic conversion diagram is available. See order form.)

BLUEPRINT PRICE CODE: E

UPPER FLOOR

BASEMENT STAIRWAY LOCATION

MAIN FLOOR

TO ORDER THIS BLUEPRINT, CALL TOLL-FREE 1-800-547-5570

Plans P-7664-4A & -4D

PRICES AND DETAILS ON PAGES 12-15

Ornate Design

- This exciting home is distinguished by an ornate facade with symmetrical windows and a columned entry.
- A beautiful arched window highlights the two-story-high foyer, with its open-railed stairway and high plant shelf. The foyer separates the two formal rooms and flows back to the family room.
- With an 18-ft. ceiling, the family room is brightened by corner windows and warmed by a central fireplace.
- Columns introduce the sunny breakfast area and the gourmet kitchen, which features an angled island/serving bar and a butler's pantry near the dining room. A laundry room and a second stairway to the upper floor are nearby.
- Ceilings in all main-floor rooms are 9 ft. high unless otherwise specified.
- Upstairs, a dramatic balcony overlooks the family room and the foyer.
- The master suite boasts a 10-ft. tray ceiling, a sitting room and an opulent garden bath with a 12-ft. vaulted ceiling. Three more bedrooms, each with a walk-in closet and private bath access, complete the upper floor.

Plan FB-5347-HAST

Bedrooms: 4+	Baths: 4
Living Area:	
Upper floor	1,554 sq. ft.
Main floor	1,665 sq. ft.
Total Living Area:	**3,219 sq. ft.**
Daylight basement	1,665 sq. ft.
Garage	462 sq. ft.
Exterior Wall Framing:	2x4

Foundation Options:

Daylight basement

(All plans can be built with your choice of foundation and framing. A generic conversion diagram is available. See order form.)

BLUEPRINT PRICE CODE:	E

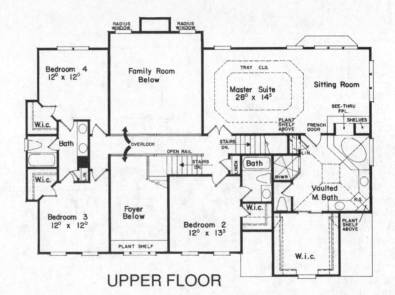

UPPER FLOOR

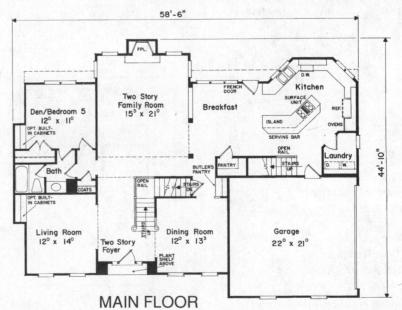

MAIN FLOOR

Set in Stone

- Sure to impress, this home features a stucco finish set off by a two-story entry faced with stone.
- Inside, a stunning 18-ft. vaulted foyer separates the formal living spaces. The secluded living room flaunts a 15-ft. vaulted ceiling and a boxed-out window. Columns outline the dining room, which has French doors to a covered porch.
- The casual spaces begin with a wonderful Great Room that features a two-story-high ceiling and a fireplace flanked by tall arched windows.
- Window walls and a French door to the backyard brighten the breakfast nook, which has a 14-ft. vaulted ceiling. The adjoining kitchen offers a work island, a corner sink and a walk-in pantry.
- The superb master suite includes a 10½-ft. tray ceiling in the angled sleeping area and a 16-ft. vaulted ceiling in the luxurious master bath.
- Ceilings in all main-floor rooms are 9 ft. high unless otherwise specified.
- Upstairs, a balcony hall leads to three nice-sized bedrooms, each with an ample walk-in closet and private access to one of two compartmentalized baths.

Plan FB-5348-BARR

Bedrooms: 4	Baths: 3½
Living Area:	
Upper floor	776 sq. ft.
Main floor	2,165 sq. ft.
Fourth bedroom/bonus room	281 sq. ft.
Total Living Area:	**3,222 sq. ft.**
Daylight basement	2,165 sq. ft.
Garage and storage	456 sq. ft.
Exterior Wall Framing:	2x4

Foundation Options:

Daylight basement

(All plans can be built with your choice of foundation and framing. A generic conversion diagram is available. See order form.)

BLUEPRINT PRICE CODE: E

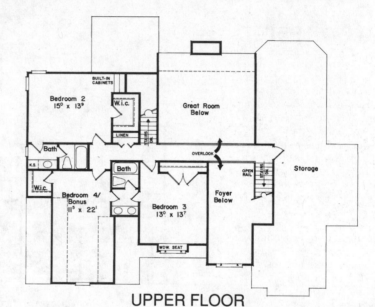

UPPER FLOOR

MAIN FLOOR

TO ORDER THIS BLUEPRINT, CALL TOLL-FREE 1-800-547-5570

Plan FB-5348-BARR

PRICES AND DETAILS ON PAGES 12-15

Smart Two-Story

- This simple yet classically designed two-story is functional and spacious.
- The recessed entry opens to a wide reception foyer that offers dual closets and access to each of the living areas.
- The enormous sunken living room with an optional fireplace stretches from the front of the house all the way to the back! Charming French doors open to the backyard.
- The big family room also provides easy outdoor access. A fireplace would look nice between the corner windows.
- The efficient kitchen features an island range, a work desk and a handy pantry. The adjoining breakfast area is enhanced by a lovely bay window that opens to the backyard.
- Four big bedrooms and two baths are housed on the upper floor.
- The master bedroom boasts a private sitting area and the option of a fireplace. Two walk-in closets and an elegant skylighted bath with a cathedral ceiling are also included.

Plan AX-87105

Bedrooms: 4	Baths: 2½
Living Area:	
Upper floor	1,552 sq. ft.
Main floor	1,734 sq. ft.
Total Living Area:	**3,286 sq. ft.**
Standard basement	1,734 sq. ft.
Garage	434 sq. ft.
Exterior Wall Framing:	2x4

Foundation Options:

Standard basement

(All plans can be built with your choice of foundation and framing. A generic conversion diagram is available. See order form.)

BLUEPRINT PRICE CODE: E

UPPER FLOOR

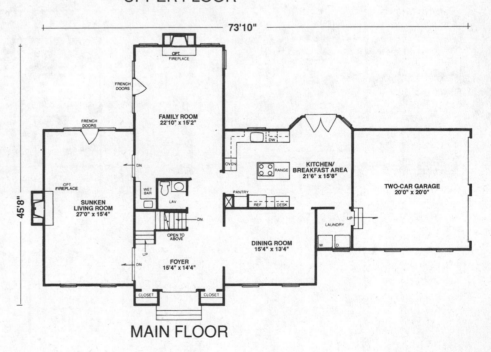

MAIN FLOOR

Tremendous Tri-Level Living

- Perfect for a scenic or sloping lot, this stunning home offers three levels of living space for maximum privacy and flexibility.
- At the heart of the main floor is the sunken living room, which boasts a cozy woodstove, skylights and French doors to a deluxe library.
- Just off the formal dining room is a gourmet kitchen, complete with a pantry closet, a boxed-out window and an angled snack bar overlooking the

nook. The glassed-in nook includes a built-in desk and access to the huge, wraparound backyard deck.
- Located near the garage entrance is an oversized utility room with space for a freezer, an ironing center and a laundry tub. A half-bath is nearby.
- An open stairway leads up to the very private master suite. Featured here are a raised sleeping area, a walk-in closet, a private deck and a luxurious bath with a step-up spa tub and a corner shower.
- Two more bedrooms are housed in the daylight basement, which also offers a game room, a wine cellar and a central family room with a woodstove and access to a ground-level patio.

Plan NW-855	
Bedrooms: 3	**Baths:** 2½
Living Area:	
Upper floor	549 sq. ft.
Main floor	1,388 sq. ft.
Daylight basement	1,371 sq. ft.
Total Living Area:	**3,308 sq. ft.**
Garage	573 sq. ft.
Exterior Wall Framing:	2x6

Foundation Options:

Daylight basement
(All plans can be built with your choice of foundation and framing. A generic conversion diagram is available. See order form.)

BLUEPRINT PRICE CODE:	E

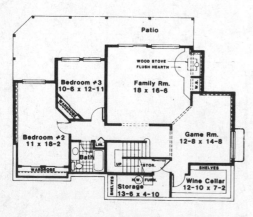

DAYLIGHT BASEMENT

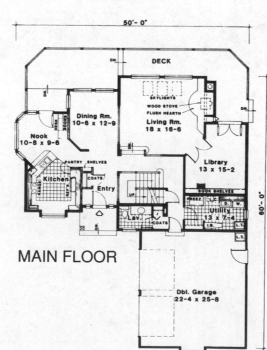

MAIN FLOOR

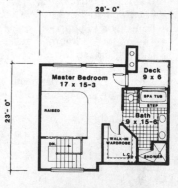

UPPER FLOOR

TO ORDER THIS BLUEPRINT, CALL TOLL-FREE 1-800-547-5570   Plan NW-855   *PRICES AND DETAILS ON PAGES 12-15*

Attractive European Look

- Arched windows with keystones, the stucco finish with corner quoins and many other fine flourishes give this European-style home its good looks.
- The two-story foyer flaunts a handsome open stairway to the upper floor. A second stairway is offered in the family room.
- Columns act as dividers between the formal living spaces to the left of the foyer. Double doors in the dining room close off the kitchen, which features a center island, a walk-in pantry and a handy freezer room.
- A bright, bayed breakfast area is nestled between the kitchen and the family room and offers access to the deck.
- The vaulted family room also opens to the deck and has a fireplace and two built-in bookcases.
- A bonus room or fourth bedroom shares the upper floor with three other bedrooms, three full baths and a convenient laundry room.

Plan APS-3302

Bedrooms: 4+	Baths: 4
Living Area:	
Upper floor	1,276 sq. ft.
Main floor	1,716 sq. ft.
Bonus room	382 sq. ft.
Total Living Area:	**3,374 sq. ft.**
Standard basement	1,716 sq. ft.
Garage	693 sq. ft.
Exterior Wall Framing:	2x4

Foundation Options:
Standard basement
(Typical foundation & framing conversion diagram available—see order form.)

BLUEPRINT PRICE CODE: E

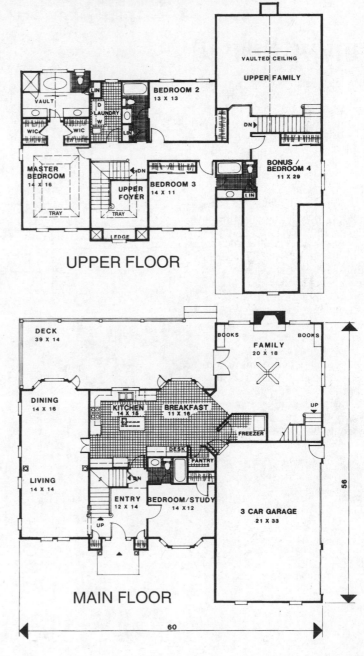

UPPER FLOOR

MAIN FLOOR

Nicely Adorned

- This nostalgic brick design is adorned with lovely columns, arches and half-round windows.
- Interior columns set off the main living areas from the foyer and gallery.
- A columned gallery directs traffic to a half-bath and the elegant dining room.
- The central family room offers a nice fireplace and a built-in media center.
- The focal point of the kitchen is its large island, which includes a handy bar sink.
- The fabulous morning room flaunts a 15-ft., 8-in. cathedral ceiling. Unless otherwise specified, 10-ft. ceilings are found throughout the main floor.
- The master suite boasts a dramatic corner fireplace, a sitting room and a private courtyard. The master bath hosts a Jacuzzi tub and a neat dressing table.
- Upstairs, an open game room offers French doors to an outdoor balcony.
- All three secondary bedrooms feature private bath access. A vaulted ceiling enhances the front bedroom, while 9-ft. ceilings are found in the rear bedrooms.
- The area above the stately porte cochere could be finished as a media room or a teen's bedroom. The ceiling slopes up from 5 ft. to 9 feet.

Plan GML-593

Bedrooms: 4+	Baths: 4½
Living Area:	
Upper floor	1,125 sq. ft.
Main floor	2,300 sq. ft.
Total Living Area:	**3,425 sq. ft.**
Media/teen room (unfinished)	303 sq. ft.
Exterior Wall Framing:	2x4

Foundation Options:

Slab

(All plans can be built with your choice of foundation and framing. A generic conversion diagram is available. See order form.)

BLUEPRINT PRICE CODE: E

UPPER FLOOR

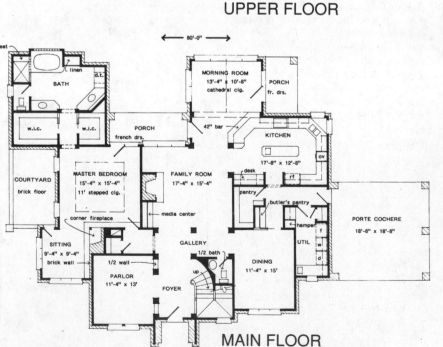

MAIN FLOOR

TO ORDER THIS BLUEPRINT, CALL TOLL-FREE 1-800-547-5570

Plan GML-593

PRICES AND DETAILS ON PAGES 12-15

Superb Views

- This superb multi-level home is designed to take full advantage of spectacular surrounding views.
- The two-story-high entry welcomes guests in from the covered front porch. An open-railed stairway and a 23-ft. domed ceiling are highlights here.
- The sunken living and dining rooms are defined by archways and face out to a large wraparound deck. The living room has a 13-ft. cathedral ceiling and a nice fireplace. The dining room offers a 9½-ft. domed ceiling and a wet bar.
- The octagonal island kitchen hosts a Jenn-Aire range, a sunny sink and a bayed breakfast nook. Nearby, the utility room reveals a walk-in pantry, laundry facilities and garage access.
- The quiet den boasts a second fireplace, a cozy window seat and deck access.
- The entire upper floor is occupied by the master bedroom suite, which has a spacious bayed sleeping room with a 12½-ft. cathedral ceiling. Other features include a huge walk-in closet, separate dressing areas and a private bath with a curved shower and a Jacuzzi tub.
- The exciting daylight basement has a recreation room, an exercise room and another bedroom, plus a sauna and a hot tub surrounded by windows!

Plan NW-229

Bedrooms: 2+	Baths: 2½
Living Area:	
Upper floor	815 sq. ft.
Main floor	1,446 sq. ft.
Daylight basement	1,330 sq. ft.
Total Living Area:	**3,591 sq. ft.**
Garage	720 sq. ft.
Exterior Wall Framing:	2x6

Foundation Options:

Daylight basement

(All plans can be built with your choice of foundation and framing. A generic conversion diagram is available. See order form.)

BLUEPRINT PRICE CODE: F

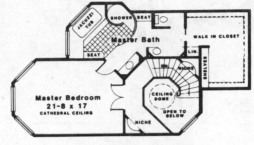

UPPER FLOOR

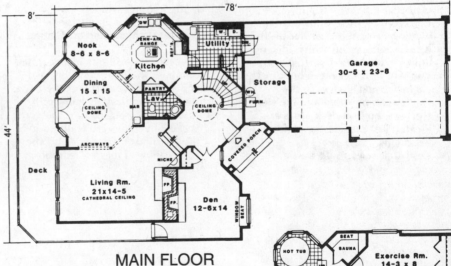

MAIN FLOOR

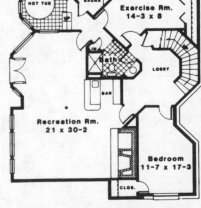

DAYLIGHT BASEMENT

Curved Glass Class

- It is difficult to pigeonhole this unique design with its skillfully blended traditional and post-modern elements.
- Eye-catching floor to ceiling windows round the corner of the formal living room which includes built-in cabinetry and fireplace.
- You will discover more built-in cabinetry and shelves in the vaulted dining room and the study. Upstairs, built-in desk areas are located just outside the children's bedrooms.
- Dual staircases route traffic

directly to the formal and informal living areas of the home.
- The kitchen includes a walk-in pantry, corner window sink, built-in desk, and large island counter with cooktop and eating bar.
- Skylights are skillfully incorporated into both the bathrooms upstairs and are also located over the back stairwell and upstairs hallway.
- A walk-in closet, spa tub, shower, and dual vanities are featured in the luxurious master bath off the cove-ceilinged master bedroom.

Plan CDG-2019

Bedrooms: 3-4	Baths: 2½
Space:	
Upper floor:	1,426 sq. ft.
Main floor:	1,891 sq. ft.
Bonus area:	255 sq. ft.
Total living area:	3,572 sq. ft.
Garage:	676 sq. ft.
Exterior Wall Framing:	2x6
Ceiling Heights:	
Upper floor:	8'
Main floor:	9'
Foundation options:	
Crawlspace. (Foundation & framing conversion diagram available — see order form.)	
Blueprint Price Code:	F

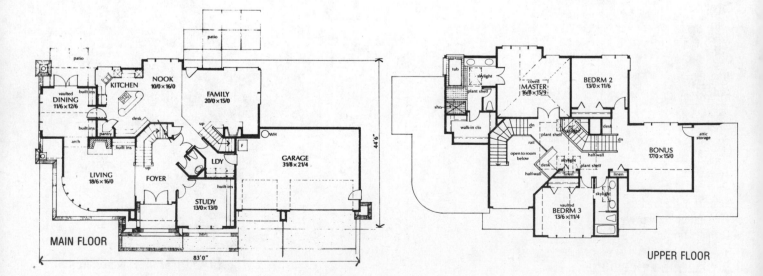

TO ORDER THIS BLUEPRINT, CALL TOLL-FREE 1-800-547-5570   Plan CDG-2019   **PRICES AND DETAILS ON PAGES 12-15**

Luxury Suite

- A distinctive roofline, a pair of porches and a wonderful exterior of stone and stucco give this elegant home an inviting European look.
- The two-story-high foyer is flanked by the living room and the formal dining room, which are defined by columns.
- The bright and airy island kitchen adjoins a two-story-high breakfast area. A laundry room, a powder room and a versatile butler's pantry are nearby.
- The bay-windowed family room is enhanced by a 20-ft., 9-in. vaulted ceiling and a handsome fireplace.
- Double doors lead into the spectacular master suite, which has an 11-ft. tray ceiling and boasts a morning kitchen and a private porch.
- The bedroom's see-through fireplace adds warmth to the master bath, which features a 17½-ft. vaulted ceiling, a spa tub, a designer shower, dual vanities with knee space and a walk-in closet.
- Upstairs, a balcony bridge overlooks the foyer and the breakfast area below. Four bedrooms offer private access to the two additional full baths.

Plan FB-3676

Bedrooms: 5	Baths: 3½
Living Area:	
Upper floor	1,405 sq. ft.
Main floor	2,271 sq. ft.
Total Living Area:	**3,676 sq. ft.**
Daylight basement	2,271 sq. ft.
Garage and storage	528 sq. ft.
Exterior Wall Framing:	2x4

Foundation Options:

Daylight basement

(All plans can be built with your choice of foundation and framing. A generic conversion diagram is available. See order form.)

BLUEPRINT PRICE CODE:	F

UPPER FLOOR

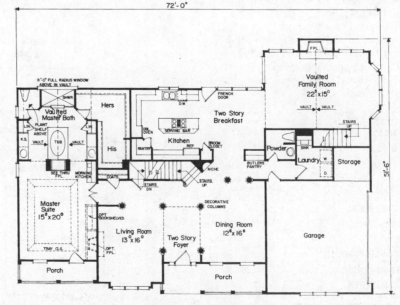

MAIN FLOOR

Stately Stone and Stucco

- A graceful combination of stone and stucco creates a warm and stately appearance for this charming home.
- The ornate, columned porch welcomes guests into the two-story-high foyer. Flowing to the right, the living room features a fireplace and a 15½-ft. vaulted ceiling. Decorative columns to the left set off the formal dining room.
- More columns introduce the two-story Great Room, which offers another fireplace and a handy back stairway.
- The open kitchen includes a work island and an angled serving bar to the bayed breakfast nook. French doors open to a covered backyard porch.
- The private master suite boasts a three-sided fireplace and a 10½-ft. tray ceiling in the bedroom; the sitting room and the luxurious garden bath each have a 16-ft. vaulted ceiling.
- Ceilings in all main-floor rooms are 9 ft. high unless otherwise specified.
- Upstairs, three more bedrooms share two full baths. The optional bonus room is a nice extra.

Plan FB-5345-JERN

Bedrooms: 4+	Baths: 3½
Living Area:	
Upper floor	928 sq. ft.
Main floor	2,467 sq. ft.
Bonus room	296 sq. ft.
Total Living Area:	**3,691 sq. ft.**
Daylight basement	2,467 sq. ft.
Garage	531 sq. ft.
Exterior Wall Framing:	2x4

Foundation Options:

Daylight basement

(All plans can be built with your choice of foundation and framing. A generic conversion diagram is available. See order form.)

BLUEPRINT PRICE CODE: F

UPPER FLOOR

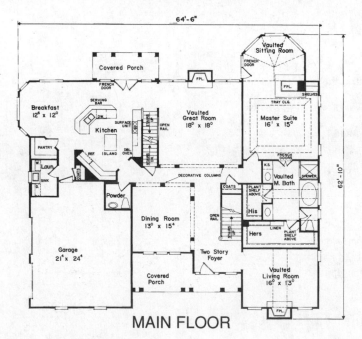

MAIN FLOOR

TO ORDER THIS BLUEPRINT, CALL TOLL-FREE 1-800-547-5570   Plan FB-5345-JERN   *PRICES AND DETAILS ON PAGES 12-15*

Design Leaves Out Nothing

- This design has it all, from the elegant detailing of the exterior to the exciting, luxurious spaces of the interior.
- High ceilings, large, open rooms and lots of glass are found throughout the home. Nearly all of the main living areas, as well as the master suite, overlook the veranda.
- Unusual features include a built-in ale bar in the formal dining room, an art niche in the Grand Room and a TV niche in the Gathering Room. The Gathering Room also features a fireplace framed by window seats, a wall of windows facing the backyard and a half-wall open to the morning room. The cooktop-island kitchen is conveniently accessible from all of the living areas.
- The delicious master suite includes a raised lounge, a three-sided fireplace and French doors that open to the veranda. The spiral stairs nearby lead to the "evening deck" above. The master bath boasts two walk-in closets, a sunken shower and a Roman tub.
- The upper floor hosts two complete suites and a loft, plus a vaulted bonus room reached via a separate stairway.

Plan EOF-61

Bedrooms: 3+	Baths: 4½

Living Area:

Upper floor	877 sq. ft.
Main floor	3,094 sq. ft.
Bonus room	280 sq. ft.
Total Living Area:	**4,251 sq. ft.**
Garage	774 sq. ft.

Exterior Wall Framing: 2x6

Foundation Options:

Slab

(All plans can be built with your choice of foundation and framing. A generic conversion diagram is available. See order form.)

BLUEPRINT PRICE CODE: G

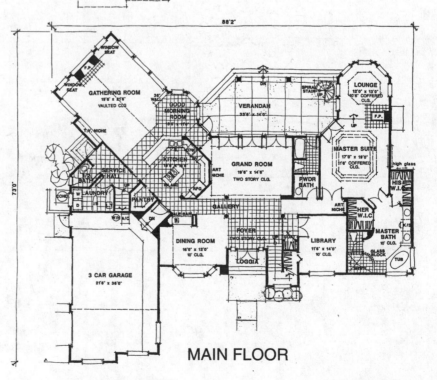

UPPER FLOOR

MAIN FLOOR

TO ORDER THIS BLUEPRINT,
CALL TOLL-FREE 1-800-547-5570

Plan EOF-61

PRICES AND DETAILS
ON PAGES 12-15

377

Estate Living

- This grand estate is as big and beautiful on the inside as it is on the outside.
- The formal dining room and parlor, each with a tall window, flank the entry's graceful curved staircase.
- The sunken family room is topped by a two-story-high ceiling and wrapped in floor-to-ceiling windows. A patio door opens to the covered porch, which features a nifty built-in barbecue.
- The island kitchen and the bright breakfast area also overlook the porch, with access through the deluxe utility room.

- The master suite has it all, including a romantic fireplace framed by bookshelves. The opulent bath offers a raised spa tub, a separate shower, his-and-hers walk-in closets and a dual-sink vanity. The neighboring bedroom, which also has a private bath, would make an ideal nursery.
- The upper floor hosts a balcony hall that provides a breathtaking view of the family room below. Each of the two bedrooms here has its own bath.
- The main floor is expanded by 10-ft. ceilings, while 9-ft. ceilings grace the upper floor.

Plan DD-4300-B	
Bedrooms: 4	**Baths:** 4½
Living Area:	
Upper floor	868 sq. ft.
Main floor	3,416 sq. ft.
Total Living Area:	**4,284 sq. ft.**
Standard basement	3,416 sq. ft.
Garage and storage	633 sq. ft.
Exterior Wall Framing:	2x4 or 2x6
Foundation Options:	
Standard basement	
Crawlspace	
Slab	

(All plans can be built with your choice of foundation and framing. A generic conversion diagram is available. See order form.)

BLUEPRINT PRICE CODE:	G

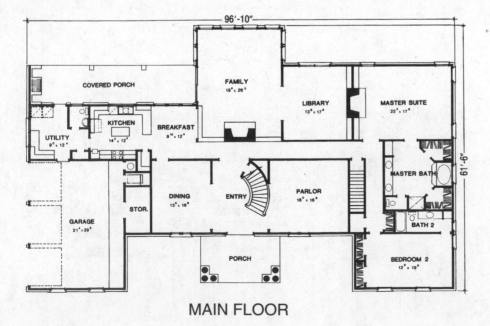

MAIN FLOOR

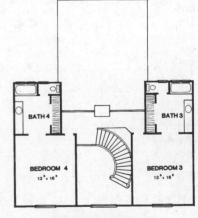

UPPER FLOOR

TO ORDER THIS BLUEPRINT, CALL TOLL-FREE 1-800-547-5570

Plan DD-4300-B

PRICES AND DETAILS ON PAGES 12-15

Elegance Perfected

- The grand style of this luxurious home brings elegance and grace to perfection.
- The contemporary architecture exudes an aura of grandeur, drawing the eye to its stately 2½-story entry portico.
- The interior is equally stunning with open, flowing spaces, high ceilings and decorative, room-defining columns.
- The formal zone is impressive, with a vast foyer and a sunken living room highlighted by dramatic window walls and a 20½-ft. ceiling. Round columns set off a stunning octagonal dining room with a 19-ft., 4-in. ceiling. A curved wet bar completes the effect!
- The informal areas consist of an island kitchen, a breakfast nook, a large family room and an octagonal media room. Activities can be extended to the covered back patio through doors in the breakfast nook and the family room.
- The fabulous master suite shows off a romantic fireplace, a 12-ft. ceiling, an enormous walk-in closet and a garden bath with a circular shower!
- Two more main-floor bedrooms, an upper-floor bedroom and loft area, plus two more baths complete the plan.

Plan HDS-90-819

Bedrooms: 4+	Baths: 3½
Living Area:	
Upper floor	765 sq. ft.
Main floor	3,770 sq. ft.
Total Living Area:	**4,535 sq. ft.**
Garage	750 sq. ft.
Exterior Wall Framing:	2x4

Foundation Options:

Slab
(All plans can be built with your choice of foundation and framing. A generic conversion diagram is available. See order form.)

BLUEPRINT PRICE CODE:	G

UPPER FLOOR

MAIN FLOOR

Spectacular Executive Estate

- The unique angular design of this executive home focuses attention on the spectacular entrance, which is enhanced by two balconies above.
- Beyond the vestibule, a 19-ft. ceiling presides over the columned Great Room and the sunny dining room. A two-story window wall overlooks the expansive backyard pool area.
- The gourmet island kitchen and breakfast nook open to a side deck and offer easy service to both the dining room and the family room.
- A nice-sized media room or library boasts two walls of built-ins.
- The master suite is a masterpiece, with its 15-ft. vaulted ceiling, romantic fireplace and sliding glass doors to a secluded sun deck and hot tub. The luxurious bath offers a whirlpool tub, a separate shower and two vanities.
- A classy, curved staircase accesses the upper floor, where three more bedrooms each have a private bath. A lounge with a window seat and a central area with outdoor balconies are other special appointments found here.

Plan B-05-85

Bedrooms: 4+	Baths: 4 full, 2 half
Living Area:	
Upper floor	1,720 sq. ft.
Main floor	3,900 sq. ft.
Total Living Area:	**5,620 sq. ft.**
Standard basement	3,900 sq. ft.
Garage	836 sq. ft.
Exterior Wall Framing:	2x6

Foundation Options:

Standard basement

(All plans can be built with your choice of foundation and framing. A generic conversion diagram is available. See order form.)

BLUEPRINT PRICE CODE: G

REAR VIEW

UPPER FLOOR

MAIN FLOOR

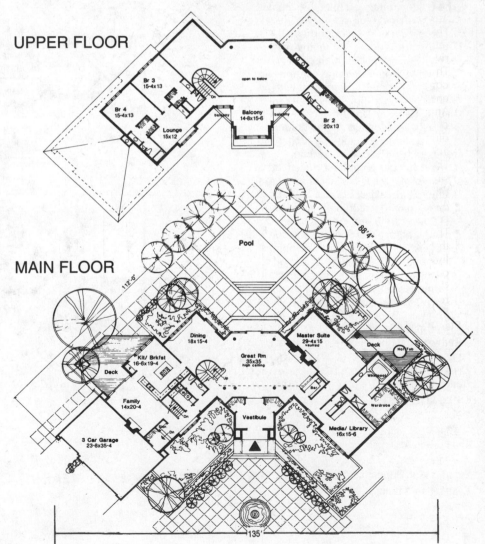

TO ORDER THIS BLUEPRINT, CALL TOLL-FREE 1-800-547-5570

Plan B-05-85

PRICES AND DETAILS ON PAGES 12-15

Cozy, Cost-Saving Retreat

- This cozy cabin is the perfect vacation retreat for that special mountain, lake or river location.
- The design is large enough to provide comfortable living quarters and small enough to fit a modest building budget.
- An 18½-ft. vaulted ceiling and expanses of glass add volume to the living and dining area. Double doors provide access to an inviting deck or patio.
- The U-shaped kitchen offers a bright sink and a convenient pass-through to the dining area.
- A quiet bedroom and a hall bath complete the main floor.
- The upper floor consists of a railed loft that provides sweeping views of the living areas below and the scenery outside. The loft could serve as an extra sleeping area or a quiet haven for reading, relaxing and other activities.

Plan I-880-A	
Bedrooms: 1+	**Baths:** 1
Living Area:	
Upper floor	308 sq. ft.
Main floor	572 sq. ft.
Total Living Area:	**880 sq. ft.**
Exterior Wall Framing:	2x6

Foundation Options:

Crawlspace

(All plans can be built with your choice of foundation and framing. A generic conversion diagram is available. See order form.)

BLUEPRINT PRICE CODE:	**A**

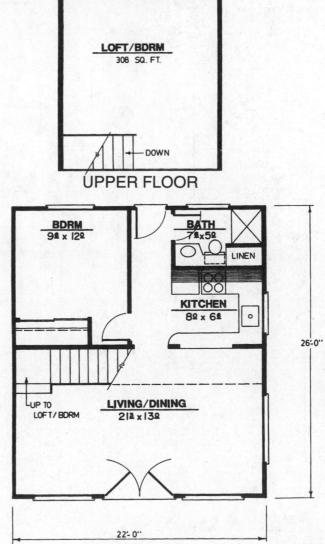

LOFT/BDRM
308 SQ. FT.

DOWN

UPPER FLOOR

BDRM
9² x 12²

BATH
7² x 5²

LINEN

KITCHEN
8² x 6²

UP TO
LOFT/BDRM

LIVING/DINING
21² x 13²

26'-0"

22'-0"

MAIN FLOOR

Relax in the Country

- This country home provides plenty of room to relax, with its covered porches and wide-open living spaces.
- Just off the front porch, the living room boasts a two-story-high cathedral ceiling and a soothing fireplace with a raised brick hearth.
- The adjoining dining room opens to the backyard porch and merges with the bright walk-through kitchen.
- In between the kitchen and the main-floor master bedroom are a pantry, a full bath with a whirlpool tub and a laundry closet housing a stackable washer and dryer.
- The master bedroom boasts two closets, views of the front porch and private access to the bath.
- An open stairway with an oak rail leads to the upper-floor bedroom, which features a window seat, a pair of closets and access to extra storage space.

Plan J-90016

Bedrooms: 2	Baths: 1
Living Area:	
Upper floor	203 sq. ft.
Main floor	720 sq. ft.
Total Living Area:	**923 sq. ft.**
Standard basement	720 sq. ft.
Exterior Wall Framing:	2x6

Foundation Options:

Standard basement
Crawlspace
Slab

(All plans can be built with your choice of foundation and framing. A generic conversion diagram is available. See order form.)

BLUEPRINT PRICE CODE:	A

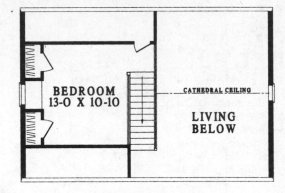

UPPER FLOOR

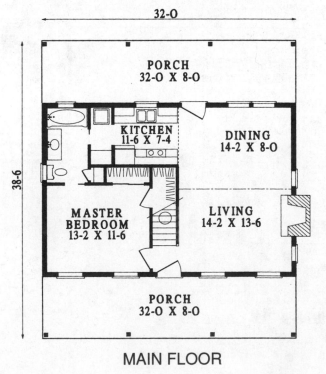

MAIN FLOOR

TO ORDER THIS BLUEPRINT, CALL TOLL-FREE 1-800-547-5570

Plan J-90016

PRICES AND DETAILS ON PAGES 12-15

Sunny Chalet

- This captivating home is designed to maximize indoor and outdoor living. It features expansive windows, an open main floor and a large deck.
- The lower-level entry leads up a staircase to the spacious living room, which features a 12-ft. cathedral ceiling, an energy-efficient fireplace, a railed balcony overlooking the foyer and sliding glass doors to the deck.
- The adjacent bayed dining room merges with the skylighted kitchen, which also boasts a handy serving bar.
- The lower floor features two spacious bedrooms that share a full bath, complete with a whirlpool tub.
- The quiet den could serve as a third bedroom or a guest room.

Plan K-532-L	
Bedrooms: 2+	**Baths:** 1½
Living Area:	
Main floor	492 sq. ft.
Lower floor	488 sq. ft.
Total Living Area:	**980 sq. ft.**
Exterior Wall Framing:	2x4 or 2x6
Foundation Options:	

Crawlspace
(All plans can be built with your choice of foundation and framing. A generic conversion diagram is available. See order form.)

BLUEPRINT PRICE CODE: A

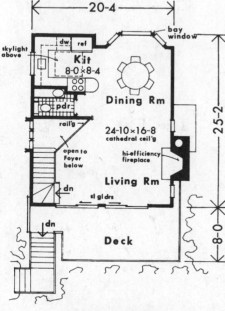

MAIN FLOOR

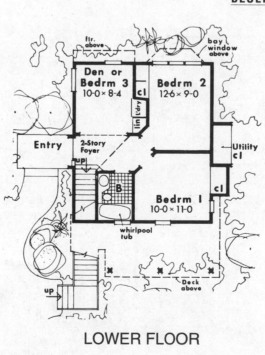

LOWER FLOOR

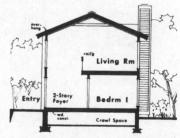

SECTION

VIEW INTO LIVING ROOM AND DINING ROOM

Casual Flexibility

- This beautifully designed vacation or year-round home is spacious and flexible.
- The interior is brightened by an abundance of windows.
- The open, vaulted living room boasts a central fireplace that makes a great conversation place or a cozy spot for spending cold winter evenings.
- The kitchen opens to the dining room and the scenery beyond through the dramatic window wall with half-round transom.
- The sleeping room and loft upstairs can easily accommodate several guests or could be used as multi-purpose space.

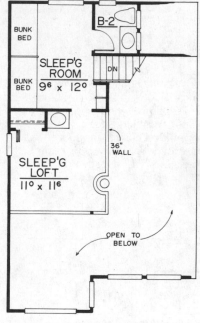

UPPER FLOOR

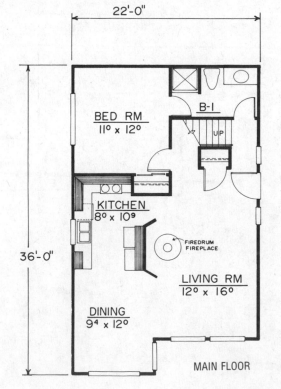

MAIN FLOOR

Plan I-1032-A

Plan I-1032-A	
Bedrooms: 2-3	**Baths:** 1½
Living Area:	
Upper floor	288 sq. ft.
Main floor	744 sq. ft.
Total Living Area:	**1,032 sq. ft.**
Exterior Wall Framing:	2x6
Foundation Options:	
Crawlspace	
(Typical foundation & framing conversion diagram available—see order form.)	
BLUEPRINT PRICE CODE:	A

Weekend Retreat

For those whose goal is a small, affordable retreat at the shore or in the mountains, this plan may be the answer. Although it measures less than 400 sq. ft. of living space on the main floor, it lacks nothing in comfort and convenience. A sizeable living room boasts a masonry hearth on which to mount your choice of a wood stove or a pre-fab fireplace. There is plenty of room for furniture, including a dining table.

The galley-type kitchen is a small marvel of compact convenience and utility, even boasting a dishwasher and space for a stackable washer and dryer. The wide open nature of the first floor guarantees that even the person working in the kitchen area will still be included in the party. On the floor plan, a dashed line across the living room indicates the limits of the balcony bedroom above. In front of this line, the A-frame shape of the living room soars from the floor boards to the ridge beam high above. Clerestory windows lend a further note of spaciousness and unity with nature's outdoors. A huge planked deck adds to the indoor-outdoor relationship.

A modest-sized bedroom on the second floor is approached by a standard stairway, not an awkward ladder or heavy pull-down stairway as is often the case in small A-frames. The view over the balcony rail to the living room below adds a note of distinction. The unique framing pattern allows a window at either end of the bedroom, improving both outlook and ventilation.

A compact bathroom serves both levels and enjoys natural daylight through a skylight window.

First floor:	391 sq. ft.
Upper level:	144 sq. ft.
Total living area:	535 sq. ft.

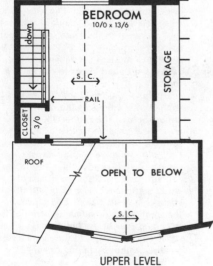

UPPER LEVEL
144 SQUARE FEET

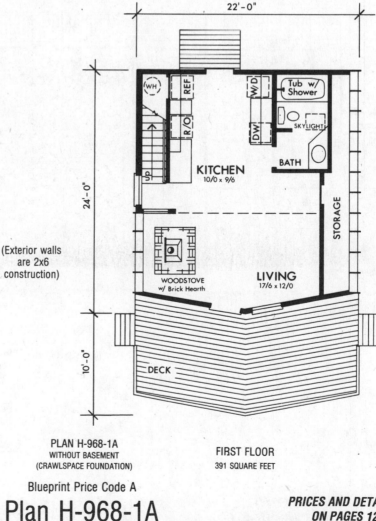

(Exterior walls are 2x6 construction)

PLAN H-968-1A
WITHOUT BASEMENT
(CRAWLSPACE FOUNDATION)

FIRST FLOOR
391 SQUARE FEET

Blueprint Price Code A

Plan H-968-1A

PRICES AND DETAILS ON PAGES 12-15

Carefree Vacation Home

Scoffers and non-believers had a field day when the A-Frame first began to appear. Impractical, some said; uncomfortable, declared others; too expensive, ugly and more. And yet people built them and enjoyed them — and like the Volkswagen Bug, found them to be economical and practical, and yes, even beautiful to many beholders. Through the years, there has been a steady demand for these ubiquitous structures, and Plan H-15-1 is one of our more popular models. With this design, you will not be experimenting or pioneering because it has been built sucessfully many times.

Though it covers only 654 sq. ft. of main floor living space, it boasts an oversized living/dining room, a U-shaped kitchen, large bedroom and closet spaces, fully equipped bath plus a standard stairway (not a ladder) to the large second floor balcony dormitory. An old fashioned wood stove or a modern pre-fabricated fireplace adds warmth and cheer to the main living room.

The huge glass wall that dominates the front facade enhances the romantic atmosphere of the vaulted interior. And in ideal locations, where this wall can face south, a surprising amount of solar energy can help minimize heating costs.

One particular advantage of the A-Frame as a part-time or holiday home is easy maintenance. Use of penetrating stains that resist flaking and powdering on the small areas of siding and trim at the front and rear of the building is all that is required. The rest is roofing which resists weather without painting or other treatment.

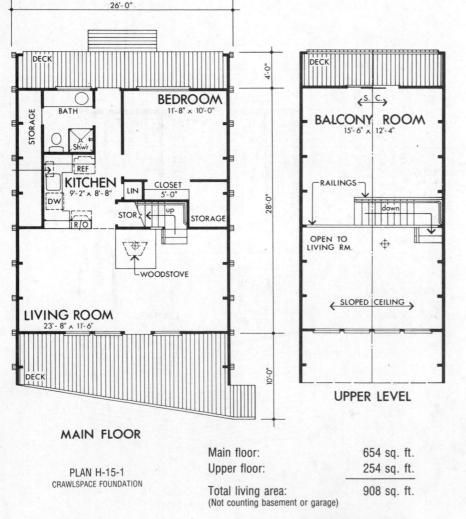

MAIN FLOOR

PLAN H-15-1
CRAWLSPACE FOUNDATION

UPPER LEVEL

Main floor:	654 sq. ft.
Upper floor:	254 sq. ft.
Total living area:	908 sq. ft.

(Not counting basement or garage)

Blueprint Price Code A

Plan H-15-1

PRICES AND DETAILS
ON PAGES 12-15

Build It Yourself

- Everything you need for a leisure or retirement retreat is neatly packaged in this affordable, easy-to-build design.
- The basic rectangular shape features a unique wraparound deck, entirely covered by a projecting roofline.
- A central fireplace and a vaulted ceiling that rises to 10 ft. visually enhance the cozy living and dining rooms.
- The efficient kitchen offers convenient service to the adjoining dining room. In the crawlspace version, the kitchen also includes a snack bar.
- Two main-floor bedrooms share a large full bath.
- The daylight-basement option is suitable for building on a sloping lot and consists of an extra bedroom, a general-purpose area and a garage.

Plans H-833-7 & -7A

Bedrooms: 2+	Baths: 1
Living Area:	
Main floor	952 sq. ft.
Daylight basement	676 sq. ft.
Total Living Area:	**952/1,628 sq. ft.**
Tuck-under garage	276 sq. ft.
Exterior Wall Framing:	2x6
Foundation Options:	**Plan #**
Daylight basement	H-833-7
Crawlspace	H-833-7A

(All plans can be built with your choice of foundation and framing.
A generic conversion diagram is available. See order form.)

BLUEPRINT PRICE CODE:	**A/B**

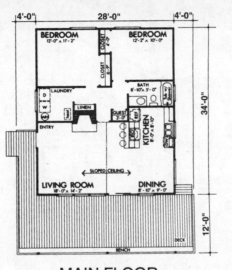

MAIN FLOOR
Crawlspace version

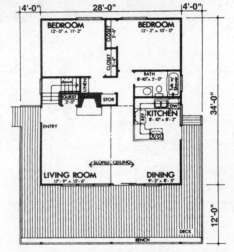

MAIN FLOOR
Basement version

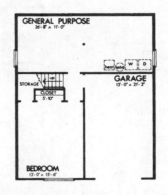

DAYLIGHT BASEMENT

UPPER FLOOR

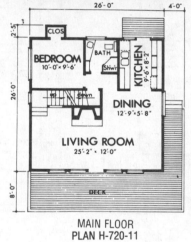

MAIN FLOOR
PLAN H-720-11

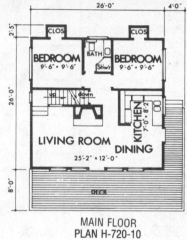

MAIN FLOOR
PLAN H-720-10

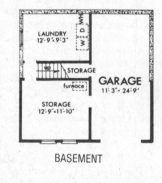

BASEMENT

Chalet with Variations

- Attractive chalet offers several main level variations, with second floor and basement layouts identical.
- All versions feature well-arranged kitchen, attached dining area, and large living room.
- Second-floor amenities include private decks off each bedroom and storage space in every corner!

MAIN FLOOR
PLAN H-720-12A
WITHOUT BASEMENT

Plans H-720-10, -11 & -12A

Bedrooms: 3-4	Baths: 2

Space:	
Upper floor:	328 sq. ft.
Main floor:	686 sq. ft.

Total living area:	1,014 sq. ft.
Basement:	approx. 686 sq. ft.
Garage: (incl. in basement)	278 sq. ft.

Exterior Wall Framing:	2x4

Foundation options:
Daylight basement
   (Plans H-720-10 or -11).
Crawlspace (Plan H-720-12A)
(Foundation & framing conversion
diagram available — see order form.)

Blueprint Price Code:

Without basement:	A
With basement:	B

Plans H-720-10, -11 & -12A
PRICES AND DETAILS
ON PAGES 12-15

Compact, Easy to Build

This compact vacation or retirement home is economical and easy to construct. Only 24' x 46' for the daylight basement version, it nonetheless contains all the necessities and some of the luxuries one desires in a three-bedroom home. The non-basement version measures 24' x 44'.

Overall width for both versions including deck and carport is 50'.

One luxury is the separate, private bath adjoining the master bedroom; another is the double "His & Hers" wardrobe closets for the same room. The other two bedrooms are equipped with good-sized closets and share a second bathroom. Even if you choose the basement version, the convenience of first floor laundry facilities is yours.

The open stairway to the basement adds 3' to the visual size of the living room. A

pre-fab fireplace is located to allow enjoyment of a cozy hearth and a beautiful view from the same chair.

The plans are so completely detailed that a handyman amateur might frame this building (with the help of a few friends). Why not try it? (Be sure to order a materials list, too!).

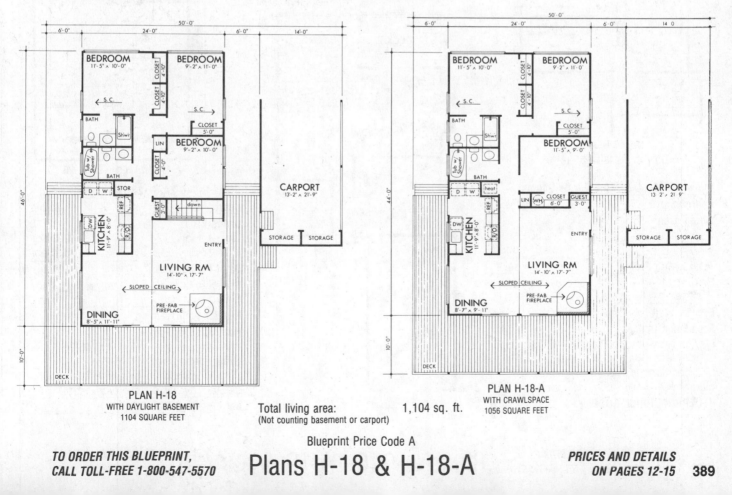

PLAN H-18
WITH DAYLIGHT BASEMENT
1104 SQUARE FEET

Total living area: 1,104 sq. ft.
(Not counting basement or carport)

PLAN H-18-A
WITH CRAWLSPACE
1056 SQUARE FEET

Blueprint Price Code A

Plans H-18 & H-18-A

Narrow-Lot Solar Design

- This design offers your choice of foundation and number of bedrooms, and it can be built on a narrow, sloping lot.
- The passive-solar dining room has windows on three sides and a slate floor for heat storage. A French door leads to a rear deck.
- The living room features a sloped ceiling, a woodstove in ceiling-high masonry, and sliding glass doors to the adjoining deck.
- The kitchen is open to the dining room but separated from the living room by a 7½-ft.-high wall.
- The upper-level variations include a choice of one or two bedrooms. Clerestory windows above the balcony railing add drama to both versions.

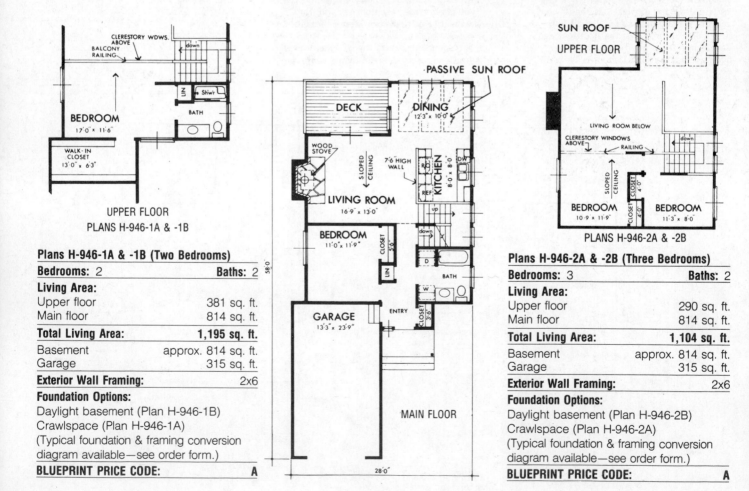

UPPER FLOOR
PLANS H-946-1A & -1B

Plans H-946-1A & -1B (Two Bedrooms)

Bedrooms: 2	Baths: 2
Living Area:	
Upper floor	381 sq. ft.
Main floor	814 sq. ft.
Total Living Area:	**1,195 sq. ft.**
Basement	approx. 814 sq. ft.
Garage	315 sq. ft.
Exterior Wall Framing:	2x6

Foundation Options:
Daylight basement (Plan H-946-1B)
Crawlspace (Plan H-946-1A)
(Typical foundation & framing conversion diagram available—see order form.)

BLUEPRINT PRICE CODE: A

UPPER FLOOR

MAIN FLOOR

PLANS H-946-2A & -2B

Plans H-946-2A & -2B (Three Bedrooms)

Bedrooms: 3	Baths: 2
Living Area:	
Upper floor	290 sq. ft.
Main floor	814 sq. ft.
Total Living Area:	**1,104 sq. ft.**
Basement	approx. 814 sq. ft.
Garage	315 sq. ft.
Exterior Wall Framing:	2x6

Foundation Options:
Daylight basement (Plan H-946-2B)
Crawlspace (Plan H-946-2A)
(Typical foundation & framing conversion diagram available—see order form.)

BLUEPRINT PRICE CODE: A

Plans H-946-1A/1B & -2A/2B

PRICES AND DETAILS ON PAGES 12-15

Active Living Made Easy

- This home is perfect for active living. Its rectangular design allows the use of truss roof framing, which makes construction easy and economical.
- The galley-style kitchen and the sunny dining area are kept open to the living room, forming one huge activity space. Two sets of sliding glass doors expand the living area to the large deck.

- The secluded master bedroom offers a private bath, while the remaining bedrooms share a hall bath.
- The two baths, the laundry facilities and the kitchen are clustered to allow common plumbing walls.
- Plan H-921-1A has a standard crawlspace foundation and an optional solar-heating system. Plan H-921-2A has a Plen-Wood system, which utilizes the sealed crawlspace as a chamber for distributing heated or cooled air. Both versions of the design call for energy-efficient 2x6 exterior walls.

Plans H-921-1A & -2A	
Bedrooms: 3	**Baths: 2**
Living Area:	
Main floor	1,164 sq. ft.
Total Living Area:	**1,164 sq. ft.**
Exterior Wall Framing:	2x6
Foundation Options:	**Plan #**
Crawlspace	H-921-1A
Plen-Wood crawlspace	H-921-2A

(All plans can be built with your choice of foundation and framing. A generic conversion diagram is available. See order form.)

BLUEPRINT PRICE CODE:	**A**

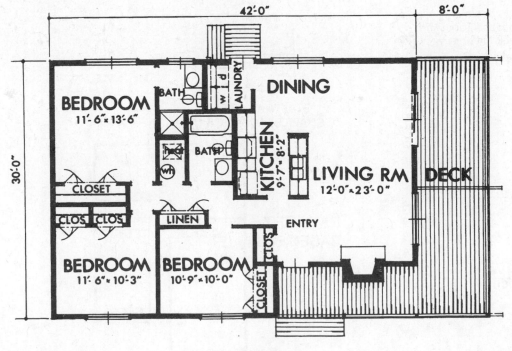

MAIN FLOOR

Suspended Sun Room

- This narrow-lot design is a perfect combination of economical structure and luxurious features.
- The living and dining rooms flow together to create a great space for parties or family gatherings. A 16-ft. sloped ceiling and clerestory windows add drama and brightness. A fabulous deck expands the entertaining area.
- An exciting sun room provides the advantages of passive-solar heating.
- The sunny, efficient kitchen is open to the dining room.
- A full bath serves the two isolated main-floor bedrooms.
- The optional daylight basement includes an additional bedroom and bath as well as a tuck-under garage and storage space.

Plans H-951-1A & -1B

Bedrooms: 2+	Baths: 1-2
Living Area:	
Main floor	1,075 sq. ft.
Sun room	100 sq. ft.
Daylight basement	662 sq. ft.
Total Living Area:	**1,175/1,837 sq. ft.**
Tuck-under garage	311 sq. ft.
Exterior Wall Framing:	2x6
Foundation Options:	**Plan #**
Daylight basement	H-951-1B
Crawlspace	H-951-1A

(All plans can be built with your choice of foundation and framing. A generic conversion diagram is available. See order form.)

BLUEPRINT PRICE CODE:	**A/B**

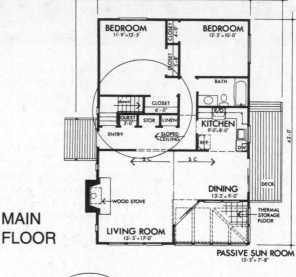

MAIN FLOOR

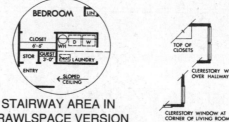

STAIRWAY AREA IN CRAWLSPACE VERSION

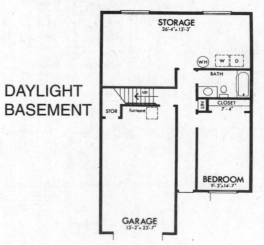

DAYLIGHT BASEMENT

Plans H-951-1A & -1B

PRICES AND DETAILS ON PAGES 12-15

FRONT VIEW

REAR VIEW

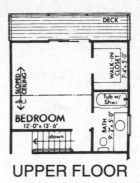

UPPER FLOOR

Easy Living

- The living is easy in this affordable home, which is perfect for a scenic lot.
- Five steps down from the entry, the main living areas look out over an inviting wraparound deck. The living room offers a 16-ft.-high sloped ceiling, a handsome fireplace and deck access. A snack bar separates the sunny kitchen from the spacious dining area. Additional deck access is provided near the laundry area.
- Two bedrooms near the main entrance share a bath and feature 13-ft. sloped ceilings.
- The secluded upper-floor master suite boasts a 14-ft. vaulted ceiling, a walk-in closet, a full bath and a private deck.

Plans H-925-1 & -1A

Bedrooms: 3	Baths: 2
Living Area:	
Upper floor	288 sq. ft.
Main floor	951 sq. ft.
Total Living Area:	**1,239 sq. ft.**
Daylight basement	951 sq. ft.
Garage	266 sq. ft.
Exterior Wall Framing:	2x4
Foundation Options:	**Plan #**
Daylight basement	H-925-1
Crawlspace	H-925-1A

(All plans can be built with your choice of foundation and framing. A generic conversion diagram is available. See order form.)

BLUEPRINT PRICE CODE: **A**

MAIN FLOOR

STAIRWAY AREA IN CRAWLSPACE VERSION

Sun-Soaked Leisure Home

- This eye-catching leisure home is accented with vertical and diagonal siding and soaked in sunlight from dynamic clerestory windows.
- A generous amount of living space and three bedrooms are neatly packaged to maximize the home's square footage.
- The exciting Great Room covers half of the main floor and is open to the upper floor. A dramatic woodstove serves as the focal point of the room, which adjoins the dining area, the kitchen and a large deck. This entire area is enhanced by a 16½-ft. vaulted ceiling and clerestory windows.
- The main-floor master bedroom offers two closets and a nearby bath. A nice laundry room is just off the entrance.
- The upper floor includes two more bedrooms that are separated by a full bath. The balcony hall provides a dramatic view to the rooms below.

Plan P-520-D	
Bedrooms: 3	**Baths: 2**
Living Area:	
Upper floor	448 sq. ft.
Main floor	823 sq. ft.
Total Living Area:	**1,271 sq. ft.**
Garage/Shop	702 sq. ft.
Exterior Wall Framing:	2x6
Foundation Options:	
Daylight basement	

(All plans can be built with your choice of foundation and framing. A generic conversion diagram is available. See order form.)

BLUEPRINT PRICE CODE: **A**

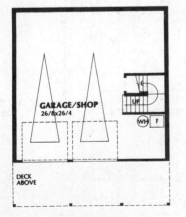

DAYLIGHT BASEMENT

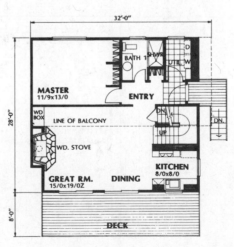

MAIN FLOOR

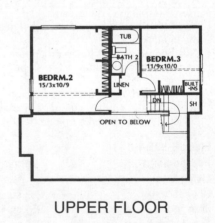

UPPER FLOOR

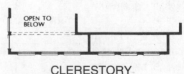

CLERESTORY WINDOWS

Spacious
Swiss Chalet

- Three decks, lots of views and Swiss styling make this three-bedroom chalet the perfect design for that special site.
- A stone-faced fireplace is the focal point of the huge central living area. Sliding glass doors between the living room and the dining room lead to the large main-level deck. The space-saving kitchen conveniently serves the entire entertaining area.
- The main-floor bedroom is close to a full bath. The oversized laundry room doubles as a mudroom.
- Upstairs, each of the two bedrooms has a sloped ceiling, accessible attic storage space and a private deck.
- The optional daylight basement provides space for utilities as well as the opportunity for expansion. In the crawlspace version of the design, the furnace and water heater are located in the laundry room.

Plans H-755-5E & -6E	
Bedrooms: 3	**Baths: 2**
Living Area:	
Upper floor	454 sq. ft.
Main floor	896 sq. ft.
Daylight basement	896 sq. ft.
Total Living Area:	**1,350/2,246 sq. ft.**
Exterior Wall Framing:	2x4
Foundation Options:	**Plan #**
Daylight basement	H-755-6E
Crawlspace	H-755-5E
(All plans can be built with your choice of foundation and framing. A generic conversion diagram is available. See order form.)	
BLUEPRINT PRICE CODE:	**A/C**

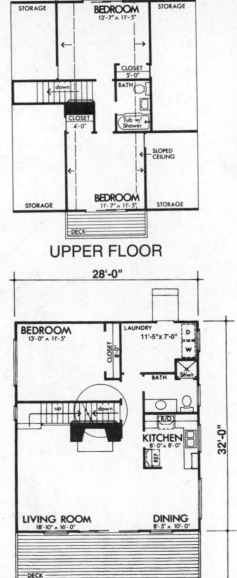

UPPER FLOOR

DAYLIGHT BASEMENT

MAIN FLOOR

STAIRWAY AREA IN
CRAWLSPACE
VERSION

Vacation Home with Views

- The octagonal shape and window-filled walls of this home create a powerful interior packed with panoramic views.
- Straight back from the angled entry, the Great Room is brightened by expansive windows and sliding glass doors to a huge wraparound deck. An impressive spiral staircase at the center of the floor plan lends even more character.
- The walk-through kitchen offers a handy pantry. A nice storage closet and a coat closet are located between the entry and the two-car garage.
- The main-floor bedroom is conveniently located near a full bath.
- The upper-floor master suite is a sanctuary, featuring lots of glass, a walk-in closet, a private bath and access to concealed storage rooms.
- The optional daylight basement offers an extra bedroom, a full bath, a laundry area and a large recreation room.

Plans H-964-1A & -1B

Bedrooms: 2+	Baths: 2-3
Living Area:	
Upper floor	346 sq. ft.
Main floor	1,067 sq. ft.
Daylight basement	1,045 sq. ft.
Total Living Area:	**1,413/2,458 sq. ft.**
Garage	512 sq. ft.
Storage (upper floor)	134 sq. ft.
Exterior Wall Framing:	2x6
Foundation Options:	**Plan #**
Daylight basement	H-964-1B
Crawlspace	H-964-1A

(All plans can be built with your choice of foundation and framing. A generic conversion diagram is available. See order form.)

BLUEPRINT PRICE CODE:	**A/C**

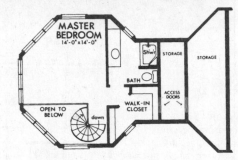

UPPER FLOOR

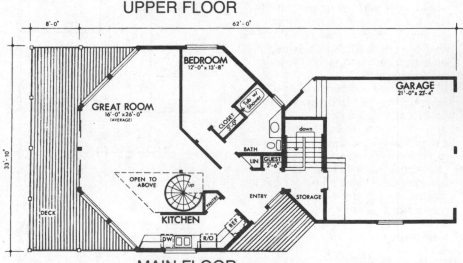

MAIN FLOOR

DAYLIGHT BASEMENT

TO ORDER THIS BLUEPRINT, CALL TOLL-FREE 1-800-547-5570 Plans H-964-1A & -1B **PRICES AND DETAILS ON PAGES 12-15**

Eye-Catching Chalet

- Steep rooflines, dramatic windows and wide cornices give this chalet a distinctive alpine appearance.
- The large living and dining area offers a striking 20-ft.-high vaulted ceiling and a breathtaking view of the outdoors through a soaring wall of windows. Sliding glass doors access an inviting wood deck.

- The efficient U-shaped kitchen shares an eating bar with the dining area.
- Two main-floor bedrooms share a hall bath, and laundry facilities are nearby.
- The upper floor hosts a master bedroom with a 12-ft. vaulted ceiling, plenty of storage space and easy access to a full bath with a shower.
- The pièce de résistance is a balcony with a 12-ft. vaulted ceiling, offering sweeping outdoor views as well as an overlook into the living/dining area below. Additional storage areas flank the balcony.

Plans H-886-3 & -3A	
Bedrooms: 3	**Baths:** 2
Living Area:	
Upper floor	486 sq. ft.
Main floor	994 sq. ft.
Total Living Area:	**1,480 sq. ft.**
Daylight basement	715 sq. ft.
Tuck-under garage	279 sq. ft.
Exterior Wall Framing:	2x6
Foundation Options:	**Plan #**
Daylight basement	H-886-3
Crawlspace	H-886-3A

(All plans can be built with your choice of foundation and framing. A generic conversion diagram is available. See order form.)

BLUEPRINT PRICE CODE:	**A**

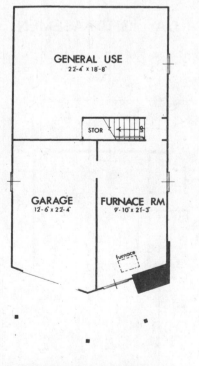

DAYLIGHT BASEMENT

MAIN FLOOR

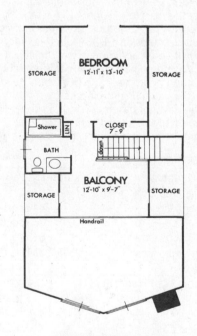

UPPER FLOOR

Unique and Dramatic

- This home's unique interior and dramatic exterior make it perfect for a sloping, scenic lot.
- The expansive and impressive Great Room, warmed by a woodstove, flows into the island kitchen, which is completely open in design.
- The passive-solar sun room collects and stores heat from the sun, while offering a good view of the surroundings. Its ceiling rises to a height of 16 feet.
- Upstairs, a glamorous, skylighted master suite features an 11-ft. vaulted ceiling, a private bath and a huge walk-in closet.
- A skylighted hall bath serves the bright second bedroom. Both bedrooms open to the vaulted sun room below.
- The daylight basement adds a sunny sitting room, a third bedroom and a large recreation room.

Plans P-536-2A & -2D

Bedrooms: 2+	Baths: 2½-3½
Living Area:	
Upper floor	642 sq. ft.
Main floor	863 sq. ft.
Daylight basement	863 sq. ft.
Total Living Area:	**1,505/2,368 sq. ft.**
Garage	445 sq. ft.
Exterior Wall Framing:	2x6
Foundation Options:	**Plan #**
Daylight basement	P-536-2D
Crawlspace	P-536-2A

(All plans can be built with your choice of foundation and framing. A generic conversion diagram is available. See order form.)

BLUEPRINT PRICE CODE:	**B/C**

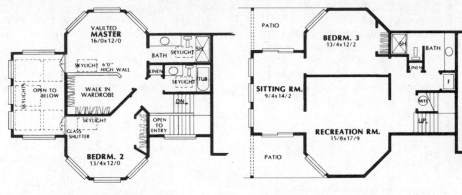

UPPER FLOOR

DAYLIGHT BASEMENT

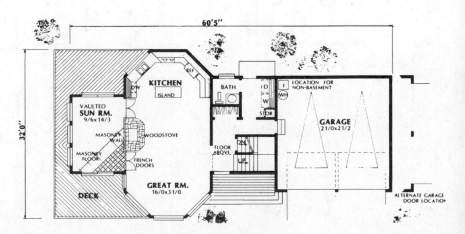

MAIN FLOOR

Hillside Design Fits Contours

- The daylight-basement version of this popular plan is perfect for a scenic, sloping lot.
- A large, wraparound deck embraces the rear-oriented living areas, accessed through sliding glass doors.
- The spectacular living room boasts a corner fireplace and a 19-ft. vaulted ceiling with three clerestory windows.
- The secluded master suite upstairs offers a walk-in closet, a private bath and sliding doors to a sun deck.
- The daylight basement (not shown) includes a fourth bedroom with a private bath and a walk-in closet, as well as a recreation room with a fireplace and access to a rear patio.
- The standard basement (not shown) includes a recreation room with a fireplace and a room for hobbies or child's play.
- Both basements also have a large unfinished area below the main-floor bedrooms.

REAR VIEW

UPPER FLOOR

STAIRWAY AREA IN CRAWLSPACE VERSION

Plans H-877-4, -4A & -4B

Bedrooms: 3+	Baths: 2-3
Living Area:	
Upper floor	333 sq. ft.
Main floor	1,200 sq. ft.
Basement (finished area)	591 sq. ft.
Total Living Area:	**1,533/2,124 sq. ft.**
Basement (unfinished area)	493 sq. ft.
Garage	480 sq. ft.
Exterior Wall Framing:	2x6
Foundation Options:	**Plan #**
Daylight basement	H-877-4B
Standard basement	H-877-4
Crawlspace	H-877-4A

(All plans can be built with your choice of foundation and framing. A generic conversion diagram is available. See order form.)

BLUEPRINT PRICE CODE: B/C

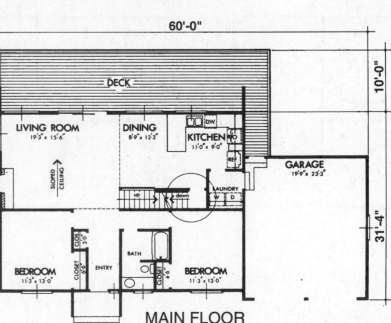

MAIN FLOOR

Romantic Retreat

- The romance and appeal of the Alpine chalet have remained constant over time. With more than 1,500 sq. ft. of living area, this chalet would make a great full-time home or vacation retreat.
- The L-shaped living room, dining room and kitchen flow together for casual living. This huge area is warmed by a

freestanding fireplace and surrounded by an ornate deck, which is accessed through sliding glass doors.
- The main-level bedroom, with its twin closets and adjacent bath, could serve as a nice master suite.
- Upstairs, two large bedrooms share another full bath. One bedroom features a walk-in closet, while the other boasts its own private deck.
- The daylight basement offers laundry facilities, plenty of storage space and an extra-long garage.

Plan H-858-2

Bedrooms: 3	Baths: 2
Living Area:	
Upper floor	576 sq. ft.
Main floor	960 sq. ft.
Total Living Area:	**1,536 sq. ft.**
Daylight basement	530 sq. ft.
Tuck-under garage	430 sq. ft.
Exterior Wall Framing:	2x6

Foundation Options:

Daylight basement

(All plans can be built with your choice of foundation and framing. A generic conversion diagram is available. See order form.)

BLUEPRINT PRICE CODE:	B

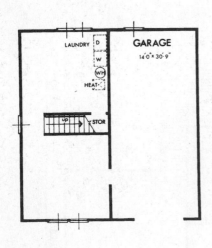

DAYLIGHT BASEMENT

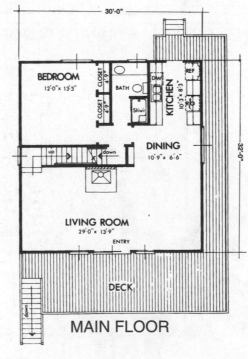

MAIN FLOOR

UPPER FLOOR

TO ORDER THIS BLUEPRINT, CALL TOLL-FREE 1-800-547-5570　　Plan H-858-2　　*PRICES AND DETAILS ON PAGES 12-15*

At One with the Sun

- This two-bedroom ranch home combines an open floor plan with large expanses of glass to get the most out of the sun.
- The vaulted kitchen faces a cheerful sun porch on one side and opens to the dining and living rooms on the other.
- The dining and living rooms are combined to create one huge area, which is enhanced by vaulted ceilings and views of the large rear deck. A corner fireplace radiates warmth to the entire living area.
- The master bedroom has twin walk-in closets and a private bath. Another full bath, a laundry closet and a den or second bedroom complete the efficient plan.
- The full basement offers more potential living space.

Plan B-91012

Bedrooms: 2	Baths: 2
Space:	
Main floor	1,421 sq. ft.
Total Living Area	**1,421 sq. ft.**
Basement	1,421 sq. ft.
Garage	440 sq. ft.
Exterior Wall Framing	2x4

Foundation options:

Standard Basement
(Foundation & framing conversion diagram available—see order form.)

Blueprint Price Code	A

REAR VIEW

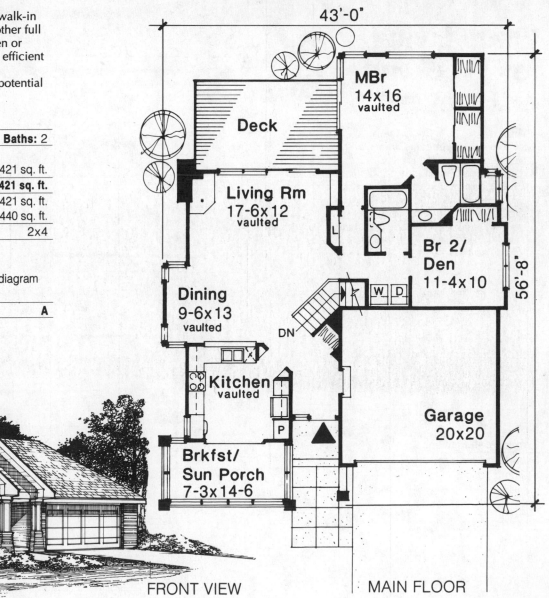

FRONT VIEW

MAIN FLOOR

TO ORDER THIS BLUEPRINT,
CALL TOLL-FREE 1-800-547-5570

Plan B-91012

PRICES AND DETAILS
ON PAGES 12-15

401

Open Living for Weekend or Forever

- This cozy, 1 1/2 story home is perfect for a weekend retreat, summer home, or casual permanent residence.
- A large, open living area on the first level combines the kitchen, dining area and living room for a spacious setting; sliding doors to the front offer an outdoor relaxing or dining alternative.
- Two bedrooms and a full bath are located at the rear, both with closet space.
- The upper loft would be ideal for a private master bedroom or quiet study area.

Plan CPS-1095

Bedrooms: 2-3	Baths: 1
Space:	
Upper floor	320 sq. ft.
Main floor	784 sq. ft.
Total Living Area	**1,104 sq. ft.**
Basement	784 sq. ft.
Exterior Wall Framing	2x6
Foundation options:	
Standard Basement	
(Foundation & framing conversion diagram available—see order form.)	
Blueprint Price Code	**A**

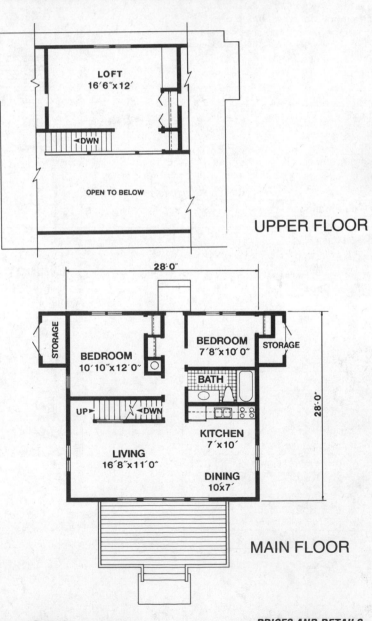

UPPER FLOOR

LOFT
16'6"x12'

DWN

OPEN TO BELOW

MAIN FLOOR

28'-0"

28'-0"

STORAGE

BEDROOM
10'10"x12'0"

BEDROOM
7'8"x10'0"

STORAGE

BATH

UP   DWN

KITCHEN
7'x10'

LIVING
16'8"x11'0"

DINING
10'x7'

Affordable Alternative

- A rustic contemporary exterior surrounds an efficient plan to create an affordable rec home.
- The design would be well-suited to a ski or water location for winter or summer enjoyment.
- The heart of the plan is the dramatic vaulted fireside living room with fireplace and an optional built-in sofa.
- The informal galley ktichen serves the dining room while enjoying plenty of views on three sides.
- The sleeping quarters upstairs can accommodate up to two bedrooms with a second full bath in-between.

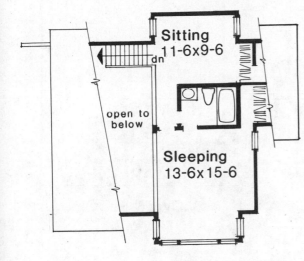

Sitting 11-6x9-6

dn

open to below

Sleeping 13-6x15-6

UPPER FLOOR

Plan B-7635

Bedrooms: 1-2	**Baths:** 2

Space:

Upper floor:	452 sq. ft.
Main floor:	700 sq. ft.
Total living area:	1,152 sq. ft.
Exterior Wall Framing:	2x4

Foundation options:
Crawlspace.
(Foundation & framing conversion diagram available — see order form.)

Blueprint Price Code: A

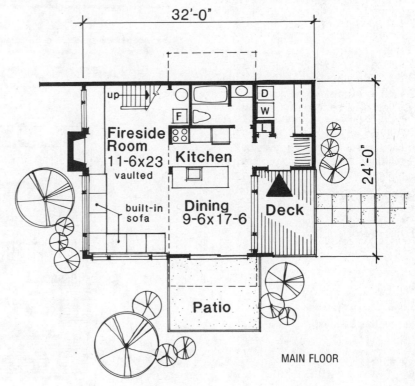

32'-0"

24'-0"

up

Fireside Room 11-6x23 vaulted

Kitchen

built-in sofa

Dining 9-6x17-6

Deck

Patio

MAIN FLOOR

Space-Saving Tri-Level

- This clever tri-level design offers an open, airy interior while taking up a minimum of land space.
- The Great Room features a spectacular 15-ft. vaulted and skylighted ceiling, an inviting woodstove and sliding glass doors to a full-width deck.
- The Great Room also incorporates a dining area, which is easily serviced from the efficient, space-saving kitchen.
- The main-floor bedroom boasts two closets. A compact laundry closet, a guest closet and a storage area line the hallway to the spacious main bath.
- The large loft offers infinite possibilities, such as extra sleeping quarters, a home office, an art studio or a recreation room. Clerestory windows and a sloped ceiling enhance the bright, airy feeling.
- The tuck-under garage saves on building costs and lets you make the most of your lot.

Plan H-963-2A

Bedrooms: 1+	Baths: 1
Living Area:	
Upper floor	432 sq. ft.
Main floor	728 sq. ft.
Total Living Area:	**1,160 sq. ft.**
Tuck-under garage	728 sq. ft.
Exterior Wall Framing:	2x4

Foundation Options:

Slab
(All plans can be built with your choice of foundation and framing. A generic conversion diagram is available. See order form.)

BLUEPRINT PRICE CODE: A

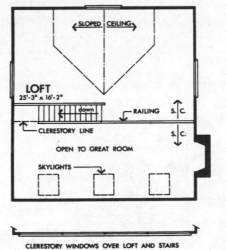

UPPER FLOOR

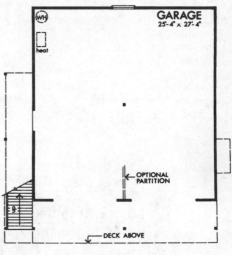

LOWER FLOOR

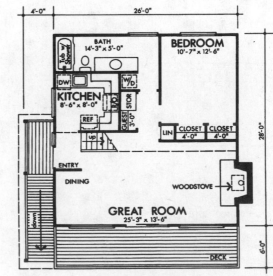

MAIN FLOOR

TO ORDER THIS BLUEPRINT, CALL TOLL-FREE 1-800-547-5570

Plan H-963-2A

PRICES AND DETAILS ON PAGES 12-15

Super Chalet

- The charming Alpine detailing of the exterior and the open, flexible layout of the interior make this one of our most popular plans.
- In from the large front deck, the living room wraps around a central fireplace or woodstove, providing a warm and expansive multipurpose living space. Sliding glass doors open to the deck for outdoor entertaining.
- The adjoining dining room is easily serviced from the galley-style kitchen. A convenient full bath serves a nearby bedroom and the remainder of the main floor.
- Two upper-floor bedrooms have 12-ft.-high sloped ceilings, extra closet space and access to another full bath. The larger bedroom offers sliding glass doors to a lofty deck.
- The blueprints recommend finishing the interior walls with solid lumber paneling for a rich, rustic look.
- In addition to a large general-use area and a shop, the optional daylight basement has space for a car or a boat.

Plans H-26-1 & -1A	
Bedrooms: 3	**Baths:** 2
Living Area:	
Upper floor	476 sq. ft.
Main floor	728 sq. ft.
Daylight basement	410 sq. ft.
Total Living Area:	**1,204/1,614 sq. ft.**
Tuck-under garage	318 sq. ft.
Exterior Wall Framing:	2x4
Foundation Options:	**Plan #**
Daylight basement	H-26-1
Crawlspace	H-26-1A

(All plans can be built with your choice of foundation and framing. A generic conversion diagram is available. See order form.)

BLUEPRINT PRICE CODE:	**A/B**

DAYLIGHT BASEMENT

GARAGE 12'-1" x 26'-4"

SHOP 12'-1" x 9'-9"

WH

STOR

up

GENERAL USE 12'-1" x 13'-2"

CLOSET CANTILEVER

STORAGE

STAIRWAY AREA IN CRAWLSPACE VERSION

MAIN FLOOR

26'-0"

4'-0"

28'-0"

10'-0"

KITCHEN 7'-2" x 8'-1"

REF

DW

BATH

BEDROOM 10'-0" x 10'-0"

Shw'r

DINING 6'-10" x 9'-8"

down

up

MASONRY BACKED PRE-FAB FIREPLACE

LIVING ROOM 25'-2" x 13'-5"

DECK

down

UPPER FLOOR

CLOSET 4'-10"

CLOSET 4'-10"

STORAGE

BEDROOM 13'-7" x 10'-0"

SLOPED CEILING

STORAGE

Tub w/ Shower

BATH

down

CLOSET 5'-7"

STORAGE

STORAGE

S.C.

CLOSET 7'-5"

BEDROOM 13'-7" x 11'-5"

STORAGE

DECK

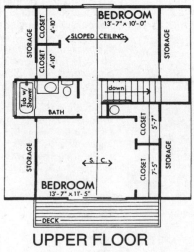

A-Frame Chalet with Popular Features

Ski chalets bring to mind Alpine comforts and evenings by the hearth. Schussing down nearby slopes is much more enjoyable when you don't have to worry about long drives home. Also, being on hand means you won't miss the fresh snowfall. In addition, summer time finds the mountain setting ideal for refreshing weekends away from the crowds and heat.

This class A-Frame is designed for optimum comfort and minimum cost, yet allows for variety and individual taste in setting and decor. Your home away from home can vary from plush to rustic, depending on personal preferences.

A special feature of this plan is the natural stone fireplace located where it can be enjoyed from indoors and outdoors. It serves the dual function of being a standard fireplace indoors and a handy barbecue outdoors. Two sleeping rooms on the main floor are a further advantage. Upstairs, there is a third bedroom plus a half bath. A balcony room provides space for overflow guests or a playroom for the kids. All the rooms in the house have "knee walls" so the space is usable right to the wall. These walls provide handy storage places as well as space for insulation.

First floor:	845 sq. ft.
Second floor:	375 sq. ft.
Total living area:	1,220 sq. ft.

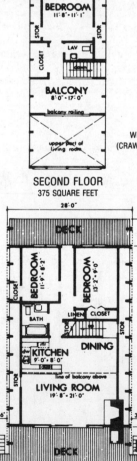

PLAN H-6
WITHOUT BASEMENT
(CRAWLSPACE FOUNDATION)

SECOND FLOOR
375 SQUARE FEET

FIRST FLOOR
845 SQUARE FEET

Blueprint Price Code A
Plan H-6

PRICES AND DETAILS
ON PAGES 12-15

Unexpected Amenities

- Surprising interior amenities are found within the casual exterior of this good-looking design.
- A dramatic fireplace warms the comfortable formal areas. The living and dining rooms share a 20-ft. cathedral ceiling and high windows that flank the fireplace. Sliding glass doors access an expansive side patio.

- The efficient walk-through kitchen provides plenty of counter space, in addition to a windowed sink and a pass-through to the living areas.
- A large bedroom, a full bath and an oversized utility room complete the main floor. The utility room offers space for a washer and dryer, plus a sink and an extra freezer.
- Upstairs, the spacious and secluded master suite boasts a walk-in closet, a private bath and lots of storage space. A railed loft area overlooks the living and dining rooms.

Plan I-1249-A	
Bedrooms: 2	**Baths:** 2
Living Area:	
Upper floor	297 sq. ft.
Main floor	952 sq. ft.
Total Living Area:	**1,249 sq. ft.**
Standard basement	952 sq. ft.
Exterior Wall Framing:	2x6
Foundation Options:	
Standard basement	
Crawlspace	

(All plans can be built with your choice of foundation and framing. A generic conversion diagram is available. See order form.)

BLUEPRINT PRICE CODE: **A**

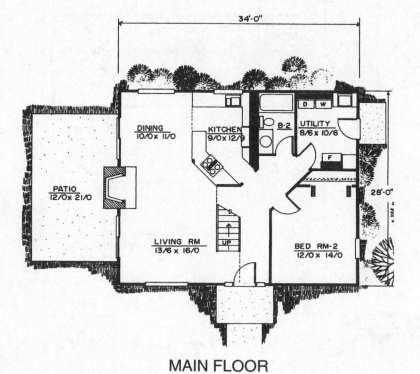

MAIN FLOOR

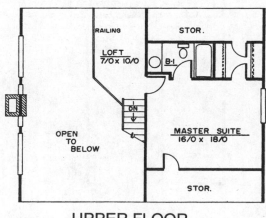

UPPER FLOOR

Clean-Lined Design for Narrow Lot

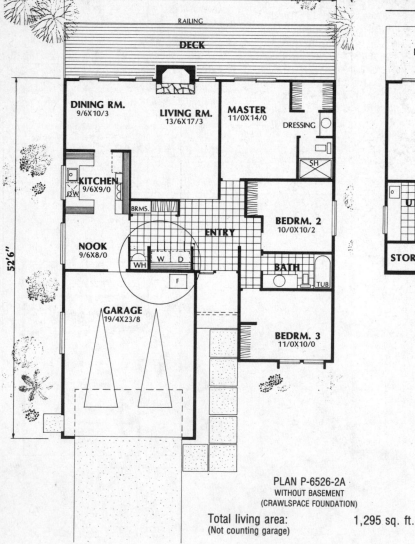

40'0"

RAILING

DECK

DINING RM. 9/6X10/3

LIVING RM. 13/6X17/3

MASTER 11/0X14/0

DRESSING

SH

KITCHEN 9/6X9/0

BRMS.

ENTRY

BEDRM. 2 10/0X10/2

NOOK 9/6X8/0

WH W D

F

BATH

TUB

GARAGE 19/4X23/8

BEDRM. 3 11/0X10/0

52'6"

PLAN P-6526-2A
WITHOUT BASEMENT
(CRAWLSPACE FOUNDATION)

Total living area: 1,295 sq. ft.
(Not counting garage)

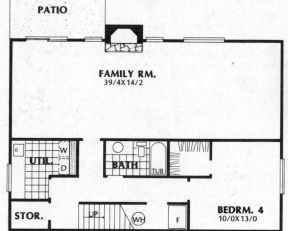

PATIO

FAMILY RM. 39/4X14/2

UTIL. W D

BATH TUB

STOR.

UP WH F

BEDRM. 4 10/0X13/0

NOOK

UP

GARAGE

PLAN P-6526-2D
WITH DAYLIGHT BASEMENT

Main floor: (Not counting garage)	1,295 sq. ft.
Basement level:	1,120 sq. ft.
Total living area with daylight basement:	2,415 sq. ft.

Blueprint Price Code A Without Basement
Blueprint Price Code C With Daylight Basement

Plans P-6526-2A & -2D

PRICES AND DETAILS
ON PAGES 12-15

A Chalet for Today

- With its wraparound deck and soaring windows, this chalet-style home is ideal for recreational living and scenic sites.
- The living and dining rooms are combined to take advantage of the dramatic cathedral ceiling, the rugged stone fireplace and the view through the spectacular windows.
- A quaint balcony above adds to the warm country feeling of the living area, which extends to the expansive deck.

- The open kitchen features a bright corner sink and a nifty breakfast bar that adjoins the living area.
- The handy main-floor laundry area is close to two bedrooms and a full bath.
- The study is a feature rarely found in a home of this size and style.
- The master suite and a storage area encompass the upper floor. A cathedral ceiling, a whirlpool bath and sweeping views from the balcony give this space an elegant feel.
- The basement option includes a tuck-under garage, additional storage space and a separate utility area. A family room may be finished later.

Plan AHP-9340	
Bedrooms: 3+	**Baths: 2**
Living Area:	
Upper floor	332 sq. ft.
Main floor	974 sq. ft.
Total Living Area:	**1,306 sq. ft.**
Basement	624 sq. ft.
Tuck-under garage	350 sq. ft.
Exterior Wall Framing:	2x4 or 2x6

Foundation Options:
Standard basement
Daylight basement
Crawlspace
Slab
(All plans can be built with your choice of foundation and framing. A generic conversion diagram is available. See order form.)

BLUEPRINT PRICE CODE:	A

BASEMENT

MAIN FLOOR

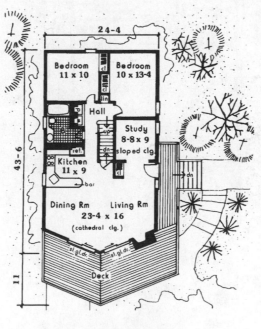

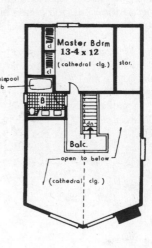

UPPER FLOOR

Windowed Great Room

- This attractive, open design with a wonderful windowed Great Room can function as a cabin, a mountain retreat or a permanent residence.
- The main level of the home is entered via a split-landing stairway to a wraparound deck.
- The kitchen and the Great Room merge to form a huge family activity area under a soaring 22-ft. cathedral ceiling.
- Two quiet main-floor bedrooms share a hall bath.
- Upstairs, an open balcony loft offers elevated views through the massive front window wall.
- The large sleeping loft could be split into two smaller bedrooms.

Plan I-1354-B

Bedrooms: 2+	Baths: 2
Living Area:	
Upper floor	366 sq. ft.
Main floor	988 sq. ft.
Total Living Area:	**1,354 sq. ft.**
Daylight basement	658 sq. ft.
Tuck-under garage	260 sq. ft.
Exterior Wall Framing:	2x6

Foundation Options:

Daylight basement

(All plans can be built with your choice of foundation and framing. A generic conversion diagram is available. See order form.)

BLUEPRINT PRICE CODE: **A**

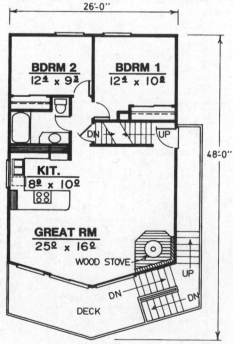

MAIN FLOOR

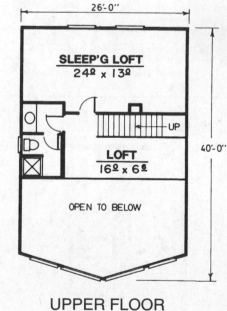

UPPER FLOOR

Plan I-1354-B

**PRICES AND DETAILS
ON PAGES 12-15**

Dramatic Skewed Prow

- This cleverly modified A-frame design combines a dramatic exterior with an exciting interior that offers commanding views through its many windows.
- The central foyer opens to a spacious living room and dining room

combination with a soaring 23-ft. cathedral ceiling and a massive stone fireplace. Sliding glass doors open to an inviting wraparound deck.
- Directly ahead is the L-shaped kitchen, which also accesses the deck.
- Two bedrooms are located at the rear, near the laundry room and a full bath.
- A third bedroom, a second bath and a balcony loft that could sleep overnight guests are found on the upper level.

Plan HFL-1160-CW

Bedrooms: 3+	Baths: 2
Living Area:	
Upper floor	400 sq. ft.
Main floor	1,016 sq. ft.
Total Living Area:	**1,416 sq. ft.**
Exterior Wall Framing:	2x4

Foundation Options:

Crawlspace
(All plans can be built with your choice of foundation and framing. A generic conversion diagram is available. See order form.)

BLUEPRINT PRICE CODE: A

VIEW INTO LIVING ROOM

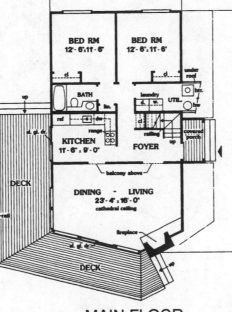

MAIN FLOOR

UPPER FLOOR

REAR VIEW

Angled Solar Efficiency

- Dramatically angled to maximize the benefits of passive-solar technology, this compact one-story home can be adapted to many sites and orientations.
- South-facing rooms, including the combination sun room and den, absorb and store heat energy in thermal floors for nighttime radiation.
- Heavy insulation in exterior walls and ceilings, plus double glazing in windows, keep heat loss to a minimum. During the summer, heat is expelled through an operable clerestory window and through an automatic vent in the sun room.
- The entrance vestibule provides an immediate view of the sun room and the outdoors beyond.
- The living lounge boasts a warm fireplace, a bright bay window and a 14-ft. vaulted ceiling.
- The kitchen features an eating bar, while the attached dining area opens to a large rear terrace.
- The bedrooms are isolated for total privacy. The master suite features a private bath and a large walk-in closet.

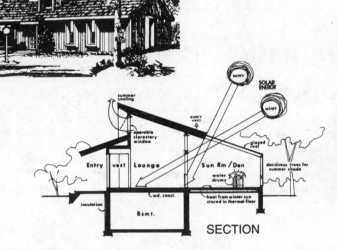

FRONT VIEW

SECTION

Plan K-505-R

Bedrooms: 3	Baths: 2
Living Area:	
Main floor	1,261 sq. ft.
Sun room	164 sq. ft.
Total Living Area:	**1,425 sq. ft.**
Standard basement	1,030 sq. ft.
Garage	466 sq. ft.
Exterior Wall Framing:	2x4 or 2x6

Foundation Options:

Standard basement

Slab

(All plans can be built with your choice of foundation and framing. A generic conversion diagram is available. See order form.)

BLUEPRINT PRICE CODE: A

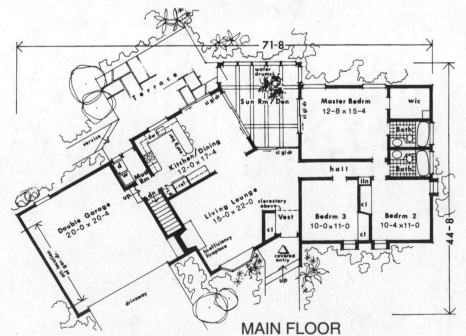

MAIN FLOOR

 Plan K-505-R   *PRICES AND DETAILS ON PAGES 12-15*

Simple, but Dramatic

- A dramatic sloped roof exterior and interior living room with sloped ceiling, floor-to-ceiling windows, an adjoining deck and wood stove give this home an interesting, but easy and affordable structure under 1,500 square feet.
- The attached kitchen and dining area also has access to the deck, for an outdoor dining alternative; a pantry and convenient laundry room is secluded to the rear.
- The main-level bedroom could ideally be used as the master; it offers dual closets and nearby bath.
- Off the two-story foyer is the stairway to the second level which ends in a balcony area that overlooks the living room. Two good-sized bedrooms, one with unique dressing vanity, share the upper level with a second bath.

Plan HFL-1382

Bedrooms: 3	Baths: 2

Living Area:	
Upper floor	465 sq. ft.
Main floor	963 sq. ft.

Total Living Area:	1,428 sq. ft.
Standard basement	811 sq. ft.
Garage	220 sq. ft.

Exterior Wall Framing:	2x6

Foundation Options:
Standard basement
Slab
(Typical foundation & framing conversion diagram available—see order form.)

BLUEPRINT PRICE CODE:	A

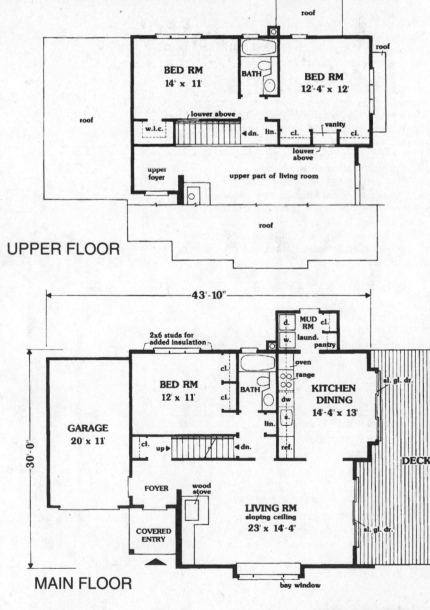

UPPER FLOOR

MAIN FLOOR

Plan HFL-1382

Loft Lookout

- Unique lakeside living is possible with this getaway home that can be built on posts.
- Inside, a large living and dining space with a dramatic cathedral ceiling is surrounded by an expansive deck.
- A nice-sized kitchen, two baths and three bedrooms complete the main floor.
- The versatile loft could be used as a rec room, a lookout station or extra sleeping space.

Plan PH-1440

Bedrooms: 3	Baths: 2
Space:	
Upper floor	144 sq. ft.
Main floor	1,296 sq. ft.
Total Living Area	**1,440 sq. ft.**
Exterior Wall Framing	2x6
Foundation options:	
Crawlspace	
Pole	
Slab	
(Foundation & framing conversion diagram available—see order form.)	
Blueprint Price Code	**A**

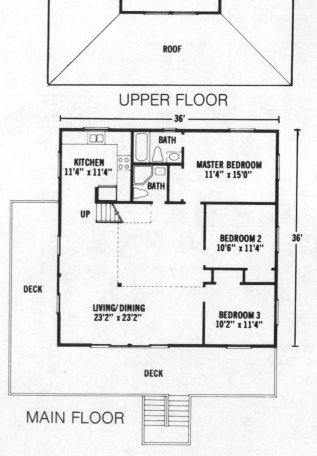

UPPER FLOOR

MAIN FLOOR

Plan PH-1440

PRICES AND DETAILS ON PAGES 12-15

Rustic Appeal

- Stone and wood combine with high angled windows to give this rustic home an appealing facade.
- The entry opens directly from a wide front deck to the majestic living room, which is accented by a 15-ft. cathedral ceiling with exposed beams. A massive central stone fireplace is the focal point of the room, while tall windows overlook the deck.
- Behind the fireplace, the cathedral ceiling continues into the adjoining dining room, which offers ample space for formal occasions.
- The galley-style kitchen features a sunny sink and easy service to the dining room. Just a step away, a pantry, a laundry closet and access to the carport are also available.
- The master suite boasts a walk-in closet, a private master bath and sliding glass doors to the deck.
- Across the home, two additional bedrooms share another full bath.
- Two handy storage areas are attached to the carport.

Plan C-7360

Bedrooms: 3	Baths: 2
Living Area:	
Main floor	1,454 sq. ft.
Total Living Area:	**1,454 sq. ft.**
Daylight basement	1,454 sq. ft.
Carport	400 sq. ft.
Storage	120 sq. ft.
Exterior Wall Framing:	2x4

Foundation Options:

Daylight basement
Crawlspace
Slab
(All plans can be built with your choice of foundation and framing. A generic conversion diagram is available. See order form.)

BLUEPRINT PRICE CODE: A

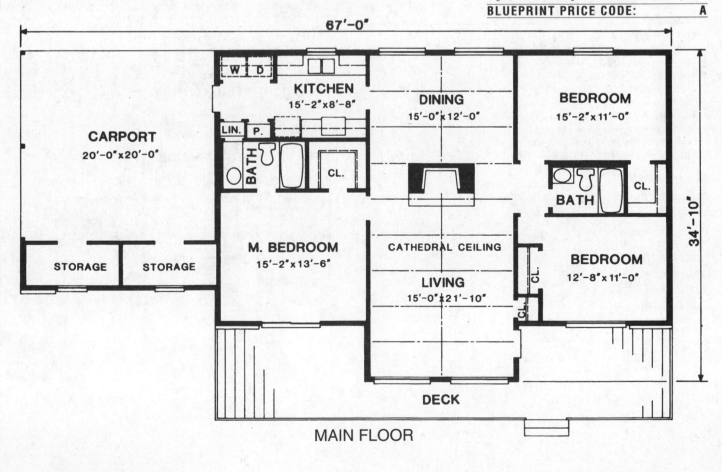

MAIN FLOOR

REAR VIEW

All Decked Out!

- All decked out to take full advantage of the outdoors, this stylish home is perfect for a scenic site.
- Entered through a front vestibule, the bright and open floor plan provides an ideal setting for casual lifestyles.
- The sunken living room features a handsome fireplace, a skylighted 19-ft. ceiling and three sets of sliding glass doors that open to an expansive backyard deck.
- The efficient kitchen has a sunny sink and a pass-through with bi-fold doors to the adjoining dining room.
- The main-floor bedroom has a walk-in closet and sliding glass doors to the deck. A half-bath is nearby.
- Upstairs, a railed balcony overlooks the living room. The smaller of the two bedrooms has private access to the bathroom and another deck.

Plan CAR-81007

Bedrooms: 2+	Baths: 1½
Living Area:	
Upper floor	560 sq. ft.
Main floor	911 sq. ft.
Total Living Area:	**1,471 sq. ft.**
Standard basement	911 sq. ft.
Exterior Wall Framing:	2x6

Foundation Options:

Standard basement

(All plans can be built with your choice of foundation and framing. A generic conversion diagram is available. See order form.)

BLUEPRINT PRICE CODE:	**A**

UPPER FLOOR

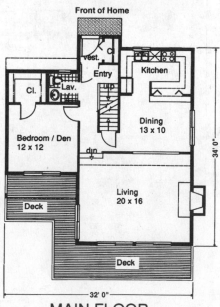

MAIN FLOOR

  Plan CAR-81007 *PRICES AND DETAILS* *ON PAGES 12-15*

Berm Home for Cozy Living

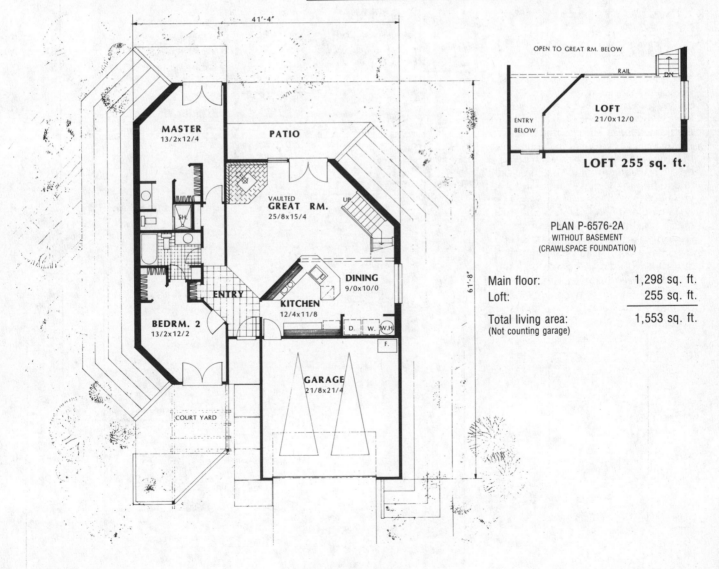

41'-4"

MASTER
13/2x12/4

PATIO

VAULTED
GREAT RM.
25/8x15/4

UP

ENTRY

DINING
9/0x10/0

KITCHEN
12/4x11/8

BEDRM. 2
13/2x12/2

D. W. W.H

F.

GARAGE
21/8x21/4

COURT YARD

61'-8"

OPEN TO GREAT RM. BELOW

RAIL

DN

ENTRY
BELOW

LOFT
21/0x12/0

LOFT 255 sq. ft.

PLAN P-6576-2A
WITHOUT BASEMENT
(CRAWLSPACE FOUNDATION)

Main floor: 1,298 sq. ft.
Loft: 255 sq. ft.

Total living area: 1,553 sq. ft.
(Not counting garage)

Blueprint Price Code B

Plan P-6576-2A

Contemporary Saltbox

- This contemporary two-story saltbox is compactly designed.
- Sliding glass doors and a greenhouse bay off the dining area make the rear of the home almost all enclosed in glass.
- The huge living room at the center of the floor plan features a sloped ceiling, heat-circulating fireplace and a skylight in addition to the glass wall of the greenhouse.
- A sunny dinette and open, skylit kitchen merge together with a convenient laundry room and pantry nearby.
- The main-floor master bedroom has dual closets and an adjacent full bath.
- Two nice-sized bedrooms and a second full bath share the upper level; a railing borders the balcony that overlooks the main living areas below.

Plan HFL-1300-MS

Bedrooms: 3	Baths: 2
Space:	
Upper floor	519 sq. ft.
Main floor	1,042 sq. ft.
Total Living Area	**1,561 sq. ft.**
Basement	1,000 sq. ft.
Garage	233 sq. ft.
Exterior Wall Framing	2x6

Foundation options:
Standard Basement
Slab
(Foundation & framing conversion diagram available—see order form.)

Blueprint Price Code	B

UPPER FLOOR

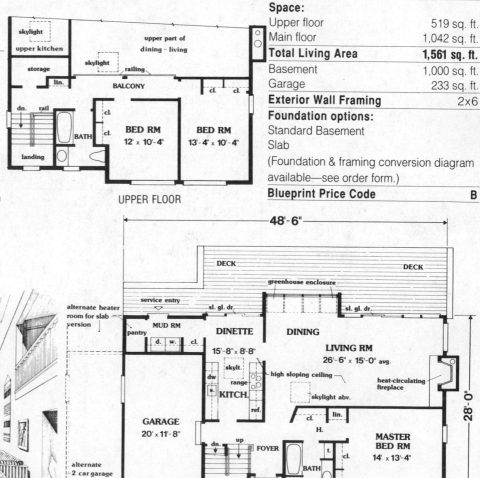

MAIN FLOOR

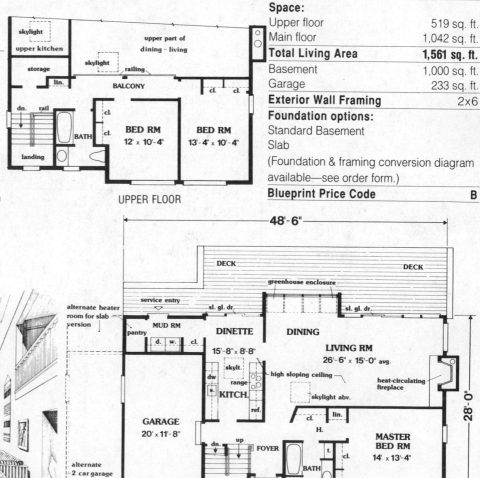

TO ORDER THIS BLUEPRINT, CALL TOLL-FREE 1-800-547-5570

Plan HFL-1300-MS

PRICES AND DETAILS ON PAGES 12-15

Lakeside Retreat Sleeps Eight

- Four bedrooms border the exterior walls of this lakeside retreat, affording a fair amount of privacy.
- A deck and a vaulted screened-in porch surround the spectacular cathedral-ceilinged Great Room and dining area. The large living space is also loaded with glass so you can enjoy your favorite scenic site.
- The adjoining kitchen features an oversized eating bar and work counter combination.
- Two full baths sit back-to-back, conveniently serving both bedroom wings. A handy main-floor laundry room is also included.

Plan PH-1600

Bedrooms: 4	Baths: 2
Space:	
Main floor	1,600 sq. ft.
Total Living Area	**1,600 sq. ft.**
Exterior Wall Framing	2x6

Foundation options:

Crawlspace
Pole
Slab
(Foundation & framing conversion diagram available—see order form.)

Blueprint Price Code	B

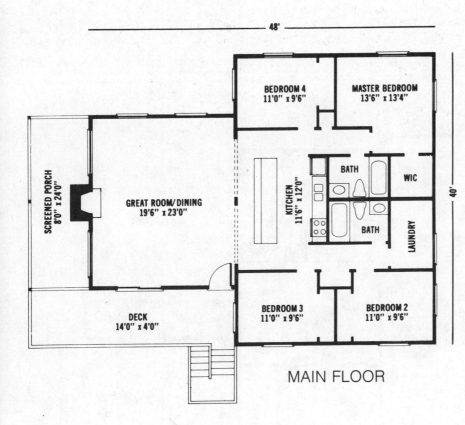

48'

40'

SCREENED PORCH 8'0" x 24'0"

GREAT ROOM/DINING 19'6" x 23'0"

DECK 14'0" x 4'0"

BEDROOM 4 11'0" x 9'6"

MASTER BEDROOM 13'6" x 13'4"

KITCHEN 11'6" x 12'0"

BATH

WIC

BATH

LAUNDRY

BEDROOM 3 11'0" x 9'6"

BEDROOM 2 11'0" x 9'6"

MAIN FLOOR

Comfortable, Open Plan

- This comfortable home defines function and style, with a sharp window wall to brighten the central living areas.
- In from the broad front deck, the living/family room boasts a fireplace, a cathedral ceiling and soaring views. The fireplace visually sets off the dining

room, which extends to the backyard patio through sliding doors.
- The galley-style kitchen offers a bright sink and an abundance of counter space, with a laundry closet and carport access nearby.
- The secluded and spacious master bedroom features private deck access, a walk-in closet and a private bath.
- On the other side of the home, two good-sized secondary bedrooms share another full bath.

Plan C-8160	
Bedrooms: 3	**Baths: 2**
Living Area:	
Main floor	1,669 sq. ft.
Total Living Area:	**1,669 sq. ft.**
Daylight basement	1,660 sq. ft.
Carport	413 sq. ft.
Storage	85 sq. ft.
Exterior Wall Framing:	2x4

Foundation Options:
Daylight basement
Crawlspace
Slab
(All plans can be built with your choice of foundation and framing. A generic conversion diagram is available. See order form.)

BLUEPRINT PRICE CODE: **B**

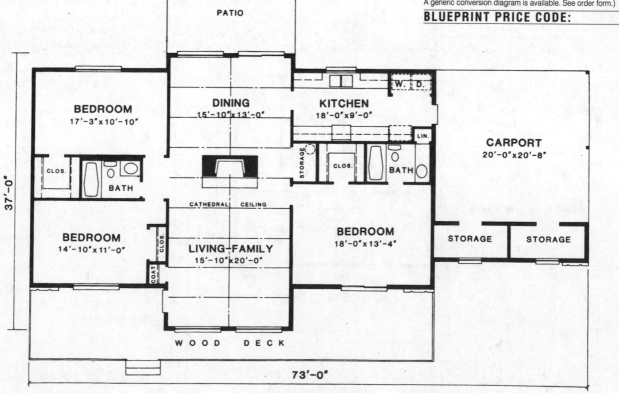

MAIN FLOOR

Plan C-8160

PRICES AND DETAILS
ON PAGES 12-15

Smart Design for Sloping Lot

- This design boasts stunning windows and a gorgeous deck, and is perfect for a narrow, sloping lot.
- The main entry opens to the spacious living areas. The Great Room shows off a soaring 12-ft. vaulted ceiling, a cozy woodstove and a boxed-out window arrangement. An 11½-ft. vaulted ceiling presides over the dining area and the kitchen. The dining area offers sliding glass doors to the deck.
- Two bedrooms and two skylighted baths are located at the back of the home. The master bedroom also has a walk-in wardrobe, a lovely window seat and deck access.
- A vaulted, skylighted hall approaches the stairway to the basement, which hosts a third bedroom and another full bath. A very large shop/storage area and a two-car garage are also included. An extra bonus is the carport/storage area below the deck.

Plan P-529-2D	
Bedrooms: 3	**Baths: 3**
Living Area:	
Main floor	1,076 sq. ft.
Daylight basement	597 sq. ft.
Total Living Area:	**1,673 sq. ft.**
Tuck-under garage	425 sq. ft.
Exterior Wall Framing:	2x6
Foundation Options:	

Daylight basement

(All plans can be built with your choice of foundation and framing. A generic conversion diagram is available. See order form.)

BLUEPRINT PRICE CODE: B

MAIN FLOOR

DAYLIGHT BASEMENT

TO ORDER THIS BLUEPRINT,
CALL TOLL-FREE 1-800-547-5570

Plan P-529-2D

PRICES AND DETAILS
ON PAGES 12-15

421

Panoramic Prow View

- This glass-filled prow gable design is almost as spectacular as the panoramic view from inside.
- French doors open from the front deck to the dining room. A stunning window wall illuminates the adjoining living room, which flaunts a 20-ft.-high cathedral ceiling.

- The open, corner kitchen is perfectly angled to service the dining room and the family room, while offering views of the front and rear decks.
- A handy utility/laundry room opens to the rear deck. Two bedrooms share a full bath, to complete the main floor.
- A dramatic, open-railed stairway leads up to the secluded master bedroom, which boasts a dressing room and a private bath with a dual-sink vanity and a separate tub and shower.

Plan NW-196

Bedrooms: 3	**Baths:** 2

Living Area:

Upper floor	394 sq. ft.
Main floor	1,317 sq. ft.
Total Living Area:	**1,711 sq. ft.**
Exterior Wall Framing:	2x6

Foundation Options:

Crawlspace
(All plans can be built with your choice of foundation and framing. A generic conversion diagram is available. See order form.)

BLUEPRINT PRICE CODE:	**B**

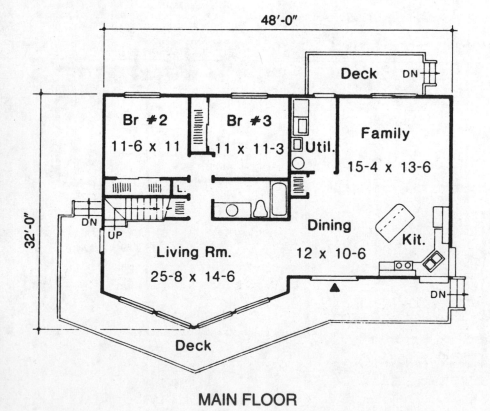

MAIN FLOOR

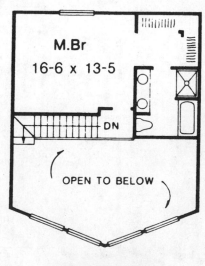

UPPER FLOOR

Plan NW-196

PRICES AND DETAILS ON PAGES 12-15

Classic Ranch-Style

- A classic exterior facade of stone and unpainted wood distinguishes this classic ranch-style home.
- A covered front entry leads guests into a welcoming gallery. At the left is the living and dining area, with its elegant 11-ft.-high cathedral ceiling. The living room has an optional entrance to the family room via folding doors.

- The open kitchen offers an adjoining dinette, which showcases a curved wall of windows overlooking a huge backyard terrace. A screen or partition separates the dinette from the family room. The family room boasts a fireplace and access to the terrace.
- To the right of the gallery lie the three bedrooms. The master suite features a skylighted dressing/vanity area, a walk-in closet and a private bath.
- The two remaining bedrooms share a convenient hall bath that features a double-sink vanity.

Plan K-162-J	
Bedrooms: 3	**Baths:** 2
Living Area:	
Main floor	1,721 sq. ft.
Total Living Area:	**1,721 sq. ft.**
Standard basement	1,672 sq. ft.
Garage and storage	496 sq. ft.
Exterior Wall Framing:	2x4 or 2x6
Foundation Options:	
Standard basement	
Slab	

(All plans can be built with your choice of foundation and framing. A generic conversion diagram is available. See order form.)

BLUEPRINT PRICE CODE:	B

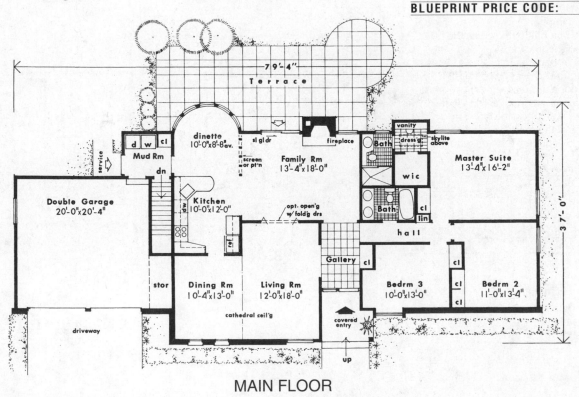

MAIN FLOOR

Very Versatile!

- You won't find a more versatile design than this one! The attractive traditional facade gives way to a dramatic rear deck, making the home suitable for a lakeside lot. With its modest width and daylight basement, the home also adapts to a narrow or sloping site.
- A nice railed porch welcomes guests into the main entry and into the Great Room straight ahead. The Great Room is enhanced by a 21-ft. vaulted ceiling, a metal fireplace and sliding glass doors to the expansive deck.
- The U-shaped kitchen offers a pantry and a serving bar.
- A convenient hall bath serves the quiet main-floor bedroom.
- Upstairs, a spacious loft allows views of the Great Room over a wood rail.
- Double doors introduce the posh master suite, which boasts a walk-in closet, a whirlpool bath and attic access.
- The loft and the master bedroom are visually expanded by 12-ft. ceilings.

Plan PI-92-373

Bedrooms: 2	Baths: 2

Living Area:

Upper floor	546 sq. ft.
Main floor	1,212 sq. ft.
Total Living Area:	**1,758 sq. ft.**
Daylight basement	1,212 sq. ft.
Garage	475 sq. ft.
Exterior Wall Framing:	**2x6**

Foundation Options:

Daylight basement
(All plans can be built with your choice of foundation and framing. A generic conversion diagram is available. See order form.)

BLUEPRINT PRICE CODE:	**B**

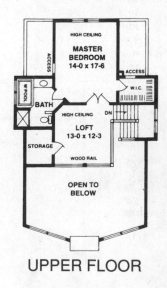

REAR VIEW

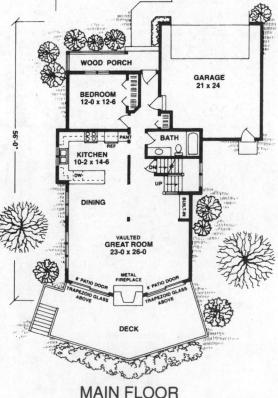

MAIN FLOOR

UPPER FLOOR

TO ORDER THIS BLUEPRINT, CALL TOLL-FREE 1-800-547-5570

Plan PI-92-373

PRICES AND DETAILS ON PAGES 12-15

Multi-Level Ideal for Difficult Lot

- This compact design is well suited for a lot that slopes steeply up to the rear.
- Massive open spaces and windows create a light and airy feeling inside.
- A mid-level landing at the entry takes you to the vaulted living room, which offers a pass-through to the kitchen; completing the main level are a dining room, two bedrooms and a bath.
- The master bedroom is an upper level loft arrangement. The attached master bath is entered through double doors and features dual vanities, large tub and separate toilet.
- The basement/lower level houses the garage, utility room and fourth bedroom.

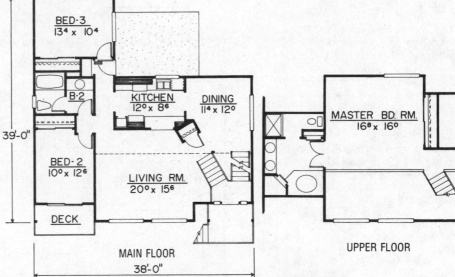

BED-3
13⁴ x 10⁴

B-2

KITCHEN
12⁰ x 8⁶

DINING
11⁴ x 12⁰

39'-0"

BED-2
10⁰ x 12⁶

LIVING RM.
20⁰ x 15⁶

DECK

MAIN FLOOR
38'-0"

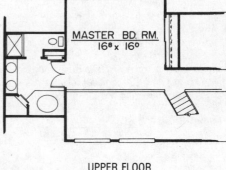

MASTER BD. RM.
16⁸ x 16⁰

UPPER FLOOR

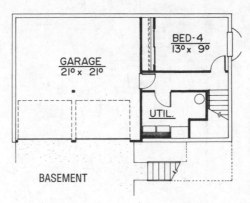

GARAGE
21⁰ x 21⁰

BED-4
13⁰ x 9⁰

UTIL.

BASEMENT

Plan I-1769-T

Bedrooms: 4	Baths: 2

Space:

Upper floor:	418 sq. ft.
Main floor:	1,021 sq. ft.
Lower floor:	330 sq. ft.
Total living area:	1,769 sq. ft.
Garage:	441 sq. ft.
Exterior Wall Framing:	2x6

Foundation options:
Daylight basement.
(Foundation & framing conversion diagram available — see order form.)

Blueprint Price Code:	B

Deck and Spa!

- Designed for relaxation as well as for active indoor/outdoor living, this popular home offers a gigantic deck and an irresistible spa room.
- A covered porch welcomes guests into the entry hall, which flows past the central, open-railed stairway to the spectacular Great Room.
- Sliding glass doors on each side of the Great Room extend the living space to the huge V-shaped deck. The 22-ft. sloped ceiling and a woodstove add to the stunning effect.
- The master suite features a cozy window seat, a walk-in closet and private access to a full bath.
- The passive-solar spa room can be reached from the master suite as well as the backyard deck.
- The upper floor hosts two additional bedrooms, a full bath and a balcony hall that overlooks the Great Room.

Plans H-952-1A & -1B

Bedrooms: 3+	Baths: 2-3
Living Area:	
Upper floor	470 sq. ft.
Main floor	1,207 sq. ft.
Passive spa room	102 sq. ft.
Daylight basement	1,105 sq. ft.
Total Living Area:	**1,779/2,884 sq. ft.**
Garage	496 sq. ft.
Exterior Wall Framing:	2x6
Foundation Options:	Plan #
Daylight basement	H-952-1B
Crawlspace	H-952-1A

(All plans can be built with your choice of foundation and framing. A generic conversion diagram is available. See order form.)

BLUEPRINT PRICE CODE: B/D

REAR VIEW

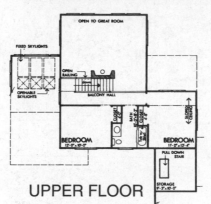

UPPER FLOOR

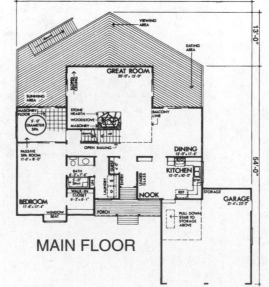

MAIN FLOOR

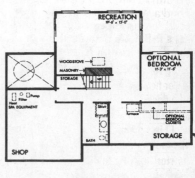

DAYLIGHT BASEMENT

Plans H-952-1A & -1B

PRICES AND DETAILS ON PAGES 12-15

Octagonal Home Has Lofty Views

- There's no better way to avoid the ordinary than to build an octagonal home and escape from conventional square corners and rigid rooms.
- The roomy main floor of this exciting home offers plenty of space for full-time family living or for comfortable second-home recreation.
- The two-story entry hall leads to the bedrooms on the right and to the Great Room around to the left.
- Warmed by a woodstove, the Great Room offers a relaxing retreat that includes a 12-ft. ceiling and a panoramic view of the outdoors.
- At the core of the main floor are two baths, one of which boasts a spa tub and private access from the adjoining master bedroom.
- A roomy kitchen and a handy utility room are also featured.
- The upper floor, surrounded by windows and topped by a 12-ft. ceiling, is designed as a recreation room, with a woodstove and a wet bar.
- The optional daylight basement adds a fourth bedroom, another bath, a garage and a large storage area.

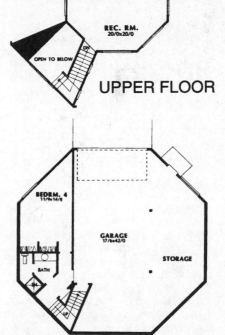

UPPER FLOOR

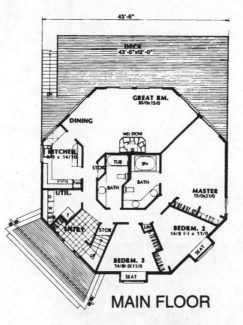

MAIN FLOOR

DAYLIGHT BASEMENT

Plans P-532-3A & -3D

Bedrooms: 3+	Baths: 2-3
Living Area:	
Upper floor	355 sq. ft.
Main floor	1,567 sq. ft.
Daylight basement	430 sq. ft.
Total Living Area:	**1,922/2,352 sq. ft.**
Opt. tuck-under garage/storage	1,137 sq. ft.
Exterior Wall Framing:	2x6
Foundation Options:	**Plan #**
Daylight basement	P-532-3D
Crawlspace	P-532-3A

(All plans can be built with your choice of foundation and framing. A generic conversion diagram is available. See order form.)

BLUEPRINT PRICE CODE:	**B/C**

REAR VIEW

Plans P-532-3A & -3D

PRICES AND DETAILS ON PAGES 12-15

Light-Filled Interior

- A stylish contemporary exterior and an open, light-filled interior define this two-level home.
- The covered entry leads to a central gallery. The huge living room and dining room combine to generate a spacious ambience that is enhanced by a 15½-ft. cathedral ceiling and a warm fireplace with tall flanking windows.
- Oriented to the rear and overlooking a terrace and backyard landscaping are the informal spaces. The family room, the sunny semi-circular dinette and the modern kitchen share a snack bar.
- The main-floor master suite boasts a 13-ft. sloped ceiling, a private terrace, a dressing area and a personal bath with a whirlpool tub.
- Two to three extra bedrooms with 11-ft. ceilings share a skylighted bath on the upper floor.

Plan K-683-D

Bedrooms: 3+	**Baths:** 2½+

Living Area:	
Upper floor	491 sq. ft.
Main floor	1,475 sq. ft.
Total Living Area:	**1,966 sq. ft.**
Standard basement	1,425 sq. ft.
Garage and storage	487 sq. ft.
Exterior Wall Framing:	2x4 or 2x6

Foundation Options:

Standard basement

Slab

(All plans can be built with your choice of foundation and framing. A generic conversion diagram is available. See order form.)

BLUEPRINT PRICE CODE:	**B**

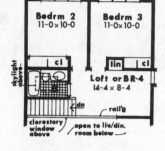

UPPER FLOOR

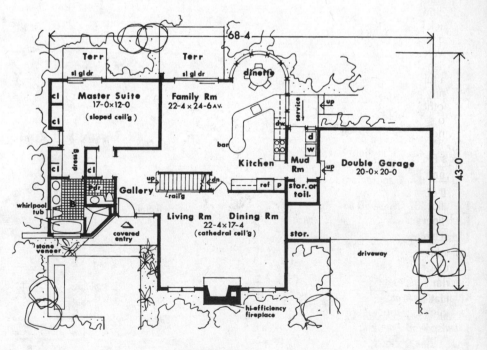

MAIN FLOOR

TO ORDER THIS BLUEPRINT, CALL TOLL-FREE 1-800-547-5570   Plan K-683-D   *PRICES AND DETAILS ON PAGES 12-15*

Deluxe
Master Bath

- Stylish decks, bay windows and a deluxe master bath are just some of the amenities found in this modern home.
- Recessed double doors open into the inviting skylighted entry, which views the backyard beyond.
- Past the entry, the spacious sunken living room offers a unique fireplace with a built-in wood bin. Sliding glass doors open from the living and dining rooms to a handsome backyard deck.
- A dramatic skywall illuminates the exciting kitchen, which also features a snack bar to the adjoining dining room.
- The fantastic master suite boasts a private backyard deck, in addition to a lavish bath that showcases a step-up spa tub, a designer shower, a dual-sink vanity and a roomy walk-in closet.
- Another full bath is convenient to the two secondary bedrooms, each with a window seat in a split bay.

Plans P-6600-4A & -4D

Bedrooms: 3	Baths: 2
Living Area:	
Main floor (crawlspace version)	2,050 sq. ft.
Main floor (basement version)	2,110 sq. ft.
Total Living Area:	**2,050/2,110 sq. ft.**
Daylight basement	2,080 sq. ft.
Garage	794 sq. ft.
Exterior Wall Framing:	2x6
Foundation Options:	**Plan #**
Daylight basement	P-6600-4D
Crawlspace	P-6600-4A

(All plans can be built with your choice of foundation and framing. A generic conversion diagram is available. See order form.)

BLUEPRINT PRICE CODE:	C

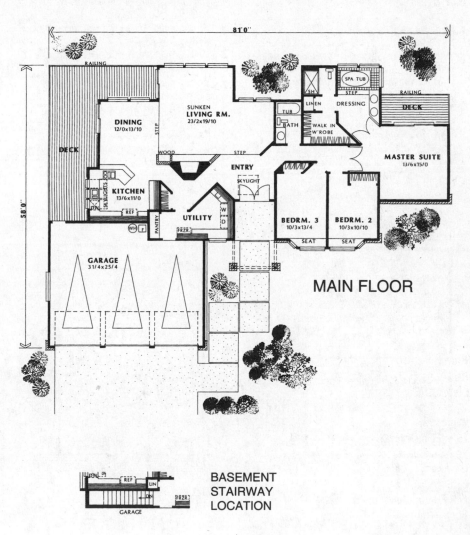

MAIN FLOOR

BASEMENT
STAIRWAY
LOCATION

Chalet for Town or Country

- Vertical siding, spacious viewing decks with cut-out railings and exposed beams in the interior give this home the look of a mountain chalet.
- The design of the home lends itself to year-round family living as well as to part-time recreational enjoyment.
- The expansive Great Room features exposed beams and an impressive fireplace. The large wraparound deck is

accessed through sliding glass doors. The dining area is expanded by an 18-ft. vaulted ceiling.
- The well-planned kitchen is open and easily accessible.
- Two main-floor bedrooms share the hall bath between them.
- The upstairs offers an adult retreat: a fine master bedroom with a private deck and bath, plus a versatile loft area. An airy 13-ft. ceiling presides over the entire upper floor.
- The daylight-basement level includes a garage and a large recreation room with a fireplace and a half-bath.

Plan P-531-2D

Bedrooms: 3+	Baths: 2½
Living Area:	
Upper floor	573 sq. ft.
Main floor	1,120 sq. ft.
Daylight basement	532 sq. ft.
Total Living Area:	**2,225 sq. ft.**
Tuck-under garage	541 sq. ft.
Exterior Wall Framing:	2x6

Foundation Options:

Daylight basement
(All plans can be built with your choice of foundation and framing. A generic conversion diagram is available. See order form.)

BLUEPRINT PRICE CODE: C

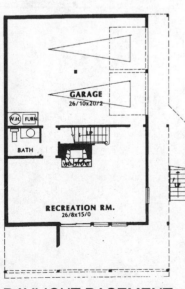

DAYLIGHT BASEMENT

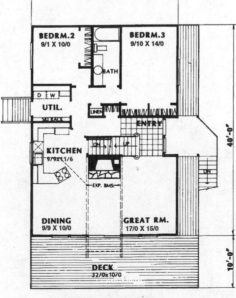

MAIN FLOOR

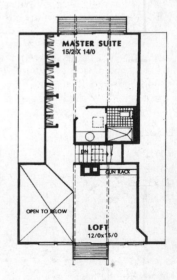

UPPER FLOOR

Plan P-531-2D

PRICES AND DETAILS ON PAGES 12-15

Large Deck Wraps Home

- A full deck and an abundance of windows surround this exciting two-level contemporary.
- The brilliant living room boasts a huge fireplace and a 14-ft.-high cathedral ceiling, plus a stunning prow-shaped window wall.

- Skywalls brighten the island kitchen and the dining room. A pantry closet and laundry facilities are nearby.
- The master bedroom offers private access to the deck. The master bath includes a dual-sink vanity, a large tub and a separate shower. A roomy hall bath serves a second bedroom.
- A generous-sized family room, another full bath and two additional bedrooms share the lower level with a two-car garage and a shop area.

Plan NW-579

Bedrooms: 4	Baths: 3
Living Area:	
Main floor	1,707 sq. ft.
Daylight basement	901 sq. ft.
Total Living Area:	**2,608 sq. ft.**
Tuck-under garage	588 sq. ft.
Shop	162 sq. ft.
Exterior Wall Framing:	2x6

Foundation Options:

Daylight basement
(All plans can be built with your choice of foundation and framing. A generic conversion diagram is available. See order form.)

BLUEPRINT PRICE CODE:	D

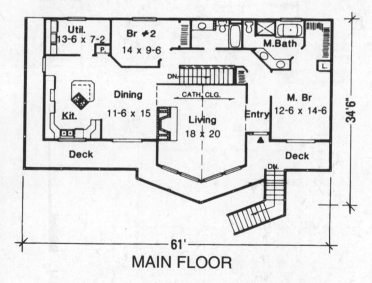

MAIN FLOOR

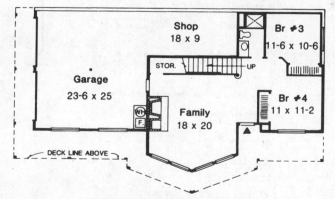

DAYLIGHT BASEMENT

VIEW INTO LIVING ROOM

REAR VIEW

Stunning Estate for Scenic Sites

- A tiered roofline, expansive windows and a magnificent wraparound deck adorn this fantastic home, which is perfect for scenic building sites.
- The main floor is a masterpiece of open design, beginning with the sunny dining room that flows into the unique kitchen. The kitchen features an angled island cooktop/snack bar, a corner sink framed by windows and a nice pantry closet.
- The sunken living room is bordered by railings on two sides, keeping it visually open. A window-filled bay overlooks the deck, while a 12-ft. ceiling heightens the room's spaciousness. Other highlights include built-in bookshelves and a fireplace with a raised hearth and a built-in log bin.
- The luxurious master suite boasts a cozy window seat, a plush bath and a private sitting room with access to the deck.
- Downstairs, the recreation room offers another fireplace and double doors to a covered driveway or patio. One of the two bedrooms here offers a private bath and walk-in closet.
- Ceilings in most rooms are at least 9-ft. high for added spaciousness.

Plan NW-779

Bedrooms: 3	Baths: 3½
Living Area:	
Main floor	1,450 sq. ft.
Daylight basement	1,242 sq. ft.
Total Living Area:	**2,692 sq. ft.**
Exterior Wall Framing:	2x6

Foundation Options:

Daylight basement

(All plans can be built with your choice of foundation and framing. A generic conversion diagram is available. See order form.)

BLUEPRINT PRICE CODE: D

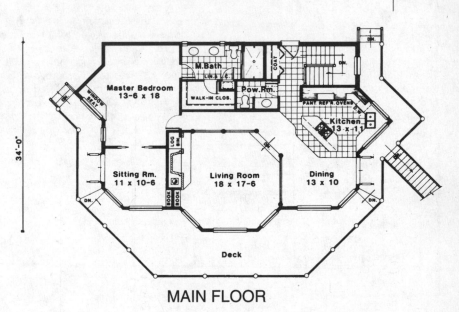

MAIN FLOOR

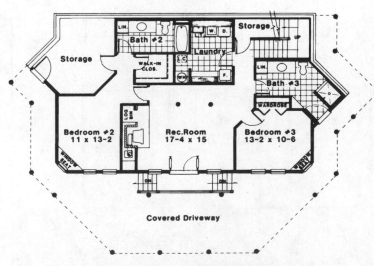

DAYLIGHT BASEMENT

 Plan NW-779 *PRICES AND DETAILS ON PAGES 12-15*

Wraparound Deck Featured

- An expansive covered deck wraps around this home from the main entrance on the left side to the kitchen door on the right side.
- An oversized fireplace is the focal point of the vaulted living and dining room area. The living room's 10-ft.-high sloped ceiling is brightened by corner

windows, while the dining area has sliding glass doors to access the adjoining deck.

- The kitchen is tucked into one corner, but the open counter space allows visual contact with the adjoining living areas beyond.
- Two good-sized main-floor bedrooms, each with sufficient closet space, are convenient to the hall bath.
- The basement level adds a roomy third bedroom, plus a huge general-use area and a tuck-under garage.

Plan H-806-2	
Bedrooms: 3	Baths: 1
Living Area:	
Main floor	952 sq. ft.
Daylight basement	673 sq. ft.
Total Living Area:	**1,625 sq. ft.**
Tuck-under garage	279 sq. ft.
Exterior Wall Framing:	2x6
Foundation Options:	
Daylight basement	

(All plans can be built with your choice of foundation and framing. A generic conversion diagram is available. See order form.)

BLUEPRINT PRICE CODE: B

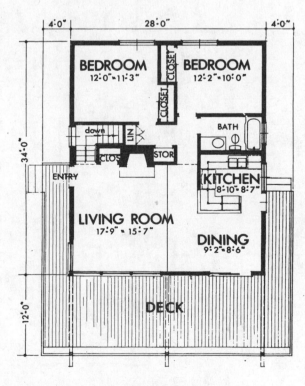

MAIN FLOOR

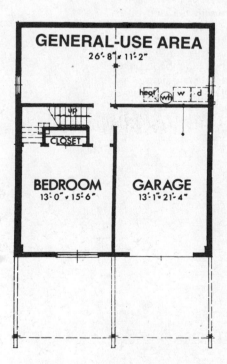

DAYLIGHT BASEMENT

Indoor/Outdoor Pleasure

- For a scenic lake or mountain lot, this spectacular design takes full advantage of the views.
- A three-sided wraparound deck makes indoor/outdoor living a pleasure.
- The sunken living room—with a 19-ft. cathedral ceiling, a skylight, a beautiful fireplace and glass galore—is the heart of the floor plan.
- Both the formal dining room and the kitchen overlook the living room and the surrounding deck beyond.
- The main-floor master bedroom has a 12-ft. cathedral ceiling and private access to the deck and hall bath.
- Upstairs, two more bedrooms share a skylighted bath and flank a dramatic balcony sitting area that views to the living room below.

Plan AX-98607

Bedrooms: 3	Baths: 2
Living Area:	
Upper floor	531 sq. ft.
Main floor	1,098 sq. ft.
Total Living Area:	**1,629 sq. ft.**
Standard basement	894 sq. ft.
Garage	327 sq. ft.
Exterior Wall Framing:	2x4

Foundation Options:

Standard basement
Slab
(All plans can be built with your choice of foundation and framing. A generic conversion diagram is available. See order form.)

BLUEPRINT PRICE CODE: **B**

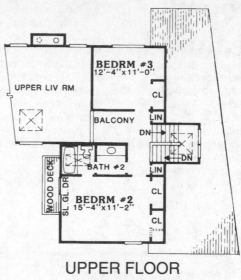

UPPER FLOOR

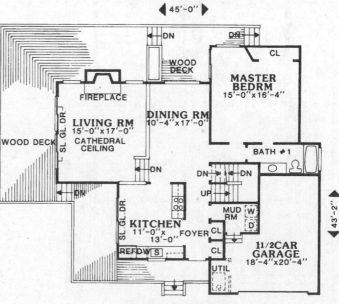

MAIN FLOOR

FRONT VIEW

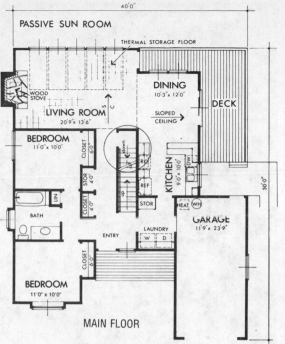

MAIN FLOOR

Sunny Family Living

- Pleasant-looking and unassuming from the front, this plan breaks into striking, sun-catching angles at the rear.
- The living room sun roof gathers passive solar heat, which is stored in the tile floor and the two-story high masonry backdrop to the wood stove.
- A 516-square-foot master suite with private bath and balcony makes up the second floor.
- The main floor offers two more bedrooms and a full bath.

UPPER FLOOR

WITHOUT BASEMENT
(CRAWLSPACE FOUNDATION)

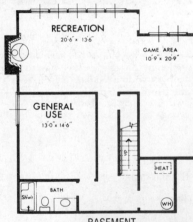

BASEMENT

Plans H-947-1A & -1B

Bedrooms: 3	**Baths:** 2-3

Space:	
Upper floor:	516 sq. ft.
Main floor:	1,162 sq. ft.
Total without basement:	1,678 sq. ft.
Daylight basement:	966 sq. ft.
Total with basement:	2,644 sq. ft.
Garage:	279 sq. ft.
Exterior Wall Framing:	2x6

Foundation options:
Daylight basement (H-947-1B).
Crawlspace (H-947-1A).
(Foundation & framing conversion diagram available — see order form.)

Blueprint Price Code:

Without basement:	B
With basement:	D

Five-Bedroom Chalet

Realizing that there are situations that require the maximum number of bedrooms, we have created this modest-sized home containing five bedrooms. One of these, especially the one over the garage, would serve very well as a private den, card room or library. The plan is available with or without basement.

This is an excellent example of the classic chalet. Close study will reveal how hall space has been kept at an absolute minimum. As a result, a modest first floor area of 952 sq. ft. and a compact second floor plan of 767 sq. ft. make the five bedrooms possible.

Also notice the abundance of storage space and built-ins with many other conveniences. Plumbing is provided in two complete bathrooms, and a washer and dryer has been tucked into one corner of the central hall on the main floor.

A clever technique has been used in the design of the staircase as it progresses halfway up to a landing midway between the two floors. From here it branches in two directions to a bedroom over the garage and to a hallway common to other rooms.

First floor:	952 sq. ft.
Second floor:	767 sq. ft.
Total living area:	1,719 sq. ft.
(Not counting basement or garage)	

FIRST FLOOR
952 SQUARE FEET

SECOND FLOOR
767 SQUARE FEET

PLAN H-804-2
WITH BASEMENT
PLAN H-804-2A
WITHOUT BASEMENT
(CRAWLSPACE FOUNDATION)

Blueprint Price Code B
Plans H-804-2 & -2A

PRICES AND DETAILS
ON PAGES 12-15

Dynamic Design

- This dynamic five-sided design is perfect for scenic sites. The front (or street) side of the home is shielded by a two-car garage, while the back of the home hosts a glass-filled living area surrounded by a spectacular deck.
- The unique shape of the home allows for an unusually open and spacious interior design.
- The living/dining room is further expanded by a 20-ft.-high vaulted ceiling. The centrally located fireplace provides a focal point while distributing heat efficiently.
- The space-saving galley-style kitchen is connected to the living/dining area by a snack bar.
- A large main-floor bedroom has two closets and easy access to a full bath.
- The upper floor is highlighted by a breathtaking balcony overlook. Also, two bedrooms share a nice-sized bath.
- The optional daylight basement includes a huge recreation room.

Plans H-855-1 & -1A

Bedrooms: 3	Baths: 2
Living Area:	
Upper floor	625 sq. ft.
Main floor	1,108 sq. ft.
Daylight basement	1,108 sq. ft.
Total Living Area:	**1,733/2,841 sq. ft.**
Garage	346 sq. ft.
Exterior Wall Framing:	2x6
Foundation Options:	**Plan #**
Daylight basement	H-855-1
Crawlspace	H-855-1A

(All plans can be built with your choice of foundation and framing. A generic conversion diagram is available. See order form.)

BLUEPRINT PRICE CODE:	**B/D**

UPPER FLOOR

DAYLIGHT BASEMENT

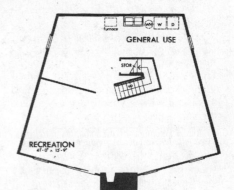

STAIRWAY AREA
IN CRAWLSPACE
VERSION

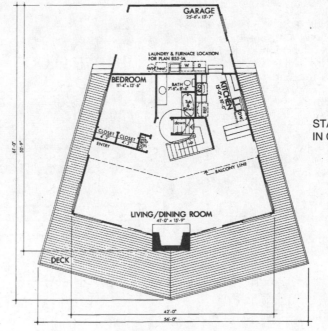

MAIN FLOOR

REAR VIEW

FRONT VIEW

Bright Ideas!

- Four clerestory windows, a boxed-out window and wing walls sheltering the entry porch give this home definition.
- Inside, an open room arrangement coupled with vaulted ceilings, abundant windows and a sensational sun room make this home a definite bright spot.
- The living room features a 22-ft.-high vaulted ceiling, a warm woodstove and a glass-filled wall that offers views into the sun room. A patio door in the sun room opens to a large backyard deck.
- The adjoining dining room flows into the kitchen, which offers a versatile snack bar. A handy laundry room is just steps away, near the garage.
- Upstairs, the intimate bedroom suite includes a 14-ft.-high vaulted ceiling, a view to the living room, a walk-in closet and a private bath.
- The optional daylight basement boasts a spacious recreation room with a second woodstove, plus a fourth bedroom and a third bath. A shaded patio occupies the area under the deck.

Plans H-877-5A & -5B

Bedrooms: 3+	Baths: 2-3
Living Area:	
Upper floor	382 sq. ft.
Main floor	1,200 sq. ft.
Sun room	162 sq. ft.
Daylight basement	1,200 sq. ft.
Total Living Area:	**1,744/2,944 sq. ft.**
Garage	457 sq. ft.
Exterior Wall Framing:	2x6
Foundation Options:	**Plan #**
Daylight basement	H-877-5B
Crawlspace	H-877-5A

(All plans can be built with your choice of foundation and framing. A generic conversion diagram is available. See order form.)

BLUEPRINT PRICE CODE:	**B/D**

UPPER FLOOR

DAYLIGHT BASEMENT

MAIN FLOOR

BASEMENT STAIRWAY LOCATION

Plans H-877-5A & -5B

PRICES AND DETAILS
ON PAGES 12-15

Raised Interest

- The raised living and deck areas of this design take full advantage of surrounding views. A sloping lot can be accommodated with the shown lower level retaining wall.
- The lower level foyer feels high and is bright with a two-and-a-half-story opening lighting the stairwell.
- A two-car tuck-under garage and two bedroom suites complete the lower level.
- At the top of the stairs, guests are wowed with a view into the Grand Room, with high vaulted ceiling, fireplace and atrium doors and windows overlooking the main deck.
- The kitchen incorporates a sunny good morning room.
- The master suite dazzles with a vaulted ceiling, plant shelves, a private deck and a splashy master bath.

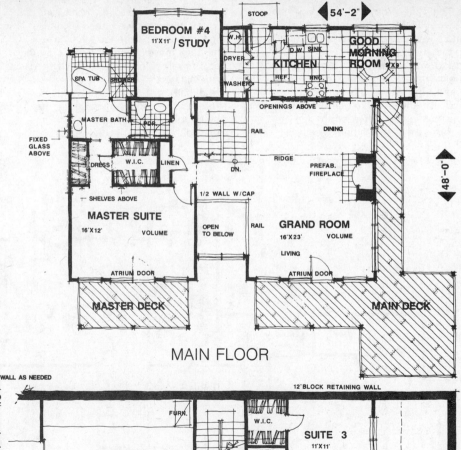

MAIN FLOOR

Plan EOF-44

Bedrooms: 4	Baths: 2
Living Area:	
Main floor	1,256 sq. ft.
Daylight basement	541 sq. ft.
Total Living Area:	**1,797 sq. ft.**
Garage	460 sq. ft.
Exterior Wall Framing:	2x4

Foundation Options:
Daylight basement
(Typical foundation & framing conversion diagram available—see order form.)

BLUEPRINT PRICE CODE:	B

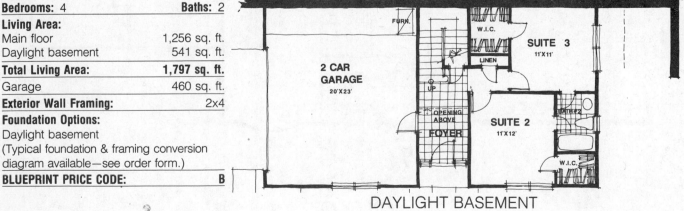

DAYLIGHT BASEMENT

Plan EOF-44

Sunny Surprises

- A clean-lined roof with wide overhangs blends this home into the landscape, and a low-walled entrance court adds to the effect.
- Inside, you'll find many sunny surprises, including bow windows in the living and dining rooms, a beautiful kitchen and a bright semi-circular dinette area.
- The spacious family room or den features a 10½-ft. cathedral ceiling.

A large fireplace is centered on a bright wall of glass. Sliding glass doors provide access to a lovely backyard terrace. A decorative screen separates the family room from the main hall.

- The quiet master suite includes a private bath, a walk-in closet and a skylighted dressing area.
- A hall bath with a dual-sink vanity serves the two front-facing bedrooms.
- The double garage offers two storage areas, plus a choice of door locations.

Plan K-167-R	
Bedrooms: 3	**Baths: 2**
Living Area:	
Main floor	1,834 sq. ft.
Total Living Area:	**1,834 sq. ft.**
Standard basement	1,768 sq. ft.
Garage and storage	619 sq. ft.
Exterior Wall Framing:	2x4 or 2x6
Foundation Options:	
Standard basement	
Slab	

(All plans can be built with your choice of foundation and framing. A generic conversion diagram is available. See order form.)

BLUEPRINT PRICE CODE: **B**

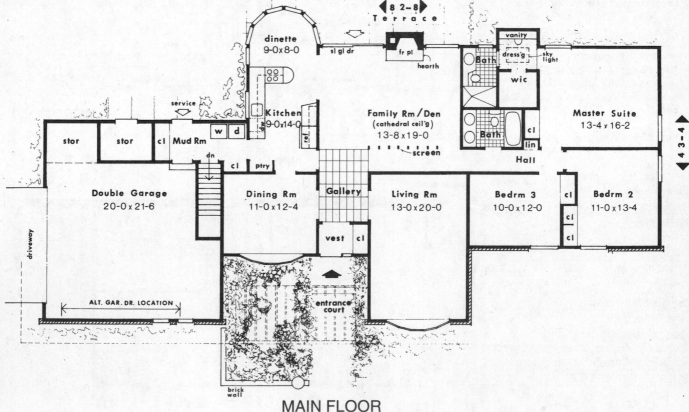

MAIN FLOOR

Plan K-167-R

PRICES AND DETAILS
ON PAGES 12-15

Spacious Octagon

- Highly functional main floor plan makes traffic easy and minimizes wasted hall space.
- Double-sized entry opens to spacious octagonal living room with central fireplace and access to all rooms.
- U-shaped kitchen and attached dining area allow for both informal and formal occasions.
- Contiguous bedrooms each have independent deck entrances.
- Exciting deck borders entire home.

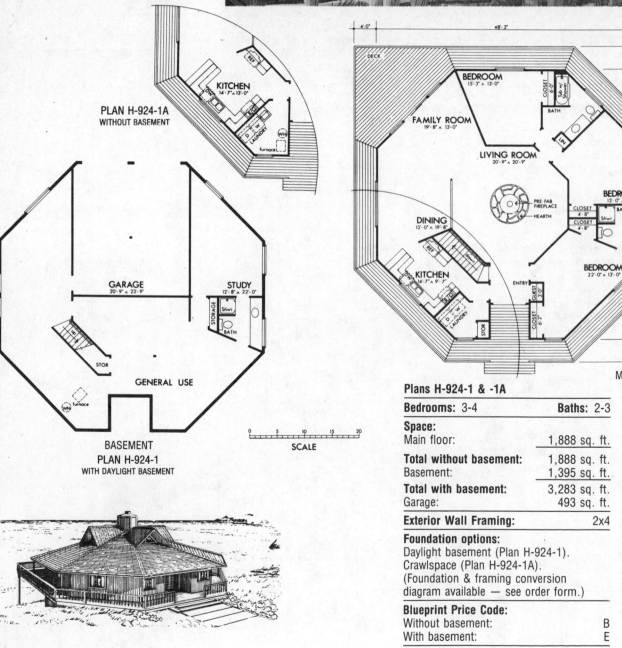

PLAN H-924-1A
WITHOUT BASEMENT

KITCHEN
14'-7" x 13'-0"

BASEMENT
PLAN H-924-1
WITH DAYLIGHT BASEMENT

GARAGE
20'-9" x 23'-9"

STUDY
12'-8" x 22'-0"

GENERAL USE

SCALE

MAIN FLOOR

DECK

BEDROOM
15'-3" x 13'-0"

FAMILY ROOM
19'-8" x 13'-0"

LIVING ROOM
20'-9" x 20'-9"

PRE-FAB FIREPLACE

HEARTH

BEDROOM
13'-0" x 18'-0"

DINING
13'-0" x 19'-8"

KITCHEN
14'-7" x 9'-7"

BEDROOM
22'-0" x 13'-0"

ENTRY

Plans H-924-1 & -1A

Bedrooms: 3-4	Baths: 2-3
Space:	
Main floor:	1,888 sq. ft.
Total without basement:	1,888 sq. ft.
Basement:	1,395 sq. ft.
Total with basement:	3,283 sq. ft.
Garage:	493 sq. ft.
Exterior Wall Framing:	2x4

Foundation options:
Daylight basement (Plan H-924-1).
Crawlspace (Plan H-924-1A).
(Foundation & framing conversion diagram available — see order form.)

Blueprint Price Code:

Without basement:	B
With basement:	E

Photo by Carren Strock

Proven Plan Features Passive Sun Room

- A passive sun room, energy-efficient wood stove, and a panorama of windows make this design highly economical.
- Open living/dining room features attractive balcony railing, stone hearth, and adjoining sun room with durable stone floor.
- Well-equipped kitchen is separated from dining area by a convenient breakfast bar.
- Second level sleeping areas border a hallway and balcony.
- Optional basement plan provides extra space for entertaining or work.

Plans H-855-3A & -3B

Bedrooms: 3	Baths: 2-3

Space:	
Upper floor:	586 sq. ft.
Main floor:	1,192 sq. ft.
Sun room:	132 sq. ft.

Total living area:	1,910 sq. ft.
Basement:	approx. 1,192 sq. ft.
Garage:	520 sq. ft.

Exterior Wall Framing:	2x6

Foundation options:
Daylight basement (Plan H-855-3B).
Crawlspace (Plan H-855-3A).
(Foundation & framing conversion diagram available — see order form.)

Blueprint Price Code:
Without basement	B
With basement	E

**NOTE:
The above photographed home may have been modified by the homeowner. Please refer to floor plan and/or drawn elevation shown for actual blueprint details.

GARAGE
26/0 x 20/0

BEDROOM
10/6 x 12/0

KITCHEN
13/0 x 14/0

LIVING / DINING
42/0 x 15/0

WOODSTOVE   STONE HEARTH

SUN ROOM
132 SQUARE FEET
12/0 x 11/0

STONE FLOOR

MAIN FLOOR
PLAN H-855-3B
WITH DAYLIGHT BASEMENT

PLAN H-855-3A
WITHOUT BASEMENT
(CRAWLSPACE FOUNDATION)

BEDROOM
11/6 x 16/6

BEDR'M
8/6 x 14/6

OPEN TO LIVING RM

RAILING

PASSIVE SUN ROOF

UPPER FLOOR

GENERAL USE
12/0 x 14/6

RECREATION ROOM
42/0 x 15/0

WOODSTOVE   STONE HEARTH

BASEMENT

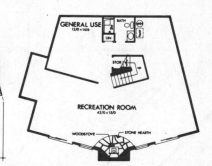

Plans H-855-3A & -3B   *PRICES AND DETAILS*
ON PAGES 12-15

Soaring Design

- Dramatic windows soar to the peak of this prowed chalet, offering unlimited views of outdoor scenery.
- The spacious living room flaunts a fabulous fireplace, a soaring 26-ft. vaulted ceiling, a striking window wall and sliding glass doors to a wonderful wraparound deck.
- An oversized window brightens a dining area on the left side of the living room. The sunny, L-shaped kitchen is spacious and easily accessible.
- The secluded main-floor bedroom has convenient access to a full bath, a linen closet, a good-sized laundry room and the rear entrance.
- A central, open-railed staircase leads to the upper floor, which contains two more bedrooms and a full bath.
- A skylighted balcony is the high point of this design, offering a railed overlook into the living room below and sweeping outdoor vistas through the wall of windows.
- The optional daylight basement provides another fireplace in a versatile recreation room. The extra-long, tuck-under garage includes plenty of room for hobbies, while the service room offers additional storage space.

Plans H-930-1 & -1A	
Bedrooms: 3	**Baths:** 2
Living Area:	
Upper floor	710 sq. ft.
Main floor	1,210 sq. ft.
Daylight basement	605 sq. ft.
Total Living Area:	**1,920/2,525 sq. ft.**
Tuck-under garage/shop	605 sq. ft.
Exterior Wall Framing:	2x6
Foundation Options:	**Plan #**
Daylight basement	H-930-1
Crawlspace	H-930-1A

(All plans can be built with your choice of foundation and framing. A generic conversion diagram is available. See order form.)

BLUEPRINT PRICE CODE: **B/D**

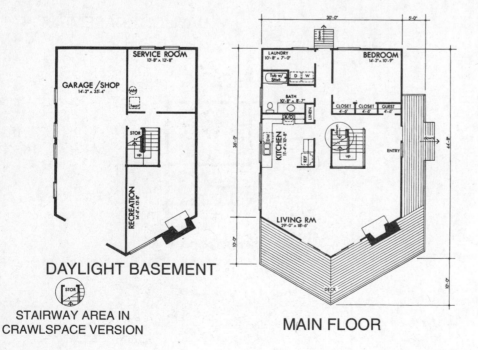

DAYLIGHT BASEMENT

STAIRWAY AREA IN CRAWLSPACE VERSION

MAIN FLOOR

UPPER FLOOR

NOTE:
The above photographed home may have been modified by the homeowner. Please refer to floor plan and/or drawn elevation shown for actual blueprint details.

Decked-Out Chalet

- This gorgeous chalet is partially surrounded by a large and roomy deck that is great for indoor/outdoor living.
- The living and dining area shows off a fireplace with a raised hearth, plus large windows to take in the outdoor views. The area is further expanded by a 17½-ft.-high vaulted ceiling in the dining room and sliding glass doors that lead to the deck.
- The kitchen offers a breakfast bar that separates it from the dining area. A convenient laundry room is nearby.
- The main-floor master bedroom is just steps away from a linen closet and a hall bath. Two upstairs bedrooms share a second full bath.
- The highlight of the upper floor is a balcony room with a 12½-ft.-high vaulted ceiling, exposed beams and tall windows. A decorative railing provides an overlook into the dining area below.

Plans H-919-1 & -1A

Bedrooms: 3	Baths: 2
Living Area:	
Upper floor	869 sq. ft.
Main floor	1,064 sq. ft.
Daylight basement	475 sq. ft.
Total Living Area:	**1,933/2,408 sq. ft.**
Tuck-under garage	501 sq. ft.
Exterior Wall Framing:	2x6
Foundation Options:	**Plan #**
Daylight basement	H-919-1
Crawlspace	H-919-1A

(All plans can be built with your choice of foundation and framing. A generic conversion diagram is available. See order form.)

BLUEPRINT PRICE CODE:	B/C

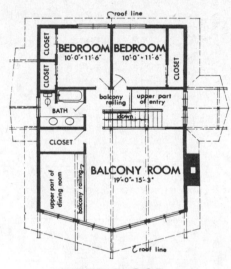

UPPER FLOOR

DAYLIGHT BASEMENT

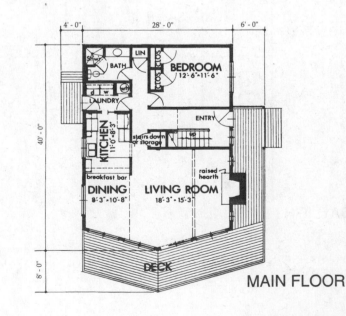

MAIN FLOOR

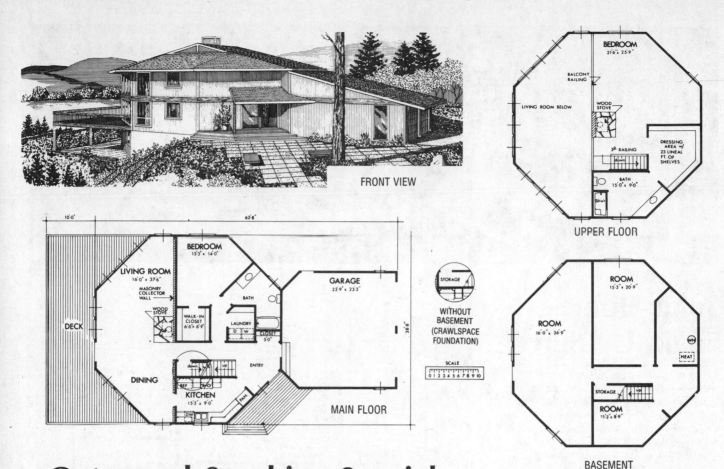

FRONT VIEW

UPPER FLOOR

MAIN FLOOR

WITHOUT BASEMENT (CRAWLSPACE FOUNDATION)

SCALE
0 1 2 3 4 5 6 7 8 9 10

BASEMENT

Octagonal Sunshine Special

- Octagon homes offer the ultimate for taking advantage of a view, and are fascinating designs even for more ordinary settings.
- This plan offers a huge, house-spanning living/dining area with loads of glass and a masonry collector wall to store solar heat.

- The 700-square-foot upper level is devoted entirely to an enormous master suite, with a balcony overlooking the living room below, a roomy private bath and a large closet/dressing area.
- Scissor-trusses allow vaulted ceilings over the two-story-high

living room and the master suite.
- A second roomy bedroom and full bath are offered downstairs, along with an efficient kitchen, a laundry area and inviting foyer.
- A daylight basement option offers the potential for more bedrooms, hobbies, work rooms or recreational space.

REAR VIEW

Plans H-948-1A & -1B

Bedrooms: 2-4	Baths: 2

Space:

Upper floor:	700 sq. ft.
Main floor:	1,236 sq. ft.
Total without basement:	1,936 sq. ft.
Daylight basement:	1,236 sq. ft.
Total with basement:	3,172 sq. ft.
Garage:	550 sq. ft.
Exterior Wall Framing:	2x6

Foundation options:
Daylight basement (H-948-1B).
Crawlspace (H-948-1A).
(Foundation & framing conversion diagram available — see order form.)

Blueprint Price Code:

Without basement:	B
With basement:	E

Solar Home Soaks Up Sun

- This dramatic passive-solar home is finished in eye-catching vertical and angled wood siding, and is adaptable to many sites and conditions.
- Solar energy is soaked up and stored in the sun garden's thermal wall and the thermal floors of the south-facing activity areas and the master suite. In the summer, overhanging eaves keep out unwanted heat, and high, operable clerestory windows give the home natural ventilation.
- Cathedral ceilings in the family, dining and living rooms keep an open air flow.
- The sheltered entry, air-lock vestibule, high-efficiency fireplace and heavy insulation are other economies.
- An expansive terrace extends along the back of the home and wraps around an exciting solarium.
- Isolated in a private wing are three bedrooms and two baths.

Plan K-395-T

Bedrooms: 3	Baths: 2½
Living Area:	
Main floor	1,921 sq. ft.
Solarium	128 sq. ft.
Sun garden	104 sq. ft.
Total Living Area:	**2,153 sq. ft.**
Partial basement	807 sq. ft.
Garage	476 sq. ft.
Exterior Wall Framing:	2x4 or 2x6

Foundation Options:

Partial basement
Slab
(All plans can be built with your choice of foundation and framing. A generic conversion diagram is available. See order form.)

BLUEPRINT PRICE CODE: C

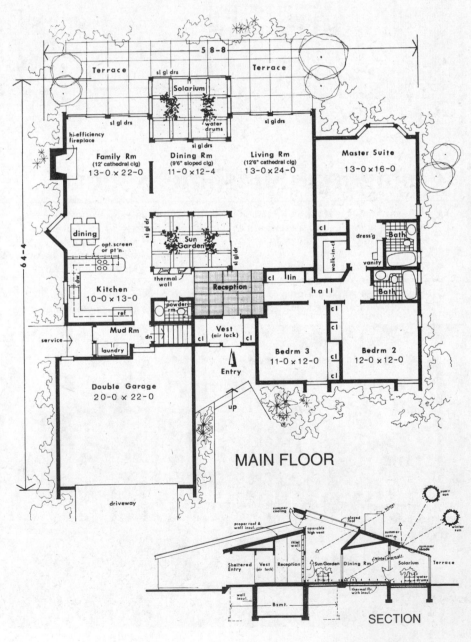

MAIN FLOOR

SECTION

Hot Tub, Deck Highlighted

- Designed for indoor/outdoor living, this home features a skylighted spa room with a hot tub and a backyard deck that spans the width of the home.
- A central hall leads to the sunny kitchen and nook, which offer corner windows, a snack bar and a pantry.
- Straight ahead, the open dining and living rooms form one huge space, further pronounced by expansive windows. The 16-ft. vaulted living room also features a fireplace and sliding glass doors to the deck.
- The master suite includes a cozy window seat, a large walk-in closet, a private bath and access to the tiled spa room. The spa may also be entered from the deck and an inner hall.
- Upstairs, two more bedrooms share a full bath and a balcony that overlooks the living room below.
- The optional daylight basement offers a deluxe sauna, a fourth bedroom, a laundry room and a wide recreation room with a fireplace. A large game room and storage are also included.

REAR VIEW

Plans H-2114-1A & -1B

Bedrooms: 3+	Baths: 2½-3½
Living Area:	
Upper floor	732 sq. ft.
Main floor	1,682 sq. ft.
Spa room	147 sq. ft.
Daylight basement	1,386 sq. ft.
Total Living Area:	**2,561/3,947 sq. ft.**
Garage	547 sq. ft.
Exterior Wall Framing:	2x6
Foundation Options:	**Plan #**
Daylight basement	H-2114-1B
Crawlspace	H-2114-1A

(All plans can be built with your choice of foundation and framing. A generic conversion diagram is available. See order form.)

BLUEPRINT PRICE CODE:	D/F

UPPER FLOOR   DAYLIGHT BASEMENT

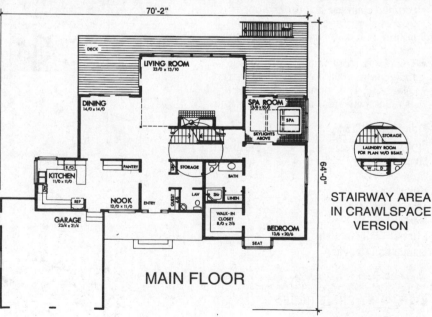

MAIN FLOOR

STAIRWAY AREA IN CRAWLSPACE VERSION

Photo by Mark Englund/HomeStyles

Take the Plunge!

NOTE: The above photographed home may have been modified by the homeowner. Please refer to floor plan and/or drawn elevation shown for actual blueprint details.

- From the elegant portico to the striking rooflines, this home's facade is magnificent. But the rear area is equally fine, with its spa, waterfall and pool.
- Double doors lead from the entry into a columned foyer where a 12-ft.-high ceiling extends into the central living room beyond. A sunken wet bar juts into the pool area, allowing guests to swim up to the bar for refreshments.
- The dining room boasts window walls and a tiered pedestal ceiling. The island kitchen easily services both the formal and the informal areas of the home.
- A large breakfast room flows into a warm family room with a fireplace and sliding glass doors to the patio and pool.
- The stunning master suite offers an opulent bath, patio access and views of the pool through a curved window wall.
- A railed staircase leads to the upper floor, where there are two bedrooms, a continental bath and a shared balcony deck overlooking the pool area.
- The observatory features high windows to accommodate an amateur stargazer's telescope. This room could also be used as an activity area for hobbies or games

Plan HDS-99-154

Bedrooms: 3+	Baths: 3
Living Area:	
Upper floor	675 sq. ft.
Main floor	2,212 sq. ft.
Total Living Area:	**2,887 sq. ft.**
Garage	479 sq. ft.
Exterior Wall Framing:	2x4

Foundation Options:

Slab

(All plans can be built with your choice of foundation and framing. A generic conversion diagram is available. See order form.)

BLUEPRINT PRICE CODE: D.

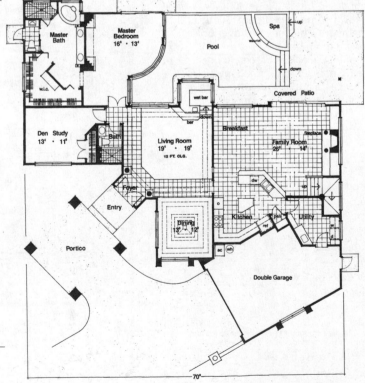

UPPER FLOOR

MAIN FLOOR